John R Black

Young Japan

Yokohama and Yedo - A Narrative of the Settlement. Vol. 1

John R Black

Young Japan

Yokohama and Yedo - A Narrative of the Settlement. Vol. 1

ISBN/EAN: 9783337166571

Printed in Europe, USA, Canada, Australia, Japan

Cover: Foto ©ninafisch / pixelio.de

More available books at **www.hansebooks.com**

YOUNG JAPAN.

YOKOHAMA AND YEDO.

A NARRATIVE

OF

THE SETTLEMENT AND THE CITY

FROM THE

SIGNING OF THE TREATIES IN 1858,

TO THE

CLOSE OF THE YEAR 1879.

WITH

A GLANCE AT THE PROGRESS OF JAPAN

DURING A PERIOD OF TWENTY-ONE YEARS.

BY

JOHN R. BLACK,

Formerly Editor of the "JapanHerald," and of the "Japan Gazette"; Editor of the "Far-East," Illustrated Monthly Magazine. Also the Proprietor and Editor of the "Nisshin Shinjishi"—the first Newspaper (worthy of the name) ever published in the native language in Japan.

IN TWO VOLUMES.

VOL. I.

NEW YORK:
BAKER, PRATT & COMPANY.
LONDON: TRUBNER & CO. | YOKOHAMA: KELLY & CO.
1883.

PRINTED
AT THE PRIVATE PRINTING OFFICE OF THE AUTHOR,
NO. 16, YOKOHAMA, JAPAN.

TO ONE
WHO,
ALL HER LIFE LONG,
HAS DEVOTED HER ENERGIES
TO THE WELFARE OF OTHERS,
DISREGARDING HERSELF;
AND WHO,
FOR MORE THAN THIRTY YEARS
HAS MADE
MY WELL-BEING AND HAPPINESS
HER FIRST CARE.

TO MY DEAR WIFE:
MY COMPANION: MY COMFORT: AND MY CROWN:
THIS NARRATIVE
OF A PERIOD,
THE GREATER PART OF WHICH WE HAVE SPENT TOGETHER
IN THIS
LAND OF PROMISE,
IS DEDICATED
WITH THE
DEEPEST AFFECTION AND RESPECT.

PREFACE.

To the dignity of history this book makes no pretension. It is a simple narrative of the most prominent events that have taken place in the beautiful 'Land of the Rising Sun,' in which foreigners have been more or less interested, and with which they have been more or less connected, during the twenty-one years that have elapsed since the existing treaties were entered into in 1858.

If asked to account for the origin of the book, I can truly say, with Topsy, "I specs it growed." The 'prospectus' circulated to announce its intended publication, may be quoted to shew how literally this is correct:—

"When in June last the author of the present work arrived in Japan, out of health, and looking for a restoration from the mere sea-trip, backwards and forwards, between Yokohama and Shanghai, he had no idea but that, after a sojourn of ten days, he would return—he hoped better for the change.

"Instead of this being realised he found himself at the end of that time, obliged to place himself under medical care, and compelled to remain a while longer.

"As he approached convalescence, he was scanning over the pages of the *Far East*, and came, at the close of the sixth volume, upon a "Retrospect," written in June 1875, of all the events that had been recorded in the pages of the magazine since its establishment in May 1870. It interested him so much, and, although he had himself written it, mentioned so many circumstances in the progress of Japan within that short period, which had passed from his mind, that he thought it was worth republishing in pamphlet form; and then, remembering that Japan was just completing its majority, since, by the Treaties of Mr. Harris and Lord Elgin, for the United States and England respectively, she was born into the family of nations, he determined to amplify it, and give a historiette, more particularly with regard to Yokohama and Yedo, of the whole period of twenty-one years. He intended to do this in a pamphlet, expecting it would occupy about 120 pages, and supply him with occupation during the remainder of his stay.

"But when once he commenced his task, he found it of such absorbing interest, that it gradually grew, until it was evident the idea of a mere pamphlet must be given up. He did not as yet, however, expect it would extend to more than one volume *Octavo*, containing about 400 pages. As he proceeded he found it impossible to condense his materials even to bring the book within these limits; and, as a fact, the First Volume, now completed and "in the Press," will be over 400 pages, and finishes with the Commercial year—June 1866; just after the Ratification of the Treaties by His Imperial Majesty the Mikado; leaving the story yet to be told of the later thirteen years, during which the greatest progress has been made."

So much for the origin of the work. As for its plan, I would particularly call attention to the fact that it professes to be a narrative of the Settlement of Yokohama and the City of Yedo, since the year 1858. I purposely adopted the narrative form, first as allowing a lighter and more readable style than that of history; and then, as permitting personal reminiscences to be introduced, which recall to mind many 'weel-kent faces' of the olden time; and at once secure a host of sympathizers, not only in Japan, but in almost every other country. For what country can be named that has not in it either some old resident of Yokohama of the early days, or some who were, or are, collaterally connected with them.

To these, the chapters of the smaller local and social events, it is hoped, will be agreeable. The chapter on Municipal affairs may be deemed as altogether too minute in its details. But I have given them that those who condemn our non-possession of any power to control our own settlement's affairs, may see that efforts have been made in that direction; by whom those efforts were made; and why they failed. Thus, the chapter will probably have a wide circle of interested readers; though it is of course certain that all these matters will be of very secondary importance with the outside world, to whom mere localisms cannot be of any moment. But the political affairs have in themselves, so much that is unique: so much that the history of no country but Japan can show: that the narrator must be clumsy indeed, who, in relating them, deprives them of the absorbing interest they intrinsically possess. I have dwelt upon some of them at greater length than I originally intended, because they have been brought powerfully under public notice, and much discussed, within the last five years; and I thought that, if I gave both sides of certain vexed questions, I might be justified in pointing out the feelings of all foreigners with regard to them, at the time of their occurrence.

My own personal sympathies are so strongly with Japan and the Japanese, that I would have been glad if I could have avoided some of the more sombre tints which I have been obliged to use but too frequently in the series of pictures I am sending forth. As it is, I know that there are many who will think I have occasionally spoken too favourably. But it is not so. In good truth, it would be easy to go to greater lengths, both in blame and in praise, and still leave considerable margins.

The opening chapter is, as will at once be understood, nothing but a rapid survey, in as few words as possible, of the state of things in Japan from the establishment of the Empire to the period at which my narrative proper begins. For those who are tolerably well acquainted with Japan, it was unnecessary; but it was written after the greater part of the book was penned, in order that any who might not be familiar with Japanese history, into whose hands the book might come, should be able to understand generally what the system was that had such a violent wrench when the Treaties were made; and a total subversion shortly after their ratification, and in their fulfilment.

With respect to my sources of information, I must confess that some portions of my narrative might justly be called a compilation; but, if so, it is from my own writings. As a maker of history, my course has indeed been infinitessimal; but, as a recorder of current events from day to day, I have had to pay greater attention to all occurrences, social and political, than those engaged in other professions are called upon to do. As Editor, for many years, of newspapers published in Japan, I have had to seek the best sources for every kind of information: to sift the numerous statements that are apt to be made on all subjects: to put the information thus gathered and sifted, into a concise and presentable form; and oftentimes to give expression to personal feeling or public opinion upon the facts related. It is natural, therefore, that I should draw largely upon the papers I have so written; but I have in most cases avoided giving any important facts from them, when my memory could not recall the source from whence I had them; or when that source was not absolutely reliable, or was debateable.

But I have also derived much assistance from the labours of others, who have published works on Japan or on Japanese affairs. Mr. OLYPHANT and Sir RUTHERFORD ALCOCK I have quoted largely. The translation of *The Legacy of Iyeyas'*, by Mr. J. F. LOWDER, has, not only in this book, but also on many occasions, been invaluable to me. Mr. ERNEST M. SATOW's papers on many subjects, have also, not only given me a fund of important information on themes that less ardent students of Japanese lore than he, hardly even know where to look for; but, in particular, for the purposes of this work, it will be seen that his translation of *Kinsé Shiriaku* has been freely drawn upon.

I have to acknowledge the kindness of Mr. DOHMEN, H. M. Acting Consul in Yokohama, in placing at my disposal, blue-books and other requisite documents. To the proprietors of the newspapers, the *Japan Herald* and *Japan Mail*, for the use of their files; and to Mr. HOUSE, for permission to make free use of his pamphlets, *Kagoshima* and *Shimonoseki*, I am much indebted. Above all is my gratitude due to the proprietors of the *Japan Gazette*, who kindly placed not only their files, but their type, at my service.

But, it is impossible in this place to thank, as they ought to be thanked, all who have aided me, and made my labour light, in bringing out this book.

My only hope is, that, being so far completed, they will find that, as a narrative, it is generally correct; and that the interest of the subject justifies the labour bestowed on it: the encouragement they have afforded me: and the expectations they have so kindly and generously expressed.

J. R. BLACK.

Yokohama, 8th January, 1880.

CONTENTS.

PRELIMINARY CHAPTER.

PAGE

Introductory.—Japan as it appears to a superficial observer now.—Very different twenty-one years ago.—Where is the difference ?—The Imperial Dynasty.—Jinmu Tenno.—Antoku Tenno.—Commencement of the Modern History of Japan.—The dual system of Government.—The Emperor's supremacy never questioned.—The Tycoon. Sei-i Tai Shôgun.—Yoritomo. —Kamakura.—Complete isolation of the Mikado ; and Government by the Military Chief —Efforts of Mikado to recover his authority.—Temporary success of Godaigo.—Ashikaga Taka-uji.—Ota Nobunaga.—Taico Sama.—Iyeyas' founder of the last dynasty of Shôguns.—Japan open to foreigners from 1542 to 1637.—Finally closed to all but the Dutch Factory at Nagasaki —The Kugé, or Court Nobles.—The Daimios—Kokushiu, Fudai and Tozama.—Hatamotos.—The Samurai.—The common people. --The Government at a glance. 1-12

CHAPTER I.

The Majority of foreign intercourse with Japan.—Arrival of Lord Elgin to make a treaty for England.—Commodore Perry's U. S. Treaty.—Followed by others.—The treaties, though peacefully obtained, effected by intimidation.—Lord Elgin's Mission. —Arrival of Mr. Alcock. H. B. M. Envoy.—Tozenji.—Kanagawa.—Dispute between Japanese and foreign representatives as to site of the settlement.—Practically settled by the Merchants.—Yokohama, old and new.—Respective capabilities of the two ports 13-29

CHAPTER II.

The British Minister's first three difficulties.—The locality of the settlement.—Attempts to prevent free use of the Tokaido.—The currency question.--Mr Alcock's own record of the opening day.—Completeness of arrangements made by Government.—The "Receipt of Custom."—Curio street.—Attempted purchases.—Disappointment and its cause.—Ingenious if not fair.—Relative value of gold and silver.—Japanese wide-awake but mistaken.—Silver and copper coin,—Japanese first year's experience of foreigners not encouraging.—Efflux of gold,—Assimilation of values to those of other countries... 30-37

CHAPTER III.

Distaste for foreign intercourse.—The first assassinations.—The mission of Count Mouravieff Amoorsky.—His large retinue.—Three Russians murdered.—Butchery.—No previous apprehensions of such attacks.—Rudeness of samurai.—Apology. Probable motives—Greed of foreigners.—Effect on the Japanese mind.—Another cold-blooded murder.—Destruction of the Tycoon's palace in Yedo.—Gloomy aspect of affairs.—Not shared by all.—Noble aspirations of the Japanese................. 38-44

CHAPTER V.

More disasters.—Great fire in Yokohama.—Earthquake.—Murder of Mr. Alcock's interpreter Daukitchi.—Demand among Japanese for firearms.—Destruction of French Legation by fire.—Pleasant rumours and prospects.—Two Dutch captains cut down.—Crowning catastrophe.—The assassination of the Regent. 45-52

CHAPTER VI.

More attacks.—The case of Mr. Moss.—His trial and sentence.—Mr. Alcock alters the sentence.—Result.—Fire at English Legation.—Apprehensions.—Ronin.—Relations of daimios and their retainers.—The Government powerless.—Meeting of foreign representatives.—Resolve to retire from Yedo.—Murder of Mr. Heusken.—Suicide of Oribe-no-Kami............. 53-57

CHAPTER VII.

Ministers. Mr. Harris excepted, leave Yedo.—Effect upon the government.—Invitation to return.—Mr. Alcock visits Nagasaki.—Returns overland to Yokohama and Yedo.—Mr Olyphant.—Attack on British Legation.—Officers wounded.—Ronins in possession.—Mr J. F. Lowder.—Mr. Macdonald... 58-62

CHAPTER VIII.

Enquiry as to attack on British Legation.—Paper found on one of the ronin—Subsequent report.—Failure of the enterprise. Hara-kiri—Japanese code of honour.—Foreign Legation Guards.—Necessity for a naval force within reach of Japan.—Mr. de Witt refuses to reside in Yedo.—More bloodshed.—The governor of Yedo.—Request to Consuls resident in Kanagawa to remove to Yokohama.—Facts and rumours.............................. 63-68

CHAPTER IX.

Inability of Government to protect foreigners.—Government anxiety as to opening Yedo.—Closer relations.—Proposals to defer the opening of Yedo, Hiogo, Osaka and Ni-igata.—Autographic letter from Tycoon to the Queen.—Mr Olyphant its bearer.—Embassy to treaty powers determined on.—Establishment of the Japan Herald.—Japanese Embassy leaves for Europe.—Its results.—Dedication of Roman Catholic church, Yokohama.—English Church.—Attempted closing of the Tokaido to foreigners.—Mr. Alcock's action—Conflagrations.—Water supply.—Land rental.—Progress of trade.—Imports.—The Dutch Consul and the Customs.................. 69-75

CHAPTER X.

Assault on Ando Tsushima-no-Kami.—Yokohama residents demand Municipal Government.—Newspaper Correspondence. —Prospects of improvement.—Japanese intolerance.—Water scheme for Yokohama.—Mr. Alcock leaves for England.— Foreigners on the opening of the Ports.—Their mistaken views.—French and English Ministers defer the opening.— The English Notification.—Portuguese treaty ratified.— Municipal committee formed.—Arrival of new U. S. Minister and Consul.—Mr. Townsend Harris. 76-90

CHAPTER XI.

Amusements of foreigners.—Races.—Indication of Japanese desire for progress.—Establishment of a college in Yedo for foreign languages, history, science, &c.—News received of postponement of opening the treaty ports.—Dissatisfaction.— Arrival of Lieut.-Colonel St. John Neale.—Offer of Governor of Kanagawa to allot Bluff land for foreigners' residences.— Rejection on plea of its being too limited.—Murder of two Marines at H.B.M.'s Legation, Yedo.—Real desire of Japanese Government to protect foreigners —Thwarted by disaffected daimios, ronins, &c.—Casualties endured by themselves in our cause.—Constant bloodshed.—Foreigners, ignorant of the real facts, had grounds for discrediting statements made to them. —Marriage of the Shogun to the sister of the Mikado — Mission of Ohara as special Envoy from the Mikado to the Shogun.—Accompanied by Shimadzu Saburo, father of prince Satsuma.—Doubts as to Shimadzu's animosity against foreigners.—Incident at Himéji—ronins demand his leadership in the expulsion of foreigners. 91-99

INTERPOLATORY CHAPTER.

Reason for this interpolation.—The Daimio of Satsuma.— Shimadzu Saburo.—His son adopted, and himself appointed Guardian of the state.—Active in Public Affairs.—Scheme for the unification of the empire under the Mikado, and the advancement of Satsuma.—Visits Kioto....Proclamation before leaving Kagoshima.—Jealousy of Daimios.—His firmness — Proffered co-operation of ronins in attacking foreigners.—His reply.—Agrees to send messengers to them at Fushimi.— Their determination.—The interview.—Brave conduct of Satsuma men.—Its results.—Saburo proceeds with his plans ; and is sent by the Mikado with a nobleman of the Imperial Court, on a mission to Yedo. 100-110

CHAPTER XII.

Japanese officials wish to trade with foreign countries.— Purchase of barque Armistice.—Yokohama municipality languishes.— Consuls willing to delegate to it certain powers.—Measles epidemic in Yedo.—General exaggeration in Japanese statistics.—Sanitary state of Yokohama — Filthy canals intersecting the Native town.—General cleanliness of the people. -Public tubbing.— Native bath-houses.—Simplicity of Japanese life.— The toilet.—Golden lacquer.—Field work.—Mountebanks.— Priests.—Kagura.—Firemen 111-123

CHAPTER XIII.

The sad tale must be told.—Shimadzu Saburo's threat to murder foreigners.—Doubts as to its truth.—If true, probable reason. —The murder of Mr. Richardson.—Mrs. Borrodaile's statement: Mr. Clarke's and Mr. Marshall's evidence.—Unchallenged until 1875.—The Satsuma version.—Effect on the residents on the news reaching the settlement.—Colonel Neale and the mounted escort.—H. B. M.'s Consul takes the escort without orders.—The body of Mr. Richardson found; and statement of Japanese on the spot, respecting his actual death. —Colonel Neale the only person who kept within the bounds of prudence.—The body conveyed to Kanagawa.—Meeting of the residents.—Resolutions passed.—Deputation to Admiral Kuper on board H.M.S. Euryalus.—Also to captains of French and Dutch men-of-war.—And to Colonel Neale.— Meeting at the French Minister's house.—Colonel Neale's refusal to act as proposed by the residents.—Approval of his conduct by his Government, and subsequently by his countrymen.—Original condemnation of it by all foreigners and by the press.—Probable results of immediate action.—Colonel Neale's prompt communication with the Japanese Government.—Perplexity of Yedo Government. 124-144

CHAPTER XIV.

State of public feeling in Yokohama.—Enrolment of a volunteer corps.—Meeting of landrenters.—Autumn race meeting.— Terrible visitation of cholera in Yedo and Yokohama.—No foreigners attacked by it.—Attractions to Japan.—Change among the Japanese at the open ports.—Injudicious familiarity.—Still much that was agreeable preserved.—The samurai or military class—their privileges; prohibition from any but special occupations; officials selected from them; their idleness; conceit; code of honour.—Remark of a daimio to Sir Rutherford Alcock on this point.—Japan no paradise before opened to foreigners.—On the subject of foreign intercourse samurai generally adopted the views of their prince.—Shogun obliged to place a large guard for the protection of foreigners. —The dangerous class.—Incident in Tokio in 1872, and conversation with an official. 145-157

CHAPTER XV.

Ohara's mission.—Various reasons assigned for Shimadzu Saburo accompanying it. Abolition of enforced residence of the daimios in Yedo.—Exodus of daimios, their families and retainers from the city.—The consequent effect on the capital. —Doings of the ronins.—The ex-Prince of Tosa arrives in Kioto.—Sat-cho-to.—Two later missions from the Mikado to the Tycoon.—Tycoon resolves to comply with the order to visit Kioto.—Agitation among foreign residents kept up by flying rumours.—Consular notification.—Indignation of foreigners.—Great changes that have taken place on the Tokaido – now deserted in consequence of the construction of a railway between Yokohama and Yedo.—Picture of it as it was in 1863.—Description of it as seen by Kœmpfer two centuries ago. 158-172

CONTENTS. IX

CHAPTER XVI.

PAGE

Rumour, at the commencement of 1863, that the ronins intended to slay all the foreign representatives.—Preventive measures.—Rumour proves to be false.—Another request of the Governor of Kanagawa that foreigners should avoid the Tokaido.—Burning of the British Legation building at Go-ten-Yama, Yedo, and a lengthened detail of the circumstances that led to it.—Those who now judge their countrymen who passed through those times should put themselves in their place.—Knowledge now attained not then existing.—What foreigners did know.—Facts as they appeared before them had alone to be considered.—As a rule foreigners were quiet and well-conducted; and most favourably disposed towards the country and people of Japan.—The true nature of the government begins to reveal itself.—The Tycoon no emperor, but yet a real potentate.—Combination of circumstances that led to his downfall 173-185

CHAPTER XVII.

The protection of the Mikado.—Competitive examinations.—Anxiety of the government.—Daimios encouraged to purchase steamers.—Provision for protecting the foreign settlement.—Admiral Kuper arrives with a squadron.—Yokohama harbour well filled with foreign men-of-war.—Shimadzu Saburo's report of the Richardson episode calls forth the approval of the Mikado.—Clamour of ronins at Kioto for expulsion of foreigners.—Satsuma placed in charge of Go-ten-Yama.—Colonel Neale receives replies from his government to his dispatches on the subject of the Richardson murder.—The Tycoon's hurried departure for Kioto.—Colonel Neale sends in his note to the Japanese Ministers for Foreign Affairs, with the demands of the English Government.—Extracts from the note.—Twenty days ultimatum expand into many weeks.—Tycoon arrives at Kioto.—Intense excitement in Kioto and Yokohama.—Many natives leave Yokohama.—The American Legation in Yedo burnt.—Ruse by which the U.S. Minister was induced to leave Yedo, and the U.S. Consul to quit Kanagawa.—Japanese evidently trying to carry out the orders from Kioto.—Court deliberations; and appointment of a day for the expulsion of foreigners and closing of Yokohama.—Intimation from the Governor of Kanagawa to the consuls, that extra precautions being necessary, more guards would be employed and a strong detachment posted on the Eastern Hatoba.—This last objected to.—In spite of delays negotiations continue and the Government agrees to pay the indemnity demanded of them by the British Government, leaving Satsuma to be subsequently settled with.—A hitch.—Correspondence.—Satisfactory settlement —Fresh troubles.—Letter from Gorojin Ogasawara to the foreign Ministers announcing determination of the Government to close the ports.—Reply—The letter—sent under pressure. The Mikado always acted through the Tycoon—The Tycoons not all "puppets."—The Government's apology to Great Britain.—Assassination of Ane-no-Koji..................186-206

CHAPTER XVIII.

PAGE

More excitement.—The Choshiu forts and steamers fire upon foreign vessels in the Straits of Simonoseki.—Details of reprisals by the French, Dutch and American men-of-war. The Japanese navy in the year 1863. 207-219

CHAPTER XIX.

Fire in the Oshiro, Yedo, and destruction of the Tycoon's palace. —The Tycoon returns to Yedo by sea.—Unpleasant episode at Kanasawa.—Charge brought in the English Consular Court and dismissed.—Changes among foreign officials.—The Yokohama contribution to the Lancashire Cotton famine relief fund.—Establishment of banks in Yokohama.—The close of the Satsuma episode—Admiral Kuper to proceed to Kagoshima.—The Gorojiu now urge that no further delay should take place.—Departure of squadron.—The battle of Kagoshima.—The proceedings of the British Admiral misunderstood by Satsuma officials.—Damage suffered by Satsuma.—Effect of the battle on the clan.—Payment of all the demands of the British Government, and close of the Richardson episode. —Lieut. Colonel Neale's services rewarded by the Queen, and acknowledged by the public. 220-238

CHAPTER XX.

Change of theme.—' Out of bounds.'—Treaty limits.—Occasional transgressions.—A trip across the gulf of Yedo in search of scenery and game.—First effect on the natives on seeing foreigners.—Difficulties.—Surmounted.—The kind hearts of the people easily won.—Visit of officials.—The Yakunin's melted.—Subsequent civility and attention.—Return to settlement 239-246

CHAPTER XXI.

What is Japan like?—All who visited it charmed with it. —The Government and princes condemned but the country and people universally approved of—Preparations made by Government for the reception of foreigners at opening of the port, a proof of the intention to act up to treaty engagements. —The Tycoon's power limited as against the most powerful daimios.—The court nobles join the disaffected daimios.— Their influence with the Mikado.—The youth of the Tycoon prevents vigourous action.—Endeavour to obey the Mikado to the letter only.—Official interference to business between Japanese and foreigners.—Silk to Yokohama restricted in quantity.—Silkworms eggs sale forbidden.—General Public meeting on the subject.—Letter to the Consuls.—Steps taken by the Consular board, and the reply from the Consuls to the merchants. 247-255

CHAPTER XXII.

Meetings of the great daimios in Yedo and Kioto.—Report of one of them.—Rumour of the confinement of the Tycoon.—Ogasawara's expedition to release him.—Ogasawara advances to Fushimi, but finding the rumour to be untrue, returns to Osaka: is dismissed from the Gorojiu, and ordered to be confined in the Tycoon's castle.—Correspondence between the Tycoon's Government and the foreign representatives.—The French Minister's suggestions.—Distressing news from Osaka of the assassination of merchants.—Notices posted in Kioto and Osaka forbidding merchants to do business with foreigners.—Letter from the Ministers of Foreign Affairs to Dr. Winchester.—Amusements.—Bad news from Nagasaki.—Murder of Lieut. Camus.—Gorojiu expresses its regret to the French Minister.- Opening of the English Episcopal Church.—Another branch bank established.—Effects of the presence of the allied squadron.—Foreign sailors and Japanese..256-266

CHAPTER XXIII.

Another attempt to yield obedience to Kioto.—U.S. and Dutch Ministers, invited to meet Gorojiu, proceed to Yedo.—The interview.—Informed that foreigners must leave Yokohama and the port be closed, but that the letter sent by Ogasawara was retracted, and trade with Nagasaki and Hakodadi permitted.—Translation by Mr. Enslie of Japanese official documents.—Proposal of Japanese Government to erect fort at Benten.—Not permitted by foreign officials.—Choshiu and the Bakufu.—Proposal to Mikado that he head the army for the expulsion of foreigners.—Disgrace of Choshiu and the Court nobles.—Flight of the latter.—The Kioto palace gates.—Suspicion of Choshiu's ambition.—Appeal on behalf of Choshiu.—The clan's attack on the palace.—Destruction of a great part of Kioto.—Government proposes another embassy to Europe.—Satisfactory rumours, unsatisfactory facts.—Ronins.—Japanese order ships from America and Europe.—Suicidal order of Government to prevent trade in Silkworm's seed.—State of parties in Japan.—Choshiu expected in Yedo to make submission.—Palace of Tycoon again burnt.—Money plentiful in Yokohama.—The Ichiboo exchange.—The naval force in harbour.—The United Service Club.—Municipal matters.—The Swiss embassy's exhibition.—Murder of a Portuguese by a British subject.—Recall of Mons. de Bellecourt 267-280

CHAPTER XXIV.

Hopeful dawn of 1864.—Interview between British Chargé and Japanese officials.—Ominous hints.—Russian Envoy arrives.—Ratifications exchanged.—Signature of Swiss treaty.—Japanese Government fulfils promises made in Europe by the former Embassy.—Departure of new Embassy for France.—Yokohama personal changes.—Liberality but want of public spirit in Eastern communities.—Public Hospital.—General salubrity of Yokohama.—Japanese and small-pox.—Sanitary Committee.—Trade.—The Japanese New Year............281-292

CHAPTER XXV.

Life in Yokohama.—Progress of trade.—Yokohama unfortunate in Municipal matters —Fire.—Sir R. Alcock's return to Japan.—Lieut. Colonel Neale's departure—Scheme for iron floating dock.—French Hatoba completed.—Attack on Mr. Sutton of Nagasaki.—Foreign ministers call on the Tycoon's Government to destroy the Choshiu batteries and open the Inland Sea:—Communications with the Government.—Peace policy reported as prevalent at Kioto.—Satsuma and Silk.—Consular changes.—Arrival of M. Leon Roches, the new French Minister —Sir R. Alcock obtain's promise for a recreation ground.—Departure of M. de Bellecourt.—Arrival of Conqueror with Royal Marines, and Semiramis with French Fusiliers.—Return of Tycoon to Yedo.—Commercial.—Decided improvement of relations between Japanese and foreigners. 293-302

CHAPTER XXVI.

Arrival of H.B.M.'s XX Regiment.—Ultimatum respecting Shimonoséki.—The Tycoon's difficulties.—Peace dispatches from Earl Russell arrive too late.—Japanese visit Europe for education:—Return of Ito Shiunske and Inouyé Bunda.—Bearers of a letter to the prince of Choshiu from the foreign ministers.—Conveyed to their province on board H.M.S. Barossa and Cormorant.—Ill success.—The ineffectual appeal on behalf of Choshiu to the Mikado.—The attack on the palace.—Owari appointed Commander-in-chief to punish the clan.—Indignation against Choshiu in Yedo.—His yashikis burnt.—Sudden return of the envoys.—Their agreement with France not ratified—Departure of expedition against Shimonoséki.—Friendly intercourse between the foreign and native soldiers.—The battle of Shimonoséki—Details.—Peace concluded.—The indemnity.—Alternatives proposed by foreigners and rejected by Japanese Government.—Sir R. Alcock ordered home to explain matters to the Foreign Office.........303-314

CHAPTER XXVII.

The changes that have happened since the battle of Shimonoséki. —Effects of the battles of Kagoshima and Shimonoséki on the clans of Satsuma and Choshiu.—Bitterness of Choshiu against the Yedo Government. —The bravery and patriotism of the clan.—Adoption by Satsuma and Choshiu of foreign arms.—Desire of Tycoon to do the same, but unwillingness of many of his retainers to use them.—Present prejudice of fighting men in favour of the sword.—The sword and the rule that it should not be unsheathed except to shed blood.—A personal reminiscence.—One more proof of the deadly character of the sword.—Excursions of foreigners. 315-321

CHAPTER XXVIII.

Kamakura.—Description and history.—Yoritomo its founder.—Yoritomo's descendants.—Hojo Yoshitoki.—Recapitulation of the foregoing—Yoritomo's successors, and end of the dynasty. Kamakura no longer the Governmental capital................322-330

CHAPTER XXIX.

Another tragedy.—Attack at Kamakura on Major Baldwin and Lieut. Bird.—Manner of the attack.—Consternation throughout the settlement.—Determination.—The funeral. —Justice.—The assassins caught and decapitated.—First doubts of foreigners as to the true culprits cleared up.— Shimidzu Seiji.—Procès Verbal.—Sentence.—Public exposure in the streets of Yokohama.—The execution ground.—The executioner.—The prisoner's demeanour.—His anathema against foreigners.—His death ; and the exhibition of his head for three days.—Capture and decapitation of his miserable accomplice.—Fatal fracas in the Yoshiwara.—A Frenchman killed—but without *malice prepense*. 331-339

CHAPTER XXX.

Proposal to establish a Chamber of Commerce.—Apparent need of such an institution.—Interference of Japanese officials in every transaction.—Visit of foreign representatives to Yedo has a salutary effect.—Yokohama and literary institutions.— Municipal.—Good feeling between the Japanese and foreign troops.—Field day in presence of high functionaries native and foreign.—Another incident.—Japanese make the road by Homoku valley and Mississippi bay.—The Rifle Range.— Improved relations, and departure of Royal Marines.—Sir R. Alcock appointed ambassador to China.—Sir Harry Parkes to succeed him:—Report of determination of Tycoon to punish Choshiu, and of the latter to resist.................................340-347

CHAPTER XXXI.

Evidences of Japanese acceptance of a progress policy.— Incident that proved it to the author.—Proclamations of the Tycoon before starting for the West.—General proclamation. —Proclamation to the Gorojiu.—The Tycoon's passage through Kanagawa, as witnessed by foreigners.—Appeal of the Tycoon for supplies to defray the expenses of the present expedition. —Circumstances showing the test his retainers were put to in their sympathy with Choshiu.—Many plead sickness.—Matsudaira Idzu-no-Kami's reply and its effect.—Letter from a Colonel of Artillery in the army to his brother in Yedo.— Peril of Tycoon *en route*.—Plot for his assassinaton at Dzézó discovered.—One of the ringleaders executed in Yedo. 348-357

CHAPTER XXXII.

Exclusively Municipal. 358-376

CHAPTER XXXIV.

The "Japan Times" started.—Chamber of Commerce.—Yokohama Rifle Association and *Tir National*.—Yokohama enjoyments.—Ichiboo Exchange.—Arrival of H. M. S. "Princess Royal."—Departure of Royal Marines.—H. B. M. Supreme Court.—Close of the year 1865...............................377-384

CHAPTER XXXV.

Sir Harry Parkes, and his practical measures.—The ratification of the treaties the 'sine qua non.'—Accord between foreign representatives.—Trade benefits by the general accord.—Export of silkworm's seed, virtually the salvation of Italian silk enterprise.—Squadron ordered to Hiogo.—State embarkation of ministers.—Proceedings at Hiogo, Osaka and Kioto.—Visit of members of Gorojiu to the squadron.—Occupation of the officers of the Legations.—Ten days given for a final reply.—Excitement at Kioto.—Threats against the Tycoon and the Mikado.—Mikado requests that the squadron will leave Hiogo.—Disgraces two members of Gorojiu.—The foreign representatives remain firm.—Letter written to the Mikado by the Tycoon offering to resign, fortunately stopped.—In its stead, document prepared entreating the Mikado to give his sanction to the treaties.—The Tycoon sends troops to Kioto.—Mikado still unfavorable.—Tycoon proceeds to Kioto ; orders apprehension of daimio's officers, and assembles representatives of daimios.—Excitement excessive.—Foreign Ministers hourly informed of passing events.—Still firm.—Crisis at hand.—Final interview between the Gorojiu, and high officials of the Tycoon, with Hitotsubashi at their head, and the Mikado.—Their resolution.—Hitotsubashi's action.—The Mikado yields.—The treaties are ratified.—Instantaneous effect.—Letter of the Satsuma clan to the Mikado, protesting against the opening of Hiogo, and demanding to be placed in van of the army to oppose it...385-395

CHAPTER XXXVI.

Affairs in Yokohama.—Arrival of the Fusiyama.—Fire in Yedo.—Schools.—Native peculiarities.—Professor Risley.—Many useful schemes afloat.—General progress.................396-407

CHAPTER XXXVII.

Proposal for a public garden.—Violent death of a French sailor and its consequences.—English and Japanese troops parade together.—Military arrivals and departures.—Death of Mr. John Macdonald.—Clemency towards a Japanese soldier.—Government permit Japanese subjects to visit foreign countries. 408-418

EXPLANATIONS.

THE Mikado's titles are numerous. In this work he is generally called either Mikado or Emperor.

The proper title of the Yedo ruler was Shogun. Though sometimes using this title, I have more generally referred to him by that always formerly used by foreigners—Tycoon.

The last Tycoon was known at the time of his accession as HITOTSUBASHI; afterwards as YOSHI-HISA or YOSHI-NOBU. Subsequently as KEIKI-Sama; and his name now he is in retirement, is—ICHIDO.

The Kugé were nobles of the Court of the Mikado; and were hereditarily noble, from the fact of their blood relationship, (however distant), to the Mikado.

SHIMADZU SABURO, who figures largely in the story of foreign intercourse with Japan, is spoken of at different periods under different names. First SHIMADZU IDZUMI-NO-KAMI; then SHIMADZU SABURO; then SHIMADZU OSUMI-NO-KAMI; then SHIMADZU HISAMITSZU, by which he is now known. From 1872 to 1876 he occupied the position of Sa-Daijin—Prime Minister of the right; the third subject in the realm.

CHOSHIU, in the following pages, is named in several different ways. First by his name and rank—MOWORI or MORI DAIZEN-NO-DAIBU; then as the Prince of Choshiu; the prince of Nagato; or simply CHOSHIU, NAGATO.

Bakufu, was the term commonly used for the Shogun's Government.

ERRATA.

PAGE	FOR	READ.
15...............	Yedo, Osaka, Hiogo and Niigata on the 1st January 1863.	Niigata and Hiogo on the 1st January 1863, and foreigners were to be allowed to reside for the purposes of trade in Yedo from the 1st January 1862, and Osaka from the 1st January 1863.
83 (9th line from top)	twelve	fourteen.
314 (3rd ,, ,,)	$50,000	$500,000.
322 (Heading)	Chapter VIII.	Chapter XXVIII.
386 (10th line from bottom.)	high officials and the Tycoon.	and high officials of the Tycoon.

YOUNG JAPAN.

PRELIMINARY CHAPTER.

INTRODUCTORY.—JAPAN AS IT APPEARS TO A SUPERFICIAL OBSERVER NOW.—VERY DIFFERENT TWENTY ONE YEARS AGO.—WHERE IS THE DIFFERENCE?—THE IMPERIAL DYNASTY.—JINMU TENNO.—ANTOKU TENNO.—COMMENCEMENT OF THE MODERN HISTORY OF JAPAN.—THE DUAL SYSTEM OF GOVERNMENT.—THE EMPEROR'S SUPREMACY NEVER QUESTIONED. THE TYCOON, SEI-I TAI SHÔGUN.—YORITOMO.—KAMAKURA.—COMPLETE ISOLATION OF THE MIKADO; AND GOVERNMENT BY THE MILITARY CHIEF.—EFFORTS OF MIKADO TO RECOVER HIS AUTHORITY.—TEMPORARY SUCCESS OF GODAIGO.—ASHIKAGA TAKA-UJI.—OTA NOBUNAGA.—TAICO SAMA.—IYEYAS' FOUNDER OF THE LAST DYNASTY OF SHÔGUNS.—JAPAN OPEN TO FOREIGNERS FROM 1542 TO 1637.—FINALLY CLOSED TO ALL BUT THE DUTCH FACTORY AT NAGASAKI.—THE KUGE, OR COURT NOBLES.—THE DAIMIOS—KOKUSHIU, FUDAI AND TOZAMA.—HATAMOTOS.—THE SAMURAI.—THE COMMON PEOPLE.—THE GOVERNMENT AT A GLANCE.

I PROPOSE to write of YOUNG JAPAN. It is necessary, therefore, that I should, in as few words as possible, give my readers some idea of the Japan of antiquity; that they may clearly understand the transition that has taken place the course of which I am about to describe.

Travellers who should bend their steps hitherward in this year of grace 1879, and land at either of the open ports of Yokohama, Kobe or Nagasaki, and who should look only at the surface of things, without going out of the way to seek and to find the people and places which give a distinct interest to the country, might easily pass on without emotion; and truthfully record their convictions in the statement, that, from what they saw of Japan, it was a quiet hum-drum region. Very little movement. Very little business. The people so little diverse from others, that there is nothing more to be said about them.

Yet only twenty-one years ago it was far otherwise.

Then anyone who arrived here, however superficial an observer he might be, found everything strange, and every human being he met, full of interest and attraction.

Where is the difference?

Why are the *then* and *now* so unlike?

The answer is, that, at that time, Japan experienced a new birth.

She now attains her majority!

Then, boasting herself as one of the most ancient Empires in the world, with an Imperial Dynasty extending over two thousand five hundred years, she was for the first time born into the family of nations. In the most literal sense may she have been said previously to speak and think and act as a child; but now she is of age she has put away childish things.

Twenty five years ago the knowledge of Japan by the outer world, was little indeed; but the knowledge of the outer world by Japan, amounted to almost nothing.

The acquaintance that has since spring up has been of a very intimate character. It is to be hoped that as this intimacy ripens it may prove beneficial to all.

The Empire of Japan claims an existence of two thousand five hundred and thirty nine years, during which period there has been but one dynasty of imperial rulers, whose source was from the gods.

The first mundane emperor was JINMU TENNO, the son of TENSHIU DAIJIN, the Sun goddess. The sanctity of this celestial descent and its universal acceptance by the people has been throughout all ages the one irrefragable pillar that has supported, and still continues to support, the Imperial House; and, amid all the changing scenes of life—through all the fierce civil contests that have blazed in the land—not once has any ambitious power-seeker dared to put forth his hand to appropriate the supreme office to himself. Emperors have been dethroned and rivals placed in their seats, but never once has it been attempted to raise any to the dignity who were not of the descent of JINMU TENNO, son of AMA TERASU ONGAMI, the benevolent dispenser of light.

JINMU at first exercised his power only over the southeast portion of Kiushiu; but that island being overrun with robbers and lawless people, he formed the resolution to bring it into order; and having accomplished this successfully, he determined to effect the same amelioration over the whole cluster of islands. Crossing over to what is now known as Aki, the adjoining province to Choshiu, he brought the whole country under his sway; then, taking up his residence at Kashiwabara in Yamato, he made it the seat of his government; and from his days downwards to 1868, the *miako* or metropolis continued to be in that province. He assumed the title of Tenno or Tenshi—Son of Heaven, which has been preserved from that day to this.

For more than eighteen centuries the successors of JINMU both reigned and ruled; but in the reign of ANTOKU (A.D. 1181), the struggle commenced which ended in transferring the governing power to a lieutenant, who, professing to receive his authority from the Emperor, kept him closely immured within the precincts of his residence at Kioto, and arbitrarily governed the country from a capital far removed from the old time-honoured centre, in which still resided the true nobility—the descendants, and the branches, of the imperial family.

It is at this time that the modern history of Japan commences.

From this time forward that dual system which was such a puzzle to foreigners, and which was not clearly understood until it was on the very eve of overthrow, was maintained.

It was as follows :—

The Mikado, Tenno, heaven-born Emperor, was supreme.

This was never questioned, and never lost sight of. He was always the fountain of honour ; the source of authority. But practically this was reduced to the delegation of power to one individual, who, from exercising all the duties, proudly appropriated to himself all the attributes, of sovereignty.

This was the chief known to foreigners as the Tycoon (tai kun, great ruler). His real title was Sei-i Tai Shôgun (barbarian-controlling generalissimo). By rights he was not entitled to the first name ; and it is probable that he only obtained it accidentally by the use of the two words in conversation between Japanese officials and some of the early foreigners. To a Japanese, until very recently, his country was the universe ; its sovereign the great ruler ; and the real emperor had so completely sunk out of the knowledge of the people that the only ruler they knew was the Sei-i Tai Shôgun ; of whom they might speak as the great ruler, and foreigners might suppose that it was his title.

The title " Shôgun " is of some antiquity, but not until the year 1184 did its bearer assume sovereign powers.

Yoritomo was the first to invest it with this importance. He it was, who, while admitting himself to be a vassal of the Mikado, deprived him of power; and who, gathering all the great military leaders around him at Kamakura, the new governmental city of his own creation, so cemented his strength by the sagacious rules of government he established, that thenceforward he was virtually to all intents and purposes the real ruler in Japan. It is true that theoretically the sanction of the Mikado had to be obtained to all that was done by the Shôgun; and it was usually given as a matter of course when sought; but it was only on rare or very special occasions that it was thought necessary to seek it.

On two or three occasions, the Mikado of the day made a fitful effort to break the yoke, but always unsuccessfully; and so things continued for seven centuries. It has of late become the fashion to speak of the Tycoon as an arch-usurper, a *parvenu*, as a mere vassal, an arrogant military tyrant, exercising powers he did not legally possess, and assuming titles to which he had no right.

But all this seems really absurd. For if the actual wielding of the governing power during seven centuries does not justify the position not only assumed by the Shôguns, but claimed for them and acknowledged by the people, then it is hard to say when parvenuism ceases, or when the title of usurper may be set aside.

Yoritomo established the dual system; and fondly hoped he had founded a dynasty. This, however, proved fallacious. His two immediate successors were his descendants, but totally lacking his ability, were unable to retain his power. At their death the office was transferred to a scion of a rival family. A series of minors were appointed, each of whom was somehow or other disposed of before attaining manhood: and the government was administered by the powerful Hojo family, who played an important part in the history of the empire from A.D. 1219 to 1333, when the emperor GODAIGO made a vigorous effort to break the thraldom in which he was held.

It was unfortunate for him that he had no military following; and he had also no money or means of raising it. He was dependent solely on the provision made for him by the government of Kamakura.

He found some powerful friends, however; and one or two of them are to this day mentioned among the most honourable names recorded in Japanese history. At one time it appeared as if success had crowned their struggle; and for about a couple of years, 1333-5, the government was carried on in the name of the Emperor, from Kioto. One of those, however, who had been the most prominent of his generals, succeeded in having the title of Sei-i Tai Shôgun conferred upon himself; and once in possession of the title, he proceeded to act with all the arbitrariness and resolution of his predecessors. ASHIKAGA TAKA-UJI, thus invested with power, the office remained in his family for two hundred and forty years, from 1335 to 1574, during which time the disputes between rival chieftains ran so high that the sword was never at rest; but from one end of the Empire to the other, blood flowed like water.

To put an end to this state of things OTA NOBUNAGA buckled on his armour; and after a brilliant series of victories, in which he was mainly assisted by HIDEYOSHI, he brought the ASHIKAGA dynasty to an end, and exercised the ruling power on behalf of the Mikado from 1574 to 1582. During this period there was no Shôgun, but the Mikado was still kept within his palace boundaries; sovereignty being administered in reality, though not in name, by the Ota chief.

At his death Towotomi Hideyoshi took the reins. He was of humble origin; but having entered the service of Nobunaga as a stable boy, rose by degrees, until he became the most renowned of all his generals. For sixteen years he wielded the supreme power; appropriating to himself the title of Taico, or great man; and he is now generally known by the name of Taico Sama, and spoken of by all classes of Japanese as the greatest hero in the annals of their country.

His successor was Tokugawa Iyeyasu, who received the title of Sei-i Tai Shôgun in 1604, and was the founder of that dynasty which lasted until 1868, when it was overthrown, and the dual government was closed for ever, by the events which I have undertaken to record.

By Iyeyas' the dual government was perfected. By him was formed that wondrous system, which, creating a host of military chieftains wielding semi-royal authority in their own dominions, made of each, for the Shôgun, a bulwark against all the rest.

A system of espionage was also established, by which every act of every chieftain throughout the country, was reported to the Central Government. Yedo was made the capital, and there every territorial prince large and small, was obliged to reside during six months of every year, maintaining in the city, for the service of the Shôgun, a number of armed retainers, ready at call, to do the behests of the Yedo chief.

From the year 1604 the Mikado became of less account than ever. One after another lived and died at Kioto, of whom all that can be said is, that their names are recorded, and their line was preserved unbroken; but so utterly useless were they as rulers, that their very existence was unheard of by many of the common people, and doubted by more, who looked upon the Shôgun as their sole sovereign.

Japan was first visited by Europeans in 1542 or thereabouts. A Portuguese named MENDEZ PINTO has the credit of its discovery. Such was the cordiality of his reception, that, on his tale being heard at home, many of his countrymen, merchants and missionaries, sought its shores, the one to win gold, the other souls. And great success rewarded the efforts of both.

They were followed by Dutch and English traders, and by Spanish missionaries; and for a while all were welcomed. But the time came when the jealousies and rivalries of the foreigners militated against themselves.

NOBUNAGA in his hatred of the Buddhists,—whom he made every effort to destroy, and thousands of whom he caused to be massacred in cold blood,—encouraged the missionaries, whose disciples multiplied, until it seemed that the whole land would be speedily converted. The result was that they became arrogant and overbearing; and the converts so regardless of native authority, that IYEYAS' first, and finally IYEMITZ', the third of the dynasty, ordered the expulsion of the missionaries, and subsequently of all foreigners. In 1637, the country was closed against them, so that from that time forward, with the exception of the few members of the Dutch Factory, not one was found in the whole empire. The Dutch were limited to the little islet of Deshima at Nagasaki, which they were rarely permitted to leave at all; and even on the particular occasions, few and far between, when they did obtain permission to cross the boundary, it was only under the closest guard and supervision. To them came one ship in the course of each twelve-months; and this ship's cargo out and in, with those of a few Chinese junks, represented the whole of the foreign trade of Japan during two centuries and a quarter—i.e. from the year 1637 until the date at which my narrative commences.

Having explained the exact position of the Mikado and the Shógun, it remains to speak of the body politic.

The nobles, in the eyes of foreigners, on their first arrival here, appeared to be the daimios—territorial princes or chieftains; but although these possessed all the power and wealth, they were not the true, legitimate, nobility. This was confined to the Kugé—relatives, close or distant, of the sovereign; who all resided in, or in the neighbourhood of, Kioto. Some were members of his council; some occupied posts of honour and nominally of authority; whilst others were placed in positions of great eminence in connection with religion, and lorded it over the sects with all the pride of the proudest of prelates elsewhere. But there were others who were poor and obliged to earn their bread by the labour of their hands or the exercise of their intellects, or by their accomplishments and graces; yet even these were noble, and ranked above the very Shògun himself.

The daimios were for the most part the creation of the Shógunate; their nobility, therefore, was not even acknowledged by the Kugé. So much was this felt, that the proudest of them were wont to seek office conferring rank from the Mikado; and were prouder of such imperially-bestowed dignities than of all other honours.

The daimios were of three classes:—Kokushiu, Fudai, and Tozama.

The Kokushiu were semi-independent chieftains, who, although compelled to submit to Iyeyas', were sufficiently powerful to prevent their territorial possessions being alienated or disturbed; and who were treated by Iyeyas' rather as equals than as vassals. He insisted on their coming to Yedo as the rest of the daimios did; but it was his custom to go to Goten Yama, outside the city limits, to meet and welcome them. This custom was continued during the lifetime of his successor; but Iyemitz', who followed, felt himself strong enough to discontinue it, being disinclined to acknowledge any equality.

The Fudai are described by Iyeyas' himself,—in his "Legacy," as translated by Mr. F. J. Lowder, formerly of H. B. M.'s Consular service, but now legal adviser to the Japanese Customs,—as, "those samurai who followed me, and proffered me their fealty before the overthrow of the castle of Osaka, in the province of Sesshiu."

The Tozama are "those who returned and submitted to me after its downfall."

To the Fudai alone were entrusted the highest offices of state; the others, however able, being excluded.

Iyeyas' further decreed :—"Although the collected Fudai are numerous, I put on record those whom I brought from my ancient seat, Mikawa." (Here follow the names of eighteen daimios). "This is a separate class, from among the male issue of which are to be chosen such as possess talent and ability, and entrusted with the direction of the business of the Shôgun's Government. They are denominated 'Koshiu' (or Gorojiu); and even though there may be some among the Tozama of extraordinary ability, it is not permitted to appoint them to this office."

Again :—"The Fudai-samurai, great and small, all have shown the utmost fidelity, even suffering their bones to be ground to powder, and their flesh chopped up for me. In what way soever their posterity may offend,—for anything less than treason,—their estate may not be confiscated."

The revenues of the daimios varied from 10,000 to 1,000,000 *kokus* of rice (of the value, at the time foreign intercourse recommenced, of about fifteen shillings a *koku*.) Each one was obliged to supply a certain number of fighting men for the service of the Shôgun, in proportion to his registered income; and they took precedence also in accordance with their revenues.

But there was a large class of samurai, called Hatamoto—supporters of the flag; who were the immediate retainers of the Shôgun. Upon these devolved the heaviest duties, military and civil, in carrying out the Government. They received incomes varying from 3,000 to 10,000 *kokus*, and had to furnish their contingent of fighting men as required.

The daimios, hatamotos, and their retainers, formed the samurai, or military caste. They were deemed altogether superior to all other classes, and possessed many privileges. IYEYAS' thus provides for them:— "The samurai are the masters of the four classes. Agriculturists, artizans and merchants may not behave in a rude manner to samurai. The term for a rude man is 'other-than-expected:' and a samurai is not to be interfered with in cutting down a fellow who has behaved to him in a manner other than is expected. The samurai are grouped into direct retainers, secondary retainers and nobles and retainers of high and low grade; but the same line of conduct is equally allowable to them all towards an 'other-than-expected fellow.'"

The samurai, high and low, were the two-sworded men, of whom so much has to be said in the following pages. All the progress that has taken place, and all the opposition to it, has been their work; and literally the whole interest of Japanese history centres in them.

The common people were divided into agriculturists, artizans and merchants; ranking in that order. Below these were actors and beggars; and as the lowest of all, not admitted to be named among the people, and living apart as a race separate and proscribed, were the *yétas*, or people whose trade or occupation was in any way connected with the handling of skins of beasts.

It only remains to mention in this introductory chapter, that to all intents and purposes the following was the scheme of Government :—

At the head the Shôgun (Tycoon).

The Gotairo, or Regent, hereditary in the family of the daimio Ii KAMON-no-KAMI.

The Gorojiu, or Council of State, which really held the reins of government. Usually the decisions of the Gorojiu were absolute; but if necessary they were submitted to the Shogun or Regent. In cases of extreme importance, such as arose after the making of the foreign treaties, a Council of the eighteen great daimios was called; and the result was communicated to the Mikado by the Shogun's representative, resident in Kioto.

Above these was the DAIRI or Imperial Court at Kioto. In sublime impotence, but with undisputed majesty, the Mikado reigned—the most helpless, but the most venerated, of all the sovereigns of the East.

CHAPTER I.

THE MAJORITY OF FOREIGN INTERCOURSE WITH JAPAN.—ARRIVAL OF LORD ELGIN TO MAKE A TREATY FOR ENGLAND.—COMMODORE PERRY'S U. S. TREATY.—FOLLOWED BY OTHERS.—THE TREATIES, THOUGH PEACEFULLY OBTAINED, EFFECTED BY INTIMIDATION.—LORD ELGIN'S MISSION.—ARRIVAL OF MR. ALCOCK, H. B. M. ENVOY.—TOZENJI.—KANAGAWA.—DISPUTE BETWEEN JAPANESE AND FOREIGN REPRESENTATIVES AS TO SITE OF THE SETTLEMENT.—PRACTICALLY SETTLED BY THE MERCHANTS.—YOKOHAMA, OLD AND NEW.—RESPECTIVE CAPABILITIES OF THE TWO PORTS.

OMNIA MUTANTUR! The changes to which all mundane things are subject, and which Japan has so long and so strenuously resisted, have at last reached her islands and proved her amenable to nature's universal law. "Those who have turned the world upside down have come hither also," may be her cry, when she sees the rapidity with which old things are passing away, and her people bestirring themselves to compete for some of the prizes held out to enterprise and intelligence.

The intercourse between Japan and the outer world has attained its majority. It is over twenty-one years since the commercial treaty between America and Japan, which opened the way for subsequent treaties with other foreign nations, was signed. Little more than twenty-one years have elapsed since H. M. S. *Furious*, in command of Captain SHERARD OSBORN, R. N., bore Lord ELGIN to Yedo for the purpose of arranging a treaty of amity, commerce, and friendship between the Queen of Great Britain and the Emperor of Japan; and less than twenty-one years have passed since the ratification of these treaties was exchanged formally in Yedo. Yet, in this short period, how many and how great have been the changes. Experience has been gained by all parties; but Japan has received lessons that it has taken European nations centuries to acquire; and the antiquated notions with which the people were imbued, are fast crumbling to dust beneath the wands of science and of commerce.

I am about to give a short recapitulation of the course of events in Japan, more particularly with regard to Yokohama and Yedo, now called Tokio, since the signature of Mr. HARRIS's and Lord ELGIN's American and English treaties in 1858.

The first treaty between America and Japan, in which Commodore PERRY, U. S. N., was the accredited agent of the United States' government, was made in 1854. Yokohama was the place where the negociations were carried on, and this alone must always render it notable in Japanese history. Commodore PERRY's expedition was composed of nine men-of-war, three of which were steamers and six sailing-ships. These, anchoring in line-of-battle off Yokohama, preparations were made by the Japanese for the reception of the Commodore and the opening of the conferences. A spacious wooden building had been hastily erected, which had been fitted up with every regard to the comfort of the strangers. Commodore PERRY, assuming as he had on all occasions from his first arrival off Uraga the preceding year, a high and aristocratic tone, claimed the treaty not as a concession but as a right ; and after many objections had been made, which he firmly refused to attach any weight to, he gained his point. An agreement was signed by which the Japanese were bound to extend kindness and assistance to any American subjects who might happen to be shipwrecked on the coast, and supply provisions to any American ships that might require them ; and further to open the ports of Shimoda, Hakodadi, and Napha in the Loochoo islands, to American trade. Commodore PERRY had only gone a few months, when Admiral STIRLING appeared, and on behalf of England obtained a similar treaty. Mr. DONKER CURTIUS arranged a convention ameliorating the condition of the Dutch at Nagasaki ; and, in 1857, Count POUTIATINE concluded a treaty for Russia. But all these were but preliminary. A fuller commercial treaty was made in 1858 between Mr. HARRIS, as the plenipotentiary for America, and the Tycoon. This was quickly followed by that between Great Britain and Japan ; and a little later by the treaties with France, Holland and Russia. By these treaties, Kanagawa, Nagasaki and Hakodadi were to be opened on the 1st July 1859 ; and Yedo, Osaka, Hiogo and Ni-i-gata on the 1st January, 1863.

As one effect of this narrative will be, to show, by the progress made by Japan during the past twenty-one years, that the intercourse with foreign nations has been beneficial to her, perhaps the manner in which the treaties were obtained need not be objected to. The end will be held to justify the means. The decided movements and resolute demeanour of each of the diplomatists engaged in framing the treaties with the Japanese, were absolutely requisite in dealing with the proud and unveracious people they had to encounter, and no treaties would have been obtained to this day in any other way.

Commodore PERRY has received great laudation for the manner in which he succeeded in obtaining his ends, and for the treaty he made with Japan. Yet it is quite certain that if theorists and humanitarians are supported in their principles, he was altogether wrong in " riding the high horse " in the way he did, from his arrival to propose a treaty in 1853, to his departure with a treaty in 1854. As a mere matter of fact he undoubtedly fulfilled the objects of his mission; and the world approves of the course he took. Strictly speaking, however, his action in visiting the gulf of Yedo, against the law of the land, and choosing his own anchorage in spite of the remonstrances of the Japanese government officials, was most reprehensible. If a Japanese ship should attempt to anchor in an American port in any manner or place inconsistent with the harbour regulations, very short work would be made with it. Yet we read in the pages of a professed " comrade and friend " of the Japanese, who dedicates his book to their searchers after knowledge and truth both in the past and the present, " with fraternal regard : "—

" Then came PERRY, the moral grandeur of whose peaceful triumph has never been challenged or compromised."

And the same writer adds :—

"The United States introduced Japan to the world, though her opening could not have been long delayed. The American, TOWNSEND HARRIS, peer and successor to PERRY, by his dauntless courage, patience, courtesy, gentleness, firmness, and incorruptible honesty, won for all nations treaties, trade, residence and commerce."

I leave this for the present as I find it. Probably I may have more to say on the subject in a later chapter.

That Commodore PERRY and Mr. TOWNSEND HARRIS concluded their treaties peacefully is admitted. But in both cases it was a triumph of might over right. The first came with a force sufficient to overawe the gentle beings, who were "compelled by foreigners for the sake of their cursed dollars, to open their country;" and it did overawe them. The second attained his end, by picturing to the said gentle minds the terrors to be apprehended from an English and French fleet recently victorious in China, bearing down upon Japan with ambassadors from their respective sovereigns, to enforce a treaty from Japan as they had done in China. So much for the "peaceful triumph." So much for the "gentleness, firmness and incorruptible honesty." No! Commodore PERRY himself makes this manly avowal:—

"In conducting all my business with these very sagacious and deceitful people, I have found it profitable to bring to my aid the experience gained in former, and by no means limited, intercourse with the inhabitants of strange lands, civilised and barbarian; and this experience has admonished me, that, with people of forms, it is necessary either to set all ceremony aside, or to out-Herod Herod in assumed personal consequence and ostentation."

This was in extenuation of his having refused to anchor at Uraga or Kamakura, both of which were urged by the Japanese, and his insisting on conducting his business at some place nearer to Yedo than either. He carried his point, and Yokohama became the honoured spot; though what advantage there was in Yokohama over Uraga it would be hard to tell; except that it marked one, to the side of the "peaceful triumph.

In like manner, we see Lord ELGIN's delightful experience, which ended in "many demonstrations of affection on both sides." That experience "had been marked by an interest and novelty not to be surpassed, and by a success, in a political point of view, scarcely to have been anticipated."

Lord ELGIN had written home from China his oft-quoted declamation against the injustice of his countrymen against Asiatics; and yet he arrives in Japan, and, like PERRY, immediately sets the Japanese Government at defiance, by refusing to treat with them anywhere else than at Yedo; persists in going there in the teeth of the most strenuous opposition on the part of the officials; and having come so far, signifies that he has come to make a treaty, in such terms that the Government see plainly enough that very little choice is left them.

A yacht as a present from the Queen of England to the Emperor (Tycoon) of Japan is made the pretext for his visit to Yedo. Mr. OLYPHANT, his private secretary, (whose narrative of the mission, sanctioned by Lord ELGIN, is worthy of perusal by all who are interested either in the Celestial Empire, or that of the Rising Sun), thus writes:—

"As Lord ELGIN depended chiefly for an excuse for proceeding to Yedo, upon the necessity for delivering the yacht, if possible, to the Emperor himself, he assured the Governor (of Nagasaki) that it was not in his power to part with the yacht except at the capital."

On leaving Nagasaki, then,—after a stormy passage, during which they were driven, by stress of weather, to take refuge in "a slight indenture of the coast" in "the deep unsurveyed bay of Kagosima," they reached Shimoda.

Here they found Mr. HARRIS, the American Consul-General, whose flag, the Stars and Stripes, proudly waved over his temple-residence at Kakisaki—a village about a mile and a half from a town of Shimoda. They were immediately visited by Mr. HEUSKEN, the Dutch interpreter and secretary of Mr. HARRIS, who brought Lord ELGIN "an offer of services on the part of the American Consul."

Mr. OLYPHANT dilates on the hermit-like existence led by Mr. HARRIS and Mr. HEUSKEN in this "retreat." It must undoubtedly have been felt to be so by themselves; for not even the society of the few (two or three) Americans who went to, and for a time located themselves at, Shimoda, could have made it anything else. And yet there must have been in it much to relieve the monotony. The country to which they had come, the people among whom they moved, in themselves offered a great deal of most interesting employment for the mind. There is a vast difference between being so placed in Japan, and in any other eastern country; and in the early days of foreign intercourse, at a distance from the capital, this was so to a greater extent even than now. The Japanese are by nature such sociable beings, that those willing to form friendships among them have no difficulty in doing so; and as the life of the nation twenty one years ago was so different to anything known to Europe in modern times, and yet possessed so much of what we know obtained in Europe in bygone days— (the days of romance—the days we characterise as the 'good old times')—there was novelty, there was real enjoyment, in studying it. To this day there are a great many foreigners in Japan, who are content to spend all their time among Japanese, and to whom the idea of "hermit life" and isolation never occurs; and the manner in which Mr. HARRIS laid himself out to obtain the friendship and confidence of the people may satisfy us that it did not much oppress him. As yet he had none of the difficulties to contemplate that afterwards became such a strain upon foreign diplomatists. He had certain matters of some importance to settle—such, for instance, as the right of his countrymen to reside for purposes of trade at Shimoda—but these were trifles light as air, and gave him but little trouble.

The success of the British and French arms, which resulted in the Treaty of Tientsin, materially aided him in making his treaty. By representing the certainty of the ambassadors of these two nations following up their high-handed proceedings in China with similar action in Japan, he so wrought upon the fears of the Government that he obtained what he had so strenuously worked for, under a promise to use his best influence as a mediator between the two mighty powers and Japan, should it be requisite. Of course it was not necessary.

Mr. OLYPHANT dismisses the subject of Mr. HARRIS's treaty in a few words, but very amusingly:—

" Mr. HARRIS had only recently returned from Yedo, where he had only just succeeded in negotiating a more favourable treaty with the Japanese Government than had been made since the days of Captain SARIS. He had passed some months in that city, during which time both he and Mr. DONKER CURTIUS had been engaged in fruitless efforts to induce the Government to accede to their terms. In 1855, the latter gentleman had concluded a mercantile arrangement, by which certain concessions were allowed to foreigners; but the cumbersome machinery of the Geldkammer was still retained, and the monopoly of the trade was reserved to the Japanese Government, under conditions which rendered the concessions worthless to nations engaged in commerce upon enlightened principles. Mr. HARRIS, however, was determined to make a treaty worthy the progressive people whom he represented; and Mr. DONKER CURTIUS, finding him so engaged, repaired to Yedo, determined if possible not to be outdone. It so happened that his precautions were unavailing.

" Finding the Japanese cabinet inexorable, both gentlemen left in despair,—Mr. DONKER CURTIUS upon a long overland journey of two months to Nagasaki, Mr. HARRIS to return to Simoda. He had scarcely reached it, however, before the Powhattan arrived with intelligence of the Treaty of Tientsin. Mr. HARRIS then lost not a moment in himself carrying the news to the capital; and while Mr. DONKER CURTIUS was journeying laboriously to Nagasaki, ignorant of the great events that had taken place, his rival had signed his treaty, and was back again at Simoda, reposing on his laurels."

I am not aware whether any account of Mr. HARRIS's mode of passing his time at Shimoda has been published. The view of his residence here given, will show the beauty of its surroundings. It lies about a mile and a half or a little more from the town of Shimoda, at a village called Kakisaki, (Oyster Point), and is not above five minutes' walk from the beautiful bay of Shimoda.

But to return to Lord ELGIN. We read:—

"The day following our arrival at Simoda, Lord ELGIN received a visit from the Governor. He had learnt that we proposed going up the Bay of Yedo, and his object now was to exert all his powers of persuasion to induce Lord ELGIN to forego this intention. He brought a large suite on board with him, all of whom seemed to appreciate an English luncheon. I was rather startled to hear one of them refuse Curaçoa, and ask for Maraschino instead. The Governor himself was a man of a most jovial temperament. He indulged in constant chuckles, and rather reminded one of Mr. WELLER, senior. He seemed to consider everything a capital joke—even Lord ELGIN's positive refusal to comply with his request to hand over the yacht at Simoda and remain at that place. He used every possible argument to carry his point, but without avail. He said he dreaded the consequences to himself, and chuckled; still more did he dread the consequences to us, and chuckled again."

The British Embassy left Shimoda on the 12th of August, having on board Mr. HEUSKEN, who had been obligingly lent by Mr. HARRIS to Lord ELGIN, to act as his Dutch interpreter. The course of communication between the English and Japanese, was then, and for some time afterwards, somewhat circuitous. First the utterances of the ambassador were repeated by the Dutch interpreter to the Japanese interpreter, who understood Dutch but no other foreign language, and he retranslated it into Japanese; and *vice versa*. It is hardly possible that with this double filtration, the exact sense of the original can have been always conveyed, but it was the best that could be done at the time, and on the opening of the ports, until the student interpreters, sent out by England and France to acquaint themselves with the language, had succeeded in mastering it (which they did in a remarkably short time, considering its difficulties), Dutch gentlemen were employed by both legations, as well as by the American.

It is needless to follow Lord ELGIN in each step of his progress. With the great object steadily kept in view, of making a treaty of friendship and commerce, he did as all others had done. He deliberately refused to observe the laws of the country; pushed on to Yedo; demanded a residence on shore for himself and suite; refused to listen to the voice of the charmer, who represented to him the greater safety of Yokohama harbour, and its better adaptability for the desired conference; and in the easiest and "most delightful" manner, gained his point.

Three scenes described by Mr. OLYPHANT shall be presented, and then we will pass on.

H. M. S. Furious, with Lord ELGIN on board, had managed to find its way to the anchorage off Yedo, "not far from the Japanese fleet, at a distance of about three miles from the shore, and five from the capital of the empire." Of course she was immediately visited by a bevy of officials, "the burden of whose song was, 'Go back to Kanagawa.'" Lord ELGIN, instead of complying, sent a letter on shore the same afternoon to the Prime Minister, detailing the object of his visit—"to make a treaty and to present the yacht to the Emperor;" and requesting that he might be furnished with a suitable residence on shore. The Japanese fleet spoken of, "consisted of two large square-rigged ships, a pretty little paddle-wheel steamer, which they had purchased from the Dutch Government, and a three masted schooner."

The next day the frigate moved to an anchorage nearer the shore, and about noon-day certain dignitaries went on board. "They were plainly dressed, and accompanied by the usual retinue. * * * Most of these were engaged during the whole period of the interview with Lord ELGIN, in reporting in note books precisely every word that passed." * * * "One fellow was actually discovered to be "making a sketch of his Excellency."

Next day but one, a favourable answer was received to the application for a shore residence, and on the 17th of August they landed.

"On the morning of that day" writes Mr. Olyphant, "great preparations were made, in order that the event might take place with due eclat. It had been arranged that some Japanese officials should come off to accompany his Excellency on shore. They were evidently under the impression that we were going to land in their boats, and were not a little startled to find themselves on board the Lee, in company with the greater part of the squadron, all in full dress, and with thirteen ships' boats in tow, looking spruce and gay, with their neat crews, and their ensigns flying. The Retribution, Furious, and yacht were all dressed out; and as the little Lee steamed boldly on past the forts, and threaded her way among the junks beyond, the faces of our Japanese friends elongated at finding our entire indifference to shallow water and sand-banks.

"At last soundings in seven feet reminded us that even the Lee had a bottom, and we dropped anchor and got into our boats. As we did so, the ships thundered forth a salute, the band of the Retribution, in a paddle-box boat, struck up 'Rule, Britannia,' the rest of the boats formed in procession, Lord ELGIN's barge in the centre, between four paddle-box boats, each with a brass gun in the bow; and in this order we pulled along the shore for about three miles, a spectacle such as Japanese eyes had never before witnessed, and the novelty of which induced numerous boats to push off and take a nearer view of us as we moved steadily and rapidly along. The landing-place was about the centre of the city, which is here protected along the sea-face by green batteries: the grassy slopes, dotted with handsome trees, would rather lead us to suppose that we were approaching a park than the most populous part of a densely-crowded city. We turned off from the waters of the bay into a little creek, spanned by a bridge. So shallow, however, was the water, that we had some difficulty in forcing even the smaller boats to the foot of the stairs: we were consoled for the inconvenience by being informed that this was the landing-place reserved for the exclusive use of the highest officers of state."

They found that Count Poutiatine had been in the capital during the preceding fortnight, on behalf of his Imperial master, but the Russian squadron had remained off Kanagawa.

I have dwelt on this subject, in order that it may not be forgotten, that in obtaining their treaties, all of the foreign negociators—Commodore PERRY, Mr. HARRIS and Lord ELGIN—set the laws of the country at defiance; and, under the appearance of friendship, really did obtain their ends through intimidation.

The Japanese officials saw the squadron with which Commodore PERRY visited them in 1853, ominously enlarged, when, according to promise, he returned in 1854; and, backed by that powerful display of war-vessels, they found that with all the external *suaviter in modo*, the determined sailor-diplomatist exercised a very decided *fortiter in re*. His words were sweeter than honey; but his manner, and the actual presence of the ships, carried everything before them.

Mr. HARRIS had no fleet to support him. He adroitly, therefore, made use of the fame of the success of the British and French victories in China; pointing to the certainty of the diplomats who had won a Treaty at the point of the bayonet in China, coming to Japan to effect a similar object; and promising that if a treaty were made with America, the President would act as a mediator in case of trouble arising between Japan and the two powerful western nations.

Lord ELGIN was not attended by a powerful squadron; but he came "with the sunshine of fame" surrounding him; and even he, one of the most just and conscientious of England's diplomatists, did not scruple to use the only means that offered any likelihood of success.

Having said so much, it only remains to be told, that, finding or fancying they could not help themselves, the Government yielded with a good grace; and made the short visit of the English Embassy one of the most complete enjoyment.

The treaty was signed on the 26th August Mr. OLYPHANT says:—"The signing of the Treaty was a most solemn and serious operation, inasmuch as there were copies made in Dutch, Japanese, and English, of which each were in triplicate, and each required the signatures of Lord ELGIN and the six Commissioners, besides sundry additional clauses to be signed separately; no fewer than eighty-four signatures had to be appended. Some of the Commissioners were, moreover, very particular in making pretty signatures, and painted away at the hieroglyphics which represented their names, with evident care and anxiety. Others—friend Higo, for instance—dashed away with his brush, perfectly regardless of the opinion which people in England might form of his handwriting. The process of sealing, unknown to them, created a good deal of interest and curiosity; and afterwards, when Lord ELGIN proposed an interchange of pens, he having purposely made use of six different ones, the Admiral appropriately remarked, that he gladly availed himself of this opportunity of inaugurating the interchange of the products of the two countries, which he trusted might ever be marked with that interchange of good feeling which had characterized our mutual intercourse hitherto."

And now all having been happily effected within fourteen days of Lord ELGIN's arrival, he left for Shanghai on the 26th August.

In accordance with the English treaty, Mr. RUTHERFORD ALCOCK arrived in Yedo, in H. M. S. Sampson, in June 1859, duly accredited as her Britannic Majesty's Envoy Extraordinary, Minister plenipotentiary and Consul-general. Mr. HARRIS, the U. S. Minister had remained in Japan, after having accomplished his treaty in 1858, residing principally at Shimoda, a port near the entrance to the gulf of Yedo; but he also arrived at Yokohama in anticipation of the opening day.

Mr. ALCOCK, having secured the commodious temple of Tozenji as his residence and legation in Yedo, and after exchanging the ratifications of the treaty between his country and Japan, paid a visit to Kanagawa, to inaugurate the opening of the port on the appointed day.

Kanagawa itself is a long straggling town, skirting both sides of the famous Tokaido or Eastern sea road that runs between Yedo, Osaka—the central commercial city of the empire, and Kioto—the metropolis. It lies at the head of a fine bay, that forms a deep indentation on the eastern side of the gulf of Yedo, and, measured by a Japanese standard, has long had a considerable trade. The bay on the Kanagawa side, however, although affording a sufficient depth of water for flat-bottomed native junks, was quite unfit even for the smaller classes of foreign ships, and this circumstance led to the ready adoption by the earliest foreign settlers of a site on the opposite side of the bay, off which the largest ship may ride in perfect safety in all states of the tide or weather. The site had been duly prepared for them by the government: but its selection led to the first passage of arms between the Japanese Government and the representatives of England and America. The dispute ended in a sort of compromise, inasmuch as the Government, after a long delay, granted a site on the Kanagawa side, where foreigners might purchase as much land or property from the Japanese owners as they liked, and the foreign consuls were provided with residences; but virtually the Japanese Government triumphed, as the merchant-pioneers of commerce could not wait while diplomacy was discussing; and the houses, godowns and allotments offered by the Government at Yokohama being readily accepted by the eager traders, local interests were quickly established that rendered it useless for any ministers to hope for the removal of the settlement.

In point of fact, Mr. Alcock, and Mr. Harris who cordially agreed with him, were right politically speaking, though less certainly so in a commercial point of view. They had before them the example of Desima ; and when they saw the locality prepared for the new settlement, they might well feel alarm, lest their countrymen should be subjected to an imprisonment similar to that so long and patiently endured by the Dutch factory at Nagasaki, and which it had been the particular object of Commodore Perry to guard against.

In the treaty, Kanagawa is mentioned as one of the ports to be opened. Yokohama was a collection of huts, that it would be almost bombastic to dignify with the name of a fishing village. It was a small strip of hard ground bounded on the north by the sea; on the south by an extensive swamp which lay between it and a fine and well cultivated plain; on the west by a creek, tidal for about a mile, at which distance from its sea mouth it is separated by sluice-gates from the fresh water stream above; and on the east by an estuary into which a river that flows from the hills empties itself. As a boundary for the foreign settlement a canal had been cut through the salt-water swamp in its rear, uniting the creek and the estuary; so that the new settlement was an island from which there were but two exits : viz, three bridges (virtually one exit, as all led into the same street,) across the creek into the village of Homura, and one bridge across the eastern estuary leading to a long viaduct, specially made across salt marshes to Kanagawa—a distance of about three miles. Each of the bridges on the west was protected by a gate, shut at sunset, and by a guard-house, in which yakunins were always on duty to watch who entered or left the settlement, examine the luggage, bundles or parcels, and to see that they conveyed nothing contraband either in or out. On the hills immediately at the back of Homura, and at the end of the paths by which they were most naturally reached from the three bridges, were large station-houses, each with a strong guard of soldiers; so that, on that side there was great provision—the Gorogiu would say, for foreigner's protection; but foreign ministers might reasonably suspect, for interference with their freedom of ingress and egress. On the eastern side also, Kanagawa could not be reached without passing through a series of gates, each with its guard-house.

It was not to be wondered at therefore, that ministers should view with something like suspicion, if not alarm, the act of the Japanese Government in removing foreigners to a distance of a league from the high road, planting their settlement on such a spot, isolating it still more effectually than had been done by nature, and guarding it so strongly,—whilst withal, it was so limited in extent, that the first settlers having on arrival, obtained appropriations of land, there were no more allotments to be got, and the later comers had to buy at enormous prices of their more fortunate fore-runners. On the Kanagawa side the settlement might have been extended to any distance, either in the valleys or on the hills enclosing them; and thus a great deal of land speculation that was afterwards loudly complained of might have been avoided. But there were other considerations.

At Yokohama the Government had gone to a vast expense in making a *hatoba* or landing place, composed of two granite-faced jetties, running out into the sea. Then the harbour was undenially good, while Kanagawa had the disadvantage of shoal water for a distance of nearly a mile from the shore. A few houses and godowns, after a fashion, had been prepared for merchants to step into at once, whilst at Kanagawa no preparation was made; and, above all, the very fact of the space being so limited gave to those who accepted allotments the certainty of a large bonus from those whom they knew to be coming, and who would only be able to get location by purchase from the original allottees. Thus, everything was against the foreign ministers, and in favour of Yokohama being retained, with all its disadvantages of enclosures and guard-houses.

CHAPTER II.

THE BRITISH MINISTER'S FIRST THREE DIFFICULTIES—THE LOCALITY OF THE SETTLEMENT.—ATTEMPTS TO PREVENT FREE USE OF THE TOKAIDO.—THE CURRENCY QUESTION.—MR. ALCOCK'S OWN RECORD OF THE OPENING DAY.—COMPLETENESS OF ARRANGEMENTS MADE BY GOVERNMENT.—THE "RECEIPT OF CUSTOM."—CURIO STREET.—ATTEMPTED PURCHASES.—DISAPPOINTMENT AND ITS CAUSE.—INGENIOUS IF NOT FAIR.—RELATIVE VALUE OF GOLD AND SILVER.—JAPANESE WIDE-AWAKE BUT MISTAKEN.—SILVER AND COPPER COIN.—JAPANESE FIRST YEAR'S EXPERIENCE OF FOREIGNERS NOT ENCOURAGING.—EFFLUX OF GOLD.—ASSIMILATION OF VALUES TO THOSE OF OTHER COUNTRIES.

The first day saw the British Envoy-extraordinary saddled with "three difficulties," as he pathetically records in his "Narrative of a three years residence in Japan," arising out of the preparations the Government had made for the opening of the port. The first—the dispute as to the locality of the settlement—I have already alluded to; the second—the attempt of the government to prevent free use of the Tokaido even to the Ministers and Consuls, between Kanagawa and Yedo; and thirdly, a more serious and lasting difficulty than either—the alteration of the native currency to meet the tenth clause in the Treaty, which ran thus:—

"As some time will elapse before the Japanese will become acquainted with the value of foreign coin, the Japanese Government will for the period of one year after the opening of each port, furnish British subjects with Japanese coin in exchange for theirs, equal weight being given, and no discount allowed for recoinage."

The second difficulty was one that did not take very long to get over; but the "Currency question" gave an immensity of trouble to every one concerned. To convey an exact idea of the shape it assumed in its first first practical working we will take the following extract from Sir RUTHERFORD ALCOCK'S work:—

"I went on shore as soon as the Sampson had cast anchor and it was impossible not to be struck with the admirable and costly structures of granite which the Japanese had so rapidly raised, in a large broad pier running far into the bay, and a long flight of steps at which twenty boats might land their passengers or cargoes at the same time. Immediately in front was a large official-looking building, which was pointed out as the Custom-house, and thither we proceeded to find some of the officials and an interpreter. The gate gave entrance into a court yard, paved with stones from the beach, and round the four sides were ranges of offices, some evidently still in the carpenters' hands. Everywhere there were signs of a rush having been made to get into some sort of occupation and preparedness by July 1st, the day fixed by our treaty for the opening of the port. In one of the large apartments we found two grave-looking officials seated on their heels at the 'receipt of Custom,' with scales and weights and a glittering heap of new coins:—the currency of Japan, we were told, ready to exchange, according to treaty, for dollars. Immediately some of the party, eager to be possessed of the currency, as they were preparing to visit the shops, threw their dollars into the empty scale, and obtained for each—two fine-looking coins weight for weight, most religiously exact, as stipulated in the treaty regulations! The government seemed to have exceeded all expectation in their preparations, with an eagerness and completeness that was calculated to disarm the most suspicious nature! After some conversation with two of the governors of Foreign Affairs, as to a location for the Consul on the opposite side of the bay, which they declared *could not be given*, we turned down the Main Street, and here witnessed a scene which could hardly have been enacted any where but in Russia, where whole villages appeared as if by magic at the mandate of Potemkin, to greet the Empress Catherine in her progress through her dominions with evidence of a flourishing and populous empire, where ten days before there was only a desert. Here, out of a marsh by the edge of a deserted bay, a wave of the conjuror's wand had created a considerable and bustling settlement of Japanese merchants. A large wide street was bordered on both sides with handsome well-built houses of timber and mud walls, but the occupants had evidently only that very morning been precipitated in—their goods were still for the greater part unpacked, while frantic efforts were being made by servants and porters, in a state of deliquescence, to make some sort of show of the saleable contents.

"Partly to encourage such devotion to our interests, and with some of the eagerness with which children of the largest growth are not quite exempt from feeling,—to spend money already in the pocket for that purpose, various articles were priced by some of the juniors. And nothing could seem more reasonable. Six itziboos for that charming glove-box! what can be cheaper? three itziboos to the dollar—why that is only two dollars. Here my friend, here is your price without haggling—two dollars.

"A suspicious look and shake of the head, with averted palm, created a momentary pause; until it was suggested that, as at Nagasaki, they could only receive Japanese money. 'Ah, all right, here it is, bright and fresh from the mint, two for the dollar; therefore two of them—what do they call them again?—two of them must be equal to three itziboos—one and a half each —aye, that is the calculation. Now my friend, there it is, four of these large bright coins: I wish I could remember their name! But the palm turned them over, and again the head shook, but this time four fingers were held up three times in rapid succession. 'Why, what does he mean? He asked six itziboos, which I have given, and now he wants twelve. What an extortionate Jew!' This evidently required the aid of language and an interpreter,—and with such help the explanation was as easy as it was unsatisfactory. Each of the bright coins was, indeed, the weight of one and a half itziboos but they bore the mint mark and value of *half an Itziboo!* There it was, clear enough, 'ni-shi,'—half. Oh what a fall was there! Had the bright silver been turned into the shrivelled leaves of the sorcerer they could not have been looked upon with more disgust and surprise. There were no purchases made that morning. One of the party who had been the most eager ruefully remarking, 'the things are remarkably pretty—but to clip the dollar of two-thirds of its value will make them rather dear to the holders of that coin!'"

This was the first attempt of the Japanese to equalise their coinage to that brought by foreigners. It was of course quickly upset—but it was ingenious if not fair. The root of the difficulty lay in the smallest space imaginable, and yet the settlement of the "currency" was for years unaccomplished. The Japanese have adopted for themselves for centuries, in all things, standards quite independent and frequently the very reverse of those of other nations. Thus the relative value of gold and silver throughout the rest of the world being about as 1 to 15, (the ounce of gold in England for instance being equal to £3.17.10½ and the ounce of silver to 5s.2d.), in Japan, according to their currency, the ounce of silver relatively with gold when converted into boos, taking gold at the English standard, was about as 1 to 6—the ounce of silver being worth 13s. 6d.

This shews, at a glance, how certain it was that confusion would arise if the tenth clause was insisted upon in its integrity. It must be clear to the weakest comprehension that unless a change were made of some kind, every grain of gold foreigners could purchase at such rates would be seized—would be fought for—with the prospect of turning the money over perhaps a dozen times in the year, and the certainty of a profit of at least 150 per cent each time.

It is evident that the Japanese had their eyes open when they allowed the obnoxious clause to pass—for they resisted it at first, declaring that their silver coinage had a nominal value far beyond its intrinsic worth; and that American or any other foreign money could only be recognized by them as so much bullion. They yielded, however, at the time; doubtless with a mental reservation, that, in the interval between the making of the treaties and their ratification, they would find means to protect themselves; and thus when foreigners demanded the exchange of their dollars for native coin, there was one specially prepared for them which was the very opposite of the old coinage. The boo represented a purchasing power far beyond its value, the new coin a purchasing power far below its intrinsic worth in silver. If the original currency therefore would not suit them, neither would the new be accepted by foreigners. It was not a part of the genuine currency of the country, nor did it bear the same relative value as that currency—and it was too much to expect that we should accept a coin intrinsically worth one itziboo and a half with a purchasing power of half a boo only.

The relative value between their silver and copper coinage was equally disproportioned—and when Mr. Alcock saw the real position they had placed themselves in he at once suggested, what nineteen persons out of twenty would say was the only feasible plan of meeting the danger,—(for it was a danger that threatened the entire sweeping away of their gold and copper coinage)— that they should assimilate their values to those of other nations. This was done at last in the case of gold and silver—but not before such an export of gold had taken place, as led to an amount of indignation and bitterness on the part of the Japanese such as it will take years to allay. The copper currency they replaced by iron—but the gold was bought up as quickly as it could be gathered together, and sent out of the country. The gold kobang, which at the opening of the ports was thus bought for four boos, is now difficult to obtain; the last I remember being sold realised seven dollars each.

During the first year, the Japanese Government must indeed have felt that they had made a great mistake in entering into treaties with foreigners. Trade there was comparatively little, except in this bullion. How could it be otherwise? The coin that the Government had invented for foreigners was in itself calculated to prevent any business in exports, for it placed the boo and the dollar on a par of value; and, as the merchants always expected to be paid in native coin, for silk or tea that had cost the native dealer 1,000 boos, (the equivalent of 333 Mexican dollars), if sold to foreigners even at the same price, the latter having to change their dollars weight for weight, and getting only the new coin, the cost to them would be $1,000, the government quietly and most philosophically pocketing the difference.

This state of things would have suited their book very well. It would have worked well either way. It would have made the treaties a dead letter, by rendering trade impossible;—and as for any foreigners who might come to the country as mere visitors, they would give to the Government a profit of two boos on every one they spent.

Ultimately this half boo was set aside; and the Government tried various expedients to save themselves from the consequence of the unequal value of their boo to its purchasing power. When once it was settled that the treaty was to be adhered to in its integrity, and that dollars were to be changed for their weight in the true currency, the evil commenced that all might have foreseen; and instead of the Government making the large profit they had calculated upon—"the biter was bit," and many foreigners made large sums by exchanging their dollars for boos, purchasing the gold coinage at its disproportionate value, shipping it to China and there selling it at its true bullion value, and thus making, as we have above said, upwards of 150 per cent. in a cash transaction covering only a month or six weeks.

The Government complained loudly of the efflux of their gold; and even the ministers blamed their countrymen for thus availing themselves of the terms of the treaty. There were indeed some who called for an amount of exchange far beyond anything that could be called reasonable: and in the rush and scuffle for the coveted traffic, these, having demanded the fullest amount even they had the face to demand in their own persons, supplemented their requirements in fictitious names, such as themselves shew the character of the scramble. This must be condemned: but that the traffic should be also complained of by ministers simply because it put the Japanese Government to its wits' end, was absurd. It was strictly in accordance with treaty. The Japanese yielded to the clause, evidently knowing quite well the consequences to themselves if the currency continued as it was at the time; and there is little doubt that they yielded only after seeing a way to meet the difficulty. That way was to rob the foreigners without any compunction by their new half boo. Foreigners did not see where the fun lay in being thus muleted, and insisted on the treaties being adhered to. The result was as we have seen. The tables were turned, and the Japanese had none but themselves to blame.

A great monetary revulsion at last was rendered compulsory, and the precious metals were assimilated in value to that of the outer world.

But the first year came to a close, and the weight for weight exchange terminated with it.

CHAPTER III.

DISTASTE FOR FOREIGN INTERCOURSE.—THE FIRST ASSASSINATION.—THE MISSION OF COUNT MOURAVIEFF AMOORSKY.—HIS LARGE RETINUE.—THREE RUSSIANS MURDERED.—BUTCHERY.—NO PREVIOUS APPREHENSIONS OF SUCH ATTACKS.—RUDENESS OF SAMURAI.—APOLOGY.—PROBABLE MOTIVES.—GREED OF FOREIGNERS.—EFFECT ON THE JAPANESE MIND.—ANOTHER COLD-BLOODED MURDER.—DESTRUCTION OF THE TYCOON'S PALACE IN YEDO.—GLOOMY ASPECT OF AFFAIRS.—NOT SHARED BY ALL.—NOBLE ASPIRATIONS OF THE JAPANESE.

We gave in our last chapter an account of the earliest difficulties with which foreign ministers had to grapple. A very little later the first of those tragedies occurred that have since thrown such an unpleasant shadow over the intercourse between the Japanese and foreigners.

The Russian Governor of Siberia, Count MOURAVIEFF AMOORSKY, arrived in the gulf, accompanied by a squadron of ten vessels. He came to settle as to the manner in which Saghalien should be jointly occupied by the Russians and Japanese. It seems a small thing for so great a minister, and with so great a display of power, to come upon; but Russia understands dealing with Eastern races better than any other European power does, and she finds her advantage in displaying her strength in the most prominent and marked manner. Thus, on taking up his residence at the temple prepared for him, "he landed with a guard of 300 men fully armed and equipped." Yet all this display availed little with the people; for several of the officers of the Russian navy were openly insulted, and at last, one night, the settlement of Yokohama was thrown into a state of excitement by the intelligence that at about 8 o'clock that evening three Russians had been murdered. "An officer, with a sailor and the steward of one of the ships had been on shore to buy provisions, and on their way to the boat, whilst the shops were still open, the party was set upon by some Japanese and hewn down with the most ghastly wounds that could be inflicted." We have since become familiarized with the mode in which the Japanese hack and cut to pieces those they succeed in bringing down—and the description, painfully minute, as given by Sir RUTHERFORD ALCOCK, of this butchery, has more recently been again and again repeated, rendering it needless for us to give it in detail. "The ruffians," says Sir RUTHERFORD, were not content with simply killing, but must have taken a pleasure in cutting to pieces." On a later occasion, when a murder was committed apparently by several assassins, a high Japanese official assured the British minister that there was only one assailant—remarking that whenever a Japanese kills with the sword, he always makes several wounds, however effectual the first may have been.

There does not seem to have been any reason for this act of barbarity, unless it be found in the fact that the Count had obtained the dismissal of some yakunins by complaining of insults offered to Russian officers a few days previously.

No one who merely resided in the settlement of Yokohama had as yet thought such a consummation of the evident dislike with which foreigners were regarded by the yakunin class, would be at all likely. Much as the currency difficulty had operated in rendering the gulf between foreigners and the government wider and wider, there were no actual apprehensions of such a tragedy. From the very first, the rudeness of the Yedo people, more particularly the two sworded race, had rendered any appearance in the streets of the city, whether on horseback or on foot, extremely disagreeable, and had called forth on the part of Sir RUTHERFORD a very strong protest. In Yokohama, however, there was not so much of this; and on the first blush of the thing expectations ran high that Count MOURAVIEFF would take a very severe and ample revenge. But no vengeful measures were taken. Certain "high officers" went on board ship and made "an apology on the part of the Government, engaging to discover and punish the offenders by a given period. It was further stipulated that the Governor of Kanagawa should be disgraced, and that they should build a mortuary chapel and keep a guard in perpetuity on the spot. It was very characteristic that this last condition was precisely the one they most resisted, as entailing on all posterity a great and endless expense." The tomb of the murdered Russians is the most prominent object in the foreign burial ground to this day.

Among other motives assigned for this deed was one that Prince MITO, having been exiled by the Regent, II KAMON-NO-KAMI, "had been left under surveillance chafing under the loss of power and the failure of his projects. Having yet a large body of officers and retainers devoted to him as their feudal chief, it was supposed he had now taken this means of bringing the existing Government and its real chief, the Regent, into collision with a foreign power, hoping in the confusion to recover his position, and perhaps seize upon the reins of power as Tycoon."

The causes most visible on the surface in Yokohama, for the animosity with which officials regarded foreigners, were connected with the efflux of gold, as alluded to in a previous chapter.

A perfect frenzy took possession of the merchants, and little else was thought worth attention than the conversion of dollars into boos, and boos into golden kobangs. A great deal of indignation was exhibited by some of the foreign merchants at the manifest partiality with which the exchanges were made by the Custom house officers, and led to the belief that they had been initiated into the secret of allaying the irritability of an itching palm. Complaints of their partiality were both loud and vehement; and they professed to be equally indignant with the insatiable avarice of crafty foreigners, who seemed in a fair way to drain the country of its gold. Strongly does the state of things bring to mind poor TOM HOOD's apostrophe to what Burns calls the "yellow dirt":—

"Gold, Gold, Gold, Gold!
"Bright and yellow, hard and cold:
"Molten, graven, hammered, rolled,
"Hoarded, bartered, bought and sold—
"Stolen, borrowed, squandered, doled—
"Spurned by the young but hugged by the old
"To the very verge of the churchyard mould!
"Price of many a crime untold—
"Gold, Gold, Gold, Gold!"

The extent to which this passion was carried may be judged by a fact recorded by Sir RUTHERFORD, that an American frigate coming into port, one officer resigned his commission and instantly freighted a ship and started a firm; and nearly every other officer in the ship, finding by the favour of the Custom house an unlimited supply of itziboos, as they were about to take the embassy over to America,—entered largely into profitable operations—for converting silver into gold!"

Again drawing on Sir RUTHERFORD, I quote some of his remarks on the subject, which bear upon events that developed themselves long afterwards.

"It would be difficult to estimate how much, and how disastrous, was the influence these unfortunate speculations and bickerings exercised on the Japanese mind. The exchange of itziboos (intended to foster legitimate trade, but systematically, and perseveringly, devoted to the buying up of their gold coinage, which was daily shipped off in large quantities, to their despair), became at last, their one absorbing thought. There can be no doubt it tended much to excite feelings of hostility, and to array all their prejudices against the foreigner, his trade, and all that belonged to him, or was connected with his presence in the country. It equally certainly and seriously warped their better judgment, in regard to the possible benefits of foreign commerce. It was about this time they first began to exhibit a desire, which soon ripened into a distinct proposition, to defer the opening of any more ports for a term of years; and even in the interval, to limit the exports from those already opened. Many were the discussions both *riva voce* and on paper, to which those reiterated attempts to nullify the treaties led; one result of which was to give a considerable insight into their system of political economy and ethics."

The excitement that followed the massacre of the three Russians was hardly allayed, when Yokohama witnessed another cold-blooded murder. The Chinese servant of Mr. LOUREIRO, vice-Consul for France, was cut down by a man with a sword, in the middle of the day, near the house of his master. Until the end of 1866 nothing was heard of the culprit or the motives for the crime. In that year, however, the Japanese officials gave out that he had been taken on another charge, and had confessed that he was the murderer of the Chinaman—his reason being that he received an insult from a foreigner, such as a Japanese wearer of two swords could not brook; and some time afterwards taking the Chinaman, who wore a kind of European costume, for the aggressor, he drew his sword and cut him down. The murderer was beheaded within the enclosure of the Tobé in 1867.

This murder was committed early in November. A few days afterwards the Tycoon's palace at Yedo was burnt to the ground. Whether the event had anything to do with foreigners was doubtful. Indeed it is not necessary to raise the question, as the time of the year was just that in which fires are affairs of every day occurrence in Yedo. Things generally began to look very gloomy, and as the new year approached they did not show any inclination to mend.

A friend, whose note-book has been placed at my disposal, gives me an incident he has therein recorded, which shows that amid the ominous appearance of things, there were some among the Japanese who already looked hopefully to the future.

"I asked a Japanese who was making rapid progress with the English language as a student interpreter, what he thought of it? He replied—'It is the language of civilization, and all Japanese will learn it.' And then as if a good idea had struck him, he laid hold of a bottle that was on the table, the cork of which was only just sufficiently in the neck to prevent it from falling out, so that there was a good inch of the cork visible. Placing his hand on the top of the cork he said—'To day England is here,'—and then putting his hand about a couple of inches from the bottom he added 'and Japan is here. In ten years time England will still be at the top, but,' placing his hand at the bottom of the cork where it entered the neck of the bottle, 'Japan will be here.'"

'Twas a noble confidence in the adaptability of his country to take its place among the great nations, and certainly a very happily illustrated ambition. The ten years are long past, and Japan is not yet in the position he prophesied for her: but she has been making more rapid progress than ever did nation before—and probably before many years are sped we may see his dream much further advanced towards realization.

CHAPTER V.

MORE DISASTERS.—GREAT FIRE IN YOKOHAMA.—EARTH-
QUAKE.—MURDER OF MR. ALCOCK'S INTERPRETER DANKITCHI.
—DEMAND AMONG JAPANESE FOR FIREARMS.—DESTRUCTION
OF FRENCH LEGATION BY FIRE.—PLEASANT RUMOURS AND
PROSPECT.—TWO DUTCH CAPTAINS CUT DOWN.—CROWNING
CATASTROPHE.—THE ASSASSINATION OF THE REGENT.

DISASTERS followed one another so rapidly, in the early days of the settlement, as to cause much anxiety among foreigners as to the influences that were working against them.

Only six months had elapsed, when, to the acts of barbarism and hatred recorded in the last chapter, there was to be added a misfortune that told very severely on some of the young mercantile houses who had established here. On the 5th of January 1860, a fire broke out in the foreign quarter, which destroyed a large portion of it, and extended itself to the native town. The Governor of Kanagawa and his officers, with the organised native fire brigade, wrought with wonderful energy, and saved much property; protecting it carefully, and exerting themselves nobly to stop the conflagration. Whilst the fire was raging a boat arrived with seventeen persons, including the captain, his wife and child, of a ship that had been wrecked, who were lighted to the settlement by the glare from the flames. They had been eight days and nights in the boat, which was undecked. The severest shock of an earthquake that had up to that time been experienced followed in a few days; and before the end of the month another murderous tragedy was enacted, the victim being a Japanese, named Dankitchi, who having been years before shipwrecked on a foreign shore, America, had returned to his country the moment he could do so under the protection of a Treaty Power, on the opening of the ports. He was employed as an interpreter at the English legation by Mr. ALCOCK, who had long feared that the animosity evidently existing against him among his countrymen would inevitably bring him to grief. He had received distinct warning of the hostility entertained towards him, and in spite of this, his overweening manner was everything that was calculated to inspire in the breasts of his countrymen hatred and contempt. He was standing close to the Legation flagstaff in Yedo, in the open day, with women and children close to him, when " one or two men stole stealthily down behind where he was, and a short sword was buried to the hilt in his body, transfixing him as he stood. He staggered a few paces towards the porter at the gate, who drew the sword out from his back, and there he fell bathed in his blood."

Before this there had arisen in Yokohama a great demand among Japanese for fire-arms, and numerous reports led to the assumption that there was something hostile to foreigners in the wind. Sir RUTHERFORD declares himself as satisfied that Government knew that the blow was about to descend upon DANKITCHI, for a Governor of Foreign Affairs, a few days previously, had spent much time in denouncing him to Mr. EUSDEN, the

Japanese secretary, urging him strongly to dismiss him.

The murderers were not, so far as is known, discoverable. The murdered man was buried with the rites and ceremonies of his own land; being followed to the grave by the members of all the foreign legations and by two Governors of Foreign Affairs.

But whilst the assassination was under discussion between the English Minister and two high officials who had called at midnight to offer their condolence on the atrocious event, a messenger arrived announcing that the French Legation was on fire. This was within a few hours of the catastrophe at the English Legation. They must have been warm times, those. Seven months had not elapsed, and what have we had to record? Four men deliberately murdered in cold blood; a fire in the settlement; a fire at the Tycoon's palace and a fire at the French Legation. Rumours were rife of the most unpleasant intentions with regard to the strangers, and, early in February, Mr. HARRIS, the United States Minister sent to the British Envoy Extraordinary, to the effect that it had been reported to him that fifty men had been seized the night before by the police—it having been discovered that they had gone down to Yokohama to murder all the foreigners. About the same time l'Abbé GIRARD was seated outside a tea-house, as his horse was being fed, when a fellow wearing two swords came up to him, and said, "You know you are all to be killed?" "No, really!"—was the reply—"when?" To which the other answered "Soon, in a single night."

All tried to hope for the best, and that there might be no ground for such rumours and that the last of the chapter of horrors had been seen. But no! On the 25th February, about 8 P.M., two Dutch captains of vessels in harbour were cut down in the Main street of Yokohama. This act was accompanied by the same features as the others, and completed the half dozen of lives taken within as many months.

The Japanese Government, by the tenacity with which their new visitors clung to the soil, might have seen how powerful is the attraction of gain.

To counterbalance these evils were the prospects of rapid fortune held out to all who could get a reasonable share of the currency; and some got more than a reasonable share. The settlement benefited by the fire: as a better class of houses and godowns was erected, and gave an appearance to the place much superior to that it had before exhibited. As yet there was but little of what we might term trade proper—for the kobang scrimmage could lay no claim to the title.

And now occurred one of those events, that mark a distinct epoch in the foreign relations with the country.

It is well known that the Tycoon is selected from three families—called the Gosankei. They are the Daimios of Kiusiu, Owari and Mito. Hitherto the last named had never had any representative attain the much coveted rank :—and the Prince of that house, on the arrival of foreign ambassadors to make treaties in 1858, saw in the jealousy the yielding to their overtures occasioned amongst the daimios against the Tycoon, an occasion that might become a stepping-stone for his house. Accordingly, on the decease of the prince who had nominally held the reins of power since 1853, he hoped to secure for one of his own sons the election to the vacant dignity. But the hereditary Regent of the Empire, an enlightened and determined man, having discovered beyond doubt the whole Mito plot, ordered him into retirement, with the promise that if he obeyed the order promptly and quietly, he would at a favorable opportunity obtain a reversal of the sentence; otherwise he should use force. Mito, checkmated, acquiesced.

But brooding in his retirement over his failure, devised a plan to rid him of his enemy.

The election had fallen upon a young prince of Kiusiu, and during his minority, II KAMON-NO-KAMI was fully invested with his hereditary office as Gotairo or Regent. In March 1860, he was on his way to the Tycoon's palace, in a norimon surrounded by his retainers. On the bridge crossing the moat, was the cortége of the Prince of Kiusiu; and coming along the road towards the same point, was the retinue of the Prince of Owari. The account of what followed we give in Sir RUTHERFORD'S own words :—

"The Gotairo was thus between them at the foot of the bridge, in the open formed by the meeting of a broad street, which debouches on the bridge. A few straggling groups, enveloped in their oil-paper cloaks, alone were near, when suddenly, one of these seeming idlers flung himself across the line of march, immediately in front of the Regent's norimon. The officers of the household, whose place is 'on each side of him, rushed forward at this unprecedented interruption—a fatal move, which had evidently been anticipated, for their place was instantly filled with armed men in coats of mail who seemed to have sprung from the earth—a compact band of some 18 or 20 men. The unhappy officers and attendants, thus taken by surprise, were hampered with their rain gear— and many fell before they could draw a sword either to defend themselves or their lord. A few seconds must have done the work * * * * * when one of the band was seen to run along the causeway with a gory trophy in his hand. Many had fallen in the *melée* on both sides. Two of the assailants who were badly wounded, finding escape impossible, stopped in their flight, and deliberately performed the *harakiru*, to the edification of their pursuers—for it seems to be the law (so sacred is the rite or right, whichever may be the proper reading) that no one may be interrupted even for the ends of justice. * * * * * Eight of the assailants were unaccounted for when it was all over;—and many of the retinue were stretched on the ground wounded and dying by the side of those who made the murderous onslaught. The remnant of the Regent's people, released from their deadly struggle, turned to the norimon to see how it fared with their master in the brief interval—to find only a headless trunk! The bleeding trophy carried away was supposed to have been the head of the Gotairo himself, hacked off on the spot. But strangest of all these startling incidents, it is further related that two heads were missing, and that which was seen in the fugitive's hand was only a lure to the pursuing party—while the true trophy had been secreted on the person of another, and was thus carried off, though the decoy paid the penalty of his life."

This boldly originated and desperately executed plot, proved to foreigners how unscrupulous were their foes, and how utterly regardless of life, if, by its sacrifice, they could serve their chief or their country. It was merit surpassing that of martyrdom to die for the honour of their feudal lord.

That the Prince Mito was thus faithfully served was evident on many occasions, and his name became the foreigners' bugbear.

The sequel of the Regent's assassination is said to have been, that his head was conveyed to the elder Mito, who "spat upon it with maledictions, as the head of his greatest enemy. It was then carried to Miaco, the capital of the Mikado, and there exposed at a place of execution in that city especially destined for princes condemned to be executed, and over it was placed a placard—'This is the head of a traitor who was violated the most sacred law of Japan—that which forbids the admission of foreigners into the country.' After two hours exposure, the same intrepid followers are said to have brought it away; and in the night to have cast it over the wall into the court of Ii Kamon's palace at Yedo, from which he sallied forth in pride and power on the morning of his death."

The first year's occupation of the settlement was completed, and on looking to the amount of trade done, we see a total of £1,000,000 sterling—the tea and silk exported being respectively 1,250,000 lbs. and 3,000 bales, which might roughly be valued, at the prices of the day, at £200,000. The greater part of the remaining £800,000 therefore must represent the trade in precious metals. All the trade left a profit, that placed men, who had come as mere adventurers, in the position of capitalists.

The profitable results of almost every transaction that was entered into, kept all in good spirits, and as the society was very limited, everybody knew everybody, and kind feeling and good fellowship were the rule. The beauty of the surrounding country, the pleasantness of the climate and the vigour of the settlers, most of them in the hey-day of early manhood, combined to make all look bright and pleasant, apart from the apprehensions ever and anon engendered by occurrences like those recorded in our two last chapters. Hearty, robust and energetic, they could equally enjoy the climate and avail themselves of business opportunities: and it is not to be wondered at that any who heard of Japan, either from the lips of those who had visited Yokohama, or the letters of residents, were charmed with the description, and pictured to themselves, if not a land of oil olives and vineyards and flowing with milk and honey, at least a terrestrial paradise, where "all but the spirit of man was divine."

It could hardly be otherwise. Many of those who were daily augmenting this world's store had experienced life in Hongkong, Shanghai, and other Chinese ports, where, in spite of the enormous fortunes made by their employers, life was little better to them than a gilded misery. They came here, and found a land in which life was not a mere existence but positive enjoyment; whilst every mercantile or financial operation had just sufficient difficulty connected with it to give it zest, and all the profits that accrued went into their own pockets. Their time was not half occupied, and the jolly rides, walks, and land and sea excursions, of those days, live pleasantly in the memory of all who enjoyed them.

At the end of the first twelve months, the weight for weight exchange ceased according to Treaty.

At first this change was a source of much complaint among the merchants, and several other matters of great importance pressing themselves on the public attention at the same time, the whole led to such representations being made to H. M. Consul, Captain Howard Vyse, that, at the instance of the British Minister, he called a Public meeting, which was presided over by him.

At this meeting which was held on the 19th February 1861,—the subjects discussed were:—

The Currency question;

The Government obstruction of trade, and their non-enforcement of Contracts;

The Custom-house shortcomings and deficiency of Wharfage accommodation.

The tenure of land, and unaccountable delays in obtaining it; and

The security to life and property.

On the first point—the Currency—the merchants themselves were divided in opinion. Mr. Clarke, the representative of Dent & Co., proposed a resolution expressive of the absolute necessity of the continuance of the old system; whilst Mr. Keswick of Jardine, Matheson & Co., warmly opposed it. Mr. Clarke's motion was negatived.

For the legitimate commerce that was hoped for between Japan and other countries, the change was decidedly an advantage, and led to an increase in the trade in imports.

CHAPTER VI.

MORE ATTACKS.—THE CASE OF MR. MOSS.—HIS TRIAL AND SENTENCE.—MR. ALCOCK ALTERS THE SENTENCE.—RESULT.—FIRE AT ENGLISH LEGATION.—APPREHENSIONS.—RONIN.—RELATIONS OF DAIMIOS AND THEIR RETAINERS.—THE GOVERNMENT POWERLESS.—MEETING OF FOREIGN REPRESENTATIVES.—RESOLVE TO RETIRE FROM YEDO.—MURDER OF MR. HEUSKEN.—SUICIDE OF ORIBE-NO-KAMI.

THE last two chapters have been anything but cheerful, and properly speaking I ought to record a series of occurrences; which, if related in detail, would give a very lugubrious tinge to my narrative. For I have spoken of murders, and a similar strain might pervade the whole of the year 1860. The French Minister's valet was attacked at the gate of the temple assigned to the French Legation in Yedo, fortunately without a fatal result; and in November of that year, the first serious conflict between a foreigner and the Japanese took place. It was the more to be lamented, as likely to add to the difficulties surrounding the opening of the country.

An Englishman, a Mr. Moss, had been out shooting; an amusement strictly prohibited by law. He was returning through Kanagawa towards the settlement with his gun over his shoulder, and followed by his servant carrying his game, when the police laid hold of the servant. Mr. Moss immediately came to his rescue, when they attempted to arrest him also. Bringing his gun down, he threatened to shoot the first that advanced to lay hands on him. A struggle ensued in which the gun went off and one of the officers was severely wounded —one arm being shattered above the elbow, the charge grazing if not entering the chest. It is wonderful that with such an excellent excuse there was no sword drawn; but a general rush was made, Moss was secured, bound tightly after the Japanese manner, and imprisoned. The Consul having been informed of the fracas went to Kanagawa at once; but it was midnight before he could ascertain the whereabouts of his countryman, and get him out of the clutches of the Japanese.

The offence of which Mr. Moss was guilty—that of shooting within 10 ri of the Tycoon's palace—had it been committed by a native, would have been punished by decapitation. Well for him was it that he was to be judged by the more merciful laws of England. The Japanese were loud in their outcry for vengeance, and the brothers of the wounded yakunin declared they would have the life of the aggressor.

Mr. Moss was tried before Mr. Consul Vyse and two assessors, and sentenced to deportation and to pay a fine of $1,000. On this being put before the British Minister he altered the sentence, on the ground that "neither the fine nor the deportation would have been any real punishment; because the first (as was ostentatiously boasted) would be subscribed for by the prisoner's friends and supporters in the community—and the deportation would have taken place in any case by a voluntary act of the accused to escape the threatened vengeance of the wounded man's relations." The Minister therefore added three months imprisonment; and had the $1,000 handed over to the maimed official. In the end this alteration of sentence proved unfortunate for Mr. ALCOCK, for Mr. Moss brought an action against him in Hongkong, and recovered damages of $2,000.

After this came a fire at the English Legation in Yeddo; and the year closed with apprehensions of violence from hundreds of ronins, who had become so for the sole purpose of molesting and attempting to slay foreigners without the daimios, their proper masters, being responsible for their acts.

A ronin is literally an outcast. Every person in Japan was supposed to belong to some daimio. He could be thrust out of the daimio's service or clan, without any further protection from him, should he become a man of bad character; but the Japanese code of honour provided that a chief should avenge insults or molestation offered to one of his kerai. The temper of the Japanese samurai, however, is so easily roused, that had the chiefs actually espoused the cause of every clansman who fancied he had reason to complain, their whole time might be occupied and all their means wasted in quarrelling and fighting with their neighbours. To remedy this evil, a former Prince SATSUMA gave to his subjects permission to slay any person who insulted them, provided they at once performed the *hara-kiri* on themselves, that he and the clan might have no more trouble on their behalf; and the wisdom of such a permission is obvious at a glance.

It was, however, allowable for men to resign their allegiance to their proper chief, and become ronins, without the right of protection from or casting any responsibility on him. And at the time we have now arrived at in our story, a number of men thus disengaged themselves from their masters; becoming ronins with the avowed intention of attacking foreigners,

The Japanese Government saw a state of things full of danger to foreigners, and by reason thereof not less so to themselves, as powerless to prevent it. The Legations were kept in a continual state of apprehension by the constant warnings they were receiving; and after the small fire at the English Minister's residence, most likely the result of accident, and the barbarous murder of Mr. HEUSKEN, the interpreter of the American Minister, in the open street, a meeting was held of the representatives of the Treaty Powers, and all but Mr. HARRIS, the Envoy of the United States, determined to leave Yedo for a time under strong protest, and reside in Yokohama. Even Count EULENBERG, who was just completing the Prussian Treaty, joined with the English, French and Dutch representatives, and all agreed that they would not return until it was seen that the Government was disposed to assert its authority and put an end to the reign of terror which it had hitherto manifested no anxiety to discourage.

The murder of Mr. HEUSKEN took place on the 15th of January 1861, on his way home from the residence of Count EULENBERG, for whom he had been acting the part of Interpreter as he had previously done for Lord ELGIN, in 1858. He was on horseback and preceded by a mounted yakunin carrying a lantern with the Tycoon's arms upon it, and followed by the ordinary guard. On entering the narrow street through which his course lay, he was suddenly set upon by some half dozen men who rushed at him with drawn swords. Deserted by his guard, who decamped at the moment danger arose, Mr. HEUSKEN dashed through the assailants, who cut wildly at him as he passed them. He had but a hunting whip to defend himself with; but was unconscious of being wounded, until he had ridden about a hundred yards; when, discovering that he had been severely injured, he called his horse boy, and attempting to dismount, fell heavily on the ground. It is not known how long he lay there; but having at last been taken to the United States Legation, Dr. MYBURGH, then Dutch interpreter as well as medical officer attached to the British Legation, was sent for, but arrived only to find him at the point of death, and after a short absence returned with the report that he was dead.

These events were followed in a few days by the suicide of the most intelligent of the Governors of Foreign Affairs, HORI ORIBE-NO-KAMI—who had been one of the most active in arranging the Prussian Treaty; and every day increased the hostile attitude of the dangerous classes, and the alarms of the Government.

CHAPTER VII.

MINISTERS, MR. HARRIS EXCEPTED, LEAVE YEDO.—EFFECT UPON THE GOVERNMENT.—INVITATION TO RETURN.—MR. ALCOCK VISITS NAGASAKI.—RETURNS OVERLAND TO YOKOHAMA. —YEDO.—MR. OLYPHANT.—ATTACK ON BRITISH LEGATION. OFFICERS WOUNDED.—RONINS IN POSSESSION.—MR. F. J. LOWDER.—MR. MACDONALD.

THE resolution come to by the Ministers of Prussia, Holland, France and Great Britain, was carried into effect. They left Yedo, and took up residence in Yokohama. Mr. HARRIS, the Minister of the United States, alone, of all the representatives of Foreign Treaty Powers, remaining in the capital. Mr. HARRIS, although the last sufferer, through the fatal attack upon his friend and interpreter Mr. HEUSKEN, hoped to bring the Government to reason by confidence; whilst his colleagues, tired out by their never-ceasing vacillations and professed weakness, thought better to frighten them, by throwing upon them the responsibility of an open rupture.

At first the Government attempted to meet this movement of the four ministers by silence, and appearing to let them go their own way; but they very soon saw the mistake of this plan: and before long they made advances towards conciliation which were responded to in a manner fairly to put them on their mettle. The British Minister, acknowledging the truth of the Government's declaration, that the measures to be adopted for securing better protection to foreigners required repeated deliberations and would occupy much time, told them that he had made up his mind to occupy a part of such interval in a journey into the interior, and a visit to the ports that were to be opened according to treaty, but to which the Government wished to postpone the admission of foreigners.

The effect of this was instantaneous. A trusty agent who was particularly approved of by the foreign Ministers, but whom the Gorojiu had refused to send down when first requested by Mr. ALCOCK to do so, was now quickly dispatched to Yokohama to make arrangements for a return to Yedo. The conclusion come to was, that a formal invitation in the name of the Tycoon should be sent to each, requesting a reoccupation of their respective legations. The invitation was sent within a couple of days, and exactly four weeks from their departure, they re-entered the capital, but under very changed circumstances; for they were received at the landing place by the Governors of Foreign affairs and conducted to their residences, each of their national flags being honoured by a salute of twenty one guns from the batteries.

By the course of proceedings adopted on this occasion the Government was led to perceive the probable consequences of dealing weakly, treacherously, or carelessly, in matters appertaining to their newly received but most unwelcome visitors.

This occurred in March 1861. But although the intimation of Mr. ALCOCK's intention to visit the ports had led to the speedy acquiescence in all the terms demanded by him and his colleagues, he did not alter his resolves.

After a visit to China of about a couple of months he visited Nagasaki, and from thence travelled in company with Mr. DE WITT, the Dutch Consul-general, overland to Yokohama. Of this journey I need take no further notice than to mention, that it was from witnessing the precautions taking to prevent the party leaving the direct line of road, in many places, that the fact of the limited nature of the Tycoon's sovereignty first dawned upon the ministers.

They arrived at Yokohama on the 2nd July, the day after the second anniversary of the opening of the Port. The 4th July saw the British Minister once more at his legation in Yedo; and accompanying him he had a new member of the staff in the person of Mr. OLIPHANT, who had arrived during his absence, as Secretary of Legation, with the prospect of shortly taking charge of British interests at the Court of the Tycoon, during the projected visit of his chief to Europe. But man proposes and God disposes!

That night, the very first after accomplishing the overland trip, the British Legation was attacked by ronins. About midnight the Minister was awoke by some one rushing into his room with the announcement that men were breaking in at the gate. Rising and seizing a revolver, he was leaving the room, when Mr. OLIPHANT suddenly made his appearance covered with blood streaming from sword-cuts in his arm and neck, followed by Mr. MORRISON the Consul of Nagasaki, who had received a wound on his forehead. Sir RUTHERFORD's account may be thus epitomised:—

"I looked for the rush of pursuers, and stood for a second ready to fire, and check their advance, while the wounded passed on to my bedroom behind. I was the only one armed at this moment, for though Mr. MORRISON had still three barrels, he was blinded and stunned with his wounds. Mr. OLIPHANT had met his assailants in the passage from his room, with only a heavy hunting whip in his hand. We had been taken by surprise, and of the hundred and fifty guards surrounding us, not one appeared to come to our rescue.

"Mr. OLIPHANT was bleeding so profusely that I was obliged to lay down my pistol and bind his wounds with my handkerchief; and while so engaged, there was a sudden crash and the noise of a succession of blows in the adjoining apartment. Some of the band were evidently breaking through the glazed doors into the court with a frightful fracas; still no yakunins seemed attracted by the noise.

"We were but five Europeans; our foes, of unknown numbers. We dare not leave our wounded; and could not tell from what direction the assailants might come upon us. Many or few they had possession of the premises for nearly ten minutes, but providentially had missed their way to my apartments, and every moment lost to them was a priceless gain to us. Unwillingness to leave Mr. OLIPHANT lying senseless on the floor prevented our leaving the room; and at length the noise subsiding gave hope that help had come, or the attack turned in another direction. Then only, I, with two of the party ventured to leave the wounded, and go to look for one of our number at a further wing of the building who had never appeared, and might have been less fortunate. While advancing I put one of the students, Mr. LOWDER, as sentry at an angle commanding a long passage leading from the entrance, and was suddenly recalled by a shot from his pistol. A group of armed men had appeared, and not answering his challenge, he very properly fired into them, and he could scarcely have missed his aim. At all events they retreated suddenly, and this was the last we saw of them.

"In a minute or two the Japanese civilian officers in charge came and congratulated us on our safety; and with them, to my great relief, Mr. MAC DONALD, the missing one of my party. His apartment being partially detached, he had rushed out on hearing, as he thought, some one breaking into his bath-room; and after in vain attempting to induce a guard to come down, made his way though a side gate to the front, where he saw a wild scene of tumult. Groups fighting—men rushing to and fro with lanterns and gathering from all sides. He was drawn aside by some of the civilian yakunins attached to the Legation, and as he was conspicuous in his white sleeping costume, they threw a Japanese dress over him. It was some minutes before he could get his demands attended to, that the guard should go to the house to our rescue; nor was it, in effect, until all the assailants outside had been beaten off or made their retreat, that any thought was given to those inside the house, or to the propriety of seeing that those for whom they were fighting outside, had not been cut to pieces and deliberately assassinated inside."

CHAPTER VIII.

INQUIRY AS TO ATTACK ON BRITISH LEGATION.—PAPER FOUND ON ONE OF THE RONIN.—SUBSEQUENT REPORT.— FAILURE OF THE ENTERPRISE.—HARA-KIRI.—JAPANESE CODE OF HONOUR.—FOREIGN LEGATION GUARDS.—NECESSITY FOR A NAVAL FORCE WITHIN REACH OF JAPAN.—MR. DE WITT REFUSES TO RESIDE IN YEDO.—MORE BLOODSHED.—THE GOVERNOR OF YEDO.—REQUEST TO CONSULS RESIDENT IN KANAGAWA TO REMOVE TO YOKOHAMA.—FACTS AND RUMOURS.

THE attack upon the British Legation having been foiled, the attention of all was turned to the examination of the facts connected with it; by whom it was attempted and at whose instigation. From a paper that was found on the body of one of the assailants who was killed on the spot, as well as on another who had been too badly wounded to allow of his escape, it appeared that the attack was committed to fourteen men who had made themselves ronins for the purpose of killing foreigners, in the manner described in a previous chapter.

The paper, a copy of which was most likely upon each of the band, ran as follows:—

"I, though I am a person of low standing have not patience to stand by, and see the sacred empire defiled by the foreigner. This time I have determined in my heart to undertake to carry out my master's will. Though being altogether humble myself, I cannot make the light of the country to shine in foreign nations, yet with a little faith and a little warrior's power, I hope within my heart separately, (by myself,) though I am a person of low degree, to bestow upon my country one out of a great many benefits. If this thing from time to time, may cause the foreigner to retire, and partly tranquilise both the minds of the Mikado and of the government (Tycoon's) I shall take to myself the highest praise.

Regardless of my own life, I am determined to set out."

This was signed with fourteen signatures.

It turned out eventually, or at any rate such was the common report, that instead of the attempt being made by lawless ronins, they were kerai of the prince of Tsussima, who had suffered some humiliation from the Captain of a Russian ship; and hearing that a great foreign minister was about to make the overland journey from Nagasaki to Yedo, thought to avenge the insult by murdering him on the road. Rumour alleged that having failed in overtaking him they arrived in Yedo, and lost no time in putting their diabolical plans into execution.

The enterprise, so far as the intentions of the conspirators were concerned, failed totally; for all they succeeded in killing were two of their own countrymen, and for these there was a set-off in the persons of two of their own number. Besides these, with the exception of Mr. OLYPHANT and Mr. MORRISON, the former of whom was very dangerously wounded, all of the eighteen men more or less injured were Japanese. And against these, there was one made a prisoner on the spot very badly wounded; and the next day three were tracked to a house in Shinagawa, who on arrival of the police committed *hara-kiru*; but one of these having done the work inefficiently was captured. Two others were at a later day declared to have been so hard pressed by the officers of justice, that they died the death of honour to avoid falling into their hands.

A fair commentary upon the Japanese code of honour is found in one of the rumours that was generally believed,—that when the three who had fled to Shinagawa arrived at the house of rendezvous, they were bitterly reproached by their chief with cowardice—*they* especially, as the only part of the band that had been in actual conflict with foreigners! To which they replied that they found them too well armed and ready to defend their lives. But not the less being ordered to kill themselves they did so on the spot.

It was this event that decided the British and French ministers to have a guard of Europeans.

In the morning Mr. ALCOCK sent a despatch to Captain CRAIGIE of H. M. S. "Ringdove," to bring his vessel up from Yokohama with all speed; and by one o'clock that same afternoon, that officer landed in Yedo with a guard of twenty picked men all armed. One particularly gratifying feature of those days, was the perfect accord and sympathy that existed between the English and French ministers. Monsieur DE BELLECOURT was in Yokohama when the intelligence arrived in the settlement, but he immediately went on board the "Ringdove," and obtaining passage for himself and a party of Marines from the French transport "Dordogne," arrived with Captain CRAIGIE at the Legation, determined to share with his colleague whatever anxieties and perils might arise.

This attack proved to the Government at home and to the Admiral of the China station, the necessity of having a sufficient naval force within hail, in case of emergencies. Mr. ALCOCK had represented this necessity often and often, but his warnings had been unheeded, and in view of the ample employment for his force in the China waters, Admiral HOPE thought but little of Japan. So unimportant indeed, did he consider the presence of his ships here, that although he had written to the Minister that he would arrive on the 15th of that very month, he had not made his appearance at the end of it; but fortunately, on the news reaching Nagasaki, Mr. ANNESLEY, the Acting Consul, without a moment's delay, sent off to a bay at no great distance, where he knew H. M. S. ACTÆON and three gunboats were lying, and they quickly arrived off Yokohama. Thus was the safety of the foreign community provided for, which, since the departure of the "Ringdove" to Yedo, had been only guarded by a Dutch man-of-war brig, the "Camelot," in attendance on the Dutch Minister, Mr. DE WITT. This latter gentleman, on hearing of the assault, wrote to the Gorojiu, that, seeing how little their protection was to be trusted, he must decline taking up his residence in Yedo for the present.

And now my readers will be hoping that all these scenes of bloodshed are at an end. I wish they were; but I must still trespass awhile on their patience. Let me give yet another page *verbatim* from Sir RUTHERFORD's book:—

"Then followed, on the 17th, a menacing placard on ANDO TSUSSIMA-NO-KAMI's door: followed on the 18th, by an attack, real or simulated, on the American Legation. MONS. DE BELLECOURT might well say 'l'esprit se déprave,' in such an atmosphere of assassinations, menaces and rumours; each day bringing its contingent. I will complete this page of our history in Japan, by a copy and memorandum made at the time, for the Foreign Office, of rumours and reports in circulation from day to day, in Yedo and Kanagawa, which reached me from other sources.

"The Governor of Yedo, a few days after the attack on the Legation, was said to have been murdered in his house, by a band of ronins, in league with those who attacked the Legation; and in revenge for the vigour with which these were being pursued! Next day, he was said only to be sick, and suspended for the moment in his office. Finally, it appeared, he had committed the *hara-kiru*, having offended by intruding his opinion at a grand Council of daimios, (he not being a daimio.) The Council was said to have been convoked to determine whether the Tycoon should obey a mandate to go to Miako to pay homage to the Mikado, as a preliminary to a marriage with the daughter of the latter, and the composition of certain difficulties for some time existing. The Governor sent in a very strong but ably drawn up opinion against it. This opinion was adopted; but a rival and former Governor took advantage of the opportunity to ruin him by charging him with a violation of the laws in offering it. Upon this had been grafted a report of a 'duel à mort,' it seems, but not a hand to hand fight.

"Three ronins were reported to have been watching the new stockades and fences putting up at the legation, and to have said with bitterness, they were too strong to be broken through. (A great mistake on their part, if they ever arrived at the conclusion, for I demonstrated to the chief officials on service, some time after this, that the separate bamboos, could all be slid upwards, and any number of ronins might enter without the least noise or difficulty.)

"The Governor of Kanagawa urged the danger of an attack on the British Consulate, and wished Captain VYSE to go over to Yokohama where he would be more easily protected: and in the meantime, to admit a party of yakunins inside his house. The ministers urged the same thing, when the interview took place.

"Three nights before, all the gates of the streets about Kanagawa were closed, and the servants spread an alarm that the ronins were at hand, and already engaged with the daimio's guard on the hill. Four were actually seized in a tea house which was surrounded, and but one escaped. There did not seem to have been any fight, but a body of them were about: giving countenance to rumours of an intended attack on the Consulate. Captain VYSE had a guard of seven men from the "Ringdove;" and a Dutch brig of war and a French armed transport were close in at Yokohama, in the absence of any British ship, for the protection of the foreign settlement.

"Yesterday a report came in, that two men had presented themselves at the Prince of Satsuma's kami-yashiki or palace, demanding refuge, and on being refused, instantly killed themselves.

"Afterwards modified into a report that 50 men demanded entrance and sanctuary, and being refused, killed the gate-keeper and dispersed. Again, that one only presented himself, asking asylum for 50, and on being refused, killed himself, sure of being denounced.

"I may as well add here, though the account reached me somewhat later, the translation of a letter, said to have been left in their house by four officers of the Prince of MITO who had made themselves ronins.

19th of 8th month.

"We become ronins now, since the foreigner gains more and more influence in the country, unable tranquilly to see the ancient laws (of Gongen-sama) violated; we become, all four, ronins with the intention of compelling the foreigner to depart.

AKIGAMI TETSONDJIRO.
TATEMI TOMIGORO.
ATSOUMI GORO.
MITSOUNGI SADUA."

"Such were the conditions under which the Legations in Yedo had to be maintained during the month succeeding the attack of the 5th of July."

CHAPTER IX.

INABILITY OF GOVERNMENT TO PROTECT FOREIGNERS.—GOVERNMENT ANXIETY AS TO OPENING YEDO.—CLOSER RELATIONS.—PROPOSALS TO DEFER THE OPENING OF YEDO, HIOGO, OSAKA AND NI-IGATA.—AUTOGRAPHIC LETTER FROM TYCOON TO THE QUEEN.—MR. OLYPHANT ITS BEARER.—EMBASSY TO TREATY POWERS DETERMINED ON.—ESTABLISHMENT OF THE JAPAN HERALD.—JAPANESE EMBASSY LEAVES FOR EUROPE.—ITS RESULTS.—DEDICATION OF ROMAN CATHOLIC CHURCH, YOKOHAMA.—ENGLISH CHURCH.—ATTEMPTED CLOSING OF THE TOKAIDO TO FOREIGNERS.—MR. ALCOCK'S ACTION.—CONFLAGRATIONS.—WATER SUPPLY.—LAND RENTAL.—PROGRESS OF TRADE.—IMPORTS.—THE DUTCH CONSUL AND THE CUSTOMS.

THE continued hostility displayed towards foreigners, culminating in the attack on the British Legation, had the effect of convincing the foreign Ministers of the absolute inability of the Japanese Government to give them efficient protection, and much anxiety was shewn by the Government, respecting the opening of Yedo on the day appointed, the first of January 1862, which was fast approaching. The opportunity was taken by the British Minister of seeking a closer and more directly personal intercourse with the Gorojiu than hitherto; for to this time all interviews were of the most public kind, being attended by the Governors of Foreign affairs, O-metskes, and a host of lesser officials, which had rendered anything like confidential interviews impossible. As, however, Mr. OLYPHANT, temporarily disabled by his wounds, was about to return home, and would be the bearer of Mr. ALCOCK's dispatches on the late attack and on the proposals now made by the Government of the Tycoon that the opening of the ports of Yedo, Hiogo, Osaka and Niigata, be deferred until a more fitting occasion; and as Mr. ALCOCK stated that the communication he wished to make had better be divulged to none but themselves, the proposal was acceded to, and a better system of official intercourse inaugurated.

The postponement of the opening of the port of Hiogo and the city of Osaka, which by treaty were to be opened on the first of January, 1863, was made the subject of an autographic letter from the Tycoon to the Queen, of which Mr. OLYPHANT became the bearer. And an embassy was determined upon, from the Tycoon to the Treaty Powers, which should have for its primary object the attainment of the same end.

It apparently mattered little whether the ports were opened or not, so far as trade was concerned; for the Government had placed so many difficulties in the way of it, that the treaties had become practically all but inoperative, and complaints both loud and frequent were made by merchants to the Consul of the annoyances and obstructions they met with.

The foreign residents were, equally with their representatives, extremely averse to the postponement; and although they were but few in number their opinions were allowed due weight.

On the 23rd November 1861, the first number of the *Japan Herald* was published in Yokohama; and its earlier numbers are taken up with these and kindred subjects. From them it is proved, that the foreign Ministers held out against the postponement of the opening of Yedo until the last moment, and only on the 27th December, 1861, did they notify their respective countrymen of their having given their consent to it. But I will allude to this in another chapter.

The Japanese Embassy took its departure in January 1862, on board H.M.S. Odin, and I may here anticipate events by saying, that the European Treaty Powers assented to the postponement of the opening of Osaka, Hiogo, Yedo and Ni-igata, for five years, as America had already agreed to it, an Embassy having gone thither previously. In a number of other matters they brought before the governments of the Treaty Powers, they were entirely unsuccessful, but this one success was to them of incalculable advantage.

To this time Yokohama had been without a church, although not without ministers of the gospel, of whom there were from very early days both American and French Missionaries. Of the latter, was he whom I have already named as having been warned of the intended massacre of foreigners—M. l'Abbe GIRARD. By his efforts mainly a French Church was built; and dedicated to "The Sacred Heart of JESUS" on 12th January 1862. The funds were raised partly by the "mission," and partly by the subscriptions of all sects and denominations. On the 16th of the same month a mass was celebrated for the repose of the soul of the murdered Mr. HEUSKEN.

The English Church service had hitherto been held at the private residence of the British Consul every Sunday morning at the usual hour. But during the past year a successful effort was made to obtain funds for a building in connection with the English Church establishment, and application was made to the Foreign Office for a Consular Chaplain to be provided, a guarantee having been given of the recognised proportion of his salary being paid by the community. The church and parsonage were commenced early in 1862.

About the middle of the month of January the British Minister had occasion to shew his teeth to the Japanese authorities, under the following circumstances.

Numerous daimios and others with large retinues were expected to pass along the Tokaido during the week, and application was made to foreign ministers to prevent their countrymen from going upon that road for a few days. The French Minister acceded to this request, and issued an *order* to his compatriots in consonance with it; but Mr. ALCOCK refused to "prevent" British subjects from travelling on the road, but went so far as to issue a circular *requesting* them to avoid the road during two days. The Japanese, however, shut the gates; thus positively infringing the Treaty. Directly Mr. ALCOCK heard this, he sent an indignant remonstrance to the Governor of Kanagawa, reminding him that the gates were there, not for the imprisonment but the protection of foreigners, and telling him that unless they were immediately opened, a force would be landed from a man-of-war and the gates destroyed entirely. The Governor made a stammering excuse that the yakunins at the gates were alone responsible; but it was too palpable that the order had emanated from higher quarters. This promptness took the officials by surprise, and has prevented anything like such a proceeding since; although they always announced when any particularly great man was about to pass with a large cortège.

Fires in the native settlement had on more than one occasion threatened the foreign quarters. In the course of the winter of '61 and '62 two large conflagrations occurred, the lesser of which consumed more than seventy houses including a large portion of Yoshiwarra; and a cry was raised for proper precautions against fire, especially with regard to a water supply This, with other wants, also caused men's minds to turn towards the acquirement of a Municipal Committee.

The subject of land-rental had for some months occupied public attention, and vigourous protests were made by all nationalities. In the case of the Dutch residents, it led to a very ill-considered letter from Mr. DE WITT, the Dutch Consul-general, resident at Nagasaki, to the Dutch Consul in Yokohama, instructing him to see that the Dutch subjects paid the rent at once, adding—" In case it may happen that some of them are unwilling to do so, I request you to inform me of their names, that I may propose to the Government their being deported." A meeting of those concerned was immediately held, and a temperate but telling reply sent, protesting against the threat held out; and further stating "that it cannot be looked upon as otherwise than highly disagreeable and offensive to the feelings of the Dutch established here; and considering their calm and composed attitude and that the Consul-general without any precedent holds out this threat they beg to record their most serious indignation against this expression."

The French Vice-Consul, in a letter to some of his countrymen—who had declared their unwillingness to pay the land-rent demanded, and that they would send him a formal letter of explanation on the subject—quietly replied he was not permitted to receive such a letter; and the plan was adopted of making the press the vehicle of protest, by publishing the whole correspondence as an advertisement; but the English Minister took the greatest pains to reason with his countrymen in hopes of avoiding any unpleasant conflict.

Trade as yet had progressed but slowly, giving employment in round numbers to about 100 vessels in the year, of which one half were British. The total value was about One Million Sterling, of which the imports might be valued at about $300,000. The bulk of the export trade, apart from bullion, in 1860, had been "edibles for the Chinese market;" but in 1861 the legitimate staples Tea and Silk had come forward more freely; and a few ventures were made in Rags—which latter, however, reached a poor market, and in the bulk left a serious loss to the speculators.

Amongst the "imports" are mentioned "two tigers'.' In the Straits they may have been worth, Sir RUTHERFORD surmises, $100, but they sold here to Japanese for purposes of exhibition for $3,000 or $4,000. "And in this, as in other things, the appetite appeared to grow by indulgence; for the tigers led to an order for a brace of elephants. But even here, as in all other novelties, there was an impediment in the first instance to be got over on the part of the Japanese authorities, and the following story was in circulation. Whether they objected because tigers were not in the Tariff or on some other equally valid ground, certain it is, they did object; and as the importer was a Dutch subject it became a matter of discussion with the Dutch Consul, who solved the difficulty with great readiness.

"When the Japanese Custom-house and the Consul seemed to have come to a dead-lock, the question arose what was to be done with the article? The Custom-house would'nt pass it,—the ship could not take it back. What was to be done with the beautiful beast? 'Oh, very well,' said the Consul seeing it was time to make a last stroke for his countryman's merchandise, ' since you say it is impossible to allow it to be entered and sold, there is nothing left but for the merchant to lose his money, and let the beast out.' 'Let it loose?' exclaimed the officials, in various tones of horror and dismay, 'why, it will eat us up!' 'Really, I don't know —perhaps he is not very hungry, but in any case, I cannot compel the merchant to keep it.'

It is superfluous to add that all further interdict was quickly removed, and instead of making a meal of the Japanese, he was sold and publicly exhibited.

CHAPTER X.

ASSAULT ON ANDO TSUSSIMA-NO-KAMI.—YOKOHAMA RESIDENTS DEMAND MUNICIPAL GOVERNMENT.—NEWSPAPER CORRESPONDENCE.—PROSPECTS OF IMPROVEMENT.—JAPANESE INTOLERANCE.—WATER SCHEME FOR YOKOHAMA.—MR. ALCOCK LEAVES FOR ENGLAND.—FOREIGNERS ON THE OPENING OF THE PORTS.—THEIR MISTAKEN VIEWS.—FRENCH AND ENGLISH MINISTERS DEFER THE OPENING.—THE ENGLISH NOTIFICATION.—PORTUGUESE TREATY RATIFIED.—MUNICIPAL COMMITTEE FORMED.—ARRIVAL OF NEW U. S. MINISTER AND CONSUL.—MR. TOWNSEND HARRIS.

I HAVE already mentioned the threatening notice that was placed on the door of ANDO TSUSSIMA-NO-KAMI's residence in Yedo. This was no idle threat; for on the 13th of February, as the daimio was proceeding, with one of the members of the Gorojiu, or Council of State, to an audience with the Shogun, the norimon in which he was seated, in spite of the retinue by which he was attended, was attacked, on reaching the inner moat of the castle, by ten or twelve ronins, who carried fire-arms and fired at him. Happily he was not struck. It was said that he got out of his norimon, and succeeded in killing five of his assailants with his sword; receiving only a few insignificant wounds in return.

As regards the foreign settlement of Yokohama, there appears to have been more public spirit among the residents at that time than there is now. Municipal government was loudly called for. A correspondent of the *Japan Herald* says :—

"The old concession abounds with wooden buildings ; at present there is no power to compel the construction of fire-proof structures. There is no organization for the purpose of preventing the spread of fire ; none for the supply of water ; none for the restriction or removal of nuisances, and no power to pass ordinances for sanitary purposes. In fact we have a town, streets, houses, and a goodly number of inhabitants, under no control, no government, no restraints, and without the power of doing good. Such an anomaly cannot be found in any other place settled by Europeans and Americans."

We shall see presently that shortly after this there appeared to be a prospect of such a state of things coming to an end. But in point of fact, although fitful attempts at municipal government have been made, all have proved futile, and the settlement, to all intents and purposes, remains as badly off as ever it was. Fires were then frequent both in the native town and in the foreign quarters ; but organisation for extinguishing such dire visitants is still very imperfect.

One feature of those times has quite passed away— persecution for religion's sake. On the 18th February 1861, thirty-three, and on the following day twenty-two, natives, supposed to be small merchants and pilgrims to the Isé shrines, were seized at the entrance of the compound of the Roman Catholic Chapel as they were leaving it, by a number of yakunins. They were conveyed to Tobé prison ; where, it was said, they would receive condign punishment for the offence of visiting the foreign place of worship, which they had done simply to gratify an idle curiosity. Representations were at once made by the foreign ministers to the Governor of Kanagawa ; who replied that it was an extreme case, and he must apply for instructions to the Gorojiu. They were released after a few days detention, but 'ordered to be under strict surveillance. The order for their release came from the Shôgun, in response to a strong remonstrance by the French Minister; but an intimation was delivered to the effect that if any similar cases should occur they would be treated with the utmost rigour.

In March 1862, Captain F. HOWARD VYSE, H.M.'s Consul, elaborated and published a scheme for supplying Yokohama with water, to be available in case of fire. It was simple, and might easily have been carried out. A reservoir at the top of the hill, on the ground reserved for the British Consulate, calculated to contain 10,600 tons of water, which would have enabled ·30 hose to be kept running with sufficient pressure to reach the highest buildings in the settlement, continuously for eleven to twelve hours. The scheme fell through, and nothing has been done in the matter from that day to this.

Mr. ALCOCK left on a visit to England on the 23rd March, and Dr. WINCHESTER became Chargé d'Affaires pending the arrival of Lieut. Colonel St. JOHN NEALE. As the time approached for the opening of the cities of Yedo and Osaka, and the ports of Hiogo and Niigata, for foreign trade and residence, notwithstanding the urgent requests of the Japanese Government for delay, (in consideration not only for the safety of foreigners, but of the certainty that their opening them at that time would lead to a civil war, and to consequences that could hardly be foreseen), the foreign residents were most anxious that the treaty should be carried out to the letter. A memorial was signed by several of the leading merchants and others, addressed to Lord JOHN RUSSELL, H. M. Secretary of State for Foreign Affairs, pointing out that—

"This clause of the Treaty has been justly regarded as one of the most important concessions made to foreign trade by the Tycoon of Japan, and a step which would, when carried into operation, exercise the greatest' influence upon the foreign relations of the country."

And after alluding to the amount of trade done since the opening of the ports they proceed :—

"We beg leave, with all due deference, to lay before your lordship our opinion that the clause in question is one of the most important in the treaty; that there are many and strong reasons why it should be carried out; and that the reasons which are alleged against it are likely to convey impressions of the weakness of the Government and the hostility of the natives, which are not consistent with our experience; and which, if they exist at all at Yedo, are not likely to exist in any force at Hiogo or Osaka."

How very much they were mistaken as to the effects of the opening of Hiogo and Osaka, subsequent events displayed; and those events fully justified the measures taken by the foreign representatives in December 1861. We have ample testimony to prove that the postponement of the opening of Yedo and the other places mentioned in the Treaties, was as unpalateable to the Ministers as it was to the merchants; but they were a little more conversant with what was going on behind the scenes, and they acted wisely in taking upon themselves the responsibility of deferring the fulfilment of the letter of the treaties until they had instructions from home. Mr. ALCOCK and M. DE BELLECOURT published simultaneously the notification of the postponement in identical terms. The English notification ran as follows :—

"Whereas, I, the undersigned RUTHERFORD ALCOCK as being Envoy-Extraordinary and Minister Plenipotentiary for Her Majesty the Queen of Great Britain in Japan, have authority to suspend and vary the provisions of the treaty now in force between Her Majesty and the Tycoon of Japan: And whereas by an Order in Council providing to the exercise of Consular jurisdiction over British subjects in Japan under 6 and 6 Victoria, Cap. 24, dated the 23rd of January 1860, power is given to the Consul-general and Consuls, or persons duly authorised in such capacities, in the dominions of the Tycoon of Japan, in the port, place or district in which they may severally reside, to make rules and regulations for the peace, order and good government of Her Majesty's subjects being within the dominions of the aforesaid Tycoon, and for the observance of the stipulations of any Treaty or Regulation appended thereto, made between Her Majesty, Her Heirs and successors, and the Tycoon of Japan.

"*Be it known* that I, RUTHERFORD ALCOCK, Her Majesty's Envoy-Extraordinary, Minister Plenipotentiary and Consul-General in Japan, in consideration of divers reasons affecting the good Government of Her Majesty's subjects in Japan, and also in consideration of divers other good and weighty reasons, do hereby make the following Rules and Regulations, to wit:—

That the provision for the opening of divers ports and places on and after the 1st of January 1862, as places of residence of and for British subjects, and for purposes of trade, is hereby suspended until further notice, in so far as respects the City of Yedo, without special warrant and authority from Her Majesty's Consul-General, by and with the consent and concurrence of the Government of the Tycoon; and that any infringement of this rule in the meantime, and until after such further notice as aforesaid shall render the offender liable to be dealt with according to the laws of Japan by the authorities appointed by the Government of the Tycoon, in the same manner as if the said City of Yedo had not been included or mentioned in the said Treaty; and further, that no such offender as aforesaid shall have any claim on Her Majesty's Minister, or on any Consul in Japan for protection from the consequences of any such offence.

Given under my hand and seal this twenty-seventh day of December, in the year of our Lord 1861.

   (Signed) RUTHERFORD ALCOCK,
*   Her Majesty's Envoy-Extraordinary,*
*   Minister Plenipotentiary, and Consul-*
*   General in Japan.*

On the 8th April 1862, the Portuguese Treaty, which had been originally signed on the 3rd August, 1860, was formally ratified at the American Legation in Yedo, and delivered to Mr. EDWARD CLARKE, H. M. F. M. Consul.

On the 10th April, at an adjourned meeting of Land-renters, presided over by the British Consul, a Municipal Committee was formed, who at once proceeded to organise sub-committees for the Streets, Lighting, Bund and Jetties, Police, Nuisances, and Cargo-boats. Mr. J. W. BROADBENT, the representative of the firm of Messrs. GEO. BARNET & Co. was elected chairman.

On the 25th April the HON. R. H. PRUYN arrived, to relieve the HON. TOWNSEND HARRIS as Minister-Resident of the United States. With him also came Mr. GEORGE S. FISHER to replace Mr. E. M. DORR as U. S. Consul, and Mr. E. E. RICE, who was to be the U. S. Commercial Agent at Hakodate.

As Mr. TOWNSEND HARRIS played a very important part in opening the intercourse between Japan and foreign nations, a few words as to his career in this country may be acceptable to those of my readers who are not well acquainted with it.

He arrived here in August 1856, and a residence was provided for him in a very pleasantly situated temple at Kakisaki, near Shimoda, one of the places which had been named in Commodore PERRY's treaty as a trading port for Americans. He was the bearer of a letter from the President to the Tycoon, and requested permission to visit Yedo to deliver it in 'person, and to present his credentials as Minister-Resident with full powers. His request was not complied with. But Mr. HARRIS was a man of patience, of temper and of resolution. He had come to secure and foster American trade with Japan.

VOL. I J

His first sight of Shimoda and its harbour showed him its impracticable character as a commercial port; and he determined to leave no effort untried by which he could get it changed for a better one—if possible Yedo itself; or, failing that, one that should be sufficiently near to the great city to secure its trade.

At that time Yedo was a very different place from what it has since become. The real seat of government was there. The hereditary Generalissimo of the Empire, virtually exercising imperial powers, and supposed by foreigners, both from the information of old writers and from the representations of all officials, and indeed of every Japanese, official or otherwise, to be the *de facto* Emperor, resided there. All knew that at Kioto, then more generally called Miaco (the metropolis), there was a mysterious being called the Mikado; but he was looked upon by the people as too holy to trouble himself with mundane affairs; and the popular belief was that he lived in a state of sublime abstraction, occupying himself from morning to night, at all times and seasons, in prayer to the gods, his ancestors, for the welfare of Japan.

In very truth, it would be easy to shew that this was far from being correct. For several years before foreigners came to Japan, the most powerful territorial princes, chafing under the oppressive government of the Shoguns, had commenced an active opposition to it; and roundly asserted the fact that the Mikado was the true and sole sovereign of Japan.

Seven centuries ago, YORITOMO had succeeded in immuring the real Emperor or Mikado at Kioto; whilst he, receiving his authority from him, ruled the nation arbitrarily, establishing his government at Kamakura— that pleasant village so frequently visited by excursionists from Yokohama, and tourists from all parts of the world.

Yoritomo made it a great city, and introduced the system, afterwards confirmed and tightened by Iyeyas'— by which the daimios were obliged to reside for stated periods at the governmental centre.

At the beginning of the 17th century, the Shogunate, after having passed through several of what may justly be called dynasties, was seized by the powerful Tokugawa prince Iyeyas'; whose descendants wielded the sovereign power for twelve generations, until the whole feudal system was swept away by the revolution of 1868, and the Mikado became once more the active, as well as the nominal, ruler of the land.

At the time of Mr. Harris's arrival, however, the old system still prevailed; and under it all the daimios, holding their territories and titles from the Shogun, were compelled to reside in Yedo every alternate year, keeping up a large retinue there always, and leaving their wives and families there even when they themselves visited their own dominions. Thus all of them had extensive yashikis, which served as residences for themselves and the chief officials of their clans, and barracks for the retainers and their families. Each of the daimios had more than one of these yashikis; some had several: the prince of Satsuma, for instance, having no less than nine. There were over 260 of these territorial chieftains, with revenues from 10,000 to 1,000,000 kokus of rice, or, at the then prices of rice and rates of exchange, from £7,500 to £750,000 sterling per annum. Their retinues were proportioned to these nominal revenues; and it was said that the Prince of Kaga (the richest, with a revenue of 1,027,700 kokus), and the Prince of Satsuma, (the second in point of wealth, with 710,000 kokus), maintained each a force of 80,000 fully equipped fighting men, of whom a large proportion were always stationed in Yedo. It is, therefore, well within the mark when the population of the city, civil and military, is stated at over two millions; and it is quite credible that it may have approached the generally reported number of three millions.

As yet the wants of these people were few, and well supplied from their national resources and productions. They had seen very little of the products of other nations, and knowing nothing of them were quite content to be without them. But Mr. HARRIS was quite alive to the fact that supply creates demand quite as surely, up to a certain point, as that demand creates supply. He believed that no sooner were foreign goods brought hither, their uses seen, and their cheapness realised, than a demand would spring up for them; and under any circumstances, there were certain commodities that Japan produced, which would certainly be eagerly bought by foreigners. His mind, therefore, was fully made up that new arrangements must be agreed to, the object of which should be, not merely friendship and mutual kindness to ships visiting the coasts, but commerce; with all the necessary facilities for carrying it on with the native merchants without let or hindrance.

In the *Kinsé Shiriaku*, translated from the Japanese by Mr. E. M. SATOW, of H. B. M's Legation, will be found the account of Mr. HARRIS' proceedings, written by an intelligent Japanese official, who served both under the old and new governments. It is sufficient here to state that after repeated efforts to obtain permission to visit the Shogun in Yedo, and encountering direct refusals, rejecting "every possible art" used "in order to dissuade him from his project," he "would not listen, and it (the government) had no resource but to give way." Written protests were sent in by the leading daimios and the Council; but, in spite of all, Mr. HARRIS " eventually reached Yedo in the 9th month (Oct. 17—Nov. 15.) He "had an interview with the Shogun and presented his credentials: after which he withdrew and returned to his lodgings. Shortly afterwards he had an interview with the Ministers, and briefly stated his demands. These were, unrestricted trade between the merchants of both countries in all articles except gold and cereals, without any official interference; the closing of Shimoda, and the opening of Kanagawa and Ozaka; the residence of a minister plenipotentiary at Yedo, to settle all diplomatic questions, and the conclusion of a treaty in detail, to be ratified by the Japanese Government."

It is generally supposed that Mr. HARRIS obtained all his demands simply by his patience, perseverance and gentle consideration for the Japanese. If the plain truth be told, although these qualities did much for him, they were not more conspicuous in him than in other ministers of foreign nations who subsequently came upon the scene, and whose patience and gentleness were put to an infinitely greater strain than he was ever subjected to. This by the way. The fact is only mentioned here, that when the proper time comes in the course of our narrative, it may be remembered.

It is the misfortune of England, that, in the far East, the protection of her extensive commerce has thrown upon her the principal portion of the burden of clearing obstructions, and of opening up and carrying on the intercourse with the jealous and exclusive inhabitants of these highly favoured regions. In China, England wrought, and other nationalities reaped the benefit of her labours; but in 1857-8 the French and English combined to punish the bad faith of the Celestial Emperor and his ministers; and, at Tientsin, dictated their own terms.

Mr. HARRIS was too astute a diplomatist to allow such an opportunity to pass. With consummate tact he availed himself of the successes of the allies in China to effect his long cherished purpose.

A writer in a New York paper, in a long letter on the subject of Mr. Harris as American Minister in Japan, says:—

"Caution and forbearance are essential qualities in the management of official relations with the government and people of Japan. Mr. Harris seemed to understand their national character by intuition. In every effort he has made to obtain amelioration of the hard conditions of the first American Treaty, he has been signally successful; and up to the present time he has enjoyed the entire confidence of the ruling princes, and exercised an influence over the minds of the people never before possessed by any foreign resident.

"These facts are remarkable, and conclusively show that good results have come from the upright and honorable course pursued by Mr. Harris, while in other quarters so different a feeling had been awakened that revolt and murder have ensued."

Acknowledging as I do, the great talents of Mr. Harris, and the services that he performed in inserting and driving home the wedge which opened the doors of Japan to foreigners, and admitting the respect with which anything emanating from Mr. P. M. Wetmore in connection with trading interests in the far East should be received, it is impossible to pass over the *bunkum* of these paragraphs. For what were the means adopted by Mr. Harris to effect the insertion of the wedge? He, as others did after him, became impatient of delay. The native writer already quoted says:—

"In the 2nd month (March 14—April 12) the American Harris, rendered impatient by the long interval that had already elapsed without anything being communicated to him about the Treaty, threatened that if his time was to be wasted in this way, he would proceed forthwith to Kioto and arrange it himself. He was surprised, after being informed that Yedo was the seat of government, to find such dilatoriness on the part of the Bakufu, and he gave it a certain number of days within which to make up its mind."

Again the some writer tells us :—

"American and Russian men-of-war came to Yokohama and gave information that the English and French squadrons would arrive in a few days with the object of concluding a treaty. HARRIS took advantage of this to point out what he thought the best course for them to pursue, and to urge the ratification of his own treaty."

But we have better authority still for what led to the success of Mr. HARRIS. The following is a

"*Circular from the Tycoon dated the 6th month of the 5th year of Ansei (August 1858), sent by order of Yamato-no-Kami by the Ometski Kouro Kawa Sadjou.*

" The Mikado having been consulted by the Tycoon's government about the making of Treaties with foreigners, he answered that the conclusion of that matter (the making the Treaties) would distress him very much. Thereupon the Tycoon requested all to send their written opinion upon the subject. Only a short time was required to gather together everyone's opinion, but in the meantime some Russian and American men-of-war came here bringing the news that in a short time English and French men-of-war would arrive here : that these two nations had fought and won many battles in China : that they would come here in the same warlike spirit, and it would be difficult for us to negociate with them. The American ambassador offered to us that if we would make a temporary treaty with him, as soon as we should have signed and given him that Treaty he could act as mediator between us and the French and English, and could save us all difficulties.

" It was impossible for us to comply with this without consulting the Mikado. However, INOUYE SHINANO-NO-KAMI and IWASA HIGO-NO-KAMI, fearing the immediate assault (or breaking out of a war), the results of which might be the same as in China, signed themselves, or were authorised to sign, the American Treaty, at Kanagawa, which Treaty was given up to the American ambassador.

" Necessity compelled the Japanese to this.

" The Mikado on hearing of this was much troubled, but to reassure him we told him we would fortify our shores.

" The Tycoon thought there was the necessity of concluding this Treaty, and he at once sent to the Mikado the messenger that everyone should fearlessly express his opinion on the subject to the Government."

And if any confirmation of the above be required it may surely be gathered from the American Treaty itself:—

"The President of the United States, at the request of the Japanese Government, will act as a friendly mediator in such matters of difference as may arise between the government of Japan and any European Power."

From this will be understood the leverage that was brought to bear by the adroit minister. But it is almost too much of a joke to use England as a cat's-paw to pluck the chestnuts from the fire, and then to speak of the high character he bears among the Japanese, and to write disparagingly of the British.

With all the admiration that may be felt for the cleverness of the minister, the generosity of the man can hardly be extolled by those who read the following extract from one of his letters, informing his Government of the attack on the British Legation.

No. 28.   Legation of the United States in Japan,
Yedo, 9th July 1861.

SIR,—It is my unpleasant duty to inform you that a daring and murderous attack was made on the British Legation in this city on the night of the 5th instant.

* * * * * * * * * *

I consider the present as a crisis in the Foreign Affairs of Japan, for if the Government be too weak to punish the instigators and agents of this nefarious affair it may be believed that it will lead to some very decided action on the part of the English Government, for the outrage was too great to be overlooked.

"There is a party in this country who are opposed to the presence of any foreigners in Japan, and, in addition to this there is a very strong dislike to the English in particular, which feeling seems to attach especially to Mr. ALCOCK. He was absent from this city for some three months, during which time the utmost quiet prevailed; yet within 36 hours of his return the attack in question was made on him.

"I am happy to say that these prejudices do not extend to our citizens in this country, and I think I am personally popular among all classes of the Japanese."

Mr. HARRIS may have been correct as to his personal popularity; but as for the dislike to the British in particular at that period of our intercourse, it is a very gratuitous assertion, and very unlikely to have been founded on fact. No special cause had been given by Englishmen as distinguished from other foreigners for such marked aversion; and judging by the manner in which the Japanese assassins and incendiaries had distributed their favours, it would not appear that any one nationality more than another could claim the honour of being most prominent in the national hatred. Russians, Dutch, French (in the person of M. DE BELLECOURT's valet), Portuguese (Mr. LOUREIRO's servant, who, by the way, was a Chinese), Mr. HARRIS's own interpreter, Mr. HEUSKEN, had all felt the keenness of the Japanese sword before the attack on Mr. ALCOCK's Legation; and subsequently, the U. S. Legation shared the same fate as did the French and English, in being burnt to the ground, not accidentally. These facts, and the murderous attacks on Japanese daimios who were favourable to foreigners, (including the assassination of the Regent II KAMON-NO-KAMI) and the burning of the Tycoon's palace, should suffice to shew that no foreigner could cast a stone at another. It was not individual foreigners that were hated, but the whole race of them; and all Japanese, whether high or low, who favoured them. It is certainly possible that Mr. ALCOCK may have been a marked man among them, for none was obliged to play so prominent a part as he did. The French minister, indeed, always acted with him, thus laying himself open, in some degree, to the same measure of popularity or the reverse; but the great *onus* rested on the British minister, and Mr. HARRIS, differing with him in policy, kept quiet in his secluded temple at Asabu, and escaped much of the danger that constantly attended his more active colleagues. As to the remark of Mr. HARRIS that during Mr. ALCOCK's absence of three months from Yedo, there was perfect quiet, that proves nothing. The French minister was also absent during the same period, and the same inference might as justly be applied to him.

Thus much I have thought it right to say, in noticing the departure from Japan of Mr. HARRIS. He was an excellent minister for his own country; and very useful in aiding others in making the treaties they sought. Lord ELGIN, Count EULENBERG and the Portuguese Envoy, all handsomely acknowledged the valuable assistance he rendered them. That he understood the Japanese character thoroughly, and, in general, dealt uprightly with them, is undeniable. He will readily be pardoned for the *ruse* he played off upon them by which he succeeded in getting his Treaty signed, even though it was calculated to create a strong prejudice against England and France in the minds of the already incensed and frightened Japanese. It is only to be regretted that he never attempted to dispel the unpleasant feeling then engendered; but seems from his letter, rather to observe with a grim satisfaction the fancied dislike of the Japanese to the British residents and their minister, as distinguished from the personal favour of the Japanese towards himself.

CHAPTER XI.

AMUSEMENTS OF FOREIGNERS.—RACES.—INDICATION OF JAPANESE DESIRE FOR PROGRESS.—ESTABLISHMENT OF A COLLEGE IN YEDO FOR FOREIGN LANGUAGES, HISTORY, SCIENCE, &C.—NEWS RECEIVED OF POSTPONEMENT OF OPENING THE TREATY PORTS.—DISSATISFACTION.—ARRIVAL OF LIEUT.-COLONEL ST. JOHN NEALE.—OFFER OF GOVERNOR OF KANAGAWA TO ALLOT BLUFF LAND FOR FOREIGNERS' RESIDENCES.—REJECTION ON PLEA OF ITS BEING TOO LIMITED.—MURDER OF TWO MARINES AT H. B. M.'S LEGATION, YEDO.—REAL DESIRE OF JAPANESE GOVERNMENT TO PROTECT FOREIGNERS.—THWARTED BY DISAFFECTED DAIMIOS, RONINS, &C.—CASUALTIES ENDURED BY THEMSELVES IN OUR CAUSE.—CONSTANT BLOODSHED.—FOREIGNERS, IGNORANT OF THE REAL FACTS, HAD GROUNDS FOR DISCREDITING STATEMENTS MADE TO THEM.—MARRIAGE OF THE SHOGUN TO THE SISTER OF THE MIKADO.—MISSION OF OHARA AS SPECIAL ENVOY FROM THE MIKADO TO THE SHOGUN.—ACCOMPANIED BY SHIMADZU SABURO, FATHER OF PRINCE SATSUMA.—DOUBTS AS TO SHIMADZU'S ANIMOSITY AGAINST FOREIGNERS.—INCIDENT AT HIMEJI—RONINS DEMAND HIS LEADERSHIP IN THE EXPULSION OF FOREIGNERS.

AMID all the troubles and dangers that accompanied residence in Japan in the earlier days it was no part of the policy of foreigners to curtail their enjoyments. Although in making excursions into the country around the settlement, within the limit of the ten ri assigned by treaty, it was usual to carry revolvers, it was rather that the dangerous class might be deterred from assaulting them by the knowledge that they carried arms, than from apprehension of having to use them. Occasions did sometimes occur which called for their being resorted to in self-defence; but they were not frequent.

Within the settlement public amusements of any kind were as yet rare; but, of course, there could be no congregation of foreigners in the East without its periodical race-meetings. In 1862 a race-course was formed on the newly filled-in Swamp Concession. It was the best that could be obtained, and on the application of the English and Dutch Consuls, the Governor of Kanagawa allowed a portion of the ground to be fenced in and prepared for two days racing. It was about three quarters of a mile round. The prizes were moderate as compared with those of the present day; but of all the old friends and acquaintance who figured as owners then, only one remains with us—Mr. MORRISON, the spirited owner of the Tartan stable.

In May 1862, the Japanese Government gave an important indication of their desire to place themselves on an equal footing with foreigners. They commenced the erection of a college in Yedo, for the instruction of students in foreign languages, history, and the sciences.

The news which reached Japan this month, that the Home Government, on the recommendation of Mr. ALCOCK, had consented to postpone the opening of the other Treaty Ports for five years, was received by the foreign residents with much dissatisfaction; but judging after the event, and by the consequences that attended the opening of Osaka and Hiogo in 1868, few will be disposed now to question the judiciousness of the step.

Lieut. Colonel St. JOHN NEALE arrived this month and assumed the duties of H.B.M. Chargé d'Affaires.

At this time, whilst the Mikado was constantly ordering the Shogun to close Yokohama and drive the ugly foreign barbarians away, and as frequently receiving his promise that it should be done, the Governor of Kanagawa was actually offering to allot 25,000 tsubos of land on the Bluff for foreign residences. The residents, however, considered so limited a space quite inadequate for the wants of the community, and suggested that the boundary should be extended to cover not less than the face of the whole Bluff, from the Canal to Treaty Point, and backward from the sea to a width not less than that of the foreign settlement—a space just about equal to that subsequently appropriated for the purpose in 1867.

On the morning of the 27th June, just twelve months, (according to the Japanese calendar), from the attack on the British Legation which has been already described, a second assault was made within the same precincts, by which two marines—the corporal of the guard and another from H. M. S. Renard, lost their lives. It seems hardly worthy of the name of a second attack on the Legation; for, so far as was ever ascertained, it was the work of one man only. Since the former attack, when the Japanese guard appointed by the Government for the minister and his attachés so signally failed in their duty, an English guard had been availed of in addition to that still provided by the Government. At this time it consisted of 80 men; namely, of the Military Train 12 men under Lieut. APPLIN, and 68 marines from H. M. S. Renard, under Captain BINGHAM and Lieuts. EDWARDS and WARREN. The Japanese guard consisted of 500 men, not one of whom was wounded. The corporal of the guard was going his rounds, when he was suddenly attacked and speared in several places. He managed to reach Colonel NEALE's door, where he fell and died. The other victim was the sentry at the door. All was done so quickly and quietly that not one of the guard was aroused until all was over and the perpetrator of the cruel deed had made his escape. On enquiry, it turned out that he was one of the native guard. The next morning he was missed from the roll, and traced to his own house, where he was found to have committed *hara-kiri*. Colonel NEALE asked to be permitted to examine the body of the murderer. He was told that it would be brought to the Legation compound; but, as the man belonged to a very high daimio, it would be escorted by his head officer and a large retinue and deposited in the Temple. This Colonel NEALE objected to. Ultimately the body was brought and deposited outside the gate, but not seen by Colonel NEALE. The Japanese asserted, that on examination, it was found to have at least one ball through the chest.

This deed does not appear to have had any further political significance than as indicating the general jealousy of the samurai against foreigners.

With the history of succeeding years plainly laid bare before us, any reasonable mind must come to the conclusion that the Government did really use every effort in its power, to act faithfully up to the spirit of the Treaties, and to protect foreigners from the assaults of the lawless desperadoes who, while the Mikado and many of the daimios were urging on the Shogun the imperative necessity of driving us away and closing the already opened ports, drew their swords and sought to make the country too hot for us, by indiscriminate murder, arson, attacks by armed bands on the Legations, and by causing us to be kept in continual apprehension of a descent upon the settlement of Yokohama by large bodies of ronins.

Already one Shogun, IYESADA, who had been in power when the treaties of PERRY, HARRIS and Lord ELGIN, were made, had been sacrificed, it is generally believed, on account of them. His successor, IYEMOCHI, a boy 12 years of age when he was called upon to assume the responsibilities of government, inherited nothing but trouble from the first. He was exalted to office in September 1858; and though the Regent, Gotairo II KAMON-NO-KAMI, was the real actor in all the proceedings that found such opposition in Kioto and among the most powerful daimios, yet the youthful ruler was early made to bear the responsibility. It was the influence of II KAMON-NO-KAMI that induced IYESADA to nominate IYEMOCHI as his successor, in opposition to the wishes of the daimios that HITOTS'BASHI should be so named. In January 1859, the Mikado confirmed the nomination, and formally appointed IYEMOCHI to the office. The conspiracies against the Shogunate became more and more numerous and more and more difficult to deal with. One "YOSHIDA SHOIN, of Choshiu, wrote to a court noble, OHARA SHIGETAMI," (of whom more presently), inviting him down to Choshiu in order to get up an agitation in the clan, for the expulsion of the barbarians, and the restoration of the Mikado. In conflicts between the opponents of the treaties and the Shogun's supporters, many good men lost their lives, and blood was spilt like water. II KAMON-NO-KAMI was himself assassinated by a band of ronins at the Sakurada gate of the castle, within sight of his own residence, as has already been told; and among the crimes alleged against him was one, that he was "frightened by the empty threats of foreign barbarians into concluding treaties" with them, without the sanction of the Mikado, and under the pretext of political necessity.

From this time onwards hardly a day seems to have passed without bloodshed among the Japanese on account of the admission of foreigners; and all the inimical acts against the new-comers were but as a drop in the ocean as compared with the trouble brought on the Empire by their presence in Japan. Of all this foreigners knew comparatively little at the time. To them it appeared that the Government of the Shogun was vacillating, hostile and treacherous. As there were undoubtedly occasions—important ones too—when they endeavoured by a distortion or hiding of facts to mislead and deceive the foreign ministers; to keep them in ignorance of what was going on, or to give a false colouring to what could not be entirely concealed, it became a settled belief that they were always mendacious; never to be relied upon; that their representations as to the difficulties that well-nigh overwhelmed them, and which, in 1868, absolutely did deprive them, as a government, of all power, and force their chief, the Shogun, into permanent retirement, were mere subterfuges; and that the appeals for delay in opening the ports of Hiogo and Ni-igata for trade, and Yedo and Osaka for residence, were made in the hope that ultimately this portion of the treaties might be abrogated altogether.

According to the light possessed by foreigners, however, their suspicions are not to be wondered at. Anyone reading Sir RUTHERFORD ALCOCK's book "Three years at the Capital of the Tycoon," must admit that he makes out a strong case for very much more vigourous action than he ever took, and that with all the provocation he had, his measures, and those of his diplomatic colleagues who held the same views, and whose policy coincided with his, were extremely moderate.

Toward the end of the year 1861, the young Shogun

now 15 years of age, had the sister of the Mikado, KAZU-MIYA, conferred upon him in marriage. It was a purely political arrangement, "to show to the world that the Imperial family and the house of TOKUGAWA agreed in their political views."

And now, in June 1862, the Shogun being only in his 16th year, a special Envoy arrives in Yedo, with the Mikado's command that he, the Shogun, "with all the daimios great and small," should repair to Kioto, and there "ascertain the opinion of the country, expel the barbarians, and so calm the indignation of the Mikado's divine ancestry." Orders were also included for "five of the great daimios to be consulted as chief ministers upon the conduct of public affairs," according to the *Kinsé Shiriaku;* "to make the sea-coast strong," according to the *Japan Herald*, "so as to be safe against foreign men-of-war." And "HITOTSUBASHI to be appointed guardian of the Shogun, and the ex-prince of ECHIZEN to be made chief minister of state" as reported in the *Kinsé Shiriaku*. "HITOTS'BASHI to be vice-Shogun, and ECHIZEN to help the Shogun, that all parties may be satisfied;" as translated from the letter delivered by the Envoy and published in the *Japan Herald*.

This mission of OHARA's led to important and unfortunate consequences. For the first time in the history of the country, the guard of an Imperial Envoy was not entrusted to the Shogun's troops, but to those of the Prince of SATSUMA. SHIMADZU IDZUMI, henceforward known as SHIMADZU SABURO, the Mikado having just honoured him by giving him this name, accompanied him. SABURO was the real father of the daimio of SATSUMA; but the previous daimio, his brother, having adopted the youth as his son, SABURO was, according to Japanese law and custom, his uncle—the uncle by adoption of his real son. He was, however, the active ruler of the clan, and from having been a great student and book-worm in early life, he had now changed and had come to be looked upon as one of the cleverest and bravest spirits in the nation. He was one of those who had been most earnest in opposing the Yedo government. Yet it is hard to believe that he was seriously or violently opposed to foreigners as such; for his territories were in the immediate vicinity of Nagasaki, the only port that for over two centuries had any foreign trade: and that trade must have benefited his people. Indeed, it was given out that he was highly indignant with the Tycoon for having restricted foreign trade to ports which would enrich the TOKUGAWA coffers alone; and that he was eager to throw open the whole of the SATSUMA dominions; in which, laudable desire, however, he was thwarted by the Yedo Government.

Whilst on his way to Kioto, *en route* for Yedo, on reaching Himéji in Harima, an incident occured which strengthens my belief that he had at that time no hostile intentions against foreigners. One HIRANO JIRO had collected a band of ronins, about two hundred in number, and wished to place himself and his band under the leadership of some noble of kindred spirit.

In Mr. SATOW's translation of the *Kinsé Shiriaku* we read :—

"They were on the look-out for an ally of the kind they wanted, when they heard of the arrival of SHIMADZU IDZUMI at HIMEJI. HIRANO, who was aware of the intrepid character of this prince, at once proceeded thither with his men, and addressed a letter to him. It said :—' The Bakufu has lately been treating the Mikado's orders with contempt, and has concluded treaties without his sanction. The empire is on the point of becoming a hell. We wish therefore to get you to become our leader, in order that we may release the Court nobles who have been confined in consequence of the Bakufu's displeasure, seize the castles of Ozaka, Hikoné and Nijō, send orders to all the clans, carry the Mikado to Hakoné, punish the crimes of the Shogun, and immediately afterwards sweep out the barbarians. Pray take our request into your gracious consideration, oh Prince, and grant it.' They then asked him to forward their letter to the Imperial Court. Idzumi felt secretly alarmed at their violence, and giving an evasive answer, pacified them as well as he could. Having left them at the town of Fushimi he went on to Kioto, and sent Hirano's letter to Konoyé, a Court noble. The Court was so frightened at the seditious style of the letter, that it retained IDZUMI in Kioto to keep the ronins in order. It happened that the ronins at Ozaka and some Satsuma samurai of the same way of thinking, heard of this, and were enraged at what they called IDZUMI's temporizing policy. Some forty or fifty started for Kioto at once, intending to put pressure on him and proceed to action. On receiving this news, IDZUMI sent some of his retainers to stop them at Fushimi, and to persuade them to remain quiet. The efforts of the retainers were unavailing, and after a long dispute, they were obliged to use force. Numbers were killed on both sides, and the town became the scene of an indescribable commotion."

This was the man of whom much has to be told; whose name was for a long time a byword among foreigners; and whose acts led to results direful indeed to his clan, and hardly less so to the Government of the Shogun.

Whilst in Yedo SHIMADZU SABURO purchased an English steamer, the Fiery Cross, for his son-nephew, the Prince of Satsuma. He visited Yokohama and went a trial trip in her; and there is no reason to imagine that he then entertained such feelings towards foreigners as should lead to any cruelty to them; especially as on that occasion he was treated most cordially, and appeared to appreciate the kindness of his reception.

Prince Shimadzu

INTERPOLATORY CHAPTER.

REASON FOR THIS INTERPOLATION.—THE DAIMIO OF SATSUMA.—SHIMADZU SABURO.—HIS SON ADOPTED, AND HIMSELF APPOINTED GUARDIAN OF THE STATE.—ACTIVE IN PUBLIC AFFAIRS.—SCHEME FOR THE UNIFICATION OF THE EMPIRE UNDER THE MIKADO, AND THE ADVANCEMENT OF SATSUMA.—VISITS KIOTO.—PROCLAMATION BEFORE LEAVING KAGOSHIMA.—JEALOUSY OF DAIMIOS.—HIS FIRMNESS.—PROFFERED CO-OPERATION OF RONINS IN ATTACKING FOREIGNERS. —HIS REPLY.—AGREES TO SEND MESSENGERS TO THEM AT FUSHIMI.—THEIR DETERMINATION.—THE INTERVIEW.— BRAVE CONDUCT OF SATSUMA MEN.—ITS RESULTS.—SABURO PROCEEDS WITH HIS PLANS; AND IS SENT BY THE MIKADO WITH A NOBLEMAN OF THE IMPERIAL COURT, ON A MISSION TO YEDO.

THE character of SHIMADZU SABURO has been so freely handled by foreigners, and, (whether rightly or wrongly will never be known), so terribly vilified, that I venture to introduce bodily, in an interpolatory chapter, a most interesting account of him, and of the incident referred to in the quotation from the *Kinsé Shiriaku* given in the preceding chapter. It was written by Mr. E. H. HOUSE, published in a pamphlet entitled *Kagoshima*, and is inserted with his permission. I doubt not the main facts were imparted to him by none other than SAIGO YORIMICHI himself, who plays an honourable part in one incident recorded.

It confirms my view respecting the probable *animus* of SABURO towards foreigners. Mr. HOUSE writes:—

The daimio of Satsuma, at this period, was one who fully shared the sentiments of his race, without ever reaching the opportunity of acting upon them. A few words only, concerning him, are necessary to explain his relation to the events about to be described. He was the legitimate inheritor of his title and position, but he had acceded to them under circumstances of much difficulty and confusion. He was not the favorite of his father, who had always expressed a determination to be succeeded by a younger son, the offspring of a concubine, whose birth would not necessarily exclude him from the inheritance. This younger son was the person now known as SHIMADZU SABURO. The project was energetically opposed by many powerful clansmen, and one of the daimio's secretaries, who openly favored it, was assassinated by the malcontents. These latter were speedily brought to trial and execution, but the course of popular feeling was now so obvious that the daimio did not venture to resist it, and, at his death, the legitimate son assumed his place.

It does not appear that the younger SHIMADZU had taken an active part in the intrigue of which he was the object, but, after his half-brother's accession, feeling himself under some degree of suspicion, or perhaps really being so, he withdrew from public notice, and led a life of almost rigorous seclusion. His only serious occupation appeared to be the study of the Chinese classics. His diversions were the composition of Chinese poetry and trials of skill in games of chance. He was not generally supposed to give the slightest heed to the political affairs even of his own province,—much less to those of the nation. He passed to a mature age without ever gaining much popular deference or esteem, and, while among men he was spoken of with careless indifference as an idle recluse, he was held in even less respectful consideration by the youth of Kagoshima, in which city he resided, and where his reputation for stolidity and his personal peculiarities, notably his extreme near-sightedness, supplied abundant opportunities for juvenile, and probably not brilliant, satire.

The brother in power had married, but was without children. Whether he had formed an independent estimate of the character of the recluse, or not, is an open question; but, in his last days, he selected the infant son of the latter to be his successor, and appointed SABURO (then known by another name) to the position of guardian of the state [Kokufu.] In 1862, this long secluded nobleman thus became the actual, though not the titular, ruler of Satsuma. To the amazement of everybody, he at once renounced the inactivity of his former life, and devoted himself to the public interests with a vigilance and an industry of which no person had supposed him capable. Within a few weeks from the time when the power of the province was placed in his hands, he had conceived and commenced the execution of a scheme which had for its double object the unification of the empire by the restoration of the Mikado's dormant rule and the establishment of the house of Satsuma in the front rank of political agencies. It is not easy, at this time, to decide which may have been the more potent motive in his mind. His adherents have always claimed that his first purpose was to ensure the re-organization of the national Government upon the only basis that promised an enduring security. However this may have been, it is certain that through his exertions and those of the allies he gathered about him at different times, both designs were accomplished before six years had passed. The Imperial Court resumed the functions which it had failed to exercise for more than six centuries, and SHIMADZU SABURO was hailed as the Warwick of the day. The Tokugawa line was even more effectually broken than he had proposed, for he had at first looked only to curtailments and limitations of its vast dominion, and, in the earlier civil contests that arose, often co-operated with its leaders for the preservation of peace in the Mikado's capital. But the fortunes of the Shoguns could not outlast the struggle. When the last of the dynasty fell, the political prestige of the family expired, and such power and influence as could be wielded by one man alone passed into SHIMADZU's possession. While the feudal system lasted, his pre-eminence was plainly acknowledged. Even after its destruction, he continued to hold a position of authority which no other representative of the old nobility maintained, or pretended to emulate in the remotest degree, and which culminated in his advancement to the highest office, with a single exception, that is filled by a Japanese subject.

Early in the spring of 1862, SHIMADZU resolved to visit Kioto, for the purpose of submitting his plans directly to the Mikado or his chief counsellors. Aggressive acts against foreigners formed no part of his calculations, and there is no evidence to show that he looked upon their expulsion from the country, or even their molestation, as the necessary outgrowth of his projects. There is evidence, on the contrary, that he used his authority to prevent deeds of violence and unsanctioned combinations even in support of what might be supposed to be his policy. Before leaving his province, he issued a proclamation to his retainers, " forbidding them to ally themselves with the ronins," (disaffected agitators and virtual outlaws) " or to do anything without the instructions of their superiors." His subsequent orders, especially applicable to the Richardson case, will appear hereafter. His self-imposed mission was not looked upon with much favor by the feudal lords in general. He was accused of claiming privileges, in the matter of asking audiences and tendering advice, that did not properly belong to any beneath the rank of daimio, and which, though they might be granted to his son (now, legally, his nephew and ward) ought not to be expected by himself. It would have needed much stronger remonstrances than these to dissuade him from his purpose. He declared that this was a time when, if traditions stood in the way of the public welfare, they must be brushed aside like cobwebs. Other difficulties, however, beset him on his way to Kioto, from which he could not so easily relieve himself. The most embarrassing of these was the proffered co-operation of a troop of turbulent ronins who, assuming that his principal design was to organize an attack upon foreigners, insisted upon accompanying him and taking part in all his movements. Appreciating the necessity of avoiding all signs of disturbance at or near the Imperial capital, he sent for the leaders of the party, eight in number, and gave them to understand that, whatever might be the merit of their enterprise, the time for executing it had certainly not arrived, and that the question of dealing with the foreigners was one that must be decided in the future. He was listened to with impatience, and assured that if he would not accept their services they would go to Kioto by themselves, and seek for authority to commence operations on their own account. The situation was critical, for it was plain that these desperate men, if left to their own devices would create a tumult in the capital that might bring discredit upon SHIMADZU's whole action. The manner in which he suddenly resolved to deal with it is worth relating in detail, as illustrating the resolute character of the man, and as showing incidentally, to what lengths he was prepared to go in preventing, at this time, instead of inciting, onslaughts upon strangers. The story has never been made public, although it is vaguely touched upon in *Kinsé Shiriaku*, and reproduced from that source, with certain variations that show a slight misapprehension of the circumstances, in Mr. ADAMS's *History of Japan*.

He announced that he would make no promises as to their adoption into his service, but agreed to send messengers to them, within a reasonable time after his arrival in Kioto, who would consult with them and convey his final decision. The ronins agreed to wait, and halted at the town of Fusimi, a few miles distant from Kioto. At the same time they declared their determination not to be thwarted, and their firm intention to advance, even against his injunction, if they could not receive his authorization. The next day, SHIMADZU selected eight of his most trusted followers, in whose diplomatic address and faculties of persuasion he had great confidence, and who had also proved themselves the most expert swordsmen in his suite. These he directed to return to the rendezvous; to hold a parley with the insurgent leaders; to convince them, by argument if possible, of the impracticability of their course, but at all hazards to prevent them from proceeding in their rebellious career. To Japanese vassals as devoted as those of SATSUMA, no further suggestions were needed. They reached Fusimi late in the evening and found the greater number of the ronins in a large house of public entertainment. The leaders joined them in a small room on the ground floor, while the others continued their carousals above. Before arriving, the principal of the SATSUMA retainers had arranged his plan and communicated it to his subordinates. Every effort should be made to bring the malcontents to reason by straightforward representations of the designs of their master, and by earnest exhortations that the disorderly campaign they contemplated should be abandoned. If these should fail, the conference could end only in a quarrel, in which event, the position and duty of seven of the SATSUMA participants was distinctly laid down. The lights were to be simultaneously extinguished, each man was to plant himself at a given distance from his neighbors, to drop upon one knee, and to sweep the space above his head with his drawn sword. The head of the party, NARABARA, would spring to the nearest corner, where he would be protected from assault in the rear or directly from the sides, and would attack in the dark any that should approach him. These precautions would not have been enjoined if an encounter upon anything like even terms had been anticipated; but the ronins were several hundred in number, and it was only through the application of some such strategy that the eight leaders could by any chance be disposed of. In case of a general conflict, some of them would have been almost sure to escape, and the mission of the retainers would have failed. It was foreseen that, in the tumult, some of the inferior ronins would rush to assist their chiefs, and join in the mêlée before the work of destruction could be thoroughly carried out; hence the necessity of having the advantage of darkness and pre-organization on the side of the militant envoys.

The interview in the tea-house was long and earnest. NARABARA and his companions were sincere in their efforts to settle the affair without violence, as, indeed, they were bound by their instructions to do, if any means could be discovered. For more than two hours they exerted such arguments and eloquence as they could command to persuade the adventurers to disband the troop and return to their homes. These endeavors were totally ineffectual. Having advanced so far, the insurgents declared, they could not and would not recede. If SHIMADZU would lead them to the fulfilment of their schemes, they would gladly exterminate the foreigners under his banner. If not, they would undertake the task in their own way. Moreover, they were convinced that the real spirit of the SATSUMA clan was in sympathy with them, in spite of all that the Kokufu might say. Several SATSUMA men had joined them within a few hours, and were heartily in unison with their plot. The discussion terminated in confusion and high words, as had been more than half anticipated. At a signal from NARABARA the paper lanterns that hung around the walls were thrown to the ground and trampled upon. The swords of all were instantly drawn. The SATSUMA leader darted to his corner, proclaiming his name and inviting attack by loud cries. His seven associates fell on their knees, and, in rigid silence, dealt fatal blows upon all that came within reach of their weapons. The ronins above, warned by the clamor of the chiefs, struggled to descend to their aid, but the ladders of communication had been removed. A few sprang from the windows and mingled blindly and ineffectively in the obscure affray. In less than five minutes from the time that the signal was given, the swords of the Satsuma men passed through the air without resistance. NARABARA called to his followers by name, and all but one replied. A light was struck, and its first ray revealed the bodies of eleven ronins and one of SHIMADZU's messengers, stretched lifeless upon the floor.

But the end of this extraordinary encounter had not yet

come. The scene that followed, though unattended by desperate strife or bloodshed, was even more startlingly dramatic. Yielding suddenly to an inspiration that could have had no prevision in his sober calculations, NARABARA, without waiting to apprise his companions of his intention, cast away his sword, threw off his upper garments to show that he was now defenceless, and, clambering up to the apartment above, flung himself, half naked, among the amazed and excited ronins, and fell upon his hands and knees with a salutation that was at the same time a gesture of appeal for momentary forbearance. Before they could recover from their surprise, he had rapidly related the whole story of what had occurred below, and begged to be heard in justification. The nearest of those who heard his words sought to destroy him without ceremony, but a young man from Satsuma, who had lately joined the troop, abruptly confronted them, and, placing himself defiantly before the prostrate body, proclaimed that he would protect the unarmed suppliant with his own life until he should obtain a hearing. In moments of critical suspense like this, a sudden demonstration of superior boldness is sure to carry all before it. Those who had hastened to avenge their leaders now instinctively yielded, and signified their willingness to listen. NARABARA at once declared that he did not mean to plead for himself, and that if, after having received his explanation, they were still determined to pursue their course, his body was at their disposal. He then hastily repeated the arguments he had used below, and said that, although he had failed to convince the chiefs, who were prepared with a regular and carefully contrived plan, his representations should surely have weight with the subordinates, who, left in ignorance of how to proceed, without commanders of experience or tried ability, and thrown into hopeless confusion at the moment when decision and unanimity were most needed, could not contend against the forces which SHIMADZU would be able to array against them. As to what he had himself done, every Japanese samurai knew that it was simply his duty, and the men of Satsuma, above all, would applaud, rather than condemn him for the fidelity and thoroughness with which he had fulfilled his mission. An appeal of this kind, made under circumstances that attested the fearlessness and faith of the speaker, and addressed to an audience composed of soldiers, who, whatever their other errors, had been trained to respect courage and devotion as the highest of human virtues, could not be ineffective. It was, in fact, triumphant. In admiration of his gallantry, NARABARA was suffered to go free. In acknowledgment of the force of his reasoning, the ronins admitted the feebleness of their position, under the new state of affairs, and pledged themselves to disperse without delay. The ready resolution of SHIMADZU, acting through the strong arm of NARABARA and his associates, had cut the knot of disaffection and mutiny with a single blow.

Thus relieved of his most pressing embarrassment, and no longer imperilled by the "entangling alliance" of a riotous mob, the Satsuma chieftain proceeded freely to the execution of his purposes. It is not essential to recount these purposes in detail. They all tended to the restoration of the national power into the hands of the Mikado, and the subordination, though not necessarily the extinction, of the Yedo Government. It does not appear that the adoption of violent measures against foreigners was ever advocated or suggested by him. His representations were so effective that in the course of a month he was sent to Yedo, together with a nobleman of the Imperial Court, to communicate the determination that had been taken by the supreme authority of the land. Having accomplished this task, and tarried in the Shogun's capital until the early part of the autumn of 1862, he set out upon his homeward journey.

The " young man from Satsuma who had lately joined the troop," and who defended the prostrate NARABARA in the courageous manner described by Mr. HOUSE, was SAIGO YORIMICHI, the Commander-in-Chief of the Japanese forces in the Formosan expedition, and now a member of the Ministry as the Chief of the War Department.

CHAPTER XII.

JAPANESE OFFICIALS WISH TO TRADE WITH FOREIGN COUNTRIES.—PURCHASE OF BARQUE ARMISTICE.—YOKOHAMA MUNICIPALITY LANGUISHES.—CONSULS WILLING TO DELEGATE TO IT CERTAIN POWERS.—MEASLES EPIDEMIC IN YEDO.—GENERAL EXAGGERATION IN JAPANESE STATISTICS.—SANITARY STATE OF YOKOHAMA.—FILTHY CANALS INTERSECTING THE NATIVE TOWN.—GENERAL CLEANLINESS OF THE PEOPLE.—PUBLIC TUBBING.—NATIVE BATH-HOUSES.—SIMPLICITY OF JAPANESE LIFE.—THE TOILET.—GOLDEN LACQUER.—FIELD WORK.—MOUNTEBANKS.—PRIEST.—KAGURA.—FIREMEN.

As REGARDS the ordinary passing events connected with Yokohama, and with the progress of foreign intercourse, there is nothing of much interest to relate. In connection with the latter, I take the following from the *North China Herald*:—

"A new feature in the trade of Japan has just transpired, which adds considerable interest to our relations with that country. It appears that for some time the Japanese Government have entertained the idea of encouraging a foreign trade amongst their own people, and, as an experiment, have launched into a commercial venture, by purchasing an English ship and loading her for the port of Shanghai on their own account. The first vessel they have purchased for this purpose is the British barque *Armistice*, Captain RICHARDSON, of 385 tons, for which they paid $34,000 and have named her the *Senzai-maru*, signifying to last a thousand years," or, freely translated, a thousand years' ship.' She arrived in harbour this morning, and has on board eight of some of the highest officials from Yedo, who are empowered by the Tycoon to trade with any port in the world that may extend their commerce. Also to purchase a number of ships of equal or superior quality to the *Armistice*, to form the nucleus of a merchant fleet."

As little more was ever heard of this scheme, it is to be inferred that either the early trading of "eight of some of the highest officials from Yedo," was not very profitable; or that the growing troubles of the empire forced the Government to attend to politics rather than to commerce.

In Yokohama, the Municipal Council that had been established soon began to languish. Yet it would appear that the Consuls were willing to give it every possible countenance, by a delegation of powers, which, however, it was very doubtful whether they themselves possessed. Three or four years later an attempt was made to induce ministers to obtain from their respective Governments, formal sanction for such powers being conferred; but it was of no avail.

There was a terrible visitation of measles, *(hashika)* in Yedo this summer. In the 56 days from June 17 to August 11, inclusive, no less than 567,713 persons were attacked, of whom 73,158 died.

On almost all occasions of such public calamities overtaking the nation, the statistics of mortality are given in such big figures as to be hardly credible. As an instance we are told in the *Kinsé Shiriaku* that " in the 6th month (July 10—August 7, 1858) an epidemic of cholera spread throughout the land, and about 30,000 persons died in Yedo alone." One thousand deaths a day is a rate remarkable even in a city of 2,000,000 inhabitants, more especially in one, where, if sanitary regulations were little thought of, yet the general airiness of the dwellings, and the cleanliness of all but the very lowest and poorest classes, struck foreigners as distinguishing characteristics of the natives. However, I only mention this to show how unreliable such statistics were; for in September in the same year, when Baron Gros arrived with the object of making a treaty for France, on demanding a residence on shore in Yedo, as Lord Elgin had done before him, all sorts of reasons were given to prove the impossibility of his wish being complied with; among the rest this being strenuously urged, that cholera was raging in the city; that *three thousand* had already died, and the deaths still continued at the rate of three hundred a day—a very different statement to the other.

As for the native settlement of Yokohama, there was a slight visitation of fever and diarrhœic complaints every summer, but nothing as compared with what might have been expected.

In laying out the land for the reception of foreigners, the native surveyors had availed themselves of the natural facilities they found to their hands.

The sea, of course, formed the frontage; and by cutting a broad canal in the rear, uniting two branches of a small river, which, parting about two miles inland, fell into the sea on the two sides of the proposed site, and by a little judicious labour in widening and deepening the embouchure of each, an island was formed, with a navigable water-way all round.

The land immediately fronting the sea was slightly above the level of that further inland, which had never been availed of even for rice-fields, but remained a simple, and oftentimes a very offensive, salt-water swamp.

The native and foreign quarters were kept quite distinct from each other; the foreign settlement being to the left looking from the sea, the native to the right. The frontage lay about south-east and north-west, the former extremity being appropriated to foreigners.

At first only the higher ground was laid out in streets, and it is a strange fact that in the native town several small canals or water courses were cut, whilst in the foreign quarter there was nothing of the kind. It is probable that these were enlargements of rivulets that made their way from the swamp to the sea; or they may have been inlets from the sea availed of as a means for small boats to penetrate into the town. One use they were turned to was to insulate the Yoshiwara; a quarter of which it will be necessary to speak hereafter.

The small canals alluded to, ramifying in various directions, although to a certain extent affected by the tides, were so to a very insufficient degree. They gradually, therefore, became black and offensive; and it was often as much as could be endured to pass them.

Yet houses were not only built on their banks, but actually overhanging them. There were streets of clean respectable-looking shops, on one side of which the back rooms of the houses—the living and sleeping apartments of the families occupying them—overhung these fetid, miasmatic canals; and it was often remarked that the rarity of any epidemic attacking the inhabitants, almost gave the lie to those who contend that stagnant pools, unripe fruit, and what foreigners would esteem low diet, are the generators of such diseases.

It is possible that the personal cleanliness of the people did much to preserve them from such illnesses; for there were few who did not take a hot bath every day, and hardly any who did so less frequently than every other day.

Those who published their Japanese experiences in those early days, speak of the public tubbing of females which came under their observation in Yedo; whilst later writers have called their statements in question: one, in particular, who has been among the most largely read and quoted, declaring, that although he had traversed the streets of Yedo at all hours of the day he had never seen anything of the kind. It is very likely not, for he arrived in Japan at the time that foreign influences had had their effect. As late as 1862 such things were seen in the vicinity both of Yedo and Yokohama; and within five years from this present writing, i.e. as lately as 1874, such a sight might have been, and was, seen every evening by passers-by, in the immediate neighbourhood of the settlement. I have seen it repeatedly both on one of the pathways leading from Homura to the Bluff, and also in the surrounding villages. By excursionists in all directions, what is called "indiscriminate tubbing" is so commonly seen, that they soon come to think nothing of it.

One of the features of the native town up to 1862, and even later, was the numerous public bath-houses, in which both sexes performed their ablutions together. This was gradually altered simply by the force of public opinion as expressed by the few foreigners then resident here. In Yedo it continued for years after it was discontinued in Yokohama; but now, although the sexes still use the same bath-houses in many instances, they are generally divided by a partition; and there are some houses where the separation is more complete still. Yet to this day, there is hardly one—if indeed there be one—where men are not in attendance even in the female division, and in which their services are not often brought into requisition to pour water over, or otherwise aid in the purifications, of the fair patronesses.

I will wind up this chapter by touching on some of the every-day scenes in Japan.

The simplicity of country life in Japan very much assimilates to what is found in other countries. As in Europe so in Japan there is much self-dependence. Although villages are abundant, the people in them have hardly got the length of resolving themselves into different trades, for the business would be quite too small. There may be in each a kind of general store, where the very simplest and most common and inexpensive necessaries may be obtained, but this is frequently kept by a family whose members farm a little piece of land themselves, and prepare on the premises many of the things they supply.

Very primitive are they in all they do. They are up with, or oftentimes before, the sun, and commence labour at once. Their toilet, rough as it is, is performed just as circumstances permit; sometimes directly they rise, often during a midday rest, but not less frequently in the evening when work is done. Every country house has its bath tub, in which the body can be purified and reinvigorated after the toils of the day by being parboiled. The temperature at which these baths are used is so high, that those who emerge from them are almost the colour of red Indians; and in the year 1872 an edict was promulgated in Tokio, that the public baths should not be heated beyond a moderate temperature— slightly below blood heat.

The men never do their own hair. There is always a barber near at hand, and the heads of the farmers and farm labourers may pass under his hand once a week or less according to their means. With the women it is almost the same, but they have to touch up a little each day, apart from the special day when they look for the visitation of the kami-san or hair dresser, whose periodical coming is preceded by letting down the hair and giving it a thorough washing. It must be a very poor person who has not the few things looked upon as necessities of the toilet. Among the wealthy, these are always supplied to a bride, of most beautiful quality, and are an important portion of her possessions.

Among the poorer or labouring class, the ordinary operations of the toilet may be seen every day; for everything is quite public. With them, of course, the requisites are but few and very common. To European eyes they look more like playthings; but small and simple as they are, to their owners they are as useful, and by them as much thought of, as the more pretentious toilet tables of the West. The diminutive cabinet of drawers suffices for them and holds all the accessories. The mirror is a disc of highly polished metal, quite effective for its purpose; and easily set up for use as required, and put away when done with. This simplicity was hardly departed from even among the highest classes. None were given to elaborate furniture at any time. The principal difference between peer and peasant in this respect, lay in the richness of the lacquer, or artistic workmanship of whatever kind, bestowed on the articles. All those pretty little cabinets and nick-nacks that are sent from Japan to other countries, were by no means playthings twenty years ago, and, indeed are not so among the mass of the people, even now.

About twenty years ago, the most honorable business among the mechanics of Yedo was that of gold-lacquerer. When the daughter of a daimio was married, it was customary to present her with a norimon, a quantity of toilet articles and boxes, all having the family mong or device in gold, on black or other lacquer. As this portion of the lady's outfit was considered very important, the artists in gold-lacquer were not permitted to do them at their own houses, but had to go to the yashikis and work there; it being understood that their charge, however exorbitant, should not be disputed. They were great people in their own way, and always wore silk clothes on such occasions, because cotton clothes were supposed to damage so fine an article. At home they had beautiful houses, generally with two or three fire-proof warehouses, and several apprentices were invariably there learning the business. It was a profession which was held in such esteem that even the learners of the trade used to refuse to be adopted into the families of flourishing merchants, because the profits of the gold lacquerers were so ample. But since the changes, there is no longer any demand for these valuable articles, and the trade has sunk into total decay. To such an extent is this the case, that actually some who a few years ago looked forward to a profitable career in this business, are now drawing jin-riki-shas. Of old a skilful artist could lacquer with gold as many as 300 badges in a single day; and as this lacquer was always in demand, they were never idle. There are still a few gold-lacquerers in the empire, but they have very little patronage. Mere common lacquerers are plentiful and a different class entirely from the workers in gold. The latter had special rules for their business, and it was a very difficult thing to become apprenticed to them. Some of the finest specimens of their workmanship are now in Europe, and ought to command high prices; for the original cost here was for the reasons above stated, very great, and the daily increasing rarity should enhance the value.

Field work throughout Japan is performed by both men and women. The fields are never large, but divided into little patches, no two of which are alike in size or shape. The rice fields are surrounded and divided from each other by low embankments, which serve to hold the water as in a basin. Rice growing is the dirtiest labour we know, in every stage the labourers working either in water or in mud. The general aspect of the agricultural districts would lead foreigners to suppose that the natives have little to learn from them in this respect. The soil, to all appearance, rich, from the care bestowed upon it for ages, is cultivated in a manner that commends itself to the admiration of all. One feature of it, however, is unpleasant—their system of manuring. During certain months of the year it is impossible to walk in the country with any pleasure on this account. The crops of every kind shew that this system is not the best; for the fruits and vegetables alike are tasteless and insipid.

Itinerant mountebanks are common in Japan. They exercise their calling from village to village with great spirit. It is astonishing in how many things the Japanese in their every-day life resemble Europeans. They have their street conjurors, their peep-shows, their acrobats, and all the tribe of such Bohemians, just as we have in the West, and they draw the money out of people's pockets by exactly the same kind of patter as we were used to of yore. Is it civilized or uncivilized people who have such *institutions?*

Priests in their peculiar garb, are also everywhere met with. Among the numerous sects of Buddhists, there are as many different forms of worship as among different sects of Christians. The pride of the sleek and pampered priests is often an exact counterpart of what may be seen elsewhere. Their worship is never without the aid of drum or bell, and these are generally struck by the servant or acolyte in attendance. In the domiciliary visits, there is often one who brings the little bronze disc with him, on which he strikes as the priest prays. The kind of self-satisfied pharisaic air of these priests is very noticeable. Without enjoying the real respect of the people, who look upon them as no better than they should be, they undoubtedly exercise a certain amount of influence, which is mainly exercised in maintaining that superstition which is their strongest hold on their flock.

On certain holidays a peculiar kind of theatrical exhibition is given in front of the temples, to entertain the Kami, or gods, the origin of which, I gather from a description of some of the customs and ceremonies of his countrymen, sent to me long ago by a young Japanese friend, was as follows:—

"In the early ages, the great goddess, called TENSHO-DAIJIN, descended from the heavens and established herself in the province or state of Hiuga. Becoming angry (for some unexplained reason) she withdrew herself from the public gaze and retired to a cave called Iwato, whose entrance was guarded by a large stone gate. Mundane affairs being thus left to take care of themselves, the other Kami, who were her servants, assembled for counsel, and agreed upon the necessity of drawing her from her seclusion. This was the formula observed. A singer, who was accompanied by every kind of musical instrument, discoursed sweet melodies, the performers leaping and dancing around the mouth of the cave, and a goddess, attired in raiment of white silk, moved slowly about, waving a paper fixed to the end of a stick, called Heisoku. Hearing this agreeable music, TENSHO-DAIJIN opened the gate a little way, and peeped through to see what was occurring. Taking advantage of the opportunity, a brave Kami, named TOGAKUSHI, exerting his utmost strength, seized the gate, wrenched it from its hinges, and threw it high into the air. Away it went, whizzing for over four hundred miles, finally resting on the centre of a high mountain, called Tsukuba-san, which can be seen from the capital of this country, Tokio or Yedo."

[The narrator of this legend says, "My father has been over this mountain, and I have conversed with him as to its situation and surroundings. I trust it may be some day my fortune to visit it. There are so many pleasant things to see on the way that I advise those travelling thither to do so on foot, as its many beauties tempt the traveller to halt every minute."]

"The stone, or gate, which was thrown by TOGAKUSHI still exists, resting on a pinnacle of the mountain, in such a position as momentarily to threaten the destruction of the beholder. It measures in length about twenty feet, and in breadth about fifteen.

"Having described the origin of the festival, let us proceed to a description of the Kagura—the celebration as now observed. As it was first used as a remonstrance to the Kami (or gods) it is sometimes called the Kami-Isami, and from its foundation it was adopted as a religious observance or festival. The Kagura is usually practiced on an edifice erected in front of a temple, and is celebrated with all kinds of musical instruments—drums, flutes or whistles, bells, and blocks of sonorous wood and bamboo. Dancers, arrayed in beautiful garments, and wearing masks, leap and gambol about to the sound of the music. In the first and middle acts of the exhibition, a woman who is called MITO (or witch) appears, dressed in loose red trowsers, slowly moving her body to and fro, whilst sounding a sort of bell which she carries in her hand. In the last act small cakes made of rice beaten in a mortar are scattered amongst the spectators, who are clamorous in their endeavours to get hold of them, believing that those who eat them will never suffer from that greatest of all the minor ills that flesh is heir to, toothache. The celebration of the Kagura is one of the most interesting of the many religious festivals of our country."

My friend also thus described the native firemen, who were, in the early days, almost constantly under the observation of foreigners.

"The Empire of Japan contains three capitals, Yedo or Tokio, Kioto, and Osaka: of these the first-named is the most extensive and populous, containing over two millions of inhabitants. This flourishing city is situated on a vast plain called Musashino, and when the Government was first established there, two hundred and fifty years ago, by the ancestor of Tokugawa, it was almost uninhabited. Since then it has undergone many improvements, and has rapidly advanced in population and wealth. The city, however, was but poorly built of bamboo and mud and inflammable materials, the roofs of the houses being composed of thatch and rushes. As a matter of course, fires were of frequent occurrence, both day and night, as many as nine in one night being not infrequent.

"In order to combat the fiery demon, a brigade was organised, selected from the lower class of citizens, and divided into twelve companies, each distinguished by a letter of the alphabet. In course of time these companies became very numerous, and, thirty years ago, they counted not less than five thousand men. When not employed in their duties as firemen, they occupied their time in building, in levelling the ground for the erection of houses, but frequently in the by no means honourable pursuit of gambling. When the alarm-bell was sounded they were on the alert and assembled at a known rendezvous. Their dresses consisted of a long quilted coat or mantle, over which was worn a shorter coat of the same kind: their hats were made of a cotton cloth, also quilted. On the alarm of fire being given, they assembled in a body, armed with long poles, to be used as fire-hooks in the demolition of burning buildings. A procession being formed they advanced in the direction of the fire, singing loudly, in the following order. First, an officer bearing an ensign made of paper, then a ladder, twenty-four or thirty feet long. Then came a band of firemen, singing their loudest strains in various voices, each of them carrying the fire-hook. Lastly came men bearing the pump. When the burning place was reached, the man bearing the ensign or banner, which was heavy and tenacious, though constructed of paper, mounted the roof of the building nearest the one a-flame—and in the direction toward which the wind was blowing—and endeavoured to protect the roof from the flying sparks. Here he would remain at his post until the flames caught the building on which he stood, and, the fire spreading rapidly from the inflammable nature of its construction, it frequently happened that he would have no time to make use of the ladders provided, and must either jump from the roof or perish in the flames. They were a brave set of men and never shrank from the flames, many paying the penalty of their devotion to duty with their lives. Their widows, whilst mourning their untimely end, submitted themselves to the decrees of fate, looking upon the event as they would upon an ordinary death. After the fire had been subdued the firemen marched back to their quarters, singing even more loudly than before. As a rule, they were, and are, a courageous body, and at the command of a superior, would undertake any work, however seemingly desperate."

Richardson Affair

CHAPTER XIII.

THE SAD TALE MUST BE TOLD.—SHIMADZU SABURO'S THREAT TO MURDER FOREIGNERS.—DOUBTS AS TO ITS TRUTH.— IF TRUE, PROBABLE REASON.—THE MURDER OF MR. RICHARDSON. —MRS. BORRODAILE'S STATEMENT ; MR. CLARKE'S AND MR. MARSHALL'S EVIDENCE.—UNCHALLENGED UNTIL 1875.—THE SATSUMA VERSION.—EFFECT ON THE RESIDENTS ON THE NEWS REACHING THE SETTLEMENT.—COLONEL NEALE AND THE MOUNTED ESCORT.—H. B. M.'S CONSUL TAKES THE ESCORT WITHOUT ORDERS.—THE BODY OF MR. RICHARDSON FOUND ; AND STATEMENT OF JAPANESE ON THE SPOT, RESPECTING HIS ACTUAL DEATH.—COLONEL NEALE THE ONLY PERSON WHO KEPT WITHIN THE BOUNDS OF PRUDENCE.—THE BODY CONVEYED TO KANAGAWA.—MEETING OF THE RESIDENTS.—RESOLUTIONS PASSED.—DEPUTATION TO ADMIRAL KUPER ON BOARD H.M.S. EURYALUS.—ALSO TO' CAPTAINS OF FRENCH AND DUTCH MEN-OF-WAR.—AND TO COLONEL NEALE.—MEETING AT THE FRENCH MINISTER'S HOUSE.—COLONEL NEALE'S REFUSAL TO ACT AS PROPOSED BY THE RESIDENTS.—APPROVAL OF HIS CONDUCT BY HIS GOVERNMENT, AND SUBSEQUENTLY BY HIS COUNTRYMEN.—ORIGINAL CONDEMNATION OF IT BY ALL FOREIGNERS AND BY THE PRESS.—PROBABLE RESULTS OF IMMEDIATE ACTION.—COLONEL NEALE'S PROMPT COMMUNICATION WITH THE JAPANESE GOVERNMENT.—PERPLEXITY OF YEDO GOVERNMENT.

THE tale has now to be told of the saddest incident that has occurred since the signing of the treaties. Saddest, because, although only one foreigner's life was at first sacrificed, it led to fighting by which numbers both of Japanese and foreigners lost their lives, and to other consequences hardly less lamentable.

I have already spoken of SHIMADZU SABURO, and shown, as I think, that there is no good reason for supposing that, on his arrival in Yedo, he was imbued with such feelings towards foreigners as should lead him to act with hostility towards individuals.

It was stated, after the event I am about to chronicle, that before leaving Yedo on his return to Kioto, he made a direct threat to the Government, that, should opportunity arise, he would assault foreigners. I have never been able to trace this to any reliable source; but at the time it was universally believed, and there are few, if any, of the foreigners then resident in Japan who do not still accept it as an indisputable fact. If it be true, it may have been uttered in the heat of the moment; and have arisen from a desire to embroil the Government with foreigners—forcing hostilities, under the impression that the latter would act in such a manner as to compel immediate steps to drive them out. Of this, however, more hereafter. Here is the original version of the sad story.

On the 14th September 1862, three English gentlemen escorted a lady, the sister-in-law of one of them, in a ride on the Tokaido. Two of the gentlemen, Mr. MARSHALL and Mr. CLARKE, were residents of Yokohama; the lady was Mrs. BORRODAILE, wife of a merchant in Hongkong; the third gentleman a Mr. RICHARDSON who had been in business in Shanghai, but, having retired, was on a visit to Japan before going home. That I may not appear to impart any colouring of my own to the affair, I shall give the statements of the lady and the two first-named gentlemen, as to what took place, simply premising, that no one who knew the parties could think of doubting them; and that the peculiarly single-minded, truthful and conscientious character of Mr. MARSHALL in particular, gave him in early days a leading position among foreign residents, which he maintained unchallenged during the remainder of his career, and until his sudden decease in September 1873.

First then, here is the account given in the *Japan Herald*, with Mrs. BORRODAILE's statement.

Yokohama, 15th September, 1862.—Yesterday afternoon about two o'clock, a party left Yokohama for a country ride, intending to cross to Kanagawa in a boat and proceed from thence on horse-back to Kawasaki, where there is a fine temple.

The party was composed of Mrs. BORRODAILE, the wife of a merchant in Hongkong; Mr. MARSHALL—her brother in law, a merchant of Yokohama; Mr. W. CLARKE —of the house of Messrs. A. HEARD & Co., and Mr. RICHARDSON, who had just retired from business in China and was on a visit to Japan, prior to his return to England.

The Community at about half past three o'clock, in the afternoon, were startled by the return of Mrs. BORRODAILE on horse-back to Mr. GOWEN's house, in a fearful state of agitation and disorder—her hands, face and clothes bespattered with blood, her hat gone, and herself in a fainting state. She informed Mr. GOWEN that she had just ridden for her life over seven miles, and had escaped, she knew not how, from a most dastardly and murderous attack upon herself and her companions; that at about four miles beyond Kanagawa, nearly halfway to Kawasaki, they had met part of a daimio's train consisting of a large body of two-sworded men coming from Yedo, some of whom signed to them to move aside, which they did. They drew up their horses at the side of the road, but in consequence of continued signs to go back, they turned their horses to return towards Kanagawa. Without a word, or the slightest further notice, some of the retainers drew their swords and fiercely attacked them. A cut was aimed at Mrs. Borrodaile's head, which she fortunately avoided by quickly stooping, though her hat was cut away by the blow. The three gentlemen were badly wounded, and being entirely surrounded and the road being for some distance lined by their assailants, and being themselves entirely unarmed, they had no course but to dash through them, and to endeavour thus to effect their escape. Mrs. Borrodaile saw Mr. Richardson fall from his horse, as she supposed dead—and the others were so badly wounded that Mr. Marshall told her to ride for her life and try to save herself, as he did not think they could keep up. She scarcely remembers what happened afterwards, but she recollects riding into the sea, preferring the risk of drowning to falling into the hands of these blood-thirsty miscreants. Her horse, however, regained the road and continued his head-long course towards Yokohama, twice falling under her. By some means she regained her seat and arrived fainting and exhausted at the house mentioned. Fortunately Dr. Jenkins and Mr. Gower's brother entered the house at the moment, the former of whom administered the needful restoratives; and Mr. Gower's brother, at her earnest entreaties, went at once to Capt. Vyse, to endeavour to obtain assistance towards the recovery of the persons of her companions, all three of whom she imagined were lying dead in the road.

Next, Mr. Woodthorpe C. Clarke, at the inquest held on the body of Mr. Richardson the following day, deposed :—

"On Sunday the 14th September a party consisting of Mrs. Borrodaile, Mr. Richardson, Mr. Marshall and myself left Yokohama for Kanagawa in a boat. Our horses were sent round to Kanagawa before us, and meeting them at the landing place at Kanagawa, we mounted and rode on towards Kawasaki. Along the road we passed several norimons surrounded each by a few attendants, each armed with two swords and occasionally a few spears. These norimons and attendants formed a continuous but irregular train broken at intervals. When these people were passing we walked our horses at a steady pace, and cantered during the intervals when no people were passing; this continued for about 3½ to 4 miles of the road from Kanagawa to Kawasaki when we met a regular procession preceded by about a hundred men in single file on either side of the road. We kept well to the near side of the road, going at a walking pace, until we arrived at the main body, which was then occupying the whole road, which at that place had, I think, a rather wide Japanese bridge across it. Mrs. BORRODAILE and Mr. RICHARDSON were about ten yards in advance, Mr. RICHARDSON riding on the off-side of Mrs. BORRODAILE. I observed, that on nearing the main body, they halted, and Mr. MARSHALL and I immediately did the same. As we did so I observed a man of large stature issued from the main body, at the same time raising both his arms, and making some gesture, whereupon both Mrs. BORRODAILE and Mr. RICHARDSON instantly turned their horses round towards Kanagawa, Mr. MARSHALL and myself doing likewise. As I was in the act of turning round, I saw a Japanese, whom I think was the same big man I saw at first issuing from the main body, cut with a sword at Mr. RICHARDSON. Upon this I observed also that a portion of the advanced guard, namely, those referred to before as advancing in single file, closed in upon us, to the number of about thirty. On seeing this I immediately put my horse to a handgallop and went through them. While doing so I received a wound on the left shoulder, and my horse received another on the near hip; I saw several swords drawn and blows aimed at me which I escaped, perhaps by bending forward, and on account of the rapid pace at which my horse moved. As soon as I had cleared the advanced guard, I checked my horse somewhat, then Mr. RICHARDSON came up with me and begged me to pull up, saying at the same time "Oh! CLARKE, they have killed me." I replied that I was wounded and I further begged him to endeavour to keep his seat, and to move on as quickly as possible as the only chance of safety. At this time Mrs. BORRODAILE and Mr. MARSHALL came up, and I then moved on at a hand-gallop with Mrs. BORRODAILE, she keeping a little ahead. I think Mr. MARSHALL stopped a moment or two with Mr. RICHARDSON, and that was the last I saw of Mr. RICHARDSON. Mrs. BORRODAILE and I kept on, and were joined by Mr. MARSHALL at Kanagawa just immediately before we came to the bridge of Kanagawa; we had then slackened our pace; but seeing Mr. MARSHALL coming on all right, and feeling myself becoming somewhat faint, I pushed on with Mrs. BORRODAILE, agreeing among ourselves to go to the American Consulate at Kanagawa. I rode on some distance until arriving at the landing place at Kanagawa, and again telling Mrs. BORRODAILE to go to the American Consulate, I became dizzy and lost my sight from loss of blood, and I remember nothing more until I found the American Consul and some-one else helping me into a chair. I then fainted, and again came to my senses as Mr. MARSHALL was brought in. I was then kindly attended to by the family of the American Consul and later in the evening we were removed to Yokohama. Very shortly before meeting the compact train by which we were attacked, I noticed in a house by the way-side two of the Japanese interpreters belonging to the Custom House at Yokohama, and who were personally known by Mr. MARSHALL and spoken to by him. I think I could recognize one of those interpreters on seeing him again. I can only recognize the uniform and crest of the advanced guard. They were dressed in dark blue and I saw on the sleeves of nearly the whole of the advanced guard, a crest, similar to the sketch which I now give in pencil, consisting of two broad white lines placed parallel."

And lastly, Mr. MARSHALL gave evidence in these words:—

"On the afternoon of Sunday, the 14th instant, Mrs. BORRODAILE, Mr. RICHARDSON, Mr. WOODTHORPE CLARKE and I, rode from Kanagawa along the Tokaido or high road in the direction of Kawasaki. When we got to that part of the road which is called by foreigners here 'The Avenue,' I saw a Japanese interpreter whom I know and two other Japanese. That interpreter I know as one of those belonging to the Custom House at Yokohama. I said to the interpreter, 'What are you doing so far away from Yokohama?' He made no reply. We proceeded about a quarter of a mile farther when on turning a corner I perceived a large procession coming towards us along the road; we did not stop but went on, taking the left hand side of the road; there was apparently no opposition until we had got about twelve men deep in the procession: then a man stepped in front of Mr. RICHARDSON and Mrs. BORRODAILE who were leading, and barred the way. Mr. RICHARDSON looked back and said, 'We are stopped.' Mr. CLARKE said 'Dont go on, we can turn into a side road.' I said 'For God's sake let us have no row.' Our horses were being quietly turned round, when I saw a man in the centre of the procession throwing the upper part of his clothes off his shoulders, leaving himself naked to the waist, and, drawing his sword, which he swung in both hands, he rushed upon Mr. RICHARDSON. I shouted 'Away;' but before our horses were started Mr. RICHARDSON was struck across the side under the left arm. The same man rushed upon me, and struck me in the same place under the left arm. By this time our horses had fairly started. The greater number of the people remained stationary, but about half-a-dozen drew their swords, and, barring our passage struck at us as we passed. Mr. CLARKE rode over one man and I rode over another. We galloped on, no person attempting to obstruct our passage until we reached the Tea-house just before the entrance to the Avenue when I saw Mr. RICHARDSON's horse begin to flag. I shouted to Mrs. BORRODAILE and Mr. CLARKE, who were leading, to go on and that I would look after Mr. RICHARDSON. I drew alongside his horse and said, "RICHARDSON, are you badly hurt?" He made no reply. I looked into his face and saw that he was all but dead if not quite so. His horse stopped and he fell to the ground. I saw then that he was quite dead, his bowels protruding, and that I could do him no good. I put my horse into a gallop and just at the entrance of Kanagawa overtook Mrs. BORRODAILE and Mr. CLARKE. Here also I met my own betto and Mr. ASPINALL's betto. The one I sent back to look after Mr. RICHARDSON's body, and mounting the other on Mr. RICHARDSON's horse sent him on to Yokohama. I felt very faint from loss of blood, and feeling comparatively safe in Kanagawa, rode quietly until I reached the American Consulate, where I received every kindness and attention. There were a great number of people coming along the road, forming, I believe, the advanced part of the procession. I observed on the dresses of most of them one or other of the three crests which I can describe, the crest prevailing most being that of Satsuma—it was a white cross in a circle thus * *; the other two were thus * * and thus * *. We did not go faster than a walking pace for at least a quarter of a mile before we came up to the procession where we were attacked. We neither spoke, nor made gestures, nor did anything else whatever to give offence to the procession: in fact we tried to get out of the way to avoid it. As far as I could see, every man belonging to or forming the procession which attacked us, was armed each with two swords, and some with long lances, and I observed in front two men carrying bows and bundles of arrows."

The jury gave as their verdict, "that the deceased CHARLES LENOX RICHARDSON was feloniously, wilfully and of malice aforethought, killed and murdered by certain Japanese (whose names are to the Jurors unknown), armed with swords, lances, and other arms after the fashion of their country; and bearing the same by authority, being officials in either the civil or military service of Japan, at a place about 4 milés from Kanagawa, on the high road between Kanagawa and Kawasaki, being within the Consular district of Kanagawa."

Observe, Mrs. BORRODAILE says that "a cut was aimed at her head, but she fortunately avoided it by quickly stooping, though her hat was cut away by the blow."

Mr. CLARKE, also, states :—" We kept well to the near side of the road, going at a walking pace, until we arrived at the main body, which was then occupying the whole road." And

Mr. MARSHALL testifies :—"Mr. RICHARDSON looked back and said 'We are stopped.' Mr. CLARKE said :—' Don't go on; we can turn into a side road.' I said :—' For God's sake let us have no row.' And again, '*We neither spoke, nor made gestures, nor did anything else whatever to give offence to the procession;'* in fact, we got out of the way to avoid it."

Such is the plain unvarnished tale, as given by the only foreigners who were witnesses of the unhappy scene; and of course the only persons present who understood the English language.

This account remained unchallenged until the year 1875, when a pamphlet, written by an American gentleman, Mr. E. H. HOUSE, appeared, giving the Satsuma version of the affair.

It is as follows:—

"On the afternoon of the 14th, four persons started from Kanagawa, to ride upon the To-kai-do toward Kawasaki, a town about ten miles distant. They were all English: Mr. C. L. RICHARDSON, a merchant who had just retired from business in China and was visiting Japan for amusement, Messrs. MARSHALL and CLARKE, residents of Yokohama, and Mrs. BORRODAILE of Hongkong. The first named gentleman, it is necessary to say, was understood to have gained a certain notoriety for violence in his dealings with the inhabitants of the country in which he had long resided. It was unfortunate that he took the lead, as he did, with Mrs. BORRODAILE, instead of some other of the party who might have better understood the character of the people they were likely to encounter. Soon after leaving Kanagawa, they found that they were in the midst of a somewhat broken, though still continuous train, composed of men variously armed with spears and swords, who were in attendance upon *norimonos*, or palanquins, evidently occupied by persons of rank. They saw certain Japanese from Yokohama, who were known to some of the party, standing beside their horses, from which they had dismounted, according to a rule which no native would have dreamed of infringing at that time. One of the most inexorable regulations of Japanese etiquette was that no casual passenger should continue to ride, either upon his horse or in any conveyance, during the occupancy of the road by a dignitary of high station. Whether this usage should or should not be held applicable to Europeans is a point hardly worth discussing. Most visitors in strange lands recognize the expediency, if not the propriety, of conforming to the established public customs. A traveller who should refuse to lift his hat at the approach of a European monarch would not escape uncomfortable treatment on the plea that he came from a distance and owed no allegiance to the sovereign in question. It is certain that no Japanese would have been suffered to pass unmolested even the advance of the procession through which Mr. RICHARDSON and his friends were allowed to move for some miles. As long as they gave no other offence than that which might have proceeded from ignorance they were unharmed, not from any disposition on the part of the retainers to treat them tenderly, but because of the orders issued by their chief. Even after the behavior of one of them had become distinctly objectionable, they were suffered to pursue their way. After the catastrophe, Mrs. BORRODAILE admitted that she had repeatedly begged Mr. RICHARDSON to be more careful in his conduct, and that he had given no heed to her remonstrances, but had continued to push his horse in and out of the groups forming the cortège, reckless of menacing glances and gestures. Finally, at or near the village of Namamugi, a more compact and regular body of attendants came in view, preceding, in two long files, the *norimono* in which SHIMADZU SABURO was seated. The officer who led this company—and who has since attained a high position in the Japanese service—turned to the left, in obedience to instructions, and drew his men to the side of the road. He is positive in declaring that if the strangers had done likewise, and moved in single file, they could have passed uninjured, as others had done before them, and as others did after. They themselves, at least the three survivors, invariably declared that they had kept well to the left, but it was not denied that they continued 'to ride two abreast. The Japanese insist that Mr. RICHARDSON did not turn at all, and that while they, though reluctantly and in great irritation, moved to one side, he persisted in holding the center of the road. He had hardly passed the head of the column when the signs of dissatisfaction became so ominous that Mr. CLARKE and Mr. MARSHALL, who were some distance in the rear, felt it necessary to interpose. 'Don't go on,' said the former, 'we can turn into a side road.'

'For God's sake,' said Mr. MARSHALL, 'let us have no row.' 'Let me alone,' answered RICHARDSON; 'I have lived in China fourteen years, and know how to manage these people.'

"A moment later, the blow fell. The commander of the SATSUMA body-guard states that it had become evident that Mr. RICHARDSON would not give way, and that his attitude indicated that he was determined to maintain his position, and compel even the *norimono* to give way to him. This is in a degree confirmed by a letter from the U. S. Minister, who wrote that it was 'supposed that the horse of one of the party forced itself between the *norimono* and the retainers who marched as a guard beside it.' At last the affront, in Japanese eyes, was unendurable. A soldier sprang from the ranks, and made an imperative sign to him to retire. The warning was now taken, but it was too late. As the party were endeavoring to turn their horses, the head of the column closed upon them. The three men were wounded almost at the same moment—Mr. RICHARDSON fatally. Mrs. BORRODAILE was not hurt. They succeeded in breaking through the group of guards, and rode back at full speed toward Yokohama. Mr. RICHARDSON soon fell from his horse and was never again seen alive by his companions. The others escaped, two with severe injuries, the lady with the shock of an agonizing terror.

"The SATSUMA officer whose statements have been above quoted is frank in the declaration that his sole regret was, since the deed was to be done, that he did not perform it himself. He had burned with indignation at what he conceived to be an insult to his master, and it was only in consequence of the restraint imposed upon him that he had held his hand. If he had foreseen that one of his command would violate the order, he himself would have struck the first blow. This is mentioned to show that the story he relates is certainly not colored by any desire to disguise the feelings by which he and his associates were actuated at the time. It is a straightforward tale, and corresponds in all essential points with those of the foreigners concerned, The depositions of Messrs. CLARKE and MARSHALL tend to confirm it, and the clear recollections of persons who conversed with and were in medical attendance upon Mrs. BORRODAILE immediately after the event are entirely in its favor."

I wish to give the two statements, that all may judge for themselves. But I am bound to say that I have conversed with the nearest and dearest of all Mrs. BORRODAILE's friends—her husband—shortly after the event, and he mentioned nothing to me of what is attributed to that lady; nor, until I read them in the pamphlet, did I ever hear of them, although well acquainted with those who are elsewhere mentioned as having reported them, and with those to whom they would be most likely to be spoken.

And now, having presented both statements of the occurrence itself, I will proceed.

On the news reaching the settlement, the excitement was, as may be readily supposed, very great. Several parties of residents mounted their ponies, and rode off as fast as they could to Namamugi. Colonel NEALE ordered the mounted Escort to hold themselves at once in readiness to start for the scene of the catastrophe; but learning that Mr. RICHARDSON was actually dead and that his companions were safe, he resolved not to send the Escort, consisting in Yokohama of only "seven men, to the Tokaido, where they would probably run the gauntlet through hundreds of armed men, fresh from the outrage and murder just perpetrated. Their officer too, Lieut. APPLIN, was absent. As, however, the very spot on the Tokaido could be safely and expeditiously reached by water, being at Namamugi directly opposite to Yokohama, he sent to H. M. S. Centaur, requesting that an armed cutter should be dispatched across the bay to bring over to Yokohama the body of Mr. RICHARDSON, and from Kanagawa the two gentlemen who had been wounded. On his return to the spot where he had left the escort, he found that they were gone, and learnt that H.B.M.'s Consul, Capt. VYSE, had taken them by the high road to Kanagawa. Lieut. APPLIN then appearing, he was told by Colonel NEALE

that the escort had gone without necessity and without
authority. The former answered that he would follow
them and see that all was right."

Lieut. APPLIN overtook Captain VYSE, the escort and a
number of the residents about two miles on the highroad.

" He ordered a halt, and stated that Colonel NEALE was
extremely incensed that the guard should have been
taken out of Yokohama without his special orders. The
British Consul, however, explained that it was his duty
at all hazards to recover and identify his missing
countryman, and that having found the guard in the
saddle ready to start, but without any instructions as to
what course they were to pursue (though Colonel NEALE
was fully aware of the urgent demand for assistance), he
had thought it his duty to order them at once to follow
him. Lieut. APPLIN, upon hearing this explanation, was
satisfied, and gave the word to advance." * * * *
The party now continued along the road till they
arrived at the half-way house between Kanagawa and
Kawasaki, where they were joined by the French
mounted guard, who had received orders from M.
DUCHESNE DE BELLECOURT, the French representative, to
act in concert with Captain VYSE and those who accompanied him."

They found the body of the Mr. RICHARDSON lying a
little off the road-side, dreadfully mangled with sword-cuts
and spear-wounds. Two old mats had been thrown over
it, but nothing had been taken from it. On enquiry it
appeared that he could not have been actually dead when
Mr. MARSHALL left him; for he is stated to have managed
to drag himself in the dreadful condition in which he
was, to the bank at the road-side, and to raise himself to
a sitting posture. He called for water; but no one
dared to approach him.

The story goes, that a young woman, the mistress of a
small road-side tea-house brought him the water he
asked for; and, with a woman's gentle sympathetic
nature, wished she could do more. This belief has
always given that woman an interest in the minds of

foreigners, who thenceforward rarely passed along that portion of the Tokaido, without stopping at "Black-eyed Susan's," the name by which to this day she is familiarly known.

Her own evidence, however, as taken by H. M. Consul, proves this to have been incorrect.

Another statement was circulated at the time, and was universally believed, to the effect that Mr. RICHARDSON had been on the bank about ten minutes, when the norimon of SHIMADZU SABURO came up, and then occurred, according to report, (which, however, I believe to have been erroneous), what most of all arouses the indignation of all who hear of it. The country-people who were examined, it was said, declared that seeing a crowd of people, SABURO asked his attendants what was the cause of it. On being informed, he ordered them to put him to death at once; which they did, cutting his throat and stabbing him repeatedly.

The following letter from Captain VYSE to Colonel NEALE tends to give a different colouring to both the above stories.

Kanagawa, September 30, 1862.

"I have the honour to inform you that, in consequence of a report being in circulation at Yokohama that the late Mr. RICHARDSON was still alive when he fell from his horse, and that he was butchered in cold blood by certain Japanese armed men on the afternoon of Sunday, the 14th of September, I deemed it to be my duty to make inquiry into the truth of this frightful aggravation of crime by which the death of C. L. RICHARDSON was hastened. I did so on Sunday, the 28th September, and it is now my painful task to lay before you the information given by a Japanese woman.

"The woman recollected seeing a foreigner fall from his horse, on the afternoon of the 14th of September; he had a large wound in his stomach; went up to him, and he immediately asked for water, but she took him none, because too much afraid. Afterwards saw him drinking from a bottle (Mr. RICHARDSON is known to have taken a bottle of champagne with him slung upon his arm). She asked him to get off the Tokaido, because, on looking up the road, she saw that a Daimio's cortège was approaching. She saw one of the advance guard of the train draw his sword and attempt to cut the wounded foreigner's throat, but was prevented by his putting up both his hands; one of his hands was then cut away; more men came up, drew their swords, and hacked him, finally, one of them caught him by the beard and cut his throat; they then covered up the body with straw and went on.

"In reply to some questions the woman said she did not recollect any orders being given by any person in a norimon; recognized that the train was composed of Satsuma's men, but does not know the name of the chief personage in the procession. The woman further stated that an interval of about ten minutes or a quarter of an hour elapsed from the time the foreigner fell until the men came up and cut Mr. RICHARDSON's throat.

"I have thought it necessary to put the foregoing information on record, with a view to having it placed before Her Majesty's Government, and I trust you will approve of my having done so."

At the post mortem examination, made by Dr. WILLIS, the Legation doctor, no less than ten wounds were found, each of which, as his evidence declared, was mortal.

A litter was constructed and the party returned with the body to Kanagawa; there they met detachments from Her Majesty's ship Centaur and the French man-of-war; the latter under the command of Captain Count D'HARCOURT, and accompanied by M. DE BELLECOURT and his body-guard. They learned that some two-sworded men had drawn their weapons upon the French guard, and had menaced a party of four other foreigners, who were only saved by one of them keeping his revolver pointed at the assailants, who thereupon retired.

It might have been expected that the most strenuous efforts would immediately have been made by the British Chargé d'Affaires to punish the assassins and their chief, and to prevent the possibility of their escape. Every one was roused to the highest pitch of indignation; and one word from Colonel NEALE would have put every available man in motion to avenge the murder, and to seize upon the chief culprit. But that word he would not speak. He was the only one who seemed to keep cool on the occasion. He looked at what would have been likely to follow such violent action as was proposed —the certain death of many of the community; the inevitable attack on the settlement by Satsuma's men if SHIMADZU were captured; and the impossibility of averting any longer that war with Japan, which, it was the general belief of foreign residents, must come ere long, but which the English Government was so anxious to avoid.

A meeting of the residents was held that evening at ten o'clock, at which nearly all the members of the foreign community were present. The chair was taken by Captain VYSE, who stated that he had that moment returned from an interview with Rear-Admiral KUPER, who had in the course of the day arrived in H.M.S. Euryalus, accompanied by the Ringdove; that the Admiral had already been informed of the fearful events of the day, and that he had announced his intention of having an interview with Colonel NEALE on the subject at noon the next day.

The following resolutions were passed:—

1.—" That the British, French, Dutch, American and Portuguese authorities, be requested to take such immediate steps as seem to them best calculated to prevent the recurrence of such a deplorable event as has occurred this evening, and that ample reparation be demanded of the Japanese Government for the murderous attack on unarmed British subjects peacefully travelling within treaty limits."

(A proposition to request the foreign authorities to

land 1,000 men with sufficient *matériel* for the purpose of arresting the guilty parties at once, and to take possession of Kanagawa, was rejected as being an attempt to dictate to the foreign authorities what steps they ought to take.)

2.—" That in consequence of the explanation given by Her Britannic Majesty's Consul of his interview with the British Admiral, it is earnestly desired by this meeting that the commanders of the foreign forces may be at once conferred with, so that immediate steps may be taken to secure, if possible, the person of the daimio whose retainers have committed the murder, or of some of his high officers, in order to guarantee speedy reparation for the horrible outrage."

3.—"That a deputation be appointed to wait on the naval and other authorities."

(The deputation was then appointed, and Captain VYSE was desired to introduce its members).

4.—" That these proceedings be for the present kept sacredly secret amongst ourselves, lest the Japanese gain any information as to the course of action proposed to be pursued."

The deputation, accompanied by the British Consul, at once proceeded on board H. M. S. Euryalus, and the Admiral rose from his bed to receive them. It was arranged that, as he did not feel justified in taking any steps without consulting H. B. M.'s Chargé d'Affaires, a meeting should be held at 6 o'clock the next morning at the residence of the French Minister.

Having then visited Captain D'HARCOURT and Captain BUYS, of the French and Dutch men-of-war respectively, and obtained their promise to attend the proposed meeting, they called upon Colonel NEALE.

"Colonel NEALE did not, they said, after having heard their statement, appear either to approve of the steps that had been taken, or concur in what was proposed to be done. Understanding, however, that the meeting was agreed to by the French Minister, the English Admiral, and other foreign officials, he said he would be present, though he considered it a most unusual proceeding, and he evinced considerable annoyance at any meeting having been held by the community."

At the meeting he said that in his opinion the proposed measures were impracticable; but that if they could be carried out with any chance of success they would be tantamount to a sudden commencement of hostilities with Japan, and result, probably, by involuntarily engaging H. M.'s Government in a course of action it had not contemplated.

I am recording events the issue of which we all know now. The English Government approved of his conduct, and so ultimately did the foreign communities in Japan; but at first the latter condemned him in no measured terms. The home papers, and the continental press, some in plain words, others in more guarded language, called him coward, and said that an enquiry must take place. The local newspaper in republishing extracts from the home papers said that doubtless he himself would demand an enquiry, to clear himself of the charge of cowardice, and to prove that certain statements of Captain VYSE and Lieut. APPLIN were false. And, noticing certain articles that appeared in the Hongkong and Shanghai papers, again and again reiterated the declaration that he had proved himself quite unfit for his post, and that he ought to be recalled. All this he had to bear for several months, until he received replies from his Government to his dispatches on the subject. His position must have been a very painful one; for he had none to sympathize with him, or to approve of the course he thought proper to take ; and he gave great offence by saying, that his countrymen could not expect to be better off than he. Attacks had been made on his Legation, and dangers threatened him, and they must not suppose that they could be exempt from sharing those dangers.

It was said by those who are believed to be the exponents of public opinion, that had he acted promptly, with such a force as would have been placed at his disposal from the men-of-war in harbour, his own Escort, the French Minister's guard, and the members of the community, he might have taken SHIMADZU SABURO and routed his band had they been ten times the number they really were. But, as already said, Colonel NEALE looked to the after-consequences; and, in the end, even those who were most bitter against him admitted that he was right.

As this was one of the most important events (from the issues it led to) of any that have occurred since the making of the Treaties, it will be well to dwell upon it at some length.

Colonel NEALE was not idle. He required that everything should be done calmly and in order. He already had the case of the murder of the two marines before the Shogun's Government, unsettled. He now had another murder for which to seek atonement. He ordered the Consul to communicate the circumstances to him officially, and then, the very day after the murder, put himself in communication with the Gorojiu.

The Yedo Government was now fairly at its wits' end. It had already frequently expressed the difficulties in its way in dealing with the more powerful of the contumacious daimios; and it was said that at a conference between the Gorojiu and the foreign representatives a wish had been expressed that the Western Powers should aid the Tycoon in curbing the turbulence of some of the disaffected princes. Be that as it may, they frankly confessed their inability to deal with SHIMADZU SABURO in the off-hand way that was demanded of them. They undertook to do all in their power to bring the real culprits, whoever they might be, to justice; and further, to take steps for the better protection of foreigners visiting the Tokaido. This they did by establishing guard-houses at intervals of 600 yards, all the way from Hodogaya to Kawasaki, which latter was the limit that foreigners were allowed to visit in the direction of Yedo.

It will be observed from what has been given above, that the Japanese justified the murder on the ground that it was compulsory for every Japanese not of the rank of samurai, to go on one side of the road and bow down with his forehead towards the ground when any great man passed by. Even officers of inferior rank must draw aside, and, if on horseback, they must dismount. The Englishmen did not dismount, and, though they say they were already close in to the side of the road, the Satsuma men say they were not; and as they seemed to act contemptuously to the proud man whose cortège they met, they were justly cut down.

This is the colouring now given to the sad affair. It certainly was not that expressed at the time by those most in contact with foreigners in Yokohama. They were as much horrified—or expressed themselves as being so—as foreigners themselves were; and certainly the Government never put forward any such excuse at the time. They expressed "extreme regret at the deplorable event that had occurred;" and further added:—

"We have been thoroughly informed of all the circumstances, and sincerely thank H. M. Chargé d'Affaires for the course which has been adopted. We are fully aware of the excitement which prevailed at Yokohama, and the coercive measures against the daimio and his cortège which have been so urgently pressed in many quarters."

It was proposed, and the scheme was partly carried out, to make a new road for the daimios and others to travel, instead of the Tokaido within the treaty limits, and foreigners agreed not to use this new road. The erection of the guard-houses, which were manned by five men each, was accomplished. But this is about the extent of what was done. And here, for the present, we leave this lamentable story.

CHAPTER XIV.

STATE OF PUBLIC FEELING IN YOKOHAMA.—ENROLMENT OF A VOLUNTEER CORPS.—MEETING OF LANDRENTERS.—AUTUMN RACE MEETING.—TERRIBLE VISITATION OF CHOLERA IN YEDO AND YOKOHAMA.—NO FOREIGNERS ATTACKED BY IT.—ATTRACTIONS TO JAPAN.—CHANGE AMONG THE JAPANESE AT THE OPEN PORTS.—INJUDICIOUS FAMILIARITY.—STILL MUCH THAT WAS AGREEABLE PRESERVED.—THE SAMURAI OR MILITARY CLASS—THEIR PRIVILEGES; PROHIBITION FROM ANY BUT SPECIAL OCCUPATIONS; OFFICIALS SELECTED FROM THEM; THEIR IDLENESS; CONCEIT; CODE OF HONOUR.—REMARK OF A DAIMIO TO SIR RUTHERFORD ALCOCK ON THIS POINT.—JAPAN NO PARADISE BEFORE OPENED TO FOREIGNERS.—ON THE SUBJECT OF FOREIGN INTERCOURSE SAMURAI GENERALLY ADOPTED THE VIEWS OF THEIR PRINCE.—SHOGUN OBLIGED TO PLACE A LARGE GUARD FOR THE PROTECTION OF FOREIGNERS.— THE DANGEROUS CLASSES.—INCIDENT IN TOKIO IN 1872, AND CONVERSATION WITH AN OFFICIAL.

Those who live in the foreign settlements of Japan in these tranquil times can form but a poor conception of the state of public feeling under the constant deadly acts and threats of violence, which their forerunners were subjected to. On the 24th September 1862, a public meeting was held at the house of Mr. E. CLARKE (DENT & Co.), for the purpose of forming a Volunteer Corps. The first resolution, proposed by Mr. S. GOWER (JARDINE, MATHESON & Co.), was :—

" That any of the Foreign community willing to join, should form themselves into a Rifle Corps for the defence of our life and property."

It may well be believed that in the angry condition of the public mind, there were very few who did not join. Mr. GOWER was elected its captain and Mr. W. C. CLARKE, one of the gentlemen so recently wounded, lieutenant.

On the same day a meeting of the land-renters was held, at which a very different subject was discussed: viz., whether the Bund, which was being formed, could not be more than fifty feet wide : a fact that shows no expectation of the port being closed, either on the part of foreigners or Japanese. It was resolved that as the Board of Consuls had already agreed for that width with the Japanese it was beyond the power of the meeting to alter it. The powers of the municipality were then brought under notice ; and Mr. SCHOYER most truly said that virtually the Municipal Council was powerless. That they were a municipality in name only, and that they had been able to do nothing whatever. It was evident that they had not sufficient funds for getting on with any really useful municipal work.

The Autumn Race meeting took place on the 1st and 2nd August. Mr. MORRISON had but one pony entered, and he was unsuccessful. It was now that the game little pony *Batavier*, that held his own against all comers for so many meetings, first showed the mettle that was in him. He won easily everything he went for. In the " Yokohama Derby," 2 miles 2 furlongs and 126 yards, carrying 10st 10 lbs., he not only did as he liked with the other ponies but with his jockey also, for the newspaper report of the race says:—" but *Batavier*, who was full of running, won easily, his rider being so exhausted that his horse made *two more* voyages round the course before he could pull him up." There being only five races on each day, they were supplemented by foot races between men of the services of various nationalities.

From Yedo accounts came of cholera; and it was stated that there were buried during a period of six weeks, according to the registers of the Buddhist temples, no less than 224,808 persons, of whom there were men 71,095, women 101,391, and children 52,322. In Yokohama and the small villages around, from the same disease, 900 died. And yet, people were coming over here from China under the impression that they escaped the risk of this fell disease. The Japanese have tried to make out that it was imported into this country by foreigners; but according to their own annals, there was plenty of it here long before the treaties were made. There were, however, attractions in Japan, that proved a strong incentive to all who could to pay it a visit. In point of fact, so far as cholera was concerned, no Europeans were attacked by it; and the beauty of the country, the general healthiness of the climate, and the pleasant cordiality of the people—apart from those who were avowedly hostile—were powerful inducements. Everything was so novel, so totally unlike anything met with elsewhere, that a strong curiosity was aroused; and the visitors, however highly their expectations had been raised, either by what they read or by what they heard, were never disappointed. Even now strangers from afar are delighted with the country and the people. The former is not liable to much change, at least in its general features; but the people, wherever they have came largely into connection with foreigners, and more particularly at the open parts, are very different in their manners and general demeanour. As a race, with all their suavity and politeness, they possess an amount of independence, which was speedily displayed when acted upon and aroused by the brusque and off-hand bearing of foreigners; and this was even intensified by the familiarity with which they were treated—so different to anything they were accustomed to among themselves. I can never forget my surprise at a scene I witnessed on the evening of the first day I landed in Japan. It was in Nagasaki. After dining at the house of some bachelor friends, when the table was cleared, and we all adjourned to the spacious verandah, to enjoy the coolness of the evening, having sat and talked for a while, nothing better offered itself as a means of pastime than for some of the young fellows to put on the gloves, or to have a bout at singlestick. Presently the "boys" who had been waiting on us came to look on, evidently with a desire to share in the amusements—a wish in which they were soon gratified; and it was quite evident from the style they shaped to their work that they were no longer novices. First they stood up to face some of their masters, and then were pitted against each other. It is very certain that all distinctions of rank would very soon disappear under such influences as these.

But everywhere the effect of intercourse with foreigners has been deleterous to the conduct of the natives. If, at the first meeting, there was an apparent amount of obsequiousness in their salutation, that speedily disappeared; and their innocent, open-hearted cordiality, their undisguised but not offensive curiosity, their jovial willingness to amuse or be amused, rendered the men agreeable; while the pretty manners and the merriment of the woman-kind were simply charming. Then there was the welcome almost universally accorded to foreigners who in passing sought to rest themselves, and the cheerful greeting, "*Ohai-o*," that was never wanting from those who were met on the roads, or from the labourers in the fields or the inhabitants of the villages;—for these never showed any hostility to foreigners, nor annoyed them by any kind of rudeness or disrespect.

But it was not always that this geniality between natives and foreigners was evinced. The military class, or samurai, were distinct from all other classes, and between them and the *heimin* or common people there was a great gulf fixed. I have already said that they were a kind of hereditary aristocracy and had special privileges. Even the lowest and poorest ranked above the richest commoner; and often did they make their power felt in the most disagreeable way.

They had the dearly-prized right to carry two swords, and to wear garments of a peculiar design. No commoner dare appear in the streets either in the *hakama* (trowsers, very loose in the leg, made of silk or cotton) or carrying two swords; although there were some wealthy men, who obtained, either by purchase or by some meritorious action, permission to carry one sword.

The samurai were the military retainers of the daimios or of the Shogun. They received their pay in kind, not in money, from their feudal master, and were forbidden to have anything to do with trade, or indeed with any other occupations but such as would fit them for official life in the service of their chief. Military tactics and exercises they were trained to from a very early age; but Chinese and Japanese literature was their principal study. Every daimio had his ministers of state and government officials, each one of whom was selected from the samurai; and it often happened that the offices descended from father to son, nothing but very special merit raising a man to the higher grades. The consequence was that most of the two-sworded men led a life of comparative idleness. They had no particular object for exertion. They read only such books as bore on military science, or on the ancient history of their own country. They knew, with a few honorable exceptions, nothing whatever of the outer world; and were puffed up with the conceit that Japan was—if not the world, at all events the greatest country in it. They had a most rigid code of honour, the central feature of which was loyalty to their chief. When his will was known, it was not for them to reason but implicitly to obey. I well remember a review of British troops which took place in 1864, before Sir RUTHERFORD ALCOCK and SAKAI HIGO-NO-KAMI, a member of the Gorojiu, who visited Yokohama under an escort of his own retainers. The latter were drawn up at the side of the parade ground—a portion of the then lately-reclaimed swamp—and watched with great interest the manœuvres of the XXth Regiment, the Royal Marines, and the two batteries of Artillery then stationed here. At the close of the review, Colonel BROWNE of the XXth Regiment, who was in command, rode forward, and asked Sir RUTHERFORD if he could prevail upon the daimio at his side to allow his men to go through their drill and tactics, which he obligingly did. But he turned to Sir RUTHERFORD, and said with an inimitable air of confidence and pride—"My retinue is small, and their tactics are not worthy of notice after what we have seen, but there is not one man among them who if I say 'Die!' will not unhesitatingly sacrifice his life at my command."

This was not a mere boast; for, unfortunately, since foreigners came to Japan, too many instances have occurred of samurai, both high and low, having to commit suicide, on the simple command of their chief or superior.

It is sometimes thought that Japan was a paradise before foreigners came to it. In reality it was not more so than other countries. In spite of severe penalties for almost all crimes, and a system of surveillance in excess of anything known elsewhere, crimes were rife, and the execution grounds were in more frequent use than was known in other lands save in times of revolution and anarchy. Besides this their moral code (if I may use the term) was of a very low standard and frequently led to most lamentable consequences. The very existence of the samurai was a frequent curse to the respectable citizens and commoners; and if the exclusion from foreign intercourse was productive of ignorance, that ignorance was—anything but innocence, and certainly not—bliss.

The advent of foreigners having raised a whirlwind about the devoted government of the Shogun, the retainers of all those daimios who were opposed to the treaties, as a matter of course took up the same views, and were most bitterly hostile to foreigners. It has already been seen how fatally so. The Shogun was obliged for our protection to have a large number of his own soldiers or those of daimios who were still obedient to him, both in and around the settlement; but it was well known that there were many ronins who were ever lying in wait, seeking opportunities to molest us. They often came into the settlement, and, as in the case of the murdered Russians and the two Dutch captains, whet their swords, even within our own precincts. The greencoated men, who were our guardians, never attempted to disperse them. Indeed until they had committed any depredations it is hard to see how they could be interfered with; and in point of fact we looked upon them all with suspicion, and spoke of all alike as the dangerous classes.

In 1872, long after this state of things had come to an end, I stood in the main street of Tokio, (the city we have hitherto called Yedo), among a crowd of Japanese who had assembled to see His Majesty the Mikado pass in his carriage, on the occasion of his paying a state visit to the first "Exhibition" held in the Confucian Temple, in the old capital of the Tycoon. I entered into conversation with a man who seemed to have a great deal to do with keeping the street clear; and I think the circumstance worth relating. He was in a very seedy kind of European dress, with certainly no pretensions to be called a uniform.

There were many police, with whom for some time he was busy, going from one to another and evidently either giving directions or suggestions. At all events they received all he said to them with great respect, and seemed to hear all he had to say as if he had a right to say it. At length he came and stood by me, and after asking my nationality and one or two questions with which Japanese often commence conversation with a foreigner, I remarked that it was a pleasant thing to see the Mikado driving about the streets among his people, as the sovereigns of other countries do. He, out of politeness, agreed with all I said; and having done so, began to give me his opinion. He thought that all this was as it should be; that the people were attaining an amount of freedom that could not have been thought of formerly; although everybody in the service of the late Shogun knew that he was devising schemes for introducing all the changes that have since taken place; not excepting the placing the Mikado in his just position as the *de facto* emperor. "But," he said, "all that might and would have been brought about without the violent upsetting of the prospects in life of hundreds of thousands of men. The plan of Yoshi-nobu he believed to be to make the Mikado in most respects what he is now. He would either have established a parliament of daimios, or have allowed them to be a kind of upper house, with a parliament consisting of men of ability appointed from each province. There would have been no civil war; the reduction of nobles into mere commoners would have been unnecessary; everything would have been settled by the parliament;" (he spoke in Japanese, but always made use of the word parliament); "and Yedo would not have been destroyed." I enquired to what he alluded in this last remark. He said, "Perhaps you did not know the city when we called it Yedo, before its name was changed to Tokio." I answered that I had visited it during that time.

"Then," said he, "you have only to look around and find a meaning for my remark."

He took me a few paces down the street and pointed to a large temple, very deserted and delapidated-looking, that stood at the end of a small street at right angles with the street in which we were, and asked:—

"Do you remember this temple as it used to be?"

"Yes, very well indeed."

"Had it the appearance then that it has now?"

"No."

"Indeed, no!" he said, bitterly. "It was always in good repair. The people flocked to it all day long; the priests were numerous and had the means and the will to do their duty to the temple and to the people; but now you may stand here for half an hour and not see a score of worshippers, and very likely not a single priest. Ah," he added as one came from the back of the temple, "there is one, but if you only read his thoughts by his looks, you can trace the altered condition of his circumstances."

He proceeded to tell me how the present Government had been persecuting not only the Christian religion but the Buddhist, which for centuries had existed with Sintooism, side by side, in the most friendly manner, often occupying the same temples. He said indignantly:—

"Why should Sintooism, which, although the religion of the Emperor, is the religion of only a small minority of the people, attempt to put down Buddhism, which is the faith of a very large majority? It may be a punishment to us, because too many of us have ceased to have any religion at all. But be that as it may, this Government has put its foot upon the neck of Buddhism, and if you go from one temple to another throughout the length and breadth of Yedo, (he called it Yedo several times, although the name had been changed), you will hardly find one Buddhist temple that retains the glory of other days. TOKUGAWA protected Sintoo temples, why cannot the Mikado respect ours?"

We returned to the spot where we had commenced our conversation, and for some time he continued to harp on this subject of the priests; at length the current of our discourse was changed by an officer passing along the street, who made a very low obeisance to him, stopping before him to show this mark of respect. He was remarkably well dressed, and I asked what was his rank. He replied, "Oh! he is only an officer of the police—like myself holding a very different position to that he formerly held."

"May I, without impertinence enquire, what rank you formerly held?"

"No impertinence, at all. I am an old TOKUGAWA hatamoto, and on one occasion was sent by the Tycoon to Kioto, the bearer of a missive from the Yedo, to the Kioto, Court. Then, as I passed along the road, the people were obliged to bow down even more submissively than you will see them do to-day when the Mikado comes."

"May I ask whether you hold any office now?"

"A very small one. My salary is under twenty rios a month, and I'm glad to get it."

As he did not tell me what his particular office was, I supposed he preferred to keep it to himself, and did not press the question.

The imperial arrival did not take place for fully an hour after our conversation commenced; but from the fact of my having fallen in with such a companion, the delay was not so wearisome as such waitings generally are.

My friend now began to put many questions to me respecting myself; my residence and business in Yokohama; my preference for Yokohama or Yedo; my opinions of the Japanese, and whether I liked the old or new state of things best. To this last I replied :—

"Long before the revolution I saw that it was inevitable; and that during the whole of it I had been favourable to the TOKUGAWA cause, because I believed that the Government of YOSHI-HISA was honestly the friend of foreigners, and most patriotically desirous of introducing reforms such as he had described in the early part of our conversation. But looking, not at what might have been, but at what actually was, I was satisfied that Japan was now in a far nobler position than she ever was before—whoever had been the author of the change. My individual position at the moment proved it. I was standing in a crowd of Japanese, in the heart of Yedo, quite unarmed, and without a thought of danger; speaking to a gentleman as friend to friend, who probably five or ten years ago would not have condescended to notice me, or if he did so at all, only to show his contempt for the "foreign barbarian."

He laughed and replied:—"Not so bad as that. You know we didn't understand foreigners then so well we as do now. When we met them we knew that they had an uneasy feeling lest we should draw our swords; but we in like manner used to look out of the side of our eye as we passed, lest the foreigner should draw his revolver and shoot us."

"But we never did anything of the kind; and your people have repeatedly cut us down."

"Yes! But most of us—I may say, all the Yedo men —regretted it. We do not admire murderers, be they whomsoever they may. But I assure you that I have seen foreigners take out their revolvers, perhaps only to shew that they had them, in a very menacing manner, and in a way that made me feel very uncomfortable at the time. Besides it has often happened that when we had to request of foreigners that they would keep out of danger that we knew of—such for instance, as keeping off of the Tokaido when particular functionaries passed along—they would answer proudly that their treaty rights were being invaded and they would not consent to abstain. They may not have been to blame, but we thought they were; and they little knew the anxiety we felt in their behalf lest any harm should come to them. There were some princes whose retainers nothing could restrain: and the refusal of foreigners to dismount from their horses, or to leave the road during the passage of a high officer or daimio, gave great offence. I remember that at the funeral obsequies of the Shogun who preceded YOSHI-HISA, one young man, an interpreter of a foreign Legation, insisted on making his way into Shiba, which was then closed not only to foreigners but to Japanese. He was remonstrated with, but he doggedly went on, and under any other circumstances than such a very solemn occasion, he would certainly have been cut down. We should have been blamed, but it would have been entirely through his own fault."

I asked if he knew the name of the young man. He told me, and the legation to which he belonged—but for obvious reasons I do not publish either the one or the other. My companion added: "He is in good favour with the existing Government, and is at present in Europe. Probably he would not act so unwisely now, as he has more experience; but I was engaged in the procession that day, and trembled for him."

Our conversation continued some time longer, only occasionally interrupted by my companion rushing forward to say something to the police, but he always came straight back, and seemed sorry at length that the word was passed for the people to *shita-ni-iro* (bow down) and the guard who preceded the Imperial carriage hove in sight. The cortège having passed, we bade each other farewell, after he had received my address, and given his promise to look me up.

CHAPTER XV.

OHARA'S MISSION.—VARIOUS REASONS ASSIGNED FOR SHIMA-
DZU SABURO'S ACCOMPANYING IT.—ABOLITION OF ENFORCED
RESIDENCE OF THE DAIMIOS IN YEDO.—EXODUS OF DAIMIOS,
THEIR FAMILIES AND RETAINERS, FROM THE CITY.—THE
CONSEQUENT EFFECT ON THE CAPITAL.—DOINGS OF THE
RONINS.—THE EX-PRINCE OF TOSA ARRIVES IN KIOTO.—SAT-
CHO-TO.—TWO LATER MISSIONS FROM THE MIKADO TO THE
TYCOON.—TYCOON RESOLVES TO COMPLY WITH THE ORDER TO
VISIT KIOTO.—AGITATION AMONG FOREIGN RESIDENTS KEPT UP
BY FLYING RUMOURS.—CONSULAR NOTIFICATION.—INDIGNATION
OF FOREIGNERS.—GREAT CHANGES THAT HAVE TAKEN PLACE
ON THE TOKAIDO.—NOW DESERTED IN CONSEQUENCE OF THE
CONSTRUCTION OF A RAILWAY BETWEEN YOKOHAMA AND YEDO.
—PICTURE OF IT AS IT WAS IN 1863.—DESCRIPTION OF IT AS
SEEN BY KŒMPFFER TWO CENTURIES AGO.—UYENO-NO-MIYA.

REVERTING to political matters, I will go back a little, and speak of the mission of OHARA from the Mikado to Yedo. I have already stated that he was accompanied by SHIMADZU SABURO and a large array of Satsuma men. I am not aware that it has ever been ascertained with any degree of certainty why it was that the old custom was departed from, and the Satsuma clan were substituted for the soldiers of the Shogun in forming this escort. Nor, to my knowledge, has it even been correctly ascertained why SHIMADZU SABURO visited Yedo in person at this particular time. Various reasons were given at the time. Some said his object was to obtain from the Shogun the removal of his son from the daimioship of the clan, and his own appointment to the office. Mr. ADAMS says it was stated that one of his principal aims was "to obtain the concurrence of the Shogun to his being invested with a certain rank at the Mikado's court (that of *jiu-go-i-no-gé*), and to his being created OSUMI-NO-KAMI." Mr. HOUSE says he was the bearer of communications directly from the Mikado. It appears that whatever his desires were, they were thwarted by the Yedo Government; and that the Shogun refused him an audience and referred him to the Gorojiu. I am inclined to the opinion that I have heard expressed among Japanese, that he came to Yedo by the imperial command at his own wish in charge of the OHARA mission; partly that he might execute some business on behalf of the clan; and partly that he might lend his powerful voice in the great question affecting the enforced residence of the daimios in Yedo. It is useless speculating on this; as it will probably never be known, unless an account should be published at some future day by his authority, giving more fully the Satsuma version of this portion of Japanese history.

The *Fukko-yumé-monogatari*, a translation of which appeared in the *Far East*, relates:—On the 15th day of the 8th month a notification was issued by the government of the Shogun to the effect that the "Sankin" (the obligatory residence of daimios and hatamotos), was abolished—i.e. that they were no longer obliged to live in Yedo with their wives and families, but might reside in their own dominions, if they liked. Several other laws also, made by IYEYAS' in order to retain full power over the daimios were abolished. No sooner was this promulgated than all the daimios with their families and retainers left the capital; and by this movement, the prosperity of Yedo which had lasted over 250 years, was lost. "With Yedo also fell the influence and power of TOKUGAWA. Many citizens shut up their shops and returned to their native provinces. The ronins of Kioto seized many TOKUGAWA officials. They were not now called ronins but *seigishi*—true or lawful samurai. In Kioto many TOKUGAWA officers were slain, and their heads exposed at Sanjo-kawara and Shijo-kawara. Indeed many of them were so discouraged as to commit suicide: whilst others fled, taking their wives and children. Those who had courage enough to stay had not courage enough to face a ronin. In the streets if they saw one, they would cross over or turn a corner in order to avoid him. To their great surprise they saw several of the large daimios arrive in Kioto to serve the Mikado, but refusing to obey the Shogun."

Amongst others YAMANO-UCHI-KE, MATSUDAIRA TOSA-NO-KAMI—a daimio of 242,000 kokus, and one of the most resolute and popular men in the Empire—came to Kioto. He was immediately ordered by the Mikado to ally himself with the chiefs of Satsuma and Choshiu in the imperial service. These three clans, acting together, attained great influence. They were spoken of as Sat-cho-to. a word coined by joining together the first syllables of their names, and it was these three clans who took the most prominent part in effecting the changes which culminated in 1868.

One of the orders contained in the Mikado's letter, it will be remembered, was, that the Shogun should repair to Kioto. This was a proceeding for which there was no precedent during more than two centuries, and there was some hesitation in obeying the mandate. In the last month of the year 1862, therefore, two other missions were dispatched to Yedo, one of which was composed of SANJO CHIUNAGON SANEYOSHI, (the present *Daijo Daijin* or prime minister), and ANE-NO-KOJI SHOSHO, who a few months later was basely assassinated.

The result of these various missions was, a resolution on the part of the Shogun, to visit Kioto in the spring.

The agitation in the minds of foreign residents in Yokohama was constantly kept up by the flying rumours, designedly and industriously circulated among them, of ronins in the neighbourhood; and further by the frequent requests of the Governor of Kanagawa that on certain days foreigners should avoid the Tokaido in consequence of the passing of some great personage with his train. Thus, on the 12th October 1862, a month after the murder of Mr. RICHARDSON, the following was issued from the British Consulate :—

NOTIFICATION.

Whereas, by a notification of the 15th September, British subjects have been generally cautioned respecting the insecurity attending riding or walking on the Tokaido until the Japanese Government have completed the measures of precaution upon which they are at present engaged, the undersigned, H. B. M.'s Consul, has received instructions from H. M.'s Chargé d'affaires to issue a further and special notification to the effect (that the Japanese Government have earnestly requested him to caution British subjects that a high personage, the son of a former Mikado, will pass along the road from Miako to Yedo, accompanied by a numerous retinue, on the 15th, 16th, and 17th instant, when he will be at the places respectively mentioned below.

The undersigned has also been instructed to inform those under his jurisdiction that although the former notification remains in force until complete measures of security are adopted, it is nevertheless advisable that this special communication should be made known to

British subjects, the Japanese Government having expressed their great fear lest any recurrence of the recent lamentable event should take place.

    (Signed) F. HOWARD VYSE,
            H. B. M.'s Consul.

Stops at Yenoshima } On the 15th instant.
Sleeps at ,,

Stops at Kanagawa } On the 16th instant.
Sleeps at ,,

Stops at Kawasaki } On the 17th instant.
Sleeps at ,,

The residents received this intimation with intense indignation. The foreign ministers took independent action upon it. Mr. PRUYN, the U. S. Minister and Mr. DE WITT, the Netherlands Minister notified their fellow-countrymen in the words of the Japanese circular, without any comment. We see above how the British Chargé d'affaires published it; and the Portuguese Consul issued a notification in somewhat similar terms. But MONS. DE BELLECOURT, Minister for France, after long conferences with the ministers for foreign affairs, in which he argued the question fully and pressed strongly upon them the advantage of making a totally new road by which daimios could reach Yedo without passing Kanagawa, issued a short notification to his countrymen of his having been informed of the passage of some dignitary on the days specified. At the same time he circulated for his countrymen's information, the letter which he had received from the authorities, and his own answer thereto, in which he pointed out to the Japanese very strongly, how they were asking for concessions to which they had no right by Treaty, and that this could not go on without some similar concessions on their parts.

His countrymen wrote a reply in which they stated that they considered that this was another of the many grievances of which they had to complain, and that they considered it was an infraction of Treaty stipulations, for which they had some right to indemnification; and, in consideration of giving up their rights they demanded, "1st, That all unfulfilled and long outstanding contracts with the natives should be fulfilled within a reasonable time, say two months.—2ndly, That the ground-rent of the French concession should be reduced one third for the year 1862. 3rdly, That the Authorities, shall, out of the ground-rent, according to previous understanding, carry out the proper sanitary and other matters for the settlement. 4thly, That two lots of ground,—the one on the newly filled-in swamp, and the other on the high ground in the vicinity, shall be appropriated to French subjects, the rental not to exceed 36 itziboos for 100 tsubos; and, finally, that if any similar concessions are asked by the Japanese, they will only be acceded to on similar further conditions. All these demands are only an attempt for indemnification to regain lost ground—ground every inch of which is guarded by Treaty stipulations."

The British portion of the community also delivered to their minister a protest, but principally in order that Colonel NEALE should have such moral support as it conferred, in resisting these frequent demands.

There is now a railway between Yokohama and Tokio, and the old road, the far-famed Tokaido, is deserted. But what a scene it used to present! How crowded with pedestrians; with norimons (the palanquins of the upper crust), and attendants; with cangoes (the modest bamboo conveyance of the humble classes); with pack-horses, conveying merchandise of all kinds to and from the capital or to the busy towns and villages along the route; with the trains of daimios or of lesser gentry entitled to travel with a retinue; and with the commonalty, men, women and children, on foot, all with their dresses turned up for facility of movement, and for the most part taking the journey pretty easily; frequently stopping at the numberless tea-houses or resting sheds by the way, and refreshing themselves with the simple little cup of weak green tea, and a cheery chat with whomsoever might stop like themselves to rest. It used to seem that distance was no consideration with them. They could go on all day, and day after day, if only they were allowed (which they generally were) to take their own time and pace. The value of time never entered into their thoughts; and even in business operations, one of the greatest annoyances of European merchants was the difficulty, I may say the impossibility, of keeping them up to time in fulfilling their engagements.

The numerous trains of armed men passing in both directions was the most striking feature of the scene. Never could one go out of one's house in any direction, but these two-sworded men were met with; but on the Tokaido, and in the streets of Yedo, they appeared to be more numerous than the common people; and it must be understood that at this time of which I am speaking, the crowds on portions of the road and in all the principal thoroughfares of the capital, were as great as in the most crowded thoroughfares of London. It took one forcibly back to the feudal times in Europe, when no noble or landed proprietor thought of going abroad unattended by his armed dependants. Added to this, there was a certain air of antiquity that imparted its charm to the scene. The old Dutch writers described the road long ago, and it was even in their day, precisely as it was in ours. A good, well macadamised, causeway, (except that the hard *stratum* was of pebbles, not of broken stones), passing through numerous populous villages, only divided from each other by short intervals, where fine old trees on both sides of the road were the sole division between the road and the paddy fields. As the decree that put an end to the enforced residence of the daimios in Yedo put an end to all this, and subsequent events have so totally swept away every semblance of it, I will quote Kœmpffer, that it may be seen how unchangeable had been the state of the country during the two centuries; and that I may put on record what we, who resided here before the change, witnessed, but which, or the like of which, we certainly shall never see again. The observant doctor says :—

"It is scarcely credible what numbers of people daily travel on the roads in this country, and I can assure the reader, from my own experience, having passed it four times, the Tokaido, which is one of the chief and indeed the most frequented of the seven great roads in Japan, is upon some days more crowded than the public streets in any of the most populous towns in Europe. This is owing partly to the country being extremely populous, partly to the journeys which the natives frequently undertake, oftener perhaps than any other nation, either willingly, and out of their own free choice, or because they are necessitated to it. For the reader's satisfaction I will here insert a short preliminary account of the most remarkable persons, companies and trains travellers daily meet upon the road.

"The princes and lords of the empire, with their numerous retinues, as also the governors of the imperial cities and crown lands deserve to be mentioned in the first place. It is their duty to go to court once a year, and to pay their homage and respect to the secular monarch, at certain times determined by the supreme power. Hence they must frequent these roads twice every year, going up to court and returning from thence. They are attended in their journey by their whole court, and commonly make it with that pomp and magnificence which is thought becoming their own quality and riches, as well as the majesty of the powerful monarch they are going to see. The train of some of the most eminent of the princes of the Empire fills up the road for some days. Accordingly, though we travelled pretty fast ourselves, yet we often met the baggage and fore-troops, consisting of the servants and inferior officers, for two days together, dispersed in several troops, and the prince himself followed but the third day attended with his numerous court, all marching in admirable order. The retinue of one of the chief daimios, as they are called, is computed to amount to about 20,000 men more or less; that of a sjomio, to about 10,000; that of a governor of the imperial cities and crown lands, to one or several hundreds, according to his revenues.

"If two or more of these princes and lords, with their numerous retinues, should chance to travel the same road at the same time, they would prove a great hindrance to one another; particularly if they should happen to come at once to the same *shiku* or village, forasmuch as often whole great villages are scarce large enough to lodge the retinue of a single daimio. To prevent these inconveniences, it is usual for great lords and princes to bespeak the several *shikus* they are to pass through, with all the inns, some time before; as, for instance, some of the first quality a month, others a week or two, before their arrival. Moreover the time of their future arrival is notified in all the cities, villages and hamlets they are to pass through, by putting up small boards on high poles or bamboos, at the entry and end of every village, signifying in a few characters what day of the month such a lord is to pass through that village, to dine or to lie there.

"To satisfy the reader's curiosity, it will not be amiss to describe one of these princely trains, cangoes and palanquins, which are sent a day or two before. But the account which I propose to give must not be understood as the retinue of the most powerful princes and petty kings, such as the lords of SATSUMA, KAGA, OWARI, KISHIU and MITO, but only those of some other daimios, several of whom we met in our journey to court; the rather as they differ but little, excepting only the coats of arms, and particular pikes, some arbitrary order in the march, and the number of led horses, fassanbacks, norimono, cangoes, and attendants.

"1.—Numerous troops of fore-runners, harbingers, clerks, cooks, and other inferior officers, begin the march, they being to provide lodgings, victuals and other necessary things for the entertainment of the prince their master and his court. They are followed by

"2.—The prince's heavy baggage, packed up either in

small trunks, and carried upon horses each with a banner, bearing the coat of arms and the name of the possessor; or else in large chests with red-laquered leather, again with the possessor's coat of arms, and carried upon men's shoulders, with multitudes of inspectors to look after them.

"3.—Great numbers of smaller retinues, belonging to the chief officers and noblemen attending the prince, with pikes, scimeters, bows and arrows, umbrellas, palanquins, led horses and other marks of their grandeur, suitable to their birth, quality and office. Some of these are carried in norimonos, other in cangoes, others go on horseback.

"4.—The prince's own numerous train, marching in an admirable and curious order, and divided into several troops, each headed by a proper commanding officer :—as, 1. Five, more or less, fine led horses, led each by two grooms, one on each side, two footmen walking behind. 2. Five or six, and sometimes more, porters, richly clad, walking one by one, and carrying fassanbacks, or lackered chests, and japanned neat trunks and baskets upon their shoulders, wherein are kept the gowns, clothes, wearing-apparel, and other necessaries for the daily use of the prince; each porter is attended by two footmen, who took up his charge by turns. 3. Ten or more followers, walking again one by one, and carrying rich scimeters, pikes of state, fire-arms, and other weapons in lackered wooden cases, as also quivers with bows and arrows. Sometimes for magnificence-sake, there are more fassanback bearers, and other led-horses follow this troop. 4. Two, three, or more men, who carry the pikes of state, as the badges of the prince's power and authority, adorned at the upper end with bunches of cock's feathers, or certain rough hides, or other particular ornaments, peculiar to such or such a prince. They walk one by one, and are attended each by two footmen. 5. A gentleman carrying the prince's hat, which he wears to shelter himself from the heat of the sun, and which is covered with black velvet. He is attended likewise by two footmen. 6. A gentleman carrying the prince's sombréro or umbrella, which is covered in like manner with black velvet, attended by two footmen. 7. Some more fassanbacks and varnished trunks, covered with varnished leather, with the prince's coat of arms upon them, each with two men to take care of it. 8. Sixteen, more or less, of the prince's pages, and gentlemen of his bed-chamber, richly clad, walking two and two before his norimon. They are taken out from among the first quality of his court. 9. The prince himself sitting in a stately norimon or palanquin, carried by six or eight men, clad in rich liveries, with several others walking at the norimon's sides, to take it up by turns. Two or three gentlemen of the prince's bed-chamber walk at the norimon's side, to give him what he wants and asks for, and to assist and support him in going in or out of the norimon, 10. Two or three horses of state, the saddles covered with black. One of these horses carries a large elbow-chair, which is sometimes covered with black velvet, and placed on a *norikago* of the same stuff. These horses are attended each by several grooms and footmen in liveries, and some are led by the prince's own pages. 11. Two pike-bearers. 12. Ten or more people carrying each two baskets of a monstrous large size, fixed to the ends of a pole, which they lay on their shoulders in such a manner, that a basket hangs down before, another behind them. These baskets are more for state than for any use. Sometimes some fassanback bearers walk among them, to increase the troop. In this order marches the prince's own train, which is followed by

"5.—Six or twelve led horses, with their leaders, grooms, and footmen, all in liveries.

"6.—A multitude of the prince's domestics, and other officers of his court, with their own very numerous trains and attendants, pike-bearers, fassanback-bearers, and footmen in liveries. Some of these are carried in cangos, and the whole troop is headed by the prince's high-steward, carried in a norimon.

"If one of the prince's sons accompanies his father in this journey to court, he follows with his own train immediately after his father's norimon.

"It is a sight exceedingly curious and worthy of admiration, to see all the persons who compose the numerous train of a great prince, the pikebearers only, the norimon-men and liverymen excepted, clad in black silk, marching in an elegant order with a decent becoming gravity, and keeping so profound a silence, that not the least noise is to be heard, save what must necessarily arise from the motion and rustling of their habits, and the trampling of the horses and men. On the other hand it appears ridiculous to a European, to see all the pike-bearers and norimon-men, with their habits tucked up above the waist, exposing their naked backs to the spectator's view. What appears still more odd and whimsical, is to see the pages, pike-bearers, umbrellas and hat-bearers, fassanback or chest-bearers, and all the footmen in liveries, affect a strange mimic march or dance, when they pass through some remarkable town or borough, or by the train of another prince or lord. Every step they make they draw up one foot quite to their back, in the meantime stretching out the arm on the opposite side as far as they can, and putting themselves in such a posture, as if they had a mind to swim through the air. Meanwhile the pikes, hats, umbrellas, fassanbacks, boxes, baskets, and whatever else they carry, are danced and tossed about in a very singular manner, answering the motion of their bodies. The norimon-men have their sleeves tied with a string as near the shoulders as possible, and leave their arms naked. They carry the pole of the norimon either upon their shoulders, or else upon the palm of the hand, holding it up above their heads. Whilst they hold it up with one arm, they stretch out the other, putting the hand into a horizontal posture, whereby, and by their short deliberate steps and stiff knees, they affect a ridiculous fear and circumspection. If the prince steps out of his norimon into one of the green huts which are purposely built for him, at convenient distances on the road, or if he goes into a private house, either to drink a dish of tea, or for any other purpose, he always leaves a cobang with the landlord as a reward for his trouble. At dinner and supper the expense is much greater."

Such was a scene on the Tokaido two hundred years ago; and although we never met with such extensive trains as some of those mentioned, those we did see had the same general features as described above.

Come we to Yedo—now called Tokio. How changed from the city to which such trains were wont to come!

VOL. I   U

There it lies stretching away along the semicircular bay, and retaining all the outlines of earlier days. There is the castle formerly the dwelling place of the Shoguns, now deserted, within its walled park and surrounded by its moat, which again is enclosed by daimios' yashikis and a second moat, the whole bounded by more yashikis and by that vast portion of the city within a third horseshoe shaped moat or canal, which, with the chord formed by the sea forms an island whose circumference is little, if any, less than nine miles. But the old glory is gone. The yashikis of the daimios are either tenantless and fast going to ruin, or they have been appropriated by the government for government offices, barracks, schools, &c. The streets are now crowded with simple citizens hurrying hither and thither in jin-riki-shas; the trains of the nobles are no more seen; and once more the population of the city is less than a million.

This is, probably, a long digression; but it will be pardoned both by those who have never become acquainted with the facts described; and certainly by readers who may have been eye-witnesses of them, and whose memories will vividly recall them. The etiquette of the road was well and rigidly defined. When the trains of two princes met, it was incumbent on the lesser of them—(measured by his income as recognised by the Government, and published in the official list), to dismount from his norimon, if he happened to be riding in one, and draw with his followers to the side of the road whilst the other passed. Whenever it was possible, therefore, such meetings were avoided; but this could not always be. With such rigid and punctilious rules for themselves, it really is not wonderful that the independent bearing of foreigners was peculiarly annoying to them. I may add that a daimio rarely rode on horseback on the public highways, because, as in the case of the norimon, the inferior must dismount on meeting a superior. It was usual to have his horse led in his train; but it was only as a part of his state equipage. For himself, he almost always either rode in his norimon or walked, accompanied by his chief retainers. Bearing this fact in mind, it may seem that we were unreasonable in taking offence at the care the Shogun's Government observed over us; but we did not understand matters then so fully as we do now; and besides, we may have been more suspicious, because it was absolutely certain that it would have relieved the minds of the Shogun and his officers of state of a heavy burden of anxiety could they have made of Yokohama a second Desima, and confined us within the limits of the settlement. With the notification given above foreigners complied; but, as it will be seen, they did so with no very good grace, and only under strong protest.

And now, ere closing this chapter, one word concerning the great man whose arrival in our neighbourhood caused all this commotion. He played a remarkable part in the time of the revolution in 1878; and although I shall only casually have to allude to him in speaking of that period, it is well that my readers should know who he was.

The shrines of the Shoguns of the TOKUGAWA dynasty, were situated, two at Nikkó, six at Shiba in the very heart of the city of Yedo, and six at Uyéno, a populous suburb of the city. They consisted of the stone or bronze urns,—built over the vaults which contain their remains, and enclosing a tablet with their posthumous names or titles—and a series of magnificent temples, which are even now, (so many of them as remain) objects of attraction to visitors from all parts of the world. Each Shogun had his own shrine and memorial temple connected with it; and at

Uyéno, in addition to the shrines, there was Toyei-san, reputed to be the largest and wealthiest temple in Yedo. It was the head-quarters of the UYENO-NO-MIYA, the high priest or bishop—who was appointed by the Mikado himself to the office and was invariably a member of the Imperial family. In rank he was far above the Tycoon, and in the very zenith of their power the Shoguns prostrated themselves before him, and occupied a lower place in his presence. He was the high priest of Nikkó, and of Rinnôji in Kioto; and no one in the empire was more venerated than he.

This was the great man, the son of a former Mikado', now passing along the Tokaido on his way to Yedo; and we have seen the excitement the circumstance caused among the foreign community.

CHAPTER XVI.

RUMOUR, AT THE COMMENCEMENT OF 1863, THAT THE RONINS INTENDED TO SLAY ALL THE FOREIGN REPRESENTATIVES.—PREVENTIVE MEASURES.—RUMOUR PROVES TO BE FALSE.—ANOTHER REQUEST OF THE GOVERNOR OF KANAGAWA THAT FOREIGNERS SHOULD AVOID THE TOKAIDO.—BURNING OF THE BRITISH LEGATION BUILDING AT GO-TEN-YAMA, YEDO, AND A LENGTHENED DETAIL OF THE CIRCUMSTANCES THAT LED TO IT.—THOSE WHO NOW JUDGE THEIR COUNTRYMEN WHO PASSED THROUGH THOSE TIMES SHOULD PUT THEMSELVES IN THEIR PLACE.—KNOWLEDGE NOW ATTAINED NOT THEN EXISTING.—WHAT FOREIGNERS DID KNOW.—FACTS AS THEY APPEARED BEFORE THEM HAD ALONE TO BE CONSIDERED.—AS A RULE FOREIGNERS WERE QUIET AND WELL-CONDUCTED; AND MOST FAVOURABLY DISPOSED TOWARDS THE COUNTRY AND PEOPLE OF JAPAN.—THE TRUE NATURE OF THE GOVERNMENT BEGINS TO REVEAL ITSELF.—THE TYCOON NO EMPEROR, BUT YET A REAL POTENTATE.—COMBINATION OF CIRCUMSTANCES THAT LED TO HIS DOWNFALL.

THE year 1863, which was to be a momentous one in the history of foreign intercourse, began inauspiciously. A rumour reached the Government which they must have placed faith in, and which must have alarmed them mightily; for, on the night of the 2nd of January, one of the Ministers for foreign affairs suddenly appeared at the British Minister's residence in Yokohama, having arrived in all haste, with his retinue, from Yedo, to impart it without delay to the foreign representatives. It was to the effect that a special band of ronins had been discovered in the neighbourhood of Yokohama, who had bound themselves with an oath that they would not rest satisfied until they had slain all the foreign diplomatic chiefs. True or false it sufficed to put everyone on the *qui vive*, and the Volunteer corps, of whose formation I have already told, turned out and took their share in the duty of patrolling the streets. At that time there seemed to be every probability that they would be called upon before many weeks, perhaps days, were over, to prove themselves worthy brothers of the Shanghai Volunteers, who had faced the Taeping rebels in 1861. In about a week this particular scare came to an end; word being brought by a colleague of the former messenger, that the rumour turned out to be false.

But if the outlaws were not actually in the vicinity of Yokohama, it was soon rendered but too palpable that there were plenty of men not enrolled in those lawless gangs, who were no less inimical to us.

It is amusing to have to report, (though we will not dwell upon it) that on the 28th January, this year, the British Consul was again called upon to warn his countrymen against using the Tokaido " during one week, or until you receive another communication from me " (the Governor of Kanagawa). The daimios who were then passing were AIDZU, the hero of the revolution on the Tycoon's side; and one of the Choshiu princes, the arch-enemies of foreigners.

On the 1st February an occurrence took place, in which happily there was no loss of life, which compels me to pause, and go back a little in point of time that it may be well understood in all its bearings. Residences were to be built in a certain locality outside of the Yedo city boundary for the five foreign legations. Those for the English and French were the most forward; indeed the former was very nearly completed—when it was wantonly, determinedly, and of malice aforethought, fired in several places simultaneously, and the work of destruction was aided by gunpowder, several discharges of which occurred in the course of the conflagration.

The circumstances were these. After the attack on the British legation a demand was made by the foreign ministers for a site on which residences might be built which should be accessible by land and sea, and at the same time capable of being protected from any renewal of the atrocious attempt at assassination. Three sites were offered by the Government—one at the mouth of the Middle river, (there being three rivers that empty themselves into the sea at Yedo); one, the shore on the sea side of the main street in Yedo; and one which it seems incredible that the Shogun would consent to give up, or that the ministers would refuse—a portion of O-Hama-Go-Ten, then known as the Tycoon's fishing ground, and now as En-rio-kuan, where all royal and distinguished foreign guests of the Emperor are lodged. But there was one spot on which the eye of desire had rested; and nothing would satisfy the representatives of the Treaty Powers but that. It was, as it were, the little pet lamb of the citizens; and though they might have had their choice of more spacious and equally defensible sites, they refused them all, and the Government in a moment of weakness yielded. Go-Ten-yama was the one spot ministerial cupidity had fixed upon. Go-Ten-yama was the one spot the Government most wished to keep for the citizens. Go-Ten-yama was yielded; and the indignation of the samurai was aroused. Go-Ten-yama, they resolved, the foreigners should not occupy.

Strangely enough, even foreign civilians saw the danger to be apprehended from the selection of this site. On the 12th and 19th July 1862, articles appeared in the *Japan Herald*, which clearly foreshadowed what might happen; and gave this interesting little bit of history concerning the locality. When IYEYAS' took up his residence in Yedo and insisted on the daimios coming there to do homage to him, in order to reconcile the higher daimios to his decrees,—to gild the bitter pill of enforced residence in his new capital, he agreed to meet them on their approach to the city, and bid them welcome. For this purpose he built a reception house on a rising ground outside the city, and gave to the site the name of Go-Ten-yama—literally 'the imperial hill of Heaven;' though some translate it 'the hill of the palace.'

"This custom was continued by his successor; but IYEMITSZ' the next in succession was a man of a different stamp. Having a position by birth so much above the daimios, whose exchequers had been exhausted; and their powers for mischief curtailed, he did not see why he should demean himself by going out to meet his inferiors. A very able and at the same time a very proud man, he removed the house entirely; and from that time the custom ceased. When the house was removed a large flat space of ground was left vacant at an elevation of perhaps a hundred feet above the level of the sea, in a very commanding situation. In a military point of view it completely commands the Shinagawa forts below. A few riflemen in the Go-Ten-yama, could effectually clear these forts, and command the Tokaido or sea-road to Yedo. No one could pass Shinagawa so long as Go-Ten-yama was in the hands of a small force. But this IYEMITSZ' did not think of. Instead of retaining the hill as a military position he gave it to the inhabitants of Yedo as a place of recreation, as a park—a pleasure-ground to which they might resort in those out-of-door parties of pleasure which they are so fond of and manage so well. He planted that part of the grounds which overlooks the sea with cherry trees; while the best part of the ground was interspersed with fine old fir-trees which had probably been planted long before. This park was the great resort of parties of pleasure from Yedo. Perhaps in no part of the world is the custom of pic-nic parties carried to the same extent as in Japan. Upon their gala days— and that seems to be six days out of the week, the beautiful lanes in the neighbourhood of Yedo are made more interesting by the groups of people—young and old, men and women, boys, girls and children, sallying out in the opening spring or in the heat of summer, to spend a few hours in the innocent enjoyment of the most beautiful scenery. There may be seen young ladies dressed in the most brilliant colours, which, peacock-like, they carry behind them, young gentlemen accompanying them in the more sober greys, and carrying their two swords like gentlemen, the pictures of happiness and thorough enjoyment, wending their way to the cherry-trees of Go-Ten-yama. There the mats are spread—the quaint picnic boxes produced—and before long the joyous shouts and the merry laugh make those outside long to be of the party.

"Nowhere in the vicinity of Yedo can the same enjoyment be obtained as in the Go-Ten-yama. There are other places of resort, but to them the sea view is wanting—the elevated position—the white sails in any direction moving over the deep blue sea—the cool breeze— the extensive view—the pleasant shade—the brilliant colours of the landscape—when these are filled up with gay dresses, bright eyes and merry laughter—alas! alas! *nous, nous avons changé tout cela.*"

The next week, the same writer at the close of a long article on the same subject, says:—

"We do not think the advantages of the Go-Ten-yama outweighed the disadvantages. The principal of these is the ill-will of the people of Yedo in the forcible appropriation of their park or place of recreation to satisfy the demands of the foreigners."

It is now admitted that it was determined from the first, by some of the most resolute haters of foreigners that they should not occupy the residences that were to be built for them on Go-Ten-yama. This was plainly declared; and the fact that it was so was published in the newspaper. It was unequivocally stated that "the buildings would be destroyed as soon as finished." And so it happened with regard to the English legation. This and the French legation were the only two in progress of construction, the Dutch and American legations not having been commenced. The English was nearest to completion, but no sooner had the last paper-hanger and plasterer put the final touches to it, than, that very day, it was burnt to the ground. "They have cut down our beloved cherry trees" said the samurai, "to make place for the houses of the foreigner, but it will be a *very red blossom* before it is full grown."

And so it was. On the 16th January, some two-sworded men presented themselves at the gate of the nearly finished legation, but on learning that there were no foreigners there, they peacefully retired, and went to a tea-house in the neighbourhood, where they put many questions to the landlord as to whether there were really any foreigners there or not. On receiving the information that there were none, one of them, laying his hand on the hilt of his sword, said fiercely, that if he attempted to deceive them they would slay him; and some of them returned to the gate to make further enquiries. On receiving the same answer as before, one of them asked that they might be allowed to view the foreigners' residence; and on being told that this was not permissible, they drew their swords, cut down the guard, as usual hacking him to pieces, and passing through, made their inspection and retired. After this the building was left almost unguarded, for it was difficult to get men to undertake the duty.

Towards the end of the month, Colonel NEALE received a very strong appeal from the Japanese Government, asking him not to occupy the newly-built edifice, and offering him almost any other site he chose to select. They had expended forty thousand dollars upon the building, but that they did not heed. The Mikado had ordered that the foreigners should not occupy Go-Tenyama, and the excitement among the people was greater than they were able to allay. But Colonel NEALE was firm. He said that all the arrangements respecting the English legation building had been made with the English Minister before he left for England. He was expected to return to Japan, and it was not for the Chargé d'Affaires to upset his dispositions. He also expressed his surprise that nothing had been said to him on the subject until the very eve of the completion of the building; and that he had never previously received any hint of there being any objection to the site.

I do not think that the Government could fairly be charged with having had any hand in the catastrophe that followed. Their information respecting the intention of certain clansmen (not ronins) to destroy it, added to the positive commands of the Mikado that the arrangement with the foreigners should not be carried through, must have put them in a position of great perplexity. At the same time, Colonel NEALE was undoubtedly right in the position he maintained. Concession after concession had been made to the Japanese authorities; and the yielding to one demand or appeal invariably led to more being asked for. Had less firmness been displayed by the English and French representatives—for, happily, M. DE BELLECOURT was a most staunch and generous supporter of his English colleague,—foreign intercourse would speedily have been a mere name—a memory of the past. It was the decisive position taken by these two Ministers, more than any others, that maintained the spirit of the treaties, and prevented their becoming a dead letter.

But passing this by as a mere abstract question, we return to the fact before us. On the 1st February, 1863, only about three or four days after the appeal to Colonel NEALE, the buildings were burnt down. Eye-witnesses reported that they observed the flames burst out in several places simultaneously, and that during the conflagration several explosions of gunpowder took place, thus making sure work of the total destruction of the building. It was not attempted to conceal that it must have been, and assuredly was, the work of incendiaries; and that, too, of men who had sympathisers watching their proceedings at a distance; for no sooner was it evident that the flames and combustibles had done their work effectually, than a salute was fired from a man-of-war at the Shinagawa anchorage.

There are many who now-a-days read of these occurrences at a distance, and some few of those who have more recently come amongst us, who are inclined to censure the proceedings of the foreign representatives who had to bear the brunt of those terrible times. For terrible they really were. I would ask those who would judge fairly, to put themselves in the position of their countrymen who had to endure them. It must never be forgotten that they did not know all the facts that we are now so well acquainted with. What they did know was,—the history of former intercourse between Japan and foreigners, and the manner of the expulsion of the latter; the long exclusion of all foreigners from the country, except the Dutch and Chinese traders at Nagasaki, the former of whom were literally and most ignominiously imprisoned in the little isle of Desima. Further, the reluctance with which they had entered into the new treaty relations, and the intense desire, not of all, but of a strong section of the nobles and territorial princes to drive out the strangers, to close the **ports**, and to put an end to the treaties.

Without going into the vast and very important question as to the right of any country to keep itself closed against intercourse with the outer world, facts as they existed had alone to be considered. Treaties had been signed. Ports had been opened. And on the faith of those treaties the ports had been resorted to by *bona fide* traders, who came, many of them as representatives of some of the most prominent and wealthy merchants of the East, to extend their operations by legitimate trading in Japan. If the anomalous state of the currency of Japan in reference to that of other countries afforded opportunities for profit which proved a temptation too great to be resisted by the new comers, it was but one episode, and that, too, a short-lived one in the new intercourse; but no blame ought to attach itself to the operators. As well might it be said that those were dishonest who bought the golden guineas, once said for a bet to have been offered on London Bridge for a penny a piece. I have already alluded to the fact that some went into this commerce which was justifiable, in a most unjustifiable, a most reprehensible, manner, and for these I have not a word to say. But this is the only sore that the Japanese complained of at the outset. As a rule the new comers were quiet, well-conducted citizens in every respect. They kept themselves, with very few exceptions, well within the conditions of the treaties; and they were so pleased with the country and the people with whom in their business and in their excursions they were brought into contact, that they thought, apart from a certain class, that Japan was the most delightful country, and the Japanese the most loveable people, in the world. I will go further—and I am not writing what may have been gathered from books or other writers, but from personal experience of the "certain class" mentioned above,—there was a large proportion even of them, favourable, or, at least, not unfavourable, to foreigners; and they were the most delightful of all.

Some time before the period at which I have now arrived the true nature of the Government began to reveal itself. It was not yet, however, clearly discerned, and only the course of events I am describing made them fully understood. Those who " know all about it " now, are inclined to sneer at the ignorance of the early-comers, who were not as wise as their successors became, because they talked of the Tycoon as a sovereign, and gave to Japan two Emperors—one spiritual and the other temporal. This error was about to be dissipated. The Tycoon was no Emperor either temporal or spiritual; but those who would give him the simple title of Sei-i-tai-Shogun, generalissimo for the expulsion of barbarians, and deny that he was a ruler exercising sovereign powers, are surely mistaken. From whomsoever he derived his powers, he was the ruler of the Empire from one end of it to the other. The Mikado was the source of honour, the imparter of authority; but the Tycoon or Shogun literally reigned by hereditary right, although he had also to be elected by certain daimios; conferred lands and titles on whomsoever he would; governed from his own capital, in his own name, by his own ministers; was upheld by his own vassals and armed forces, over whom he exercised despotic powers, totally apart from, and unconnected with, the Mikado. He levied taxes and supplied the means for all the national expenditure and for the sustenance of the court of Kioto. He appointed his own vassals as its protectors. For over two hundred years no daimio, however powerful, dared to call these facts in question. It was truly an extraordinary state of things that for nearly seven hundred years—from the time of YORITOMO—the Mikado should exist as the fountain of all power and honour in the country and yet not exercise one atom of real power himself. For two hundred and thirty years no Tycoon visited Kioto; not even for investiture. And although it was deemed necessary that the Mikado should acknowledge him and sanction his assumption of power and title, he was as much ruler of the Empire in the interval between his predecessor's death and this imperial sanction, or at all events from the day of his election, as is a European sovereign between the day of his accession and that of his coronation.

Two circumstances had, however, lately combined, which in the end were to bring this anomalous state of things to a close. One was the growing effeminacy and impotence of the later Shoguns, occasioned by their luxurious living, their self-indulgence, and their diminishing personal attention to the affairs of state. The other was, the personal jealousy of one of the greatest nobles, —as it happened, a kinsman of the Tycoon, and member of the Go-Sanké.

The story need not be very long; and it will render subsequent events more clear.

The founder of the last dynasty of Shoguns, TOKUGAWA IYEYAS', was invested with the rank and title, which he had won fairly by force of arms, in the year 1603. He had nine sons—three of whom, in particular became notable in the empire, not for any deeds of their own, but because IYEYAS' ordered that from their descendants the Shoguns should be elected in failure of heirs male of the body of any regnant Shogun. These were the 7th, 8th and 9th of his sons, whom he made princes of OWARI, KISHIU and MITO. They were always spoken of as the Go-Sanké, or the three imperial families. The prince of ECHIZEN was also descended from IYEYAS'. Now it happened that no prince of the house of MITO had ever enjoyed the high office of Shogun. But the daimio of

MITO made himself very prominent in the early days of foreign intercourse. As long ago as 1841, we are told by the *Kinsé Shiriaku*, he had been placed in confinement at one of his secondary *yashikis* in Yedo for having melted down the bells of all the Buddhist monasteries in his domain to cast cannon with, and for other similar acts. He was one of the few daimios who really governed his clan and concerned himself in state affairs. He was in 1853, when Commodore PERRY came to Japan, pardoned by order of the Shogun, and appointed Kaibo Jimu-shoku, or commissioner for the superintendence of maritime defences. Years before, he had written a pamphlet, propounding the great, but almost forgotten fact, that the Mikado was the true sovereign of the empire; and he now had always two objects at heart, namely, to secure an increase of respect for the Mikado, and to effect the expulsion of the barbarians.

At the beginning of 1857, in consequence of the dissatisfaction he felt with regard to the PERRY treaty, he declined having any further share in public affairs. When, however, on the death of the Tycoon IYESADA in September 1858, it became necessary to elect a successor, the ex-Prince of MITO was very desirous to secure the election of his favourite son HITOTSUBASHI Giobukio (who had been adopted into the family of HITOTSUBASHI.) The regent II KAMON-NO-KAMI, however, succeeded in securing the election of IYESHIGE, a youth, 12 years of age, a scion of the house of KISHIU, and he was nominated by IYESADA as his successor. This enraged the three princes of OWARI, ECHIZEN and MITO, extremely. They, with the princes of TOSA and UWAJIMA (men amongst the most active in establishing the new *régime* in 1868), were subsequently all obliged to resign their daimiates to their sons and retire into private life. MITO was ordered into perpetual confinement in his own province; and HITOTSUBASHI, for having sought the office, was also forced into retirement.

Nothing hastened the fall of the Shogunate so much as this. Other great daimios who were jealous of the arbitrary power wielded by the Shogun, speedily made their voices heard; and ultimately such a combination as had never before been known in Japan, was established, before which the Tycoon, his government, and the whole feudal system, was driven like chaff before the wind. What the effect would have been had HITOTSUBASHI been elected in 1858, it is impossible to conjecture. Certainly the course of events would have been very different, and— that is all that can be said.

CHAPTER XVII.

THE PROTECTION OF THE MIKADO.—COMPETITIVE EXAMINATIONS.—ANXIETY OF THE GOVERNMENT.—DAIMIOS ENCOURAGED TO PURCHASE STEAMERS.—PROVISION FOR PROTECTING THE FOREIGN SETTLEMENT.—ADMIRAL KUPER ARRIVES WITH A SQUADRON.—SHIMADZU SABURO'S REPORT OF THE RICHARDSON EPISODE MEETS THE APPROVAL OF THE MIKADO.—CLAMOUR OF RONINS AT KIOTO FOR EXPULSION OF FOREIGNERS.—SATSUMA PLACED IN CHARGE OF GO-TEN-YAMA.—COLONEL NEALE RECEIVES REPLIES FROM HIS GOVERNMENT.—TYCOON'S HURRIED DEPARTURE FOR KIOTO.—THE DEMANDS OF THE ENGLISH GOVERNMENT.—TYCOON ARRIVES AT KIOTO.—EXCITEMENT IN KIOTO AND YOKOHAMA.—NATIVES LEAVE YOKOHAMA.—THE AMERICAN LEGATION IN YEDO BURNT.—RUSE BY WHICH THE U. S. MINISTER WAS INDUCED TO LEAVE YEDO, AND THE U. S. CONSUL TO QUIT KANAGAWA.—APPOINTMENT OF A DAY FOR THE EXPULSION OF FOREIGNERS AND CLOSING OF YOKOHAMA.—INTIMATION FROM THE GOVERNOR OF KANAGAWA TO THE CONSULS, THAT EXTRA PRECAUTIONS BEING NECESSARY, MORE GUARDS WOULD BE EMPLOYED.—GOVERNMENT AGREES TO PAY THE INDEMNITY DEMANDED OF THEM BY THE BRITISH GOVERNMENT, LEAVING SATSUMA TO BE SUBSEQUENTLY SETTLED WITH.—FRESH TROUBLES.—LETTER FROM THE GOROJIU OGASAWARA TO THE MINISTER ANNOUNCING THE DETERMINATION OF THE GOVERNMENT TO CLOSE THE PORTS.—REPLY.—THE MIKADO ALWAYS ACTED THROUGH THE TYCOON.—THE TYCOONS NOT ALL "PUPPETS."—THE GOVERNMENT'S APOLOGY TO GREAT BRITAIN.—ASSASSINATION OF AME-NO-KOJI.

IT had been decided that the Shogun should go to Kioto in the spring of 1863; but such was the excitement in that city in consequence of the rapid influx of daimios and their followers to the city, and of ronins around it, that it became absolutely necessary to provide extra means for its security. One half of all the Yedo officers of every rank were drafted off for service there; and HITOTSUBASHI Giobukio, who had been appointed the guardian of the Tycoon, set forth early in February for the same destination. Three days later he was followed by the Prince of OWARI. From every portion of the empire the princes resorted to the metropolis, and the ancient city had never seen a period of such prosperity.

Amongst other changes and innovations now introduced was the system of competitive examinations for offices of responsibility. The Naval, Military and Civil service schools, heretofore closed to all but the families or connexions of daimios or very high officers, were thrown open to all classes, and instruction in the naval and military, farming and mechanical sciences, and in literature was imparted to all, irrespective of rank.

The anxiety of the Yedo Government must have been excessive. The princes whose territories were on the coast were not only permitted but encouraged to buy steamers and other foreign built ships; and several were disposed of to them at very high prices.

While all this was going on in the two capitals Colonel NEALE thought it necessary to provide without delay for the protection of the foreign settlements. A dispatch was sent to Admiral Kuper at Hongkong, the result of which was, that, by the end of March, the Admiral arrived in the Euryalus accompanied by the Rattler and Racehorse; and in a short time, other ships having arrived, the harbour of Yokohama was well filled with war vessels of various nationalities.

It was high time that such a demonstration should be made; for the anti-foreign party were growing more and more impatient for active steps to be taken against the hated strangers. SHIMADZU SABURO, on his arrival in Kioto after the murder of RICHARDSON, told his own tale, saying that foreigners had insulted him, and he had ordered them to be slain. Instead of being rebuked he was commended by the Mikado.

On HITOTSUBASHI's arrival he was at once beset with enquirers as to the day appointed for the forcible expulsion of the barbarians, but he put off the rabble by urging them to wait until the Tycoon himself should arrive.

In Yedo many riots took place, principally between the retainers of rival princes.

But the most curious and incomprehensible arrangement of the Government was that by which Go-Ten-yama was placed under the care of SATSUMA, whilst, at this very moment, the heavy retribution for the assault on the Tokaido by SHIMADZU SABURO's retainers, was on the point of falling on the clan. The replies from the Home Government to Colonel NEALE's dispatches had arrived; and no time was lost in communicating their contents to the Government. It was said to be the intention of the Tycoon to start for Kioto about the 9th or 10th April, but every possible effort was now made to hasten his departure; doubtless with the view of delaying any answer to whatever communication the British Chargé d'affaires had to make, by the necessity of sending it to Kioto, and the time it would take to obtain a reply from thence.

On the 29th March Colonel NEALE was officially notified that the departure would take place on the 31st instant. He replied that in two or three days he would have a communication to make respecting the instructions he had received from his Government with regard to the murder of the two marines who were slain at his own legation, and the assault on the unarmed party on the Tokaido by retainers of Satsuma. The answer to this was that the Tycoon's journey could not be delayed, and the expression of a doubt as to the possibility of settling the business speedily.

On the 6th April the note was sent by Colonel NEALE to the Japanese Ministers for foreign Affairs, in which he informed them that he had "received the explicit instructions of his Government to demand reparation from the Japanese Government for the murder and outrages committed upon British subjects on the 14th September last, on the Tokaido, near Kanagawa, by the retainers of Prince SATSUMA." Also he again peremptorily demanded "redress and compensation for the previous outrage on her Britannic Majesty's legation on the 16th June last." He pointed out to them how different had been the behaviour of the British Government to Japan, to the conduct of the Japanese towards the British. He wrote:—

"Acting under evil counsels, the Japanese Government has adopted a passive, reserved, and unfriendly policy with the British Representative not only in regard to these outrages, but in all matters of interest to British subjects.

"This unjustifiable course of action has been crowned with the destruction, by political incendiaries, of the new British Legation-residence at Go-Ten-yama.

"On the other hand the Government of Her Britannic Majesty, viewing with indulgence the obstacles and obstructions opposed to the full development of British commercial enterprise by the Japanese Government, and judging them to emanate from the great political embarrassments of the country, was the first to concede to the wishes of His Majesty the Tycoon, conveyed through his Envoys, and to consent conditionally to the postponement in the opening of Osaka and other ports, subsequently assented to by other European Treaty Powers, and to be assented to by the Government of the United States, only in consideration of counter-concessions which the Government of Great Britain has not sought to exact.

"The Tycoon's Envoys have returned and rendered an account of their mission to the Japanese Government, in relation to the foregoing negotiations, and the undersigned has just received the thanks lately expressed to him in writing by your Excellencies on behalf of the Tycoon and Government of Japan, for the attentions and cordial reception bestowed upon those Envoys by the Sovereign, Government and people of Great Britain; a record standing in painful contrast with the unfriendly demeanour of the Japanese Ministers towards the Representatives and subjects of Her Majesty in this country.

"The Undersigned, nevertheless, unhesitatingly proclaims, and challenges the Japanese Government to disprove the fact, that the subjects of no nation with which Japan is in relation have given less cause for ill-will on the part of the Japanese authorities than the authorities and subjects of the great British nation, which the Japanese Government, regardless of its duty to the interests of the Tycoon and his dynasty, has been so easily persuaded to treat with distrust and disregard.

"By a happy and rare good fortune, which could not reasonably have been expected, during the period that British subjects, of all classes, have resided in Japan, and thousands of British sailors have frequented its open ports, no noticeable instance of violence against Japanese has been complained of regarding one of them, and yet in numbers they exceed all other foreign residents in Japan.

"Such has been the anxious care of the British authorities to engage their countrymen to adopt the conduct of friendship and conciliation, and to accommodate themselves to the difficult situation of the Government of this country.

* * * * * * * * * *

"The reparation now demanded for the murders and murderous assaults committed upon British subjects has been affixed by Her Majesty's Government with a considerate regard for the difficult situation of the Japanese Government and its political embarrassments. But the penalty imposed, and the measure of compensation demanded for the sufferers and their families, now computed in thousands, will, if the Japanese Government continue to be ill-advised, inevitably expand into millions, to indemnify the costs of armaments which must be employed by Great Britain, should all serious warnings fail to ensure the redress imperatively demanded for these unprovoked and flagrant outrages.

* * * * * * * * * *

"Having thus discharged his duty and his conscience by the earnest remarks which precede, the Undersigned has the honour to state to your Excellencies that he is instructed to make the following explicit and peremptory demands on the Japanese Government.

"First, An ample and formal apology for the offence of permitting a murderous attack on British subjects passing on a road open by Treaty to them.

"Secondly, The payment of £100,000 as a penalty on Japan for this offence.

"The mode, manner and form of the apology will be regulated in conferences between the Undersigned and Commissioners appointed by the Japanese Government, as well as the mode and manner of payment of the money reparation demanded.

"Twenty days from this date is assigned to the Japanese Government for its reply, which must be of a categorical character, either consenting to or rejecting the demands here made."

It was further stated that if at the expiry of twenty days the reply should be otherwise than a positive acceptance of the reparation demanded,

"the British Admiral, now here with a considerable force, will, within twenty-four hours after the receipt of such refusal of demands, proceed to enter on such measures as may be necessary to secure the reparation demanded.

"The Undersigned, having acquitted himself of his duties in thus earnestly stating and explaining to the Tycoon's Government what is peremptorily required at its hands, and the penalties that must inevitably attend a non-compliance with the same, proceeds to acquaint your Excellencies with the further measures, which, under instructions from her Majesty's Government, will be adopted to enforce a far more important portion of the reparation rendered necessary, and required for the barbarous murder of the 14th September, from the Prince of Satsuma, by whose retainers that deed was perpetrated. * * * * * * *

"A naval force will be directed to proceed to a port appertaining to the Prince of Satsuma, where will be demanded from him :—

"1.—The immediate trial and capital execution, in presence of one or more of her Majesty's naval officers, of the chief perpetrators of the murder of Mr. Richardson, and of the murderous assault upon the lady and gentlemen who accompanied him.

"2.—The payment of £25,000 sterling, to be distributed to the relatives of the murdered man and to those who escaped the swords of the assassins on that occasion."

As a matter of course the twenty days spoken of in the letter expanded into many weeks. One excuse after another was made, and the great desire of the British Government to see the matter settled without any fighting induced Colonel Neale to listen again and again to their appeals for extension of time.

The Tycoon arrived in Kioto on the 21st April and took up his residence at Nijô, his own castle, but which had not been inhabited by any of his predecessors since it had been occupied by Iyemitz' two hundred and thirty years before.

The excitement in Kioto became intense, and extended to Yokohama. In the latter, the fact of the letter having been sent to the Government becoming known to the natives, and a day fixed for an answer, which, if unfavourable was to be the signal for war, acted on their fears to such an extent that many left the settlement. It would appear that the Governor of Kanagawa was appealed to, to know what they should do ; and he, instead of trying to allay the excitement, told them they might either go or stay, as they liked. The easily frightened people, thought they would be on the safe side, and the native town was half deserted. It was even difficult for foreigners to keep their Japanese servants; of whom probably not one fourth remained.

Throughout all these exciting times, the U S. Minister had quietly resided in Yedo, little interesting himself with the troubles of his diplomatic *confrères*; but now he was to have a gentle reminder that he was a foreigner, and as such, as much the object of popular dislike as others. The Government, for some time tried every device and used every persuasive argument they could think of, to induce him to leave Yedo, and reside in Yokohama. But he was deaf to their entreaties. The consequence was, that on the 24th May, his legation was set on fire and burnt to the ground. He only had time to save the legation archives; and lost, of his own private property, to the value of $10,000. Adjoining the residence was the large temple of JEN-PU-KU-JI, which, escaping the flames, was availed of by Mr. PRUYN as a temporary residence. On the 31st of the month, as he sat at dinner, an officer ran in to warn him that he must leave at once, as his life was in danger; and under the alarm of this intelligence he went on board a ship in the harbour and left for Yokohama forthwith.

And now, having got rid of the United States Minister from Yedo, they had yet one other object to accomplish, which was to get the U. S. Consul and the missionaries who had resided in Kanagawa ever since the opening of the port, to remove to Yokohama. This they effected by a similar *ruse* to that they had played on the minister, and they were received on board the U. S. S. Wyoming until they could procure suitable dwellings in the settlement. Originally the English Consul resided at Kanagawa; but it was found to be inconvenient, and he had removed to Yokohama long before this.

It is quite evident that the Japanese were bringing all

the efforts of their ingenious minds to bear, to carry out the orders from Kioto.

"During this time," says the *Kinsé Shiriaku*, "the Court deliberated daily upon the expulsion of the barbarians, and finally sent the prince of MITO down to Yedo, to superintend the closing of the ports. All the maritime princes were sent home to their respective provinces to make preparations for war."

The Mikado now fixed the 25th of June as the date for the expulsion of foreigners, and HITOTSUBASHI Chiunagon was sent down to Yedo to assist the prince of MITO in closing the ports.

On the same day that the United States' Minister had been so adroitly removed from Yedo, the Governor of Kanagawa notified the Consuls of all the treaty powers that the ronins had so multiplied in Yedo and the vicinity, that not only the Tokaido was unsafe but Yokohama also. Under these circumstances the Government was taking every precaution; additional guards commanded by trusty hatamotos would be placed round the settlement, and it was even proposed to post a strong detachment of them on the eastern hatoba.

The whole tale seemed to the foreigners a mere attempt to enclose them in a net from which they could not escape, as a preliminary to their total expulsion. Outside the settlement they allowed the Japanese authorities to do as they thought proper, but the placing men on the hatoba they would not consent to for a moment. Thus, if the object of the Government really was to entrap foreigners, it failed.

The delays, one after another, that occurred through the absence of the Tycoon from Yedo, may not have been his fault. He made repeated applications to the Mikado for permission to leave Kioto, pointing out in the most urgent manner the necessity of giving an answer to the British demands, but his requests were not granted.

The negotiations, however, were not allowed to slumber, and at length the Japanese Government promised to pay the indemnity and penalty demanded of it, £110,000, in weekly instalments of £10,000; leaving the demand on the Prince of Satsuma to be settled by that chief as a separate affair. But even now all was not to go smoothly, as the following extract, which I give at length from the *Japan Herald*, will show.

"On the afternoon of Saturday (20th) a meeting of British residents was convened at the Consulate by Dr. WINCHESTER H. B. M.'s Consul, who remarked that he had abstained, since the meeting he had convened about ten weeks since, from assembling those under his jurisdiction together for the purpose of communicating to them the course of events, for so many had been the changes in the aspect of things that his doing so could only have had the effect of uselessly exciting or depressing their hopes of a peaceful and satisfactory issue from the present difficulties; indeed there appeared the less occasion for his doing so because, so far as the most solemn written obligations could afford any indication, the peaceful settlement of affairs might have been reasonably anticipated. At the last moment, however, this singular people had repudiated these obligations.

"He then read the following despatch received by him from H. B. M.'s Chargé d'Affaires.

Yokohama, 20th June, 1863.

'SIR,—I have to instruct you to adopt as early as possible, such measures as may be most effectual to make known to the British community and to your colleagues the Consuls of Foreign States the present situation of affairs in regard to the subject of the British demands upon the Japanese Government.

'The patience and moderation which I have exercised in my communications with the Tycoon's Government, in the earnest desire of bringing about a peaceful settlement of the avowedly just demands for reparation preferred by Her Majesty's Government, are well known, and sufficiently manifest.

'At the most recent date, (the 18th instant) these objects which I had in view were on the very eve of being happily accomplished.

'The Japanese Government, through its Envoys, had, after innumerable difficulties, solemnly and unreservedly entered into a written engagement with me to pay the pecuniary demands at short specified intervals, the first payment to have been made on the date above referred to.

'That day has been reached and is passed, and the Japanese Ministers have flagrantly, unequivocally and designedly, broken their faith.

'In the most unjustifiable and audacious manner, the Tycoon's Government now seeks to re-open negociations previous to accomplishing their solemn assent to the settlement of the pecuniary portion of the demands, and openly declare their intention to withhold all payments; thus most effectually extinguishing all remaining faith in even their most solemn engagements.

'As Her Majesty's Representative I have now therefore to declare that the utmost limits of my patience (consistently exerted and directed to exact the reparation sought, by peaceful means, and which I had good reason to hope had been successfully exerted) is now exhausted.

'Her Majesty's subjects and your colleagues the Consuls of Foreign States have, during a period of ten weeks, at intervals been informed that the adoption of coercive measures was an impending contingency, though the probability or otherwise of their occurence was alternately stronger or feebler as matters progressed. On my part I have not failed urgently to advise through yourself British subjects and the Foreign community generally to be prepared for the worst and most regrettable emergency which could arise, namely, the necessity which might present itself (with a view to the security of their persons and property) of abandoning the open Ports, while the Vice-Admiral Commanding-in-Chief has as often and as consistently declared his inability to hold, militarily, the settlement, if coercive measures were actually resorted to effectually to enforce compliance with the demands.

'So long as a chance of honest though tardy action could be anticipated on the part of the Japanese Government, I have scrupulously deferred initiating any hostilities by an appeal to force; but I now feel myself urgently called upon to leave the adoption of the only measures which the Rulers of this country would appear to understand or appreciate,—namely, those of coercion, —to the Admiral, into whose hands I will this day consign the solution of affairs.

'Thus, within a very short period, the policy of expediency, invariably adopted by the Japanese Government, may possibly lead them to repair their broken faith, by the actual payment of the indemnities, and a more peaceful aspect of affairs may again present itself; —or, on the other hand, the Admiral may have deemed it advisable to profit by the circumstances to carry out some of the operations he may decide upon.

'Thus, also, Her Majesty's subjects and your colleagues will judge of the measures they may individually deem it practicable and expedient to adopt under all the circumstances here most unreservedly and explicitly set forth.

'I need hardly add that I shall not fail immediately to concert with Admiral KUPER and Admiral JUAREZ (whose frank and cordially proffered co-operation I am assured of), respecting such temporary measures for the safeguard of the community in this emergency, as may be practicable.

I have, &c.

(Signed)   EDWD. ST. JOHN NEALE.

To CHARLES A. WINCHESTER, Esq.,
&c.,   &c.,   &c."

"H. B. M.'s Consul then read some notes of an interview which had been held between the Governor of Kanagawa and some of the Foreign Consuls on the 20th inst., which had been kindly forwarded to him by a colleague. By this it appeared that the Governor stated that on the night of the 18th he had received commands not to pay the money the next day, but that Ogasawara would come down on the 22nd; that he had received a letter from the Tycoon commanding him not to pay the money, because it was impossible for the Gorojiu to communicate with officers of inferior rank. The Tycoon had every intention to pay the money, but if he did so he would lose his life. The Tycoon was the friend, and the Mikado the enemy, of foreigners; the latter had forbidden the Tycoon to pay; and the former had been compelled to obey, or lose his position. The Governor did not think that the money would be paid, for the rumour of such an intention had spread through the country, and the ronins and other bad people said—'·Why pay the money to these poor fools—to these bad foreigners?' The opinion of the Tycoon's government was that the money ought to be paid; and the proof of this was that when the ultimatum was sent to Yedo on the 6th April, the Tycoon, who was still there, ordered the Governor to pay it. On his way to Miako the Tycoon had received a communication from his spiritual superior which had made him reflect. Subsequently a great many things had occurred at Miako. The Governor had done nothing; therefore, he hoped the Admiral would do nothing.

"On the evening of Sunday (the 21st) another meeting of the British Residents was held at the residence of H. B. M.'s Consul, when the following despatch was read.

"*Euryalus*" at *Yokohama*,
21st June, 1863.

'SIR,—Her Majesty's Chargé d'Affaires has placed in my hands the solution of the questions at issue between the Japanese Government and that of Her Majesty, in consequence of all peaceful and diplomatic negociations having failed to bring the Government of the Tycoon to a due sense of its obligations.

'The instructions under which in this contingency, it will now be my duty to act, will necessarily involve coercive measures to be undertaken by the naval force under my command; and as such measures will probably lead to action on the part of the Japanese, which would endanger the safety not against British subjects but also of all Foreign residents in Japan, I have to request you will forthwith communicate the circumstance to all British subjects, and to the Consuls of Foreign Powers, with a view to their immediately adopting such steps as they may think desirable for the security of their persons and property, the force at my disposal being inadequate for the efficient protection of Yokohama, whilst carrying out the instructions of Her Majesty's Government in other parts of Japan.

'In order that the community may have sufficient time

to make arrangements for their personal security, I desire you will inform them that, unless called upon by any initiative act of hostility on the part of the Japanese, to maintain the dignity of the British flag, I shall not take any hostile step until the expiration of eight days from this date, inclusive.

'I have also to acquaint you that all the precautionary measures adopted some weeks since for the speedy relief of the Foreign community in the event of any sudden attack or disturbance, will be continued during the interval mentioned and subsequently, if possible, with the same vigilance as hitherto; and such additional assistance rendered as will be consistent with the duty of preserving the efficiency of Her Majesty's ships.

'Under the existing state of affairs, and the great probability of approaching strife and turmoil, I think it necessary to recommend most strongly that all those of the community who have wives and families at Yokohama, should take the earliest opportunity of removing them, at any rate from the scene of danger, should they themselves determine upon awaiting the issue of events.

I have, &c.,
(Signed) AUGUSTUS L. KUPER,
Vice Admiral and
Commander-in-Chief.

To CHARLES A. WINCHESTER, Esq.,
&c., &c., &c."

"In this position matters remained till the evening of the 23rd June.

"It may be as well before proceeding further to state that immediately upon the despatches of Colonel NEALE and Admiral KUPER being communicated to them, the most vigorous and hearty coöperation was offered by the French authorities, the Admiral, JUAREZ, expressing his determination to hold the settlement to the last extremity.

"On the above day, about noon, rumours arose of a character to have a somewhat reassuring effect, and towards night those behind the scenes had a strong inkling that the money was about to be posted. And so it proved. The Japanese Governors, shut out by the position into which the persistence of their Government in a course of procrastination had driven matters, from direct communication with the British Chargé d'Affaires, at midnight 23-24 sought and obtained an interview with the French Minister, and informed him that they were ready to pay the money. This was at once communicated to the British authorities, and at one o'clock H. B. M.'s Chargé d'Affaires communicated to them, in answer to their request to him to receive it, that as the Japanese Government had allowed things to go to such extremity, the former arrangement, for the payment in instalments, would not now be acted on, but that if they hoped the money to be received the whole amount of £110,000 must be paid down in full in 440,000 good Mexican dollars, at seven o'clock. At early dawn of the morning the cry of the coolies resounded through the streets as they dragged their heavy burthens from the treasury to the legation.

"On Wednesday morning, too, a document arrived from the Japanese Ministers of Foreign Affairs to the Ministers of Foreign Powers, informing them that they had been charged by the Tycoon, now at Miako, with the carrying out the instructions of the Mikado, that the ports should be closed and foreigners put away from Japan; and that they were willing to enter into negociations upon the subject. As may be supposed the only notice which was taken of it was an indignant protest from all the ministers, and a promise to convey the subject matter of the communication to their respective governments.

"H. B. M.'s Chargé d'Affaires caused a circular to be issued to the effect that, as the penalties are now in course of actual satisfaction, the negociations relative to the remaining portion of the instructions revert to the position which existed anterior to the 20th of June, and will be pursued with the same fixed determination as heretofore.

"H. B. M.'s Chargé d'Affaires in the same circular acknowledged the prudence and self-control which characterised the relations of the British community with the Japanese since the commencement of these negociations.

"As we now write, business and the wonted amount of comfort and sense of security are rapidly springing up, and but for the Fleet still in our harbour, and an additional sprinkling of naval and military uniforms in our streets, there is but little to indicate that so momentous a cloud is but just passing over Japan."

But actually whilst all this was being thus satisfactorily arranged at Yokohama, fresh troubles were in preparation. Any reader of all these facts must see the extreme difficulties that both the Foreign and Japanese Ministers had to encounter. It is easy to say now-a-days that all arose from the Tycoon having assumed a power, in entering into treaties, that he did not possess. Up to the time the treaties were made his power had been absolute. But as I have shown elsewhere, quoting the circular upon the subject issued by him in August 1858, he *did* appeal to the Mikado. The words are in the circular:—"*It was impossible for us to comply with this* (the demand of the United States for a Treaty) *without consultation with the Mikado.*"—" The Mikado, on hearing of this was much troubled." And the Imperial reply was that "*if it was necessary to conclude any treaties,* the Tycoon must make exceptions in favour of the neighbourhood of Miako, and that Hiogo in Setzu should be left out *if possible.*" The Mikado also said:—" You have thought it well to open the port to Foreigners, but you did not consider that Foreigners would entangle you with difficulties. We would know your opinion in this respect." This was conveyed to the Tycoon in April 1858, long before any real difficulties could have arisen, except from within; and when none but the American Minister, Mr. HARRIS, was in the country; certainly before any one of any other nationality could have given cause for complaint.

The language of the Mikado recognises clearly, as it seems to me, that the power was vested in the Tycoon.

Of course the foreign representatives could only act on the lights they possessed. Had the Japanese Government, from the first, acted in an open straight-forward manner, such as has been the case with all other nationalities with whom relations have been opened, they would not have been subjected to such suspicions and doubts as they were. But being themselves suspicious of everybody—as indeed the Japanese continue as a nation to be to this day—they made it their study how to deceive and mislead their new friends. So it was that every move they made was deemed to have an ulterior object, and, rightly or wrongly, they were distrusted.

Now, after the payment of the $440,000 in the manner described, it must have been rather startling for each of the foreign representatives to receive a dispatch, of which this is Mr. SATOW's translation :—

"I communicate with you by a dispatch.

"The orders of the Tycoon, received from Kioto, are to the effect that the ports are to be closed and the foreigners driven out, because the people of the country do not desire intercourse with foreign countries. The discussion of this has been entirely entrusted to me by His Majesty. I therefore send you this communication first, before holding a conference respecting the details.

"Respectful and humble communication.
(24th June, 1863).
(Signed) OGASAWARA DZUSHO-NO-KAMI."

The answers of all the representatives were couched in similar terms to that of Colonel NEALE. The incident is of such surpassing importance that I give *verbatim* the reply of the English Chargé d'Affaires. It is dated the very day of receiving the letter, and the day following that on which the money had been paid.

"The undersigned, her Britannic Majesty's Chargé d'Affaires, has received, in common with his colleagues, and with extreme amazement, the extraordinary announcement, which, under instructions from his Majesty the Tycoon, his Excellency has addressed to him.

"Apart from the audacious nature of this announcement, which is unaccompanied by any explanation whatever, the undersigned is bound to believe that both the spiritual and temporal sovereigns of this empire, are totally ignorant of the disastrous consequences that must arise to Japan by their determination thus conveyed through you to close the opened ports, and to remove therefrom the subjects of the treaty powers.

"For himself, as representative of her Britannic Majesty, the undersigned has to observe, in the first instance, that the rulers of this country may still have it in their power to modify and soften the severe and irresistible measures which will, without the least doubt, be adopted by Great Britain, most effectually to maintain and enforce its treaty obligations with this country, and, more than this, to place them on a far more satisfactory and solid footing than heretofore, by speedily making known and developing any rational and acceptable plans directed to this end, which may be at present concealed by his Majesty the Tycoon or by the Mikado, or both, to the great and imminent peril of Japan.

"It is therefore the duty of the undersigned solemnly to warn the rulers of this country that when the decision of her Majesty's Government, consequent upon the receipt of your Excellency's announcement, shall have in due course been taken, the development of all ulterior determinations now kept back will be of no avail.

"The undersigned in the meanwhile has to inform your Excellency, with a view that you may bring the same to the knowledge of his Majesty the Tycoon, who will doubtless make the same known to the Mikado, that the indiscreet communication now made through your Excellency is unparalleled in the history of all nations, civilized or uncivilized; that it is, in fact, a declaration of war by Japan itself against the whole of the treaty powers, and the consequences of which, if not at once arrested, it will have speedily to expiate by the severest and most merited chastisement.

With respect and consideration.
    (Signed) EDWARD ST. JOHN NEALE."

OGASAWARA was, as my readers will have perceived, a member of the Gorojiu, and no one knew better than himself the absurdity of sending this letter to the foreign representatives. But he was compelled to forward it by the positive orders received from Kioto.

Observe its date, the 24th of June. The 25th was the day appointed for the actual expulsion of the barbarians. The Tycoon was obliged to send this order to Yedo, though he knew how useless it was. In very truth, the Mikado was a prince upon whom these affairs of state were suddenly enforced; and he naturally listened to those who flattered him and urged him to assume his proper *status* in the empire—" Be a ruler in fact as well as in name. Judge the acts of your vice-gerent, and compel him to obey your infallible decrees." Ignorant of everything connected with the outer world, (as all the Japanese were, but he especially), and prejudiced as all ignorant people are, it is not to be wondered at that he allowed himself to be made an instrument in the hands of the bold and energetic spirits who professed to be maintaining his cause. Yet it must be observed, even with all the influences brought to bear upon him, that he always gave his orders to the Tycoon—to no one else. He said to him—" Do!" and left him to find the means of obeying the command. Even when it was proposed to him to place himself at the head of an army to drive out the strangers, after consenting, he withdrew and left it to the Tycoon. Further, it must be remarked —for it is most remarkable—that notwithstanding all the opposition that was made to the Tycoon and his Government, there was not one who did not yield to his judgment if sentenced to punishment; obey, at least outwardly, his behests, when ordered to fulfil any particular duty; and speak of him with the respect usually only reserved for a sovereign, in any public verbal or written communications. And if any will speak of the Tycoon as a mere puppet, I ask him to observe the importance attached to his personal visit to Kioto; the impossibility of properly carrying on the Government at Yedo without him; and the weight attached by the Mikado to the personal presence of IYEMOCHI, boy as he was (17 years of age), at his side at the metropolis. The best proof that if a Tycoon was a mere puppet, it was his own fault, is the respect with which the more active ones who made their power felt, are ever spoken of in history and by their countrymen. Doubtless sloth and luxury had crept in during some of the later reigns; but IYEMOCHI, the last but one of his dynasty, and YOSHI-NOBU (HITOTSUBASHI) his successor, and the last of that *régime*, can hardly have been such non-entities as some attempt to describe them.

Adhering now as nearly as possible to dates, on the 3rd July, Colonel NEALE received the following apology, which closed the Tokaido episode so far as the Government was concerned.

" The Japanese Ministers to Lieut Colonel NEALE.
" We communicate with you by a dispatch.
" Last year, at the British Legation in Yedo, a wicked and murderous act took place. Again, on the Tokaido, a British subject was murdered. Such unfortunate affairs were for us highly to be regretted. Thus we hope that affairs likely to break off the intercourse between the two countries may not again arise.
" We desire to inform you thus much.
" Respectful and humble communication."
(July 3, 1863.)

   (Signed) MATSUDAIRA BUZEN-NO-KAMI.
         INOUYE KAWACHI-NO-KAMI.
         OGASAWARA DZUSHO-NO-KAMI.

The different sentiments expressed in this apology written on the 3rd July and in the communication of the 24th June, are enough to show the confusion in the Councils of the Empire.

On the following day (4th July) ANE-NO-KOJI who had been associated with SANJO in the mission from the Mikado to the Tycoon at the end of the year 1862, was assassinated in Kioto—by whom, the why and the wherefore, are mere matter of conjecture.,

CHAPTER XVIII.

MORE EXCITEMENT.—THE CHOSHIU FORTS AND STEAMERS FIRE UPON FOREIGN VESSELS IN THE STRAITS OF SIMONOSEKI. DETAILS OF REPRISALS BY THE FRENCH, DUTCH AND AMERICAN MEN-OF-WAR.—THE JAPANESE NAVY IN THE YEAR 1863.

It seems that before we come to the stirring tale of the settlement of the affair still outstanding between Satsuma and Great Britain, we are to be detained awhile with other matters, not one whit less exciting.

While affairs in Yedo and Yokohama were in the unsettled condition we have described—in Yedo the public places being covered with addresses, *canards* and remonstrances of a most inflammatory character; and in Yokohama the number of Government guards being nearly trebled;—news came from a distant quarter, of more outrages, calling for immediate retribution.

On the 3rd July it became generally known that the American Minister had received intimation from the Japanese Government by a messenger from Yedo, that a merchant-steamer bearing the American flag had been fired into by either one or two Japanese armed vessels near the Western Straits of the Inland sea.

"The Pembroke was at anchor for the night near the straits at the entrance of the western end of the Inland Sea. She passed a Japanese barque, European built, at about 2 p.m. in the day. She was well armed, full of men, with no ensign set. The Pembroke had an American ensign flying. After the Pembroke anchored, and at about four o'clock, the bark came down with a fair wind with the Japanese man-of-war ensign flying. She passed the Pembroke and anchored between her and the straits about a quarter of a mile off. When she was approaching a gun was fired from a bluff about 4 miles off, and the signal was repeated all along the coast. Nothing occurred in the evening, but apparently after dark the bark warped up, and got springs on her cable, for when she opened fire she was nearer and was broadside on to the wind.

"She commenced firing on the Pembroke at a quarter before one A.M. It was dark but she could see plainly by the flashes of lightning which were frequent. After she had fired about a dozen shots one of which cut away the topmast backstay, and all passed close to the vessel, a brig, recognised as the Lanrick, suddenly appeared coming from the windward, and passed about 40 yards from the Pembroke and dropped anchor close to the barque.

"Both then fired as rapidly as they could load and discharge, but the Pembroke by that time had got steam up and ran out of fire escaping to sea through the Bungo Channel, a pass seldom used by foreign vessels. The Japanese Pilot tried to escape, but was detained by force. During the attack a great many lights were visible in motion on shore, and the noise of manning boats distinctly distinguishable. When the Lanrick passed the Pembroke a terrific yell was raised from both vessels, but they fortunately did not fire—probably because they were not ready; if they had the steamer would have been destroyed, as she was only about 100 or 120 feet off.

"The Pembroke's guns were lashed, and no attempt was made to use them, every one on board being busily engaged in aiding to get under weigh."

The whole attention of foreigners was now diverted

to the Inland sea; for the assault upon the little merchant steamer Pembroke was immediately followed by similar ones on a French despatch boat, the Kien-chang, and on H. N. M. S. Medusa.

"Scarcely had the intelligence of the assault upon the American merchant ship Pembroke become generally known, and the United States Frigate "Wyoming" left harbour in search of the piratical vessels and for the scene of attack, than a report began to spread, traceable however to no authentic source, that His Imperial Majesty's Ship "Kienchang" from Yokohama bound for Shanghai *via* Nagasaki, and carrying a general mail, had also been fired into in the same pass. This report, on the arrival of the Hellespont proved to have been well founded, for she brought intelligence that the Kienchang arrived in Nagasaki on the 10th, reporting that on the previous day, when passing through the Western entrance of the Inland (or Suwonada) sea, she was fired into by Japanese vessels, and by the forts on the Northern side, *i.e.* in the province of Nagato, commonly called Choshiu, the territory of MATZ-DAIRA DAIZEN-NO-DAIBU, Jiu-sii-no-Chiu-jio, (MOWORI). She was reported to have suffered considerable damage, which, however, fortunately does not prove to be the case.

"The "Hellespont" reporting that H.N.M.'s "Medusa" had left Nagasaki on the 9th bound for this by the Inland sea route, her arrival was looked for with some anxiety. On coming into port it soon became known that she too had been made to run the gauntlet of a heavy fire in the same passage. Every minute item of the details of present occurrences must be interesting and may have its use, we therefore give the account of this affair as furnished by the Netherlands Consul-general, D. DE GRAEFF VON POLESBROEK, Esq., who was a passenger on board, without curtailment:—

"With a view to avoid the inaccuracies generally attendant upon reports of active hostilities, I have the honor to acquaint your Excellencies with the particulars of the encounter which the Netherlands steam Corvette Medusa was compelled to sustain with the batteries and two Japanese ships in passing through the Straits of Shimonoseki, the Western entrance to the Interior Sea.

"Having left the Bay of Nagasaki on the 9th July we met, near the entrance, the French ship Kienchang, on Mail service under command of Capt. LAFONT, who had the kindness to come on board us with our despatches, giving also his report for the Admiral commanding the Naval division in China. He informed us that the batteries in the straits of Shimonoseki and two European built ships having the Japanese flag had the audacity to open fire against his steamer upon which was hoisted the French flag.

"The commander of the Medusa, before leaving Nagasaki, having decided to proceed to Yokohama by the Inland sea, had taken a Japanese pilot from the Governor of Nagasaki, and he started immediately with all sails and steam in the direction of the Straits, where we arrived on the 11th July at seven o'clock in the morning. When we came in sight two cannon shot were fired from a battery and afterwards eight others from a brig of war.

"As we were not aware of any damage being done by the balls we believed that the cannon-shot was the signal between the Japanese for the arrival of any foreign ship. But all on board the Medusa was prepared for a combat, and the batteries on both sides were charged and manned, in readiness to fire when the first balls of the enemy should be directed towards us.

"The greatest silence reigned on board, and no one believed that the Japanese would have the audacity to commit the least hostilities, when suddenly a battery of eight guns and those of two ships anchored before the town, having a flag blue and white (that of the Prince of Nagato) at her fore-royal-mast head, but no flag at the peak, opened fire of shell and ball of which the direction was fortunately a little too high, or we should have had a perfect rain of iron. At this time we had arrived into the cross fire of all their land batteries.

"All our pieces on the port side answered immediately, and owing to the short distance (only two or three cables at most), all the balls and shells carried admirably on the great land battery, and two of our balls made considerable damage on the battery of one of the ships.

"The order was given to advance as gently as possible, in order to have time to work the pieces well, and as the starboard gave no work, every one was employed at the guns at the port side continuing the fire by sections of two together; a fourth battery soon joined its thunder to that of the three others. To our great regret the Medusa could not approach sufficiently near the ships to sink them, or to take them by the board, there being a bank of sand between them and us, and the water being shallow. Exposed to so sharp a cross fire from four batteries, the Medusa was hulled by their shots, and received two shells which burst after having passed by the first board. The Commandant, seeing three men fall with one shot, horribly mutilated, and fearing fire caused by the shells, had to employ many men to extinguish the fire which had already ignited the bulwarks and the engine room. The fire of the enemy from their great battery abated a little, which raised the spirits of our men, of whom four had now fallen mortally wounded.

"The fire from the ships slackening, we could now see that our balls had seriously damaged their pieces. The Medusa advanced slowly, firing shells and ball, and was, as she advanced through the Straits, exposed successively, to five other batteries of pieces of large calibre, the correct firing of which caused the Commandant to fear for the boilers and machinery, without speaking of the danger of the rudder being damaged, in which case the corvette must have been sank in a passage so narrow and difficult. God saved us from this imminent danger; and passing the ninth battery, which like the others was concealed behind the trees or protected by the rocks, we came into the Inland sea, having passed one hour and a half in passing the Straits where we had to support a continual fire of balls and shells.

"It is wonderful that we lost four men only, and five wounded, of whom two are still in a dangerous condition, being wounded by some pieces of shell in the head. Above all when we consider the height of the ship out of the water and the little damage done by the enemy to the hull it looks like a miracle. Of the 21 shots which struck the Medusa, 17 were balls of 24 and shells of 16 c. passed by the one board; of these projectiles three had exploded—one in the battery, another in the engineers' room, a third on the deck, whilst the others passed through the long-boat, the cutter, the funnel and many other places on deck, where I was nearly killed myself by the same ball that killed a chief gunner; and at the same time the Commandant and a midshipman were slightly wounded by splinters. All the officers in the batteries and on the deck at their respective places directed the fire with perfect calmness, and considering that for the most part the seamen were for the first time called upon to vindicate the honor of their flag under so many chances of death, and they continued the fire so briskly, notwithstanding that they were obliged to change the direction of the guns at every moment, we cannot refuse to them a well deserved admiration, or to acknowledge the excellent discipline on board this ship."

All who read this account and are acquainted with the scene of action, or who only even identify it upon the charts, will be ready to add, to the Netherlands Consul-general's well deserved meed of praise to the seamen, acknowledgements of the intrepidity of the Commander of the Medusa in facing the threatened assault in despite the notice he had received from the Commander of the "Kienchang" of the reception he might expect to meet with. He worthily vindicated the honour of his flag, gallantly, unswervingly, pursuing his intended route, simply reducing his speed to the slowest possible progression, in order to have a better chance to return the compliment of his assailants, who seem, (to use Mr. POLSBROEK'S expression) to have rained "a perfect shower of iron" about his ears.

But I do not think that, looking at all the circumstances of the case, opinions will be unanimous, in respect of the right of any foreign vessel to pass through the straits; or as to the propriety of the Medusa disregarding the warning of the Kienchang, and courting a danger, about which there could be no uncertainty.

The Medusa brought particulars of the affair of

the Kienchang somewhat fuller than those reported above. It appears that on the morning of the 8th, as early as about four o'clock, two officers went on board, professedly to make enquiries as to where the ship was from, whither bound, &c., but left without making any objection to her proceeding, or other remark. Two hours after, some shots were fired from the batteries, but as they did not approach the ship they were supposed by those on board only to have been fired in some target practice, and did not excite much attention. The Kienchang passed on, but as she passed the second fort a steady fire was directed towards her, passing however over the ship. The imperial French flag was then flying. Captain LAFONT, intending to send on shore to ask what was the intention of this act, a small boat was being lowered for the purpose, but before she was manned she was struck by a shot and sank. She passed on, receiving the fire of all the forts, and having passed about one fourth of the distance through the channel, observed two armed vessels, a sailing corvette and a brig, leaving a creek or small bay. They both began to attack. The brig before commencing to fire partly hoisted the Japanese Imperial flag, but hauled it down again before it was fully hoisted. The corvette, however, hoisted it and kept it up during the whole time of the assault. The Kienchang was enabled to escape the fire of a great number of the guns on the northern side by taking a channel hitherto unknown to European vessels, through which she was conducted by the native pilot, who had fortunately been detained, though only by dint of threats, on board.

And now let us see the steps taken by the American and French senior naval officers to punish the insults to their respective national flags. Thus is it recorded in the *Japan Herald* :—

"As we have said the Wyoming left here on the morning of the 13th for the scene of the attack upon the Pembroke. H. I. M.'s Tancrede had steam up, and was off for the same spot within a few hours after the news of the Kienchang affair reached here; and Admiral Jaures left on Thursday in the Semiramis for the same port. So that without speculating at length far into the future, for which we have not now either time, inclination or space, we may make pretty sure that even at the time we now write, the daimio Mowori (and let us hope, through him, some of his haughty neighbours and compeers), have been taught that even their very strongest positions will not command immunity from punishment for such acts,—acts only to be accounted for by the supposition of their complete ignorance of the might of those nations whose flags are thus insulted and whose power is thus defied."

* * * * *

"The Wyoming arrived this morning. We compile the following account from information kindly supplied to us by E. S. Benson, Esq., who was a passenger in the corvette.

"Arriving at the straits of Shimonoseki on the 16th, immediately on passing the entrance she received the fire of a battery of three guns. The corvette had not then borne her flag, it was now hoisted; immediately another battery opened fire, three vessels, viz. a steamer, (the Lancefield), a barque (which we suppose to be the Armistice), and a brig (the Lanrick) all flying the Japanese flag at the peak and Mowori's at the main, came in sight, lying close under the northern shore. The corvette passed between the vessels, the barque and brig on the one side, that next to the forts, and the steamer on the outside; the batteries on the north side were all in full play. The barque opened fire with three broadsides of 32lbs., which was promptly acknowledged by the American, which then passed on and received the fire of the brig's 32lbs. within fifty yards range. She then passed the steamer at about 30 yards, from which she received the fire of two small guns, which she returned with two 13lbs. The corvette then kept over towards the south shore. The Japanese steamer by this time had got up steam, and ran over to the northern side close under the forts. During all this time the corvette was sustaining the fire of six batteries of 3 or 4 guns each, and also of the brig and barque.

"The corvette then manœuvred into position, and began her work in earnest. Her fine guns seem to have been admirably worked, to have silenced considerable numbers of the shore guns, whilst a 10-inch shell well pitched at the Lancefield, struck her amidships about two feet above water line : from the volumes of steam and smoke which were seen to follow it was not doubted that it had exploded her boilers.

"The corvette added two or three more shells to this and left her apparently effectually destroyed. The brig, too, appeared to be much riddled, and to be already settling by the stern.

"The corvette came out close to the batteries, receiving their fire throughout, which, however, appeared to be considerably slackened.

"The corvette's casualties are—four killed ; and seven wounded, one since dead. She received eleven shots in her hull.

"The engagement lasted one hour and ten minutes."

The account of the proceedings of the French, which I also take from the newspaper, was furnished by Mr. BLEKMAN, Dutch interpreter to the French legation, who was on board the Semiramis officially.

"I am authorised by Admiral JAURES, Commander-in-Chief of the French Forces in China and Japan, to communicate to you the following account of the proceedings of H. I. M.'s Semiramis and Tancrêde, and my own experiences in the recent retaliatory visit of those ships to the Straits of Shimonoseki.

"We left Yokohama on the morning of the 16th, and arrived in the Bungo entrance to the Inland sea on the morning of Sunday the 19th. We anchored in the channel and prepared for action. Early on the morning of Monday we ran under slow steam into the entrance of the Shimonoseki Channel, looking out for the batteries. When about two miles from the Nagato side of the Channel we saw the flashes and smoke of two guns fired from the midst of the trees, and soon after made out Kōfu, the castle of SAKI-NO-SKE, a member of MATSUDAIRA

DAIZEN-NO-DAIBU's family, and proceeding a little further on, on the same i.e. northern or Nagato side, a battery of five 25 lb. guns. The Admiral decided upon the destruction of this battery, and not of the castle. We then came to anchor about three quarters of a mile from the battery near the village of Tanoura, in the Province of Bouzen. When anchored it was found that the current put us stem on to the battery ; about half an hour was spent in putting springs on our cable, and a hawser to a Japanese junk moored at some distance from us. During all this time the Japanese gunners remained at their guns, not even pointing them at us ; had they done so they might have raked us fore and aft ; we therefore thought that the guns were fixed in the one position, viz., pointed up the narrowest part of the channel, but when we took the battery we found this not to be the case, the guns being perfectly mounted on good European fashioned carriages. When broadside on, the frigate fired a 60lb. rifle ball which went right over the battery : the second carried right into the middle of the parapet, and sent earthwork and stones, turf and sand-bags flying around in every direction. Still no answer was returned by the Japanese. We continued the bombardment till nearly eleven o'clock, sending in the shells every five minutes and making beautiful practice. I was then sent on shore in company with Mons. L'ABBE GIRARD to the town of Tanoura, to distribute the proclamation of Admiral JAURES, to the effect that the country people had nothing to fear on that side, that he had come only to punish the Prince of Nangato for having fired into a vessel under the French flag, and inviting them to send provisions on board against payment.

"We found our way to the house of the Mayor without difficulty, not being molested in any way by the people, who crowded round us in great numbers, and we were received by this official with all honors and politeness ; he thanked us for the proclamation, and in our presence sent it by a messenger to the Prince of BOUZEN. During this trip on shore I had heard both the frigate and the Tancrède recommence their fire and on going on board I learned that the Admiral had ordered the Tancrède to run in towards Shimonoseki, and that when she came into the narrowest part of the passage the battery opened fire upon her; our guns, however, soon silenced the battery. I saw one gun toppled over by a shell, and two or three Japanese gunners fly into the air. The Tancrêde was hit in three places, one shot went into her hull, one into the mizen top-mast, and one cut away the fore-top mast, which only stood there by the stays. At noon, after the men's dinner, the Admiral ordered a landing, and I had the good luck to be ordered to accompany Captain DUQUILLIOT, the commander of the troops. We landed in all 250 men—180 sailors and 70 Chasseurs of the 3rd battaillon d'Afrique.

On nearing the shore to the right of the battery, protected from her by a projecting bluff, the boat's rifled gun sent a few shells into the bushes as a precaution, but nobody stirred. We landed in good order, and made in three divisions for the battery. After we had well entered into the bushes we were attacked by the Japanese in several isolated troops of three or four, some with rifles, some with swords, but most with old Brown Bess, of Dutch manufacture. These lay concealed, aiming at us as we approached. They were immediately charged and bayoneted. Some few made a stand, but generally they took to immediate flight. I think there must have been about twenty killed this way. Passing through this brushwood we came upon the battery. It was quite deserted; the parapet was all ploughed up by our shells; one gun lay upset; another had its truncheons knocked off and pools of blood in all directions. The dead had all been carried away. In a hollow road behind the battery we found some clothes soaked with blood and some accoutrements. The guns having been spiked, the commandant ordered brushwood, mats, and all other inflammable materials to be placed under the gun-carriages, which was then fired. The powder magazine was found outside the battery, in a very safe position in a hollow road; the powder and all the ammunition was thrown into the sea. While this was going on in the battery, Mr. LAYRLE, Chef d'Etat Major of Admiral JAURES, advanced by the right of the battery (keeping up a continual fire with Japanese hid in the bushes), to a village called Aidaga-mome, which was abandoned by the peasants and evidently used as dwelling-places for the troops belonging to the batteries.

In the middle of this town there was a large building a little way up the hill, half temple half palace, in which there was found a great deal of powder and ammunition. Having been fired by us, it blew up with a tremendous noise just as we were re-embarking.

On entering the battery I went at once to the principal building where I found a good quantity of Japanese armour and arms, but no one in the house. In looking about I found several Japanese translations of Dutch books on fortification and gunnery, one of which I have now in my possession, marked at the page where it treats of attacking ships that are carried away by the current.

Having thus accomplished our object—destroyed the battery and guns, and also burned the village, (the quarters of the soldiers), we re-embarked. I must not forget to mention that during the re-embarcation the frigate, the Tancrède and the boat's guns opened a heavy fire on some spot to the right of us, but hidden by the bushes. On going on board I learned that they had seen about 2,000 men, regular infantry, some men on horseback and even field artillery, coming down upon us from Shimonoseki by the road along the shore; they fired a few shell amongst them, which, exploding in their midst, did them considerable damage and they speedily retreated. We had in all three men wounded belonging the Chasseurs, two by musket balls and one by a stab of a dagger of a Japanese who was lying wounded on the ground, and stabbed him as he passed by.

It is difficult to arrive at any estimate of the casualties of the Japanese, but there was abundant testimony in the batteries that their loss there must have been very considerable: besides that which the shell practice, at a range of 3,000 yards did upon their advanced column.

I remain, Dear Sir, &c., &c.

F. BLEKMAN,

Interpreter attached to French Admiral.

It will be seen that the prince of Choshiu had two vessels in port and engaged in these attacks. Altogether the Japanese Government and daimios—had become possessed, up to this time, of five men-of-war, two of which were royal presents; and thirteen screw steamers, six paddle steamers, two barques, two brigs, and two schooners—giving a total of thirty vessels, for which they had paid $2,357,800.

CHAPTER XIX.

FIRE IN THE OSHIRO, YEDO, AND DESTRUCTION OF THE TYCOON'S PALACE.—THE TYCOON RETURNS TO YEDO BY SEA.—UNPLEASANT EPISODE AT KANASAWA.—CHARGE BROUGHT IN THE ENGLISH CONSULAR COURT AND DISMISSED.—CHANGES AMONG FOREIGN OFFICIALS.—THE YOKOHAMA CONTRIBUTION TO THE LANCASHIRE COTTON FAMINE RELIEF FUND.—ESTABLISHMENT OF BANKS IN YOKOHAMA.—THE CLOSE OF THE SATSUMA EPISODE—ADMIRAL KUPER TO PROCEED TO KAGOSHIMA.—THE GOROJIU NOW URGE THAT NO FURTHER DELAY SHOULD TAKE PLACE.—DEPARTURE OF SQUADRON.—THE BATTLE OF KAGOSHIMA.—THE PROCEEDINGS OF THE BRITISH ADMIRAL MISUNDERSTOOD BY SATSUMA.—EFFECT OF THE BATTLE ON THE CLAN.—PAYMENT OF ALL THE DEMANDS OF THE BRITISH GOVERNMENT, AND CLOSE OF THE RICHARDSON EPISODE.—LIEUT-COLONEL NEALE'S SERVICES REWARDED BY THE QUEEN, AND ACKNOWLEDGED BY THE PUBLIC.

ON the 18th July news reached Yokohama of a great conflagration within the O-shiro, Yedo, by which the Tycoon's palace, the yashikis of three daimios and a great many residences of hatamotos and shops of merchant's were consumed. Although this was spoken of as an additional outrage of the unruly, it may or may not have been so. It had its origin in an empty house at a distance from the palace; but the wind was very strong, and the flames spread with a rapidity such as can only be witnessed in Japan.

On the last day of July the Tycoon returned to Yedo, arriving by sea in the Jinkee accompanied by three other steamers.

And now the great climax was to be put on the Satsuma episode. Yet on the very eve of the departure of the British fleet for that purpose, another unpleasantness, fortunately unattended with any fatal result, occurred to engage popular interest.

Three gentlemen, Mr. G. R. DAVIES (representative of Messrs. W. R. ADAMSON & Co.), his brother and Mr. TATHAM, were, with other gentlemen, on an excursion to Kanasawa, a very favourite jaunt, just nine miles from Yokohama, and on the road to Kamakura and DAIBUTSZ', and were about to return on horseback to the settlement. Their companions were going back to Yokohama in a boat, and the equestrians were handing over their heavier habiliments for conveyance in the boat, traversing for this purpose a public jetty. As they were returning to the roadway, a two-sworded man using some rough, offensive language, one of the party quietly asked him "What's the matter?" when the man drew his sword and made a rush at him. The Englishmen essayed to pass, but the jetty was narrow, and some stumps of trees being in the way, the man commanded the position. Seeing the desperate nature of the case, one of them drew his revolver and pulled the trigger; but it missed fire. Mr. G. R. DAVIES, seeing the life of his brother in danger, then fired his revolver at the same time as a second shot from the first pistol was heard, and the man bolted. Directly the gentlemen arrived in Yokohama they laid a complaint before the British Consul. Subsequently the man, who, it appears, was slightly wounded, brought a charge against the Englishmen—but it was clearly shown that he was the assailant, and that they acted only in self-defence ; so the case was dismissed.

I ought before this to have noticed the changes in the various Consulates. I will mention them here, and then proceed.

Captain F. HOWARD VYSE had been removed to Hakodate, and Dr. C. A. WINCHESTER (on the 1st April) took up his post as Consul at Kanagawa.

Colonel NEALE, having regard to the increasing business of H. B. M.'s Consulate, appointed Mr. M. O. FLOWERS Acting Vice-Consul pending the approval of the Foreign Office.

Mr. MORRISON, who had been wounded in the first attack on the British legation, and had been home on leave, returned to his duties at Nagasaki.

Mr. VON BRANDT, (now H. I. G. M.'s Minister at Peking), who was formerly attached to the Prussian Embassy that concluded the treaties with China, Japan and Siam, in 1860-2, took charge of the Prussian Consulate ; and Mr. D. DE GRAEFF VON POLSBROEK, who had resided in Yokohama as Netherlands Consul, was appointed Acting Consul-general.

This was the time when England was suffering in her Lancashire factories by reason of the cotton famine, the effect of the civil war in America. Yokohama contributed $2,160 towards the relief fund, which was remitted home by H. B. M.'s Consul in a draft for £558 ; a sum, which considering the extent of the population, compared more than favourably with the contributions of all other ports in the far East.

On the 7th March the first announcement was made of the establishment of a foreign bank in Japan. In the

S.S. Leemin, Mr. CHARLES RICKERBY arrived as Acting Agent of a Branch of the Central Bank of Western India, a company having its head office in Bombay.

Early in the following month a gentleman was sent from Shanghai for the Chartered Mercantile Bank; and for some years the Branch in Yokohama was among the most flourishing that bank had. It is much to be regretted that times have so far changed that last year, (1879), the directors found it necessary to close this Branch.

And now, after many delays, occasioned by the appeals and excuses of the Government, Wednesday the 5th August was appointed as the day on which Admiral KUPER should proceed to Kagosima to have a settlement with Satsuma.

On the day previous to that, however, as a result of frequent meetings of the Tycoon, the Gorojiu and several important daimios, one of the Ministers came to Yokohama and had an interview with Colonel NEALE, and, no longer urging delay, on the contrary, proposed that the squadron should start at once, promising that, in consonance with Colonel NEALE's suggestion, a high official should be sent to accompany the expedition, on board of a Japanese steamer. This promise was not fulfilled. On the 6th of August the squadron, consisting of H. M.'s ships Euryalus (35), Pearl (21), Argus (6), Havoc (2), Coquette (4), Racehorse (4) and Perseus (17), having on board the British Chargé d'Affaires and most of the members of the English Legation, weighed anchor, and shaped a course for Kagosima, which port was entered on the 11th. The bay is described as forming a splendid harbour, surrounded by lofty and picturesque scenery; and by its defenders, at least, its defences were supposed to be impregnable. The city was said to contain 180,000 inhabitants, and its factories, warehouses and commercial buildings were on an extensive scale.

On the 12th the fleet moved up, and anchored opposite the town, in 20 fathom water, about 1,200 yards from the batteries, which extend along the whole of the town front—say about two miles from the extreme south.

At 6 a.m. several of SATSUMA's high officers went on board the flag-ship. It was observed by many that their demeanour was far from of that courteous and conciliatory kind we are accustomed to; indeed that there was an amount of swaggering and bullying about their manner. They said that SATSUMA was not now at Kagoshima, but at Kirishimi, a city 20 ri off. They received, however, the letter of demands, which was as follows:—

"*To His Highness* MATSUDAIRA SHIURI-NO-DAIBU, *the daimio prince of Satsuma, or in his absence to the regent or other High Officer for the time being administering the Government of the prince of Satsuma, Fiuga, Ohosumi, and the Loo Choo Islands.*

H. B. M.'s Legation in Japan,
August 12th 1863.

"Your Highness,

'It is well known to you that a barbarous murder of an unarmed and unoffending British subject and Merchant was perpetrated on the 14th of the month of September last, 21st day of 8th month of 2nd year of Bung-kew of Japanese reckoning, upon the Tokaido near Kanagawa, by persons attending the procession and surrounding the norimon of SHIMADZU SABURO, whom I am informed is the father of your Highness.

'It is equally known to you that a murderous assault was made at the same time by the same retinue, upon a lady and two other gentlemen, British subjects, by whom he was accompanied, the two gentlemen having been severely and seriously wounded, and the lady escaping by a miracle.

'The names of the British subjects here referred to are as follows:—

CHARLES LENOX RICHARDSON, murdered,

Mrs. BORRODAILE.
Mr. WILLIAM CLARKE, severely wounded.
Mr. WILLIAM MARSHALL, severely wounded.

'This event filled with great and just indignation the British Government and people, and excited the sympathy of, and produced a painful impression upon, all civilized countries.

'Impressed with friendly and considerate feelings towards the Government of the Tycoon, with whom the Queen of Great Britain, my august Sovereign, is in relations by treaty of peace and amity, I acted with proper consideration for the Tycoon's Government by leaving in its hands the legitimate means of speedily arresting and bringing to capital punishment the murderers from among SHIMADZU SABURO's retinue.

'This necessary forbearance on my part has been entirely approved of by my Government, and appreciated and acknowledged by the Government of the Tycoon.

'A different course proposed at the moment to be adopted in the excitement attending this barbarous outrage might have resulted in the capture and perhaps death by summary retribution of SHIMADZU SABURO himself.

'Ten months have now elapsed since the perpetration of this unprovoked outrage, during which period my Government has been duly informed by me of the circumstances attending it,* while the Tycoon's Ministers have held out to me from time to time assurances and hopes that the murderers would be given up by your Highness and sent to Yedo for trial and execution.

'But I have had occasion to report to my Government that, removed in your distant domain from the direct influence of the supreme Government, and shielded also by certain privileges and immunities which belong to daimios of this Empire, you had utterly disregarded all orders or decrees of the Japanese Government, calling upon you to afford justice by sending the real criminals to Yedo. They have not been arrested nor sent; and no redress has consequently been afforded by the Tycoon's Government, however desirous it may be of doing so.

'In the meanwhile I have received the explicit instructions of my own Government how to act in the matter.

'The Tycoon's Government may be impeded by the

laws of the country, and more especially by political embarrassments from enforcing its desires upon daimios of the Empire in regard to criminal acts committed by their adherents. But when British subjects are the victims of those acts, Japan as a Nation must through its Government pay a penalty and disavow the misdeeds of its subjects, to whatever rank they may belong.

'Under instructions from my Government I demanded from the Tycoon's Government an apology, and the payment of a considerable penalty for permitting the murderous attack made by your retainers on British subjects passing on a road open to them by treaty. Both these demands have been acceded to.

'But the British Government has also decided that those circumstances constitute no reason why the real delinquents and actual murderers should be shielded by your Highness, or by any means escape the condign punishment which they merit, and which they would be subjected to for great crimes such as they have committed, in all other parts of the world.

'It has therefore been determined by the Government, and I am instructed to demand of your Highness as follows:—

'First: The immediate trial and capital execution in the presence of one or more of Her Majesty's Naval Officers of the chief perpetrators of the murder of Mr. RICHARDSON, and of the murderous assault of the lady and gentlemen who accompanied him.

'Secondly: The payment of twenty-five thousand pounds (25,000) sterling to be distributed to the relations of the murdered man, and to those who escaped with their lives the swords of the assassins on that occasion.

'These demands are required by Her Majesty's Government to be acceded to by your Highness immediately upon their being made known to you. And upon your refusing, neglecting or evading to do so, the Admiral commanding the British Forces in these seas, will adopt such coercive measures, increasing in their severity, as he may deem expedient to obtain the required satisfaction and redress.

'The Commander of Her Majesty's Ship of War charged with the delivery of this letter is made acquainted with the specific demands which I have the honour to communicate to you in this letter, and according as they are accepted or refused he has received instructions either to carry out and witness their execution, within a period of days which will be named, or in the event of a refusal, to commence at once coercive operations, pending the arrival of additional forces.

'Your Highness is therefore earnestly requested seriously to consider the course you will adopt on the receipt of this communication, the terms of which it is not in my power to modify, alter or discuss.

'I avail myself of this occasion to offer to your Highness the assurance of my respect and consideration.

(Signed)   EDWD. ST. JOHN NEALE
H. B. M.'s Chargé d'Affaires
in Japan.'

" On the following day all was quiet on board the fleet, Colonel NEALE being busily engaged in diplomatic negociations: his recently tested and proved forbearance had to endure another trial; the yakunins were constantly running backwards and forwards, always bringing with them some evasive reply, and leaving without any definite conclusion.

" On the afternoon of the 13th, the allotted time having long expired, an officer arrived, who said he had brought a letter of reply, but since he had left the shore, a messenger had been sent after him to recall it 'as there was a mistake in it.' It could not be extracted from him, and he left, saying another should be sent immediately. None arrived, until at nine o'clock that night, when one was sent. It was as follows :—

' *Translation of a Despatch in Japanese from* KAWA KAMI, TAJIMA *Minister of* MATSUDAIRA SHIURI-NO-DAIBU, *prince of Satsuma, &c., &c., &c.*

'To COLONEL E. ST. JOHN NEALE,
H. B. M.'s Chargé d'Affaires,
&c., &c., &c.

' It is just that a man who has killed another should be arrested and punished by death, as there is nothing more sacred than human life. Although we should like to secure them (the murderers) as we have endeavored to do since last year, it is impossible for us to do so owing to the political differences at present existing between the daimios of Japan, some of whom even hide and protect such people. Besides, the murderers are not one but several persons, and therefore find easier means of escape.

'The journey to Yedo (undertaken by SHIMADZU SABURO) was not with the object of committing murder but to conciliate the two Courts of Yedo and Kioto; and you will therefore easily believe that our Master (SHIMADZU) could not have ordered it (the murder). Great offenders against the laws of their country (Japan) who escape, are liable to capital punishment. If therefore we can detect those in question, and after examination find them to be guilty, they shall be punished, and we will then inform the Commanders of your men-of-war at Nagasaki or at Yokohama, in order that they may come to witness their execution. You must therefore consent to the unavoidable delay, which is necessary to carry out these measures. If we were to execute criminals condemned for other offences, and told you that they were the offenders (above referred to), you would not be able to recognize them; and this would be deceiving you and not acting in accordance with the spirit of our ancestors.

'The (Provincial) Government of Japan are subordinate to the Yedo Government, and as you are well aware, are subservient to the orders received from it.

'We have heard something about a treaty having been negociated, in which a certain limit was assigned to foreigners to move about in; but we have not heard of any stipulation by which they are authorised to impede the passage of a road.

'Supposing this happened in your country travelling with a large number of retainers as we do here, would you not chastise (push out of the way and beat) any one thus disregarding and breaking the existing laws of the country? If this were neglected, princes could no longer travel. We repeat that we agree with you that the taking of human life is a very grave matter. On the other hand the insufficiency of the Yedo Government, who govern and direct everything, is shown by their neglecting to insert in the treaty (with foreigners) the laws of the country (in respect to these matters) which have existed from ancient times. You will therefore be able to judge yourself whether the Yedo Government (for not inserting these laws), or my master (for carrying them out) is to be blamed.

'To decide this important matter, a high Official of the Yedo Government, and one of our Government ought to discuss it before you, and find out who is in the right.

'After the above question has been judged and settled the money indemnity shall be arranged.

'We have not received from the Tycoon any orders or communication by steamer that your men-of-war were coming here. Such statements are probably made with the object of representing us in a bad light. If it were not this object you would certainly have them in writing from the Gorojiu, and if so we request you to let us see them. In consequence of such misstatements great misunderstandings are caused.

'All this surprises us much. Does it not surprise you?

'Our Government will act in everything according to the orders of the Yedo Government.

'This is our open-hearted reply to the different subjects mentioned in your Despatch.

29th of the 6th Month of the 3rd year of Bunkiu.
(13th August 1863.)
(Signed   Kawa Kami Tajima,
" *Shissé* " (*Minister*.)

" Still Colonel Neale was patient. On the 14th, about 9 o'clock, two officials went on board, saying they had been sent for a receipt for the reply. They then stated that when at Kioto, Hitotsu-bashi, (the Vice Tycoon) and two members of the Gorojiu) had most distinctly ordered Shimadzu Saburo that Satsuma was not to take any step in respect to the murder of the foreigner by his retainers, and that the Tycoon's Government would settle all the matter themselves. They pretended that it was believed that the whole matter was settled at Yedo; that they had heard nothing from Yedo on the subject, and could not at first imagine what could have brought the fleet to Satsuma : and asserted that according to Japanese law and custom Satsuma had no power to settle the affair himself, either by acceding to or refusing the demands of the British.

" All hope of any peaceful settlement being crushed, deceit and subterfuge appearing to be the only aim, Colonel Neale now stepped aside, and the Admiral took the matter in hand. On the afternoon of the 14th there was a general shifting of the disposition of the fleet, the greater part of which were placed under the island, out of range of the guns on the fort in the middle of the channel, say 1,700 yards on either side.

"The Euryalus, although shifting, still remained within range, as did also the Perseus. On the morning of the 15th the Pearl, Coquette, Argus, Havoc and Racehorse, proceeded up the bay and took as hostages three steamers there at anchor :—said to be the England, (purchased by Satsuma in 1861 for $120,000) the Sir George Grey (for $40,000) and the Contest which cost him $85,000 in May 1861.

"The weather which had been stormy during the whole morning now became worse, it was raining in torrents, and the wind blowing a hurricane round the bay. At ten o'clock all the above-named vessels, English and Japanese, had returned, and at twelve the men were piped to dinner, and nothing immediate expected, when suddenly the battery on the main land covering the Euryalus, and that on the island covering the Perseus, opened fire. The three hostage steamers were forthwith fired, (their crews having been previously sent ashore. One of the head officers on board was recognised as having belonged to the staff of the late ambassadors to Europe. He and another officer, at their own request, were taken on board the flag-ship). All the ships weighed and formed line of battle. The Perseus then engaged the battery that had been firing at her, in beautiful style, knocking her antagonist's guns over, one after the other, and when she had completed that, as though she had been only getting her hand in, she passed over to the other side and engaged the battery on the opposite shore. All the batteries (10) were then engaged by the ships at point blank range, at from 400 to 800 yards respectively, (the Euryalus being within 200 yards) commencing with the northernmost [No. 8] and passing down the entire line, to the Spit battery, No. 1 at slow speed. During all this time it was blowing tremendously. About dusk the town was fired in several parts by shells, and three of the forts were silenced. All the ships then returned to their anchorage, save the Racehorse, which had got ashore within 200 yards of the nearest battery, [No. 8] of which accident she availed herself to pour her metal into it until it was effectually silenced. The Argus was sent to bring her off, which she accomplished after about an hour's delay, during the whole of which time, she was under fire from one of the other batteries.

"This was Saturday the 15th, during the whole of which day it had been raining and blowing fiercely. The loss on this day to the squadron was eleven killed and thirty-nine wounded. Amongst the former, Capt. JOSLIN of the flag-ship, and Commander Edward WILMOTT (late of the Agamemnon), met a glorious death by the same shot. They were standing on the bridge of the flag-ship about the middle of the engagement, when a shot passed through the boat and struck them both instantaneously. The Admiral escaped death by the same shot in a wonderful manner, as he and the master were standing on the narrow bridge when the Captain fell.

"About 9 P.M. the whole of one side of the town was blazing.

"The following day (Sunday) the weather cleared up, the dead, (2 officers and 7 seamen), were consigned to the sailors' grave in Euryalus Bay at 11 o'clock, and the fleet stood out, passing close to the batteries on the island, which it engaged the whole way.

"The destruction accomplished by the fleet was enormous. The whole city was now one mass of ruins including the palace, the factories and the arsenal and warehouses: the batteries also had been seriously damaged, not one of those which had been engaged during the first day fired a shot on the second day as the fleet passed out.

"The three destroyed ships alone had cost Satsuma $245,000, upwards of half of which he has paid very recently. Several large junks also were destroyed. The Japanese stood well to their guns so long as the play was at long range, but seemed somewhat taken aback when the ships came to close quarters.

"Their metal appears to have consisted of 13 in. and 8 in. shells;—four 150 lbs., ten 80 lbs., and the remainder 32 lbs., &c.

"Considering the close firing, in some cases only 200 yards, the amount of damage done to the ships was

wonderfully small. The Euryalus suffered most, and her damage was principally in her boats and rigging.
The list of casualties was :—
Euryalus, 10 killed, 21 wounded.
Pearl, 7 wounded.
Argus, 6 wounded.
Coquette, 2 killed, 4 wounded.
Racehorse, 3 wounded.
Perseus, 1 killed, 9 wounded.

"Several most pressing invites were sent to Colonel NEALE to attend with as many of his suite as he chose, on shore, at a conference, *in a place prepared to receive them ;*—a courtesy declined with thanks.

"The following is a list of the mounts of the batteries.
No. 1.—8 32 lbs., 2 mortars, and between forts numbers 1 and 2-8 field-pieces.
No. 2.—3 32s. lbs., 2 mortars.
,, 3.— 3 mortars.
,, 4.—Not known.
,, 5.—2 8 inch guns, 9 32s. 3 field-pieces.
,, 6.—3 18s.
,, 7.—2 10 inch, 5 32s. 2 field pieces.
,, 8.—1 10 inch, 5 32s. 1 18, 1 field-piece.
,, 9.—4 18s.
,, 10.—3 18s.
,, 11.—2 8 in., 4 32s.
,, 12.—15 32s., (only 3 opened fired.")

The battle was fought during a heavy typhoon, which subsequently the Satsuma officials said they purposely took advantage of to bring off the engagement; believing that no ships could stand the combined forces of nature and science—the raging elements, and the deadly hail of the forts. There was a certain amount of ignorance displayed on their part; and perhaps Admiral KUPER ought to have taken some pains to explain the truth to them. All he wanted was to enforce the rendition of the murderers of Mr. RICHARDSON, that they might meet the justice due to them; and the payment of £25,000 as indemnity to the relatives of Mr. RICHARDSON and of his companions. The Admiral's object in taking the three ships was to hold them until these demands were satisfactorily complied with. The ships had cost the clan not less than $245,000—of which about the half had been paid quite recently; and it might have been reasonably supposed that they would gladly have redeemed the ships by the payment of the $100,000—the equivalent of the required amount, and have made the arrangements they afterward did make to continue to search for, and to hand over to justice when found, the actual culprits in that most cowardly attack.

But it does not appear that they understood this. They saw their ships taken possession of, and doubtless felt the most natural indignation at such a proceeding on the part of the English.. They opened upon the fleet with shot and shell, and—the rest is told above. The damage suffered by SATSUMA was—the destruction of the town—very much to be regretted, though most of the populace had fled in anticipation of the fight; the demolition of several batteries; the consumption by fire of the Arsenal and five large Loochoo junks, the ruin of a fine temple (erroneously thought at the time to be the palace of the prince), and the burning of the three ships. It was a terrible retribution; but as, in order to secure the safety of her Majesty's ships, not from the effects of the guns in the forts but from the severity of the weather, the British Admiral, considering he had administered punishment enough, withdrew to a safe anchorage, the Satsuma people professed to believe that they had gained the victory. When, however, a few months afterwards, they sent to Yedo certain officials to pay the money and to make the written engagement which, as I have related, had they done at the time, all the loss, all the bloodshed, would have been avoided, they honestly admitted that the lesson they learnt on this occasion had the effect of showing them how mistaken they had been as to the ability of Japan to cope with western nations; and thenceforward they became more than ever desirous of cultivating European arts and sciences, with a view to placing Japan really on a platform with other nationalities.

Although anticipating the order of events, I may as well finish this strange eventful story. On the 6th November, the British Chargé d'Affaires was waited upon by the Japanese officials, to announce that envoys had arrived in Yedo from the prince of Satsuma, who desired audience of his Excellency on matters of importance. The 9th November was named by Colonel NEALE for the interview, and the appointment was duly kept. Several of the daimio's high officials, accompanied by some of the officers of the Government arrived at the Legation at 1.30 P.M., and the interview lasted until nearly 5 o'clock.

"The envoys commenced by representing to Colonel NEALE that SATSUMA felt much that he had been harshly dealt with in the seizure and destruction of his steamers at Kagoshima without due notice of the intention of the Admiral to destroy them. This opened the matter, and Colonel NEALE replied by passing in review the whole of the Kagoshima affair; pointing out that the British squadron had proceeded there for the purpose of negociating upon the matter of satisfaction required for the murder of Mr. RICHARDSON and the attack upon his companions; that during the long delay that had elapsed before sending any reply the squadron had had occasion to shift its anchorage,—that the reply, when it did arrive, was of a character which rendered some pledge or hostage necessary during further negociations; that with this view and for this purpose the steamers had been taken possession of, and not with any intention of either destroying them or of taking them away, but that the prince's people had themselves commenced the hostilities by firing upon the British ships, and that therefore the destrúction of the steamers was a consequence of their own act at the time.

"It seems that the prince's envoys quite appreciated, after the explanation given, the patience and moderation exercised by the British Minister and Admiral on the occasion.

"It was then seen that this could only be a preliminary interview, and the ground being thus partially cleared the envoys left, asking for an appointment for another occasion, which was given for the following Saturday.

"This day Colonel NEALE again gave audience to the envoys; but after several hours patient sitting, no definite conclusion was arrived at, and Colonel NEALE consented to one more adjournment. This conference lasted from shortly after mid-day to nearly six o'clock P.M.

"Terms of arrangement were at last definitely agreed upon, of a nature which the British Chargé d'Affaires considered were all he could have anticipated, and which were of an entirely satisfactory character.

"These were made and distinctly understood in the presence of the Japanese high Government officials who accompanied the Envoys.

"A vast number of propositions had however to be first encountered, combatted and declined: propositions, some for delay, some for an acknowledgement of wrong-doing in the seizure of the steamers, and others of an equally inadmissable character; but they were ultimately reduced into an entirely satisfactory compass."

The terms were as satisfactory as could have been expected. The $100,000 were paid, and the following letters passed.

The Agents of the Prince of Satsuma
to Lieutenant-Colonel NEALE.

"*Yokohama, December 11th, 1863.*.

"The money demanded by the British Government having been paid by the officers of SHIMADZU AWAJI-NO-KAMI, a branch of the family of Satsuma, we hereby promise as follows:—

"The persons who last autumn, in the eighth month, killed and wounded your countrymen at Namamugi, on the Tokaido, have escaped from that place, and although we have diligently searched for them, their place of abode has not been found out.

"And as also some time has passed, it is not possible to state with certainty whether they are still alive, but we will use every diligence in searching for them, and as soon as arrested punish the same with death in the presence of your country's officers.

"As a promise for the future we sign this.

(Signed) "Shikeno Konoshô,
"*Diplomatic Agent of the Prince of Satsuma.*
"Iwashita Saiemon,
"*Acting Minister of Satsuma.*

"Countersigned as witnesses to the above promise.

(Signed) "Ukai Taichi,
"*Officer of Department for Foreign Affairs of Tycoon's Government.*
"Saitô Kingo,
"*Assistant Ometsky.*"

[Memorandum.]

"British Legation in Japan,
December 11th, 1863.

"The basis of good will and amity being established by the settlement of the demands preferred on the Prince of Satsuma; and the Prince of Satsuma having preferred to the undersigned, her Majesty's Chargé d'Affaires, a request in presence of Officers of the Tycoon, and as a token of friendly feeling re-established, that he would facilitate the desire of the Prince of Satsuma to purchase a ship of war in England, her Britannic Majesty's Chargé d'Affaires does hereby engage to represent such request when formally and specifically preferred to her Majesty's Government, provided that at the period when such request is made or in course of examination, the relations of the Tycoon's Government with Great Britain in general, and the proceedings and disposition of the Prince of Satsuma in particular, are not inimical or directed against the rights acquired by treaties now existing between the Tycoon of Japan, Great Britain, and other friendly States.

"Given at Yokohama, this 11th day of Dec., 1863.

(Signed) "Edwd. St. John Neale,
"*Her Majesty's Chargé d'Affaires.*"

CONCLUSION OF THE RICHARDSON EPISODE.

*The Japanese Ministers for Foreign Affairs
to Lieutenant-Colonel* NEALE.

"*Yedo, December 13th, 1863.*
"We beg to make the following communication to your Excellency.

"With respect to the murder which was committed last year upon a British merchant at Namamugi, on the Tokaido, the subjects of MATSUDAIRA SHIURI-NO-DAIBU and SHIMADZU AWAJI-NO-KAMI, of the family of Satsuma, have lately had an interview with you, and the negotiation was of a peaceful nature, thus affording a proof that the subjects of SHIURI-NO-DAIBU (Satsuma) will search for and punish the murderer, as by their written engagement. The indemnity money was moreover handed over by the subjects of AWAJI-NO-KAMI of the family of Satsuma, and also as a proof of peace, the engagement entered into by you to facilitate the purchase of a man-of-war in terms of the writing was given, and everything ended satisfactorily, which we have fully understood from the communication received from our Government officers who were present.

"It gives us great pleasure, as it is a sign of the continuance of a lasting friendship between the two countries. With respect and consideration.

"The 3rd day of the 11th month of the 3rd year of Bunkiu (December 13th, 1863).

(Signed) "MIDZUNO IDZUMI-NO-KAMI.
,, "ITAKURA SUWÔ-NO-KAMI.
,, "ARIMA TÔTÔMI-NO-KAMI."

And so ended this most memorable and most melancholy episode in the history of foreign relations with Japan. Time has revealed many facts in connection with those early experiences, which have opened the eyes both of Japanese and foreigners. But time, though it may cast a doubt on certain strongly entertained opinions, can never remove the strong conviction that poor Mr. RICHARDSON, by whomsoever originally attacked, was cruelly despatched finally in the most cold-blooded manner; and that, if SHIMADZU SABURO did not actually give the original order for the assault, he, at least withheld the word, which, emanating from him, would have stopped it. It is a sad, sad story; and every sincere well-wisher of Japan, of whom I emphatically am one, must regret it probably more deeply than any other event that has to be chronicled in this narrative.

I have only to add that H. B. M.'s Government most strongly approved of Colonel NEALE's conduct throughout. The Queen conferred upon him the Companionship of the Bath, and acknowledged approvingly the services of the gentlemen of the legation who had been useful as interpreters at Kagoshima. The public also came to see and acknowledge that Colonel NEALE had acted prudently and well throughout; and he had the good sense to show no chagrin at the treatment he had received at the hands of the community, or at the hard things that had been said of him in the press. Of course the squadron under Admiral KUPER obtained the ministerial approval that was so justly their due; although an attempt was made in Parliament to obtain a vote of censure for the destruction of the town of Kagosima.

CHAPTER XX.

CHANGE OF THEME.—"OUT OF BOUNDS."—TREATY LIMITS. —OCCASIONAL TRANSGRESSIONS.—A TRIP ACROSS THE GULF OF YEDO IN SEARCH OF SCENERY AND GAME.—FIRST EFFECT ON THE NATIVES ON SEEING FOREIGNERS.—DIFFICULTIES.— SURMOUNTED.—THE KIND HEARTS OF THE PEOPLE EASILY WON.—VISIT OF OFFICIALS.—THE YAKUNINS MELTED.—SUBSEQUENT CIVILITY AND ATTENTION.—RETURN TO SETTLEMENT.

I HAVE dwelt so long on themes of a saddening character, (and I have still to continue to harp on the same string), that it will be a relief to me, and probably to my readers also, if, before proceeding with my history proper, I devote a short chapter to an incident of a different nature—more directly personal it is true, but probably allowable, as describing one feature of life in Japan, in those days.

Treaty limits used of old to be a kind of bugbear to foreigners in Yokohama, all of whom wished, but few of whom dared, to pass beyond the phantom line around the settlement, the radius of which was just 10 ri— 43,200 yards, or a little over twenty four miles and a half—except in the direction of Yedo, where they were pulled up at the distance of about five ri by the river

Rokugo, or, as it was more commonly called, Logo. Those who had the temerity to go beyond the boundary, did so with the fear of being stopped by every man they met, and sent back to the place whence they came; and it was something to talk about as a kind of feat of daring, deserving of being described to all one's friends as something very heroic and wonderful.

The following account of such an excursion was given me by one of the parties concerned. I introduce it to show the kind nature of the people, away from the influence of excited "patriots."

"We went in an open boat across the gulf of Yedo, and landed at a village the name of which has long slipped my memory—in the province of Boshiu. There were three of us—two being keen sportsmen expecting to find any quantity of game. The third was anxious to get to a certain hill, from which he had been told he could look down on such a prospect as our readers may imagine from the name "The ninety nine valleys." It had been mentioned as a spot beautiful beyond compare; so, brim-full of curiosity, we went for it. Unfortunately— ''twas ever thus since childhood's hour'—we were doomed to disappointment, not having landed anywhere near the desired spot, and none of the people to whom we addressed ourselves knowing anything about it—very few indeed understanding our vile Yokohama jargon, which rendered us, as we thought, objects of surprise to the natives, and really of contempt to ourselves. At first, when our boat reached the shore, all the natives seemed disinclined to hold any converse with us. They were evidently frightened, though their curiosity prevented their running away. We asked them in the best Japanese we could muster between the three of us, to direct us to a tea-house, but not one would answer; and had it not been for a little dirty-faced scamp who had the

boldness to touch one of the guns without being chid for
his impertinence, and who was thereby emboldened to
stand right opposite to the owner of the weapon and
grin from ear to ear, it is likely enough we should have
had some difficulty in breaking the ice. As it was, however, this urchin next allowed his curiosity to get the
better of his good manners to such an extent as to feel
the texture of a waterproof cape one of our party had
hanging over his arm, when the bearer threw it over the
lad's shoulder and held out his valise for him to carry,
telling him to lead the way to the best house in the
village, and making him understand that he should receive payment for his services. This was sufficient. The
lad trotted along, followed by us and by all those who
had assembled at the unwonted sight of three foreigners
on soil no foreigner's foot had ever before trodden.

But now came the difficulty as to where he was to lead
us. He didn't like the responsibility of taking us to any
one's house; and as I now write I wonder he didn't at
once lead us to the chief man of the village. After some
little walking, as we passed a house that seemed cleaner
than, and which was at some distance from, the rest—
we halted and went up to the door. Immediately all the
inmates ran to the back rooms, one old lady alone stay-
ing to close the sliding doors—but not being able to accomplish this before we reached the dwelling, she left her
task half-done, and ran in too.

It was now very nearly sundown; and we knew that
our night's lodging under a roof depended upon our making a favorable impression. We therefore told the boy
to put down his burden, and gave him a tip which not
only surprised him, but made him for the nonce the most
popular lad, the most desirable companion, in the whole
village. We smiled as we saw all the brats of the place
congregate about him, just like European children, the

moment he had a silver boo of his own. He laughed aloud with glee—and came half a dozen times to kow-tow and thank us; and more than that, he seemed to keep watch for us, that he might do far more should we require him. All the people who saw him receive his boo at once opened their hearts to us, and we were no longer objects of fear, but of something like wonder and admiration. Likely enough, for it is more than probable that so vast a reward as a whole boo in cash—then equal to nearly two shillings—had never been given for such a small amount of work in the village before.

But this which made us at once so popular outside of the house was not seen by the inmates; who had, as we have said, all run and hidden themselves on our approach. The last who beat a retreat, the old woman —not having been able to close the sliding doors, we put our baggage down just inside, and sat down to consult. It was evident that it would be unwise to attempt to return that night; and indeed, we did not feel at all disposed to give up the anticipated sporting pleasures we had come for, even though it appeared that we had entirely missed the scenic goal we had looked forward to. We therefore decided that we must put on a bold front, and whilst shewing the people that we perfectly understood good manners, and that we would not willingly put them about, still we must have shelter of some sort, and that in the absence of any tea-house, some of them must supply it. After therefore calling repeatedly for the inmates of the house, and none appearing, we quietly unpacked a case of provender and commenced refreshing the inner man. This must have been too much for the curiosity of the people of the house to resist—as, first the old woman came and looked on at a distance, and then some of the young fry stood by her, but not a word could we get from any of them; until at last a middle-aged woman who turned out to be the daughter of the old lady and the mother of the others, came in, and approaching us quite naturally, without any timidity, and dropping on her knees and saluting us in the ordinary Japanese way by bending her head to the earth, told us that she and her husband had been absent; but, that having heard of our arrival she had hastened home, and that he would quickly follow her. We told her that we desired nothing but shelter for ourselves and our servant—a frightened Yokohama lad, who seemed afraid to open his mouth, lest he should be seized by the yakunins for accompanying us to a place we had no business to visit. She begged us not to think her inhospitable, but to wait with patience until her husband came home, who would doubtless see that all was right. He was longer than we anticipated, but that was just as well—for it gave us time to ingratiate ourselves thoroughly with the family. It was quite dark by the time we had finished our repast, and the house being shut up, we set to work to make ourselves as agreeable as we could. One of us was an adept at twisting paper into all sorts of shapes—a favorite amusement among the Japanese themselves—but he could do twice as much as any of them could, and all got close to him to watch the twistings develope into some form or other, which invariably sent them into shouts of delight, and when the "gudeman cam' hame at e'en," he, who saw foreigners as he told us for the first time, found them sitting on the mats as happy with his household as if they had been familiar all their days.

When told that we required shelter for the night, he said that it was absolutely impossible. He did not like to refuse us, but he dare not allow us to stay under his roof—as the yakunins would be sure to hear of it and he would get into severe trouble.

Here was a pretty position for us. It was by this time black dark—one of those nights of impenetrable darkness, when nothing whatever can be seen; darkness that is not less obscure even when the eye becomes accustomed to it. What could we do? We told him, that we must decline to leave the premises. He might give us an an outhouse if he liked, if there were such a thing on the compound, but that outside of the enclosure we positively would not go, and that we were determined to have a roof over us, even if the sides were open. Seeing our determination he did not make any further resistance; but he must have sent to the head village yakunin, for after a long time—it must have been nearly 10 o'clock—two officials arrived, and entering, began to speak in a somewhat bullying voice. Candour compels us to say, that we all felt very uneasy, and two of us afterwards admitted that they made sure they were in for being tied up, and sent ignominiously back to Yokohama the next day. Fortunately the third, who was probably as apprehensive as the others, had a remarkably cool bearing at all times; and this stood us in stead now. We had brought among our provisions a few bottles of beer, a bottle of a brandy, and two bottles of sparkling Moselle—the latter with the knowledge of the fondness of the Japanese for sparkling wines—and for the very purpose of propitiating them if necessary. Whilst then the officers were excitedly addressing us and telling us we must accompany them, our cool companion quietly left us, and raising the lid of the case in which our drinkables were, exposed them to view, and taking out one of the bottles of Moselle, asked for a cup—there are no glasses in a Japanese farmer's house—and setting free the cork, sat down with some of the family who, tired of the altercation, had resumed their places on the mats. Pouring out cupfull after cupfull, he gave one to each.

(Japanese saké cups are very small, none holding much more than a liqueur glass; so that the liquor went a long way.) When the yakunins heard the cork and saw that something pleasant was going on, they turned from the other two, and approached the group on the mats. Common civility induced our friend to offer them a taste of the foreign saké, and common love of liquor, (which the Japanese go in for quite as heavily as Europeans, if not even more so), induced the officers to accept the proffered cup, which so wrought upon them that every difficulty melted away. The yakunins sat down and talked and laughed with us; paterfamilias made us welcome, and we managed to make the bottle of Moselle and a little brandy toddy occupy the male folk—(the women and bairns went to bed shortly after the men sat down together)—until the wee sma' hours ayont the twal'. When at last the time of separation came, the host showed us that a comfortable f'tong or sleeping dress (a kind of large dressing gown heavily padded with wool) had been laid down for each of us on the clean mats; and the yakunins told us that we need be under no apprehension of attack as they would take care that the house should be guarded. Whether it was so, we are not aware, but certainly we hadn't a thought of danger. In the morning, we were up with the dawn; but early as we were, all the family were before us, and preparations were being made for breakfast, which at their invitation we shared with them. As we had told overnight that the object of our visit was to get some sport, the farmer said there was plenty to be had, and sent two of the farm servants to shew us where pheasants most abounded. He also made us promise to return in the evening and again avail of his house as our resting place, adding that we were welcome as long as we found it agreeable.

The men who went with us took us to a most unpromising country for anything like game—and feeling somewhat disappointed we turned back, intending to try a bit of cover we had seen a little off the road, when one of the yakunins of the previous evening came running up, greeting us as if we were old friends, and, telling us we had overshot the mark, took us to the very ground we had spotted. He stayed with us the whole day—and we bagged a fair amount of birds; which, by the way, were carried for us by the little urchin who had carried the valise and macintosh on our arrival, and who we found waiting outside the door when we rose in the morning. We left the next morning with letters for the head men of the villages we were likely to pass on our way to the spot from which we were to see the ninety-nine valleys, which the yakunins and our host could of course tell us all about. But unfortunately the weather came on wet, and made the walking so slippery and toilsome, that we deferred that jaunt for another occasion, and that has never since turned up. This was in the old Tycoon's days, when, had we not fallen into good hands we certainly should have been sent back and hauled over the coals; but as it is, we look back upon it as one of the most pleasant experiences of the kindness and real hospitality of the Japanese that we ever received. Now-a-days, foreigners obtain passports, and go almost anywhere they like, and so long as they behave themselves they are not interfered with; but in those days there was some danger—for no one knew who were friends and who were foes of foreigners, and the orders respecting them were very stringent. The yakunins of the village ought to have sent us back, and I can hardly realize now that any could then be found to take such a responsibility on themselves as they did. However, we all got safely back, delighted with all we had seen, the little sport we had enjoyed, and the good people we had met.

CHAPTER XXI.

WHAT IS JAPAN LIKE?—ALL WHO VISITED IT CHARMED WITH IT.—THE GOVERNMENT AND PRINCES CONDEMNED BUT THE COUNTRY AND PEOPLE UNIVERSALLY APPROVED OF.—PREPARATIONS MADE BY GOVERNMENT FOR THE RECEPTION OF FOREIGNERS AT OPENING OF THE PORT, A PROOF OF THE INTENTION TO ACT UP TO TREATY ENGAGEMENTS.—THE TYCOON'S POWER LIMITED AS AGAINST THE MOST POWERFUL DAIMIOS.—THE COURT NOBLES JOIN THE DISAFFECTED DAIMIOS.—THEIR INFLUENCE WITH THE MIKADO.—THE YOUTH OF THE TYCOON PREVENTS VIGOUROUS ACTION.—ENDEAVOUR TO OBEY THE MIKADO TO THE LETTER ONLY.—OFFICIAL INTERFERENCE TO BUSINESS BETWEEN JAPANESE AND FOREIGNERS.—SILK TO YOKOHAMA RESTRICTED IN QUANTITY.—SILKWORM EGGS SALE FORBIDDEN.—GENERAL PUBLIC MEETING ON THE SUBJECT.—LETTER TO THE CONSULS.—STEPS TAKEN BY THE CONSULAR BOARD, AND THE REPLY FROM THE CONSULS TO THE MERCHANTS.

WHAT like a country is Japan? must have been a question very frequently put to those whom circumstances had directed, or enabled, to visit this country in those days. For myself, I well remember the kind of hero I considered a gentleman to be, who, on our becoming acquainted at the George Hotel, Ballarat, Victoria, told me he had just come from thence. The newspapers had, during the preceding three years, for this was in 1862, been frequently doling out intelligence from the newly-opened country, both as to its present doings and past history. At the time I had no more idea of visiting it, than I had of fraternising with the man in the moon. Nothing that my new friend told me imparted to me any special desire to go there; for, at the time my thoughts were turned in a totally different direction. But he was so charmed with his visit, that he spoke of the country and the people with a kind of enthusiasm that gave an additional interest to all he had to tell.

Yet he was here when many of these troubles that I have described were going on. I do not remember that he mentioned any of them. His one idea seemed to be that there was no country like Japan, no people like the Japanese. He told of the feudal customs; of the daimios and their retainers; of the open-hearted nature of the people. He described many of the peculiarities that came especially under the notice of the foreign sojourners in Yokohama; the system of ward surveillance; the hi-no-ban, or native night watch: the fire brigade with its extraordinary features; the wrestlers; the theatres; the tea-houses; the excursions. He did not omit the two-sworded race. And yet he had nothing to say of the danger to which life was exposed; nor of anything else that would have sobered the rose-tint with which his reminiscences of Japan were coloured.

And so, when circumstances directed my footsteps hither, I found it amongst at least the majority of the residents.

The sad episode, a narrative of which I have brought

to a conclusion, had just been closed; the settlement with Satsuma brought to a satisfactory climax; when I arrived on a visit, without an idea of becoming a permanent resident.

I found plenty of trouble on hand, between the foreigners, the native Government, and the native chiefs. No one had a word of apology for the former of the two last-named; and every one a deal of condemnation for the latter; and yet none had anything but good to say of the country and people at large.

Merchants complained, and that loudly and constantly, of the obstructions placed in the way of business by the Japanese officials, as well as of the absolute impossibility of making the Japanese merchants adhere strictly to the terms of their contracts; and yet they said that since they were doomed to live away from home, it was a good providence that had cast their lot in Japan. As to my own experience, which evidently was not exceptional but the reverse, I admit that in spite of all that I daily heard—of ronins; of the hatred for foreigners; of the hindrances to commerce; of the dangers surrounding us; and of all the disagreeables we were subject to—I was simply charmed, fascinated, and content to believe that life was all that it appeared to be on the surface.

Alas! while such were the feelings operating with the most of us, amid all those scenes that seemed to picture the primeval innocence of Eden, what deeds of darkness —what Cain-like treachery—were enacted! But there is time enough to tell of those deeds. In this chapter let me speak on other points.

In the early chapters of this narrative, it has been told how great were the preparations for the arrival of foreign merchants in anticipation of the opening of the ports.

To my mind this was always a proof that the Tycoon's

Government intended honestly to act up to all its engagements with us. No one surely could foresee such a series of casualties as arose from the fact of their making treaties with us; and increased in consequence of their steadfastly doing all in their power to be loyal to their engagements.

But how rugged was the path they cut out for themselves the preceding chapters must have revealed. The powers of the Shogunate, which had never before been questioned, were more than questioned now. Boldly men stood forward, indifferent to consequences, and asserted their acts to be illegal. And although they who did so, were obliged deferentially to submit to the punishment awarded to them, yet the Shoguns hesitated to take the lives of the greatest of them, for they felt that there was a line beyond which even they dare not go. Such men as YORITOMO, the first and third ASHIKAGA, IYEYAS' and IYEMITZ', amongst Shoguns, and NOBUNAGA and HIDEYOSHI (TAIKO-SAMA) amongst those who exercised the powers, without receiving the title, of Shogun, would probably have made short work of any who should so openly oppose them; but they were resolute men, whose position had been won by the sword; and whose authority must be maintained by it. Tycoons since 1853 were boys without the requisite personal experience, ambition or energy and those who acted for them had not the daring necessary to take extreme measures against such men as MITO, SATSUMA and CHOSHIU.

But there was another element opposed to them. Hitherto the kugés or nobles of the Mikado's Court, though holding rank in the country superior to that of the Shogun himself (until invested with special rank by the Mikado)—but without an atom of power—had kept quiescent in all affairs of state. The opening of the ports aroused them. They willingly allied themselves with the discontented daimios, and, having the car of the Mikado, easily influenced him in favour of those who made their cause the resuscitation of his ancient authority. The Tycoon was all-powerful so long as he had the Mikado on his side. With him arrayed with his enemies against him, he was impotent. Now, when he saw that the Mikado was opposed to him, his mind had to be made up. He must either obey the imperial orders; or he must buckle on his armour, boldly summon his faithful daimios, hatamotos, and their attendant hosts, and take the field, as some of his predecessors had done. He would have had to tread the bloody path over which YORITOMO strode to power; to have met his foes as YORITSUNE did when GOTOBA-NO-IN, the 82nd emperor, collected an army and sent it against him to destroy him, and recover the lost rule; or to boldly set the Mikadonic word at defiance, and like ASHIKAGA TAKA-UJI, proclaim his own sovereignty; drive before him all who might be sent against him; and, if necessary, proclaim another emperor.

But such things could not be expected of mere youths; and there were none left to act thus vigorously on their behalf. All that could be done now was, to receive the imperial commands; to obey where obedience was practicable; and passively to let the rest go by default.

I have described how they strove to obey the orders received from Kioto *to the letter*, by sending in the communication signed by OGASAWARA, announcing their desire to close the ports. We shall presently see that *the spirit* they never had any intention of acting up to.

But in one respect they more than once did appear anxious to yield obedience negatively if not positively. Their orders were to drive out foreigners. That they could not do. The treaties also provided that the Government should exercise no official interference in dealings between native and foreign merchants. But the treaties did not say that they should not put any restrictions they liked on the sending merchandise to the open ports; nor make any provision facilitating the shipment of goods purchased of native merchants.

Accordingly we find them using both these kinds of active and passive hindrances to business; doubtless with the hope of starving us out. The quantity of silk sent to Yokohama was greatly restricted; the sale of silkworm's eggs to foreigners strictly forbidden; and the inconvenience arising to merchants from the insufficient supply of cargo-boats and other causes was so great that a General Public Meeting of all the residents was held at the residence of Mr. S. MAINE, (representative of Messrs. FLETCHER & Co.), "for the purpose of considering a letter to the Consuls on sundry matters of loss and inconvenience now suffered by the community at the hands of the Japanese Government, upon which remonstrance has long been called for and frequently made in vain."

The following is the letter that was sent to the Consuls :—

Yokohama, 21st August, 1863.

GENTLEMEN,

We the undersigned, members of the Foreign Community of Yokohama, considering the present an opportune moment for again bringing before your notice grievances that have been repeatedly and in vain urged upon the notice of the Japanese Authorities, beg to recall your attention to the following points in which we consider that we have a right to look for improvement.

One of the principal causes of complaint, which has been prominently brought forward on several occasions, is the general insufficiency of the Custom House system, especially as regards cargo-boats and coolies, which are a Government monopoly, and the mal-administration of which is a constant and unnecessary impediment to trade.

The cargo-boats are inadequate in number, and defective in construction and capacity, for the requirements of the increasing trade of Yokohama. They are open and slightly built, and altogether their construction is such that goods cannot be entrusted to them with safety except in fair weather only.

This grievance has lately become so pressing, and an improvement is now so absolutely necessary, that it is seriously contemplated by the community to form among themselves a cargo-boat Company, under Foreign superintendence, that, self-supporting, shall carry out the necessary objects, which under the present system cannot be obtained. The community would therefore be glad to know if such a scheme would meet your cordial cooperation and assistance, or if you would impress upon the Japanese Government the absolute necessity of changing the present system and of introducing one similar to that in contemplation by the community. If the Japanese Government is willing to undertake the proper management of a cargo-boat system, the community will lay before you the plans and estimates they have already provided themselves with for that purpose.

Another serious cause of complaint and by no means inferior to the foregoing, is the fact that the community cannot employ coolies, except from, or with the permission of, the coolie-masters who form part of the Customhouse establishment. It has frequently happened that coolies have been applied for and not obtained, and this at a time when there were large numbers of coolies who would have been glad to have obtained employment if they had dared to do so without being told off for such a duty by the Custom House. As an instance of this monopoly of coolies, the community would beg to bring to your notice, that on the moment of the payment of the indemnity to the English Government, a double rate of hire was demanded and obtained by the coolie masters, without the participation by the coolies themselves in such an increased rate. The increased rate continues to the present moment, notwithstanding the promise made by the Governor of Kanagawa, to the Consuls, that this abuse should be discontinued.

The community would also beg to call your attention to the non-compliance on the part of the Japanese, of their obligations with respect to land-renters, accepted by the native authorities at the time of the signature of the title-deeds.

One of strong reasons urged for fixing so exorbitant a ground-rent, was that the Japanese Government had pledged itself to keep the streets and drains in thorough repair, and to form a bund in front of the Settlement. The latter, after the expiration of a long period, has been completed; but now that it is completed they have commenced to build outside it; a precedent that if not protested against might be carried out to any extent all along the Bund.

It is stated that the projected buildings on the Bund are intended for Bonded warehouses. If such is the case their position is ill-suited and their size is far too small for the purpose intended. But we would strongly urge upon you the fact, that the system of bonded warehouses would not meet the requirements of a commercial community in the same way as a system of drawbacks, similar to that organised, and for so long a time in successful operation, in China.

With regard to the promise of keeping the streets and drains in thorough repair, it is notorious to every one that up to the present moment there has been no system of drainage whatsoever. Within the last few days, some open gutters, probably intended to supply the place of drains, have been commenced: but as these are in no way adapted for carrying away the refuse of the settlement, the community would respectfully suggest that their construction should be discontinued until a competent Engineer could be obtained from China for the purpose of carrying out a proper system. The expenses of providing such an engineer would be willingly undertaken by the community.

Before concluding we would beg to call your attention to a most glaring instance of obstruction to trade. A restriction has been placed on the free introduction of Silk to Yokohama. Not more than fifty piculs per diem are allowed to be brought in to this market. This has already begun to tell upon the small native merchants, who are loud in their complaints, and who declare that it will ere long be the cause of their ruin.

We would strongly urge upon you the necessity of

sifting this matter to the bottom, and of supplying an immediate remedy, if possible; especially as we are assured by the Japanese merchants themselves, that any protest on the part of the Consuls would be followed by immediate reparation.

We have the honor to be, Gentlemen,
Your most obedient humble Servants,
[Signed by the greater part of the Foreign Community.]
[Addressed to all the Consuls.]

Immediate steps were taken by the Board of Consuls to bring the subject under the notice of the diplomatic representatives, and a month later H. B. M.'s Consul sent the following reply as regards the silk supply:—

"The undersigned was this day informed by the Governor of Kanagawa, that instructions have been received from Yedo, to the effect that measures had been taken, to render the conveyance of silk to this settlement from to-morrow and the day following, as unrestricted as it was prior to the supposed restriction.

"The undersigned, who was further authorised by the Governor to communicate the above to the British mercantile community, hopes the event may fulfil the assurance.

(Signed)   CHARLES A. WINCHESTER.
H. B. M.'s Consul.
24th September, 1863.

CHAPTER XXII.

MEETINGS OF THE GREAT DAIMIOS IN YEDO AND KIOTO.—REPORT OF ONE OF THEM.—RUMOUR OF THE CONFINEMENT OF THE TYCOON.—OGASAWARA'S EXPEDITION TO RELEASE HIM.—OGASAWARA ADVANCES TO FUSHIMI, BUT FINDING THE RUMOUR TO BE UNTRUE, RETURNS TO OSAKA.—DISMISSED FROM THE GOROJIU, AND ORDERED TO BE CONFINED IN THE TYCOON'S CASTLE.—CORRESPONDENCE BETWEEN THE TYCOON'S GOVERNMENT AND THE FOREIGN REPRESENTATIVES.—THE FRENCH MINISTER'S SUGGESTIONS.—DISTRESSING NEWS FROM OSAKA OF THE ASSASSINATION OF MERCHANTS.—NOTICES POSTED IN KIOTO AND OSAKA FORBIDDING MERCHANTS TO DO BUSINESS WITH FOREIGNERS.—LETTER FROM THE MINISTERS OF FOREIGN AFFAIRS TO DR. WINCHESTER.—AMUSEMENTS.—BAD NEWS FROM NAGASAKI.—MURDER OF LIEUT. CAMUS.—GOROJIU EXPRESSES ITS REGRET TO THE FRENCH MINISTER.—OPENING OF THE ENGLISH EPISCOPAL CHURCH.—ANOTHER BRANCH BANK ESTABLISHED.—EFFECTS OF THE PRESENCE OF THE ALLIED SQUADRON.—FOREIGN SAILORS AND THE JAPANESE.

I HAVE mentioned the meetings of the great daimios that took place in Yedo and Kioto. It is not certain how these were conducted; but the following is from a report of one of them:—

"At the principal of these meetings, the Gosanké (or three families from whom the Tycoon can be chosen,— Owari, Mito and Ki-siu) were represented. Owari was the principal speaker and the Minister Midzuno Idzumi-no-Kami repeated, word for word, the phrases used by him, to the daimios around.

'Owari spoke to this effect :—

'During the last 400 years our country had enjoyed the the calm and sweets of peace, until in the   year of Tempo, [? Perry] there came the foreign ships from the West, constantly appearing on our coasts. Recently, when it appeared probable that war would arise I [we] demanded of the daimios and the hatamotos if they were ready and could sustain it. All replied that they had not arms and were not prepared for the combat. The Mikado and the Tycoon told them this should not be so. For five years hence there is no fear of war. During this interval you must make all preparation. Up to the present time you have passed your existence in pleasure, playing the *samisen* and drinking *saké*. Now in the prospect of war you must change all this. During the next five years only have heart for the work. Perfect yourselves in the use of the sword and the lance, and the exercise of the musket. If you have not money we will provide you with it; to those of you who do not possess 10,000 kokus we will lend up to the amount of 40,000 itchibus. You can then buy all you want for the war, arms, swords, bows, muskets, lances. But you shall show all you purchase to an agent we will appoint, that we may judge the price you have paid for them."

"After the sitting was closed, on the same day, Midzuno Idzumi-no-Kami reproduced this discourse to all the hatamotos, and the day following the two documents were sent to every Governor and to all the heads of Police to be distributed through all Japan.'

NOTICE.

' To all the inhabitants of Yedo, and all other places in Japan,—who know the use of the musket, the exercise of the lance and the sword :—to ronins and the inhabitants of the mountains.

' If there are any amongst you who are capable of bearing arms, let them make themselves known to the Governors of Police, and they will be employed at the following rates.

'For men of the first selection, 400 itchibus, and 200 sacks of rice per year.

'For men of the second rank, 200 itchibus, and 100 sacks of rice a year.

'For all others, 120 itchibus and 70 sacks of rice.'

2ND CIRCULAR.

'To all those who are versed in the art of making arms, guns and cannon, swords, lances, and all things used in war.

'If you will come to us you shall be engaged on very advantageous terms."

Towards the end of the month of June, a report reached Yedo that the Tycoon was in *durance vile* at Kioto. It was therefore resolved that OGASAWARA should go down to Osaka with an armed force to free him from such an ignominious position and bring him to Yedo.

Two British steamers, the Elgin and the Rajah, were chartered for the purpose of conveying him and his troops to Osaka. Having landed they marched as far as Fushimi on the road to Kioto; but here they not only heard that there was no restraint beyond the Mikado's orders, upon the Tycoon; but also that the enraged samurai had resolved to capture and imprison OGASAWARA himself as soon as he reached the metropolis. Under these circumstances he turned back to Osaka; and shortly afterwards, at the close of a public document notifying the appointment of certain daimios as guards of the different gates of the Imperial residence, occurs this short sentence :—

"As to OGASAWARA DZUSHO-NO-KAMI, the Tycoon thinks fit to remove him from office.

By order of the Tycoon at Kioto,

(Signed)   IDZUMI-NO-KAMI.

"OGASAWARA DZUSHO-NO-KAMI is placed in confinement in the Tycoon's castle at Osaka."

In September certain correspondence took place betweeen the foreign representatives and the Tycoon's Government.

Allusion was first made to the dismissal of Ogasawara from office, and a hope was expressed that the disgrace of this minister almost immediately after the sending in the letter as to the closing of the ports, would be followed by the withdrawal of the letter itself.

A separate letter of the French Minister impressively speaks of the "good feeling and friendship evinced by the Foreign Governments towards Japan," and warns the ministry of the injurious effects of a rupture of these good relations, and the serious responsibility of those who shall work to this end. He then points out the necessary steps that should be taken to avert such a calamity from the empire, and suggests:—

"1.—That the Tycoon should declare the letter of Ogasawara to be withdrawn, and the treaties in full force.

"2.—That the Tycoon should repress all aggression, and procure complete satisfaction for the outrages committed on Foreign flags.

"3.—That the Tycoon should engage to protect Foreigners in their persons, their property and their trade. And

"Lastly, that he shall guard and endeavour to promote the extension of relations between Japan and foreign countries, especially in respect to the opening of Osaka and Hiogo."

The reply of the Government was very carefully worded; but it gave little or no indication of their future policy.

News now came from Osaka of a very distressing character. Several assassinations had taken place, the victims being merchants of the higher class, having large trading relations with Yokohama merchants. Of course these murders were attributed to the ronins; and no doubt with justice.

Notices appeared both in Kioto and Osaka to this effect:—

"The Tycoon has secret dealings with the foreigners with the aid of our wicked merchants who do business with them. These merchants go to Yokohama, sell everything—silk, tea and other produce: so that all products are very dear, and the people much troubled. If we do not take care all will be oppressed. We are charged to punish these merchants. You who may owe money to Yokohama traders, do not pay them; and if they complain to the officers at Yedo, have no fear on that account—say that you will cause them to be cut in pieces.

"Koshiu, Oshiu, Shinshiu merchants—merchants from all the silk provinces, see to this notice. Take care that you send no silk, tea or cotton, to Yedo. If you disregard this, you, your children and all your relations will be crushed."

The placard was only signed:—"The executors of justice." Rightly or wrongly it was said to have official sanction.

It is amusing, after perusing the letter of Dr. WINCHESTER on the subject of the removal of all obstructions to the entry of silk into the settlement, which letter was dated September 24th, to read the following received by the Consul on the 4th October from the Ministers for Foreign Affairs in reply to a letter written by Dr. WINCHESTER on the 26th September.

"We have received your despatch No. 38 dated 26th September. We have fully understood what you have communicated respecting the scarcity of Silk.

An order has been given to the different departments regarding the export thereof; and thus there is no reason whatever that there should be any restriction, as you make mention of in your despatches, for any article at all.

But as the trade in Silk is flourishing from day to day, we are of opinion, that it is a *ruse* of some person (or persons), who, in order to make large profits have bought up all the Silk, and then, by spreading such reports as you mention, unsettle the Foreigners, and thus expect to gain their object.

Whatever may be the cause, we have taken the above into mature consideration, and have given the necessary instructions to the proper authorities, and we therefore think that the sale of Silk will shortly take place in a proper way, and that either yesterday or to-day there will have been some signs of it.

We now trust that you will believe that what we have stated is true.

With respect &c.,
(Signed)   Minister for Foreign Affairs.
4th October 1863.

The monotony of social life was broken about this time, by the arrival of some musical artists from Australia. They were Miss BAILEY, Mr. MARQUIS CHISHOLM, Mr. SIPP and Signor ROBBIO—the last-named a violinist of exceeding merit.

And while the fleet was lying inactive in the harbour, a capital two days regatta was got up (5th and 6th October) which was the forerunner of many such amusements.

But the sweet and bitter were strangely mingled. From Nagasaki tidings came that the Governor had waited on the British Consul and warned him that a number of ronins had arrived from Choshiu's territory, who, enraged at the retribution that had recently fallen upon that clan, were expected to attack the foreign settlement. He urged that no foreigner should enter the town after dark, or go from home unarmed. A meeting of the residents was held, at which it was arranged that a strong guard of sailors from H. M. Ss. Leopard and Rattler, then in port, should patrol the settlement.

And Yokohama was once more the scene of active sorrow. If I only tell of the actual deaths that were occasioned by the attacks of the cruel cowards—cruel, for their assaults could do no good, being on single individuals, and were of a nature that showed, by the number of mortal wounds, the desperate hatred by which they were moved; and cowardly, for their attacks were always made from behind—if, I say, I should tell only of actual murders, the list were sad enough; but should I tell of the occasions on which foreigners were wantonly threatened, and escaped, they hardly knew how, the pluck of the members of the young community, in sticking to the place and making light of the atrocities they had ever to be prepared for, would appear even more remarkable. Within a few days, a lady and gentleman, quietly walking close to the town were threatened, and a gentleman riding a fine stud-bred horse on the hill leading to the Bluff was actually attacked, within hail of the guard of the British Legation, and only escaped by the spirit of his steed. And now, four weeks after the anniversary of the tragedy on the Tokaido, another barbarous murder has to be recorded.

About 4 o'clock in the afternoon of the 15th October, news was conveyed to the various consulates that "the body of a foreigner had been discovered at the village of Hodogaya on the Tokaido, about $3\frac{1}{2}$ miles distant from the settlement.

Mr. VON BRANDT, the Prussian Consul, with Lieut. APPLIN and the Military Train Escort, immediately went to the spot indicated, and the French Escort quickly followed.

Mr. BLECKMAN, of the French Legation, proceeded with two Chasseurs by the country road, traversing the plain at the back of the settlement, intending to cross the hilly ridge that separates this plain from that along which the Tokaido runs. On coming, however, to a small bridge at the turning off of the pathway that leads to Kanasawa, at a distance of only a little over a mile from Yokohama, they, with Colonel FISHER, U. S. Consul, Dr. JENKINS, and some Japanese mounted officers, whom they overtook, came suddenly upon the body of the murdered man. It was lying across the narrow bridle-road they would have had to travel, about twenty yards beyond the bridge; and to their horror they recognised it to be the horribly mutilated body of Lieut. CAMUS, a sub-Lieut of the 3rd battalion of the Chasseurs d'Afrique. On examination of the corpse, the sight that met their view was appalling indeed. Some twenty wounds had been inflicted, most of which were sufficient to cause death. The bridle-arm had been severed from the trunk, with a portion of the reins yet in hand; and this was found ten paces from the body.

The assassin was never discovered. There was no one to describe how the foul deed was done; for CAMUS was taking a quiet country ride alone. He was one of the most enthusiastic admirers of the country and its people. The idea of going out armed with a revolver was quite foreign to him. His confidence in them was complete. And he met his reward. The immediate result of this was, that Admiral JUARES landed a number of men, planted the 'tricolor' on the Bluff commanding the settlement, and declared he would hold it for the protection of foreigners.

Directly the news reached Yedo, the Gorojiu communicated to Mons. DE BELLECOURT their deep regret at the occurrence, and promised to use every effort to find the perpetrators of the diabolical crime.

Let me pass on. Are my readers as weary of reading of these deeds as I am of recording them? Then I will pause awhile and adopt another strain—but alas! I shall yet have to return to the minor key more than once before my task is ended.

On the 18th October, the English Episcopal Church, under the name of Christ Church, was opened for Divine service, which had hitherto been held, first in the private parlour of the British Consul's residence, and subsequently in the Court room of H. B. M.'s Consulate. The new edifice was 46 feet long by 30 broad, and was calculated to seat from 300 to 350 persons. Its cost was about $2,800 (£700). The REVEREND M. BUCKWORTH BAILEY, M. A., had arrived from home, with the appointment of H. M.'s Consular Chaplain, some time before. The actual consecration of the building did not take place until some years afterwards, when Bishop ALFORD, of Hongkong, being in Yokohama on a visit, performed the ceremony.

A third Bank opened a branch in Yokohama this month—the Commercial Bank of India—under the temporary charge of Mr. J. W. Mc LELLAN; but after a trial of about three years, this, and the Central Bank of Western India closed their branches here, and retired from the field.

The presence of the allied squadrons, now always amounting to from twenty to twenty-four men-of-war, made Yokohama comparatively gay. Theatrical performances were got up both by the French and English services; and nothing could exceed the cordiality existing between the fleets and the shore. One disadvantage arose to the community from the presence of so many seamen, who used by turns to be allowed ashore in large numbers every day: and that was, the springing up of a great number of grog-shops, which in certain localities became sometimes troublesome. It is, however, wonderful how rarely there was any serious quarrelling either among the foreign sailors themselves, or with the Japanese. When JACK got his stores aboard he was often enough as obstropolous as is his wont; but the

Japanese seemed to take kindly to him, and to receive all his roughness with rare good humour. The Japanese themselves are anything but tea-totalers. Whatever may be said about western ships conveying to the unsophistocated islanders of the Pacific, "missionaries and rum," the Japanese had not to be taught the art of toping. It would be well, however, for foreign sailors and others who indulge publicly, if they would take a lesson out of their book. When in his cups a Japanese of the commoner class is a model of good humour. I cannot altogether say as much for the old fighting men; for the ruling passion came out in them, and they were no better than they should be. The commoner, however, never having thoughts of violence in his mind ordinarily, they do not appear to come to him when the wine is in and the wit out. They carry on in their joyous, happy-go-lucky way, and are no more to be feared than when they are sober.

There were two or three occasions when the conduct of foreign sailors was beyond endurance, and they had to pay the penalty. Although I shall have to mention these in their proper places, I do not class them with the savage assaults I have previously had to dwell upon.

It is really marvellous that trouble did not frequently arise between the natives and the service men; for there was just the same de'il-may-care-ishness on the part of the latter, that distinguishes them the world over. Besides the grog-shops, there arose a number of livery-stables where ponies were provided with an especial view to help JACK in getting rid of some of his surplus dollars. It was one of the most favourite ways of chasing the happy hours away, of the few that were open to the holiday-makers; and it often required all the good nature their own countrymen could muster, on the consideration that a little exuberance of spirits might be allowed to men freed for a few hours from the long and strict discipline of ship-board, to pardon the vagaries of the unaccustomed equestrians. But though they galloped through the streets, endangering life and limb, and not unfrequently causing severe injuries in their course, few complaints were laid against them; and there seemed to be no disinclination on the part of the Japanese to fraternise with them.

CHAPTER XXIII.

ANOTHER ATTEMPT TO YIELD OBEDIENCE TO KIOTO.—U. S. AND DUTCH MINISTERS, INVITED TO MEET GOROJIU, PROCEED TO YEDO.—THE INTERVIEW.—INFORMED THAT FOREIGNERS MUST LEAVE YOKOHAMA, AND THE PORT BE CLOSED; BUT THAT THE LETTER SENT BY OGASAWARA WAS RETRACTED, AND TRADE WITH NAGASAKI AND HAKODATE PERMITTED.—TRANSLATION BY MR. ENSLIE OF JAPANESE OFFICIAL DOCUMENT.—PROPOSAL OF JAPANESE GOVERNMENT TO ERECT A FORT AT BENTEN.—NOT PERMITTED BY FOREIGN OFFICIALS.—CHOSHIU AND THE BAKUFU. —PROPOSAL TO MIKADO THAT HE HEAD THE ARMY FOR THE EXPULSION OF FOREIGNERS. DISGRACE OF CHOSHIU AND THE COURT NOBLES.—FLIGHT OF THE LATTER.—THE KIOTO PALACE GATES.—SUSPICION OF CHOSHIU'S AMBITION.—APPEAL ON BEHALF OF CHOSHIU.—THE CLAN'S ATTACK ON THE PALACE.— DESTRUCTION OF A GREAT PART OF KIOTO.—GOVERNMENT PROPOSES ANOTHER EMBASSY TO EUROPE.—SATISFACTORY RUMOURS; UNSATISFACTORY FACTS.—RONINS.—JAPANESE ORDER SHIPS FROM AMERICA AND EUROPE.—SUICIDAL ORDER OF GOVERNMENT TO PREVENT TRADE IN SILKWORM'S EGGS.—STATE OF PARTIES IN JAPAN.—CHOSHIU EXPECTED IN YEDO TO MAKE SUBMISSION.—PALACE OF TYCOON AGAIN BURNT.—MONEY PLENTIFUL IN YOKOHAMA.—THE ICHIBOO EXCHANGE.—THE NAVAL FORCE IN HARBOUR.—THE UNITED SERVICE CLUB.— MUNICIPAL MATTERS.—THE SWISS EMBASSY'S EXHIBITION.— MURDER OF A PORTUGUESE BY A BRITISH SUBJECT.—RECALL OF MONS. DE BELLECOURT.

WE are now to witness another throe of the Japanese Government in its attempt to obey the orders from Kioto.

On the 24th October, Mr. VON POLESBROEK and Mr. PRUYN, the Representatives of the Netherlands and the United States respectively, received an invitation to attend a conference with the Gorojiu at the house of the Governor of Kanagawa. The place of meeting was afterwards altered to Yedo, and the two ministers went thither in H. N. M.'s Medusa.

Immediately after arrival they were conducted into the presence of the Gorojiu, with whom were all the Members of the second Chamber; also the Governor of Nagasaki, (who had just arrived here) and other high officials.

In the demeanour of these officials a marked change— a sort of dogged civility, rather than that apparently hearty courtesy which had hitherto been the noticeable feature—was prevailing throughout.

The conversation commenced by a very important communication from the Gorojiu. "*The order of expulsion issued by and through* OGASAWARA *is retracted.*"

After some ordinary hesitation, however, the real gist of the sought interview came out.—"But," said, the Gorojiu, "if trade continues to be carried on in Yokohama, a revolution will ensue in the country, therefore the trade must be transferred to Nagasaki and Hakodate."

The Ministers, naturally asked if the Government were not able to put down such a revolution as they said threatened the country.

The Gorojiu answered, it was "a very great shame to Japan, but they could not."

The Gorojiu further added that they had appointed two Plenipotentiaries, to tell the Ministers of Foreign Powers why foreigners must leave Yokohama, and to negociate the terms of their leaving.

The Ministers expressed their great surprise that on

a subject of such vast importance the Gorojiu had not communicated to the British and French Ministers; to which the Gorojiu replied that they had communicated first with the Representatives of Holland and the United States, because the country had first intercourse with those nations.

The Ministers upon this, both replied that they should, of course, report this conversation to their repective Governments.

The GOROJIU :—" But cannot the Ministers or any of them consent to give up the settlement at Yokohama, without consulting their Governments? Foreigners could go to Nagasaki and then the treaties would remain in force. *The treaties with foreigners had only been made as an experiment to see if trade with foreigners would answer for Japan.*"

The Gorojiu, being asked what steps had been taken towards bringing the Prince of Nagato to punishment for his recent attacks upon foreign vessels, answered, " Nothing yet was done, but they were busily engaged in this matter. In Japan these things could not be hastened. It was the Japanese custom to do these things more quietly."

The high officers present were—MIDZUNO IDZUMI-NO-KAMI, ITAKURA SUWO-NO-KAMI, (who was the principal spokesman,) MOWORI KAWACHI-NO-KAMI, and MIWA TÔTÔMI-NO-KAMI.

It so happened that about this time Mr. JAMES J. ENSLIE, Acting-Consul at Hakodate, sent to Colonel NEALE a dispatch, under date 17th October, in which he gave translations of certain documents that had come into his hands, one of which, in particular, throws some light on the communications that were made to the British Chargé d'Affaires as above. Mr. ENSLIE writes :—

" As soon as the daimios were informed that a delay had been granted to Japan for opening the ports, they sent a Proclamation to Yedo, though the Mikado, in which they claimed the honour of having forced the foreigners to grant this delay. This is what the Mikado ordered to be written to the Tycoon, and it embodies the demands of the daimios.

" 'The honour and safety of our country, not only demand that the Te-hits-ro-a (English, French, Russians, Americans) shall not enter our sacred empire any further, but the liberties they now enjoy must be restricted. It is quite natural that they relinquished their supposed rights to Osaka and Yedo; and in doing so they showed a little common sense. I have ordered OHARA SAYEMON to inform you of the petition of the southern daimios. As the peace which has long reigned in Japan renders it impossible to enforce our orders on the Te-hits-ro-a, they must be reasoned with. Kanagawa must be closed, as their residence there is a disgrace to our nation, and the reasons assigned for Yedo and Osaka must again be adduced. Tell them this is absolutely necessary for the peace of Yedo ; and that 'when a nation experiences no change it enjoys peace.' (Extract from *Soong-Fu,* one of the four Chinese classics). You must also add that the presence of foreigners at Kanagawa (Yokohama) increases the price of the daily necessaries of life, thereby causing discontent among the people, who no longer obey their superiors.

" 'The daimios say that the Te-hits-ro-a ought to be sent back to Nagasaki, as was formerly the case. As this would perhaps be rather difficult, we must allow them to remain at Hakodate. Great difficulty will perhaps be experienced in obtaining their consent to leave Kanagawa, if, therefore, they will not listen to your reasons Shimoda can be offered to them in exchange for Kanagawa. This is all that can be done ; and if this last proposition do not please them, you must postpone your decision until you have seen us.

" '*You may let them entertain a slight hope that Kanagawa will be reopened at some future period* : for the daimios say that Japan will be able to receive foreigners without blushing in six or seven years.'"

I have mentioned the failure of the Japanese authorities in respect of placing armed men on the Eastern Hatobas, for our protection (?). They now proposed to erect a fort at, or opposite to, Benten, (a district at the extremity of the native town—so called from a temple situated there.) In this they were quickly disillusionised; the British and French Admirals telling them that no defence of the kind was needed; and that any forts either there or on the heights commanding the settlement, would be effectually prevented.

The punishment that had befallen the Choshiu clan, for firing into the foreign ships, rankled deeply in their bosoms. But the effects of the cannonading they had endured from the Wyoming, the Medusa, and more particularly the Semiramis, did not affect them so heavily as did the attempt of the Government of the Shogun to disavow them, and to deny their own responsibility in having given the orders in accordance with which the shots had been fired. As brave men they were prepared to take the consequences of having done their duty; but they indignantly deprecated the cowardice of the Government, that, having placed them in a position of trust as sentinels of the Inland sea, abandoned them in the hour of trial, when they had given such unmistakeable proof of their loyalty and patriotism.

It is an open question to this day whether they really had the orders they professed to have acted upon. It is more than probable that they had; because, when, later on, the Tycoon's Ministers were asked to punish them, and once and for all open the Straits, they hesitated, saying that the clan *might have had* orders; as much as to say that such orders might have emanated from Kioto and that the Yedo Government had not been made acquainted with the fact. They would hardly, however, have admitted so much, had they not known that such commands had been issued to them. At the same time there is room for doubt, inasmuch as from the making of the treaties, Choshiu had been one of the most earnest advocates of forcibly preventing their being carried into effect.

It will be remembered that as long ago as 1858, a Choshiu man invited OHARA SHIGETAMI to Nagato to get up an agitation in the clan for the expulsion of the barbarians. In 1861, also, the Prince of Choshiu himself wrote a letter to the Tycoon in which he said: " Since the conclusion of the treaties the people of this empire have done nothing but protest against them. They declare that you have disregarded the Mikado's wish that the country should be closed to foreigners." In 1862 the clan ordered NAGAI UTA to perform *harakiri* because he urged the necessity of the Mikado giving his imperial sanction to the treaties. And again, being in Yedo, the Prince of Choshiu continued his remonstrances in most bitter language.

Thus it is possible that in communications that took place between the chieftain and the Government, something may have passed, not intended by the latter as an order, but which the excited clan chose to consider as such; as men oftentimes talk themselves into belief in matters that are far from being facts.

Besides this it cannot be questioned that Choshiu was commanded, in conjunction with Satsuma and Tosa, to control and keep in order the ronins who had become troublesome in connection with the expulsion question both in Yedo and Kioto. It is also evident that the Court nobles of Kioto, who entered warmly into the discussions that arose on the subject of the treaties, made common cause with Choshiu; thus showing that he was looked upon more than any other daimio, as the strongest opponent of foreign intercourse; and when the ronins who adopted the curious method of warning the TOKUGAWA family by cutting off the heads of the wooden effigies of the three first ASHIKAGA Shoguns, it was Choshiu who interceded in their behalf to mitigate their punishment and save their lives; so that thenceforward "the ronins entertained great affection for the prince of Choshiu."

Be this as it may—whether they received distinct orders, or only worked themselves into the belief that they had, this much is certain:—that "the Court issued a proclamation observing that it had learnt that certain clans had put their hands in their pockets and looked on quietly when the barbarian ships had been attacked. This had profoundly distressed the Emperor, for, now that a commencement had been made by Choshiu, it was the duty of all the clans to strive to achieve the work with all possible speed; while the Bakufu at the same time despatched envoys to Choshiu, to reprimand the clan for having fired on foreign vessels without orders."

Great efforts had been made, by those who deemed that the Tycoon's Government was too slow in complying with the instructions it had received, to induce the Mikado to take the field in person. Amongst these were several of the Court nobles; but the suggestion originated with Choshiu; and none pressed the measure so urgently as did this clan. The Mikado agreed to the proposal; but, it may be supposed, unwillingly, and without any intention of acting upon it; for shortly afterwards the Choshiu men who had guarded the Sakai-machi gate of the Dairi, or imperial palace, were dismissed; and certain nobles who were acting with Choshiu were summoned to the palace. At this interview the displeasure of the Mikado was pronounced against those who had "falsified his wishes and given out that His Majesty intended to go to Yamato in order to take the field in person against the barbarians."— "Orders were then issued that the Imperial progress should not take place, and a resolution was taken to punish Sanjô and the other six Court nobles."

The result of this was that the Choshiu men left for their own province, accompanied by the seven Kugé. "The Court thereupon deprived the latter of their titles and rank, punished eighteen other official Court nobles who had been acting with Choshiu all along, and prohibited the Mori family from entering the capital."

All these circumstances served to render the Choshiu people desperate. A Satsuma vessel that had been sent with certain Government agents on board, on state business, which anchored off Tanoura, opposite Shimonoseki, was fired on by them although the national ensign was flying. Messengers were sent to remonstrate with them, and to call attention to the fact that it was one of Satsuma's ships; and even that the Government officials on board had a mission to them. They replied that, in that case, they should anchor on their side of the strait; which, on their proceeding to do, the forts poured in such a hail of shot that no less than thirty of the Satsuma men were killed. This greatly enraged the Prince of Satsuma, who proposed at once to send and demand an explanation of the outrage; but the Tycoon's Government prevented it, promising itself to obtain the necessary redress.

The following, differing in some respects from the above, is the "Report from the Prince of Satsuma's representative in Yedo, to the Gorojiu," on this circumstance:—

"The Prince of Satsuma had borrowed one of the Tycoon's steamers at Nagasaki, and she had gone to Satsuma's domain. Being in want of repairs she was sent through the Inland sea on her way to the Nagasaki foundry to be repaired, on the 22nd of the 12th moon (24th January) last year. Two days after this she came to an anchor in the straits of Shimonoseki, at 8 o'clock in the evening. Shortly after this, batteries on the northern shore opened fire upon her. Supposing that the steamer had been mistaken for a foreign vessel, the commanding officer ordered signal lanterns to be hoisted at the mast-heads, 'according to an agreement entered into among the daimios; to provide against such a misunderstanding. The signals were made and hauled down, but the firing commenced again; and as there was no attention paid when the signals were repeated, there being no help for it, the anchor was weighed, and the steamer directed towards the harbour of Shiro-no-mura, in the district called Awotoma, on the coast of Kokura. But a fire soon broke out in the ship, and she was consumed before she reached the port. Of the ship's company nine officers and nineteen others, including the engineers, lost their lives."

It may appear to some that this has nothing to do with Yokohama and Yedo. But it has to this extent—that it shows the course of events by which subsequent proceedings were arrived at, and explains in its proper sequence, what would otherwise require more lengthy explanation and the necessity of back reference hereafter.

The nine gates of the Imperial palace at Kioto were committed by the Tycoon to the charge of various daimios, of whom the Prince of Aidzu was one. He was also the Military Governor of Kioto; and my readers will observe that he, and all those who were placed in charge of the palace, received their appointments from the Tycoon. It was, however, seen at this early date, that those who were opposed to the Shogunate had designs upon the person of the Mikado—not to injure him—he was far too sacred for that—but because whoever had him on their side, and his sacred flag to display, had therein a tower of strength, which, it was supposed, none would dare to assault.

It was the conviction that Choshiu aimed at nothing short of obtaining possession of the Mikado's person, and then acting as by his authority, that led to his dismissal from Kioto. Several powerful appeals were made in his behalf, and for the seven Kugé—but all in vain. At length Choshiu sought to obtain by force of arms what he could not otherwise effect; and his retainers, collecting from all parts, marched on Kioto. They made a vigourous assault on the palace; but were met bravely by the guards in charge, and driven back after losing many men and some of their most prominent leaders. In the various encounters a large portion of the city of Kioto was burnt to the ground.

And now, leaving them awhile, I return to Yokohama. The Government availed itself of the opportunity offered by the murder of Lieut. Camus, to propose sending an embassy to France to express regret for that deplorable crime. The real object of the mission, however, was to urge upon the Governments of France and England, the necessity for closing Yokohama; any proposal for which the French and English Ministers, would not even listen to. M. DE BELLECOURT did not oppose the embassy, but only insisted on the envoys being men of suitable rank, and such as were worthy of being received by the European sovereigns.

In Yedo, among the people, a report was now freely circulated that all matters in connection with foreigners had been settled by the Government, and that it had been decided that no measures should be taken for their expulsion.

This in itself would have been gratifying; but the plans for strengthening the country against foreign attack, and the obstructions to business, still went on. The Yedo fortifications were fast proceeded with: troops vigourously drilled, and immense efforts made for the accumulation of war materials. The ronins about Yedo were a constant anxiety to the ministry; and at last a scheme was proposed and carried into effect, in accordance with which they were taken into the Tycoon's service, regularly paid and taken care of, in hopes of their being brought under control; but they were so troublesome in the city and suburbs, and acted in so violent a manner towards the citizens—robbing, cutting and wounding them at pleasure—that, at length, the Government, fairly tired out with the complaints that reached them, issued an order that the people should take the law into their own hands, and cut the marauders down wherever they should be met with. While the utmost was being done that could be for the protection of foreigners from such dangerous characters, there must have been a strong feeling in the minds of the Government that war, sooner or later, was inevitable, between Japan and foreign Powers, although it was equally clear that both parties wished to avoid it. A special agent, in the person of the Vice-Governor of Nagasaki, was despatched to China to purchase ships suitable for men-of-war; and Mr. PRUYN, minister of the United States, was requested to order men-of-war to be specially built and equipped for the Tycoon in America. Besides this, there was a man-of-war now expected to arrive shortly from Holland; and these, with the few vessels already purchased, were intended to serve as a nucleus for the Japanese navy.

At this time the business in silkworm's eggs, which later on assumed such important dimensions, had not commenced; and to limit the trade in silk, the Government officials issued an order for the destruction of three fourths of the silk cocoons; a wanton piece of suicidal destructiveness very hard to believe sane men to be capable of.

Of the true state of parties at the close of 1863, it is a little difficult to speak; because, whilst there was an evident revulsion of feeling on the part of some, rumours were so numerous, and sometimes so divergent, that it is hazardous to attempt to say which were true and which were false. The commissioners of the Prince of Satsuma who had recently concluded the business between that clan and the British, had undoubtedly spoken of a change of policy, which they honestly attributed to the experience they had of foreign arms at the battle of Kagoshima. It was now asserted that certain daimios (all of whom continued to be famous throughout the whole revolution), viz., Satsuma, Hosokawa, Chikuzen (KURODA), Mino, Nabeshima and Etchizen, had united to recommend a more liberal policy, much to the annoyance of Choshiu and Tosa, who considered themselves left in the lurch by all of them, but especially by Satsuma.

It was expected that Choshiu himself would arrive in Yedo in December 1863, to make his submission to the Tycoon; but it does not appear that he actually did so.

It was decided that the Yedo ruler should again visit Kioto early in the ensuing year. And the last event worthy of note that occurred in Yedo in the year 1863, was another great conflagration, by which the palace of the Tycoon was once more consumed.

In Yokohama things were tolerably lively. The arrangement I mentioned in chapter, by which the

Japanese allowed all foreign officials the full exchange for their dollars, extended to all the officers and men of the foreign naval and military services who visited the open ports; and as the ships alone which were now stationed at Yokohama averaged fully twenty in number, and the exchange was allowed on a very liberal scale (a common sailor, for instance, being permitted to exchange $1 a day, and officers in proportion) they all had their incomes pretty nearly doubled, and they spent their money like men. Never were such times for soldiers and sailors as those spent in Japan during the years 1862 to 1866. The Prussian officials, however, disapproved of this privileged exchange, (although it was no injustice to the Japanese), and Mr. VON BRANDT, the Prussian Consul, addressed a letter to the Ministers of Foreign Affairs, declining on the part of the Prussian Minister, Consulates and men-of-war, to avail of the right to exchange dollars for ichiboos at the Japanese Customhouses.

That the naval element was an important one in the settlement, may be gathered from the fact that the first of those "march-outs" which afterwards became so common, and so beneficial to the health of the men, took place in the middle of November, and consisted of eleven hundred and fifty men; who, being landed from several of the British ships, formed under command of Captain ALEXANDER, on the Bund, and, preceded by the band of the Euryalus, marched out some four miles from Yokohama, as far as Kanagawa, and a small distance on the Tokaido.

The United Service Club, which ultimately merged into the Yokohama United Club, was now established under the guidance of Lieut. W. H. SMITH, of the R. M. L. I., one of the most energetic and indefatigable men who ever came to this country.

The state of the settlement in respect of Municipal matters was unsatisfactory enough. The Council had been a failure; and the streets were in a lamentable condition. It was urged that it was high time the Japanese, who were bound by their covenants to keep the streets, roads and jetties, in good order, and who were receiving $17,000 a year for land rents, should do something towards fulfilling these duties.

The Swiss embassy, who now sought a treaty with Japan, although they arrived at an inopportune time, when the Government was actually declaring its intention of closing the ports, adopted a very practical method of showing the Japanese why they should yield to their wishes. They took a large godown, and, under the direction of Mr. BRENNWALD, opened a very extensive and complete exhibition of Swiss produce and manufactures. It consisted of Cottons, Silks, Silk embroideries and such like goods; Swiss rifles, Straw-work and Parqueterie; besides relief charts and photographs in great numbers, calculated to give the Japanese an excellent idea of the Swiss territory.

Two of the closing events of the year 1863 in the settlement of Yokohama, were, a large fire in the Main street, which destroyed the premises of Messrs. L. KNIFFLER & Co.; and a murder, in which the victim was a Portuguese named FRANK JOSE, and the perpetrator a British subject named A. H. BROWNING.

Finally, the whole of the foreign community heard with regret that they were to lose from their midst, the genial, able, and energetic French Minister, M. DE BELLECOURT. He had applied for leave of absence nearly a year before; and now his request was granted, with the intimation that he would afterwards be transferred to Tunis; so that he would not return to Japan, where he had played so efficient a part in upholding the interests of foreigners.

CHAPTER XXIV.

HOPEFUL DAWN OF 1864.—INTERVIEW BETWEEN BRITISH MINISTER AND JAPANESE OFFICIALS.—OMINOUS HINTS.—PRUSSIAN ENVOY ARRIVES.—RATIFICATIONS EXCHANGED.—SIGNATURE OF SWISS TREATY.—JAPANESE GOVERNMENT FULFILS PROMISES MADE IN EUROPE BY THE FORMER EMBASSY.—DEPARTURE OF NEW EMBASSY FOR FRANCE.—YOKOHAMA.—PERSONAL CHANGES.—LIBERALITY, BUT WANT OF PUBLIC SPIRIT, IN EASTERN COMMUNITIES.—PUBLIC HOSPITAL.—GENERAL SALUBRITY OF YOKOHAMA.—JAPANESE AND THE SMALL-POX.—SANITARY COMMITTEE.—TRADE.—THE JAPANESE NEW YEAR.

THE year 1864 came in hopefully if not altogether auspiciously. There were clouds still overhanging the intercourse between foreigners and the Japanese, but they did not look as if they must necessarily break forth in a violent storm; but rather as if they would easily yield to more genial influences. The Government had some difficulty in protecting the citizens of Yedo from the depredations of the lawless; but with this the foreign question was no further concerned than that the law-breakers were those who had banded together making the expulsion of the barbarians their war-cry.

An interview of a very interesting character took place early in the year between the British Chargé d'affaires and some officials of the Government, on the subject of the embassy about being dispatched to Europe.

At this interview the officers represented to Colonel NEALE that the treaty entered into with Commodore PERRY was a mere tentative measure; an experiment; which, if unsatisfactory to Japan, might at any time be reversed. They admitted that nothing of the kind appeared in writing, but asserted that it had been verbally discussed and understood. Colonel NEALE could only reply that he had heard of nothing of the kind, and that as far as the English Treaty was concerned, there was certainly no such understanding.

Allusion was then made to the determined hostility of the people to foreigners; to which it was replied that though there might exist such a feeling on the part of the samurai, there was nothing of the kind in the mind of the people in general. The officers answered that under any circumstances this hostility, by whomsoever entertained, caused a great deal of uneasiness to the Tycoon's Government, and that the only way to remove this was to close the port of Yokohama, leaving open the two ports of Nagasaki and Hakodate. As, however, the foreign Representatives had no power to agree to this, they wished to withdraw the letter that had been sent by OGASAWARA, and had resolved to send an embassy to Europe to arrange the matter with the home Governments.

Colonel NEALE called attention to the fact that obstructions to trade, of which complaints had been made, had not been removed; and particularly mentioned the closing of eighteen large native merchants' establishments in consequence of the restrictions imposed by the Government with regard to the supplies of Silk. The officials declared this to arise from the losses experienced by those engaged in the trade, as well as from the fear of ronins and other lawless people, and not from any Governmental action; but Colonel NEALE told them that the contrary was too well known to be the case; that the native dealers became rapidly wealthy through their transactions with foreigners; and that the only persons feared were the Government officials themselves. A long discussion took place, and at length Colonel NEALE warned them that they were playing a dangerous game; for, he said, "if you stop our trade, we will stop yours. If you stop our supplies we will stop yours." "By stopping our trade, do you mean our import trade with foreigners?" was the quick enquiry. And they were politely given to understand, that this was far from the meaning. That what was intended to be stopped was their own internal commerce, and the transit from place to place of those commodities which were necessary for the people. Although there was much plain language spoken, the interview was a very friendly one, and was, clearly useful in its results; as it gave the Government the assurance of the undeviating policy enjoined by his Government on the British representative.

The Prussian frigate Gazelle had now arrived, having on board Baron DE REHFUES the Envoy plenipotentiary, and Mr. VON BRANDT the Consul, to obtain the ratification of the treaty between their country and Japan. They went to Yedo and were hospitably entertained during the interval required for the ratification, at the French Embassy. An attempt was made by the Japanese officials to induce them to return to Yokohama, and remain there until the business was completed. A request was even sent to M. DE BELLECOURT, that he would get them to retire from the capital, the Gorojiu undertaking that the ratified treaty should be ready for them in a few days. His Excellency replied that he could not be guilty of such a breach of hospitality as to ask his guests to depart; but suggested that, as they would certainly leave of their own accord as soon as their business was finished, the Government should hasten it; as it really could be done as well in ten hours as in ten days if they so willed it.

The ratifications were exchanged on 21st January, on H. P. M. S. Gazelle, two members of the Gorojiu going on board, and receiving the letter of the King of Prussia to the Tycoon, whilst a third handed the ratified treaty to the Minister: and all being concluded a salute of twenty-one guns was fired. One of the Envoys about to proceed to Europe was present. After the formal proceedings were ended, the Japanese officials were courteously shown over the frigate, partook of some refreshment, and left the ship with every demonstration and profession of mutual good will.

The awkwardness of the position is strangely exhibited in all these proceedings. The treaties with Prussia and Switzerland were under negotiation at the time of the greatest pressure being brought to bear upon the Tycoon to close the ports and annul the treaties.

M. HUMBERT the Swiss Envoy, with M. BRENNWALD his secretary, and an attaché, left Yokohama for Yedo on the 5th February in H. N. M. S. Djambi, accompanied by Mr. VON POLSBROEK the Netherlands Consul-general; and on the following day the treaty with the Helvetian Republic was signed.

The Japanese Embassy being now on the eve of departure for Europe, the Gorojiu called to mind that there were certain agreements of the previous embassy with the European Governments which had never been fulfilled. They judged, and no doubt not without reason, that if these still remained unnoticed any promises made by their present representatives would be received with caution if not with distrust. They placed themselves in communication, therefore, with each of the powers to which their word had been formerly pledged, notifying them that in compliance with the promises of the Envoys they had sent in the previous year to Europe, they now reduced the duties on certain articles, specifying them in full. They can hardly claim to have acted on their engagements with a good grace; for the fulfilment was left to the very eve of the departure of the new envoys.

It will be remembered that the previous Embassy went to Europe in H. M. S. Odin. The Government refused a similar courtesy offered by M. DE BELLECOURT on the present occasion; preferring to avail themselves of the ordinary accommodation offered by the French mail steamers. They accepted a passage, however, as far as Shanghai; and accordingly, the Envoys and their suite embarked on the 6th February on board H. I. M. S. Monge, and left the harbour under a salute of seventeen guns from the Kanagawa forts.

The affairs of the settlement of Yokohama naturally occupied a good deal of attention. The fire at Messrs. KNIFFLER & Co.'s led to the formation of a Fire-brigade, the first committee of which was composed of Messrs. S. J. GOWER, E. PIQUET, W. C. CLARKE, J. C. FRASER and J. HUDSON: supplemented at a subsequent meeting by Messrs. A. J. MACPHERSON, A. REIS, O. S. FREEMAN, R. B. SMITH, N. P. KINGDON, J. O. P. STEARNS, M. J. B. NOORDHOEK HEGT, and E. KAISER. Mr. HEGT, always the foremost active assistant at any fire that occurred either in the settlement or the native town, placed at the disposal of the brigade an engine which he had imported, and kept always upon his premises, undertaking also to keep it in working order. The members of the Volunteer corps enrolled themselves as members of the Fire-brigade, almost to a man. Changes in the *personnel* of communities in the far-East have always been one of their characteristics and drawbacks. Although the Volunteer corps had been so short a time in existence, Mr. GOWER, in anticipation of an early removal to Hongkong, had resigned the captaincy, which was transferred to Mr. CLARKE, and Mr. F. H. BELL (W. R. ADAMSON & Co.) now resigned the treasurership, as he was about to reside in Shanghai. Both were elected honorary members; and Mr. E. J. SPENCE was appointed treasurer in the place of Mr. BELL.

At the first annual statutory meeting of the British episcopal Church, Mr. S. MAINE resigned his treasurership in consequence of his early departure from Japan, and Mr. W. BOURNE replaced him. Messrs. W. MARSHALL and I. J. MILLER were elected trustees, in the room of Messrs. WILLGOSS and ALCOCK. Thanks were voted to several persons for special contributions to the church— viz., to the Visitors to Yokohama for the Harmonium; to Captain VYSE for the Church stove; to Mr. EUSDEN, for the font; and to Mr. MARCUS FLOWERS for the Lectern. A resolution was also passed that was moved by Mr. A. J. MACPHERSON, "that all designs for the adornment and embellishment of the Church shall be submitted to the Committee, and shall be approved of by them; and that all gifts offered to the Church shall be sanctioned by the committee previous to being placed in the fabric, the end being the preservation of that unanimity so desirable in Church matters."

A remarkable feature in the foreign communities in China and Japan has always been the liberality with which they will subscribe for public purposes, and the unwillingness they display to attend public meetings. In the instance of the Fire-brigade in Yokohama, it was difficult to get a proper meeting together when once it had been established; and yet so liberally were the residents inclined to support it, that within one month they subscribed $1635 towards the fund for the purchase of engines, besides $975 for incidental expenses—large sums for so small a community.

Among the public institutions early established in Yokohama was a Public Hospital. Considering the nature and the size of the community, it would not have been supposed that this would have been particularly called for; but it was so in reality; and notwithstanding that drugs, stores and hospital necessaries, were supplied from the hospital ship at Hongkong at Government prices, and the additional fact that the subscriptions and donations collected in 1863 amounted to $2,065, the receipts did not meet the expenditure. Dr. JENKINS was the medical officer attached to it, and gave his services gratuitously.

As yet the settlement of Yokohama had been tolerably free from any epidemic; and, so far as foreigners were concerned, the good character for salubrity that it enjoyed was fully justified; but amongst the Japanese certain diseases were always more or less present in their respective seasons:—the much-dreaded small-pox invariably making its appearance in the native quarters in the winter and the spring. This was a disease so common among the natives that it appeared to have no terrors for them. They quite counted on having it at some time or other, and were glad if it came to their children in very early youth, as they considered that it was more easily got over in the tender years of childhood, than it was later in life. Few of them escaped, and its effects were seen on the countenances of a large proportion of the population. It carried many off by death, but nothing like so many as might have been expected; and how it happened that the disease was ever absent was a marvel to foreigners, seeing that children covered with it, and to whom foreigners would instinctively give a very wide berth, were not kept indoors, or separated from the rest of the family, but were carried *(more japonice)* on the backs of other children only a few years older than themselves, or on their mothers' backs, in the open air; their bearers mixing quite freely with their friends and acquaintance as if nothing was the matter. That they acknowledged that danger did exist was evidenced by the fact that any house in which the disease was, had to be marked by certain slips of paper suspended in a straw string across the doorway; and the children themselves had a scarlet cloth wrapped round their heads, to call attention to the fact of their being infected. There was, however, no special purification of the houses nor destruction of the clothes of those who had been afflicted, but everything was left to chance. Some slight alarm was felt by foreigners in the spring of 1864, in consequence of varioloid making its appearance in one of the ships in the harbour. The immediate effect, however, was to direct public attention more than ever to the sanitary state of the settlement. It was frankly admitted that the Municipal Council which had been elected in the preceding year had proved a total failure; and as the Japanese, however willing, were really ignorant of the best method for putting the drains and keeping the roads in proper condition, discussions arose, which culminated in the matter being placed under the charge of certain members of the community—of which more will be said presently.

At this time there were reasons for supposing that in addition to Tea and Silk, Japan would add Cotton to its regular staple exports. Under the stimulus created by high prices, the export from 1st July 1863 to January

31st 1864, amounted to 37,583 bales, against 6,227 bales for the same period in the preceding year; but although the export continued throughout the year, it gradually diminished, and the trade in Cotton from Japan to England is now—nil.

I have not yet spoken of one of the brightest periods of the Japanese year—Shôgatzu—or the New Year. It is vastly different now in its manner of observance from what it was in 1864. It was one of the most joyously kept holidays it is possible to conceive. Great preparations were made for it for some days beforehand. The houses of the wealthy, the offices of the yakunins, the shops of the traders and the humblest dwellings of the poor, were thoroughly cleansed and purified; the mats renewed; old and worn-out articles of every day use—such as the *o-hatchi* or rice-tubs, the various culinary implements, and the hundred and one things in daily household use—were repaired or replaced by new ones; *mochi*, a peculiar kind of rice-cake was prepared; and everything made 'as nice as a new pin.' The best clothes were all got in readiness; the Lares and Penates duly attended to and honoured; presents provided for especial friends or claimants; the exterior of the houses decorated very much after the fashion of Christian lands at Christmas time; and above all, every outstanding account was collected, paid or settled. Then were the people prepared for the full enjoyment of the New Year.

The streets which had been every evening, and for the last three or four days of the old year, crowded with stands for the sale of the different things in demand for the great festival—such, for instance, as the evergreens and emblems for decoration; little *miyas* or small wooden temples, which are the central objects on their household altars; lobsters and ferns, *cum multis aliis*;—were now as quiet anddeserted by daylight on New Year's day as if they had never been the scenes of animation that had only just passed away. The houses were all shut; and the people who had been experiencing such a period of toil and excitement during the preceding days, were taking a good rest before entering on the duties and pleasures before them.

It was well worth a stroll through the native quarters to see all that I have thus cursorily alluded to. The decorations were such as not only had a beautiful effect to the eye; but having a distinct meaning, they possessed more than a common interest. Our own Christmas decorations, if they ever had any particular meaning, are now nothing but evergreen adornments marking a peculiar season of festivity. The Japanese decorations are something more.

It was usual, and is so still, to place on the two sides of the principal entrance of the house a fir-tree and a bamboo, and to unite them by a piece of curiously twisted straw rope on which is hung a device called *shime-kazari*, consisting principally of a boiled lobster, an orange and a dried persimmon, a spray of fern, an oak-leaf and a piece of seaweed—the whole surmounted by a piece of charcoal wrapped in paper.

The fir-tree and the bamboo are emblems of long life, as also is the orange. The lobster typefies a hearty old age, strong though bent. The dried persimmon, very similar in appearance to, and quite as sweet as the Smyrna fig, is emblematical of the sweetness of conjugal constancy; the fern long retains its verdure; the oak-leaf does not drop until the young leaves begin to burst from their buds; and the piece of charcoal further denotes eternal stability.

The bamboos and fir-trees were generally supported in bundles of firewood; and it was usual to keep the decorations intact until the 7th day of the year, when the *shime-kazari* were burnt as an offering to the gods.

As the morning of the New Year's day advanced, the shutters were gradually taken down from the front of the houses, and the family appeared *en grande tenue* prepared to receive visitors, or in some instances all equipped for making calls. There was little visiting, however, on the first day. This was generally left for the second. Officials were seen moving about in groups, attended by their kerai, on their round of ceremonial calls—for this is strictly enjoined by authority—that all the subordinates of certain grades in official employ, do present themselves in ceremonial dress to their superiors, to offer the congratulations of the season. It was a particularly interesting and picturesque sight; the rich silk fabrics of the dresses and the peculiar wing-like robing of the shoulders imparting both beauty and originality to the scene.

Then as the day progressed the streets became more and more filled—but not with the busy anxious crowd usually seen in them. Far, very far from it. What a scene of merriment it used to be when the weather was fine! Groups of men, women and children, all flying kites or playing at battledore and shuttlecock. The kites were of all shapes and sizes, and old and young were engaged flying them. But the great game for fun and merriment was the battledore. It was played by parties of six or eight. All were dressed in their best. The hair black and glossy, and in the case of the women with some little bit of coloured crape, or coral-mounted hair pins, or tortoise-shell combs. All looked bright and happy. What screams of laughter would be heard, when, after keeping up the shuttlecock from one to another for some time, it would fall to the ground, and the luckless player who missed it would have to bear the penalty of a slap on the back from all the other players; or, in some instances, the less agreeable one of a mark down the face with an Indian ink line. But all had to endure it in turn, and naught but mirth and jollity could be seen among them. Laughter is always catching; but Japanese laughter on such an occasion surpasses anything of the kind to be heard elsewhere; and such is their heartiness and kind nature that the good folk are only too happy to see others enjoy their games as well as themselves.

These citizens certainly had not an unkind look or word for foreigners. They were glad to receive them and give them a hearty welcome in their houses, and I never heard of any one who availed himself of their hospitality being otherwise than charmed with their light hearts, open hands and good-breeding.

CHAPTER XXV.

LIFE IN YOKOHAMA.—PROGRESS OF TRADE.—YOKOHAMA UNFORTUNATE IN MUNICIPAL MATTERS.—FIRE.—SIR R. ALCOCK'S RETURN TO JAPAN.—LIEUT. COLONEL NEALE'S DEPARTURE.—SCHEME FOR IRON FLOATING DOCK.—FRENCH HATOBA COMPLETED.—ATTACK ON MR. SUTTON OF NAGASAKI.—FOREIGN MINISTERS CALL ON THE TYCOON'S GOVERNMENT TO DESTROY THE CHOSHIU BATTERIES, AND OPEN THE INLAND SEA.—COMMUNICATIONS WITH THE GOVERNMENT.—PEACE POLICY REPORTED AS PREVALENT AT KIOTO.—SATSUMA AND SILK.—CONSULAR CHANGES.—ARRIVAL OF M. LEON ROCHES, THE NEW FRENCH MINISTER.—SIR R. ALCOCK OBTAINS PROMISE FOR A RECREATION GROUND.—DEPARTURE OF M. DE BELLECOURT.—ARRIVAL OF "CONQUEROR" WITH ROYAL MARINES, AND "SEMIRAMIS" WITH FRENCH FUSILIERS.—RETURN OF TYCOON TO YEDO.—COMMERCIAL.—DECIDED IMPROVEMENT OF RELATIONS BETWEEN JAPANESE AND FOREIGNERS.

THE presence of so many ships of war in harbour imparted a wonderful life to the settlement of Yokohama; and the arrival of a portion of H. B. M.'s XXth regiment, added to it. There was a large amount of entertaining going on ashore, so far as the means at the command of the residents permitted it; but as yet few large gatherings of this kind had taken place. Mr. D. DE GRAEFF VON POLESBROECK, the Dutch Consul-general, a man of large sympathies and most hospitable proclivities, gave a magnificent diplomatic entertainment on the 19th February, in honour of the birthday of the King of Holland. It was on a scale that quite put everything of the kind that had preceded it, into the shade.

I have as yet intentionally said little about the progress of trade between Japan and foreign countries; but a few words here on the subject may not be inappropriate.

Four years before this, of course there had been no trade whatever with Japan, except the *modicum* done by the Netherlands factory at Nagasaki. In 1862 it began to show signs of future importance; for 33 vessels of 15,000 tons arrived in Kanagawa during the first six months of that year, of which 14 were British and 12 American. But in the interval between that time and the end of 1863 the trade was nearly doubled. There were 74 vessels, aggregating 25,000 tons—of which 40 were British and 19 American. This too, was in spite of the very troublous political disturbances that had been existing during nearly the entire period, and the obstructions placed in the way of trade by the Government.

In 1862 the Japanese bought imports in Yokohama to the extent of £70,000, in 1863 to the value of £112,000; thus showing the expansibility of the trade. In 1859 the Japanese supposed they had only sufficient silk in the country for their own use. In 1862 they sold to Yokohama merchants £200,000 worth, while the total value of silk bought by foreigners in the season 1863, was nearly £2,500,000. Again in Cotton no one expected to find any very large supplies in Japan; and yet, from July 1st 1863 to February 1864, they supplied us with 42,000 bales, although in 1862 they could not spare a single bale. These are remarkable figures; and more particularly so when it is considered under what circumstances the business was done.

And now respecting sanitary measures for the settlement, a public meeting was held at the residence of Mr. S. J. Gower, (where almost all such useful meetings were held in those days), especially with the view of taking action with regard to drains, sea-frontage, &c. Mr. Frank Hall (Walsh, Hall & Co.), occupied the chair. The result was the establishment of a Scavenger corps that should daily clear the streets, drains and Bund, of any offensive rubbish, and remove it to a suitable distance from the settlement; and, the formation of a corps of boats, of which one was to be at the end of each street leading to the Bund, in order to receive and convey away all the rubbish collected by the scavengers and by the coolies of private houses.

These particulars may be passed over by indifferent readers; but they are of interest to those who care to observe the progress of the settlement; for in the matter of local government it has been the most unfortunate of all foreign settlements in these seas. It has paid a heavy ground rent to the Japanese Government for all the years it has been in existence; and not until 1868 and 1869 did the Japanese take any intelligent means for improving it. Even now, the drainage is imperfect, the streets are requiring repairs, and the streets of the foreign settlement are dark at night, while the adjoining native settlement is brilliantly lighted with gas. Had it not been for the efforts of a few gentlemen, and those the representatives of the leading mercantile houses in the place, there is no knowing what epidemic or other unwholesome influence might have overtaken us; and it is doubtful if we should ever have got above the level of an ordinary ill-drained, uncared-for, Japanese town.

Messrs. GOWER (JARDINE, MATHESON & Co.), N. P. KINGDON (DENT & Co.), MACPHERSON (MACPHERSON and MARSHALL) and FRANK HALL, were appointed a Committee to carry into effect the resolution, and to make the necessary assessment. The energy with which action was taken produced the best results.

On the 23rd February a fire took place on the premises occupied by J. ALLMAND JUNIOR & Co., situated in the midst of the settlement. The engines of Messrs. KINGDON, MAINE and HEGT were quickly on the spot, but the supply of water was so small as to render them almost valueless. The Fire brigade, in the meanwhile was completely organised; subscriptions had considerably augmented, and three fine fire-engines were ordered from home. All these came out, and subsequently several more; but the water supply is very slightly improved even to the present day.

On the 2nd March, Sir RUTHERFORD ALCOCK returned from England and at once resumed the duties of his office. On the 8th a farewell dinner was given to Lieut. Colonel NEALE, and on the 11th he took his departure in H. I. M. S. Semiramis for Shanghai, there to take passage for home in the mail steamer.

A scheme for the formation of an Iron Floating dock for Yokohama was proposed at this time. A Mr. ROBINSON, representing the firm of RANDOLPH ELDER & Co. of Glasgow, arrived, bringing with him a model of a dock just completed by that firm for the French Government at Saigon. A good many persons intimated their willingness to become shareholders, but the enterprise fell through and was abandoned.

On the 29th March the new French Hatoba was opened to the public.

Professor RISLEY, who had made a great name for himself in America and Europe, many years before, as a wonderfully successful acrobat, arrived in Yokohama at this time in charge of a circus. The arrival is of no further interest than as giving the opportunity of mentioning by the way, that he was the first to introduce dairies: to build an ice-house in Yokohama: and to fill it with ice which he imported from Tientsin. It was a great boon to the public. I may further notice that he was the first who took away from here a Japanese acrobatic troupe for exhibition in America and Europe.

In Yokohama and Yedo an extraordinary calm had existed for some time. It was quite understood that wiser counsels as regards foreigners prevailed at Kioto. The obstructions to commerce, if not removed, were certainly relaxed, and but for the *malaise* in the one clan of Choshiu, all might have gone on prosperously if not altogether harmoniously. From Nagasaki there came the unwelcome news that Mr. SUTTON (now the proprietor of the "Rising Sun and Nagasaki Express") had been savagely attacked by a two-sworded man whom he had accidentally touched in quietly passing through the street. He was severely wounded, and lost his right arm. His life was for a time in danger, but happily he recovered.

The outrages on the foreign ships which had led to the punishment of the Nagato clan by individual men-of-war of the nationalities whose vessels had been fired upon, had, as it happened, been confined to American, Dutch and French ships. They were looked upon, however, by the representatives of Foreign Powers, as an attempt to carry out the Mikado's edict against all foreigners; and as early as the 28th July 1863, the British Chargé d'affaires wrote to the Japanese Ministers for Foreign

Affairs, that, acting upon this belief, he made common cause with his colleagues, and called upon the Tycoon to destroy the batteries of Choshiu and remove his guns. This was in accordance with the resolution come to at a meeting of the Foreign Ministers, held on the 25th July :—

"After discussion it has been agreed that it is indispensable for the maintenance of the sacred treaty rights concluded with Japan, to proceed immediately to the reopening of the Inland Sea, always availed of up to this time, and of which the free navigation has been wantonly interrupted by the outrageous aggressions of which the daimio of Nagato has been guilty, in firing from the batteries erected on the coasts of his territory, upon merchant-ships and men-of-war of the Treaty Powers."

Nothing, however, was done. Month after month went by. The usual promises were made; and the usual delays were requested; but now, in the spring of 1864, the Prince of Choshiu, or his clansmen on his behalf, became more troublesome than ever. It was reported that since firing on the Satsuma ship in the month of January, they had stopped every junk passing through the Straits of Shimonoseki, and if they contained cotton or other goods intended for foreigners they were burned and the crews murdered. I am not at all doubtful as to the truth of the report. It came through Japanese merchants, but it was believed and reported by the foreign Consul at Nagasaki: and it was stated that foreign merchants had been among the heavy losers; inasmuch as they had made large advances for the purchase of the cotton ' to arrive,' and it never came to hand. It was alleged, and it was evident, that the trade of Nagasaki must be stopped unless Choshiu could be curbed in these depredations.

The clan had been extremely active in constructing forts in advantageous positions. And, by forcing all boatmen, farmers, labourers and peasants in the territory, to serve in the army several days in each month, and supplying them with muskets, a nominal force of over 40,000 men had been got together.

It may have been these facts that induced Sir RUTHERFORD ALCOCK to suggest to his diplomatic confrères, the propriety of taking prompt and decisive measures, once and for all, to put an end to these proceedings of this troublesome clan, and to open the Inland Sea to the world's traffic, according to the original agreement.

And here I would observe that at the time of these transactions, all foreigners in Japan, judging by what they knew, what they saw, and what they heard, were of one opinion. They honestly and firmly believed that there was but one course to take with regard to Choshiu, and that was the course taken by the ministers. Not one of us doubted that there was truth in all we heard about his proceedings; or that the ministers knew a great deal more even than we did. I go further. I am morally convinced that if the foreign forces had not been put in movement against Choshiu, the course of events would have been very different to what it has. Of course it is impossible to say exactly what it would have been; but when, in after days, the Tycoon took it in hand to punish the clan, battle after battle was fought, almost always resulting favourably for the clan. It was altogether too strong for the Tycoon's forces; and it would have been more potent still against them had not we crippled its power in a large degree, beforehand. If then it had fairly got the upper hand, there is no knowing what would have been the result. The inveteracy of the clan against foreigners has been repeatedly described to me by an officer of the clan as something intense. "I can hardly understand now," my informant has said, "that I ever entertained such feelings towards any human beings. But we hated foreigners from the first, inherently; and then we looked upon all the misfortune that had come upon us and our prince as caused by them. At that time I should have thought it an act of the highest virtue, whatever were the consequences, to cut down a foreigner; and if more than one—so much the better."

This is quite comprehensible; and seeing the strength and influence of Choshiu, my belief is, that without some decisive display of strength on the part of foreign powers on that clan in particular, foreign affairs would have gone from bad to worse, and a much greater effort would have had to be made at a later period, against the whole nation.

The Ministers having come to a resolution to open the Inland Sea, placed themselves in communication with the Gorojiu, and told that august council of their intentions; declaring that if the Tycoon could not effect it by the punishment of Choshiu, it should be undertaken by the foreign Admirals and squadrons now in Japanese waters. The Gorojiu were powerless. They could only plead to be allowed to confer with Choshiu, and to report to Kioto. And so things stood shortly after Sir RUTHERFORD's return. The *denouement* of these matters I must relate further on.

Whilst the Ministers were hatching this scheme for sending their forces to the Inland Sea, intelligence came from Kioto that the Council of daimios had agreed upon a peaceful policy in reference to foreign intercourse. It was said that the Tycoon was to remain at the metropolis until he had fulfilled the duty now devolving upon him, of dealing with Choshiu; and no doubt he recognised the fact that in doing this duty he had hard work cut out for him.

As to the officers of the Satsuma clan, they showed the wisdom of the serpent, if not the harmlessness of the dove. Large quantities of silk now arrived in Yokohama;

and it was said that they had bought up all that came to Yedo, at a low price, and then sent it for sale to Yokohama, realising a very fine profit.

Mr. MORRISON, H. B. M. Consul at Nagasaki, who, it will be remembered, had been wounded in the first attack of the Legation, now retired from the service, and Dr. MYBURGH was appointed to succeed him. As he was permitted, however, to go home on leave, Mr. A. A. J. GOWEN went to Nagasaki as Acting Consul.

H. S. Mons. LEON ROCHES, the new French Minister, with the Comte DE TURENNE as attaché, arrived on the 27th April.

Among the labours of Sir RUTHERFORD since his return was one which has proved very beneficial to foreign residents. He succeeded in inducing the local authorities to grant a fitting site for a recreation ground, conveniently placed, in the neighbourhood of the settlement. The arrangement at first made was not carried out, but it ultimately culminated in our having the new road round by Negishi and Mississippi Bay, and in the fine race-course of which Yokohama is justly proud.

The departure of H. E. Mons. DE BELLECOURT from Japan, on board the P. & O. S. Nepaul, took place on the 27th May. He had borne with Sir RUTHERFORD ALCOCK, and Lieut. Colonel NEALE, the burden and heat of the day, in opening the ports; and he left amid the very universal regret of the residents.

The English squadron was now strengthened by the arrival of H. M. S. Conqueror, with 530 Royal Marine Light Infantry, under the command of Colonel SUTHER.

Mr. RUDOLF LINDAU returned to Japan on the 6th June, accredited as the Consul for the Swiss Confederation. In his absence he had produced his book *Un voyage au tour du Japon,*—one of the most correct of all the books which had to that time appeared on the subject of which it treats.

On the 22nd June, H. I. M. S. Semiramis brought 300 Fusiliers of the Infanterie de la Marine, to relieve the Chasseurs d'Afrique, who had already left by H. I. M. S, Dupleix, for Shanghai, *en route* for Mexico.

The Tycoon returned to Yedo by sea on the 23rd June, his own ship being attended by six others. His return was hailed as the harbinger of action. His Ministers had always excused themselves and pleaded for delay until he should once more be settled in his own capital. The time now seemed to have come; and the prospects of war with Choshiu became the universal theme of conversation.

The commercial year which closed on the 31st June, left a disappointing result as to the amount of trade done as compared with the year ending the same time in the preceding year—it being only 15,718 bales against 25,446. The total quantity of Cotton, however, was 72,134 bales, against 9,645 the previous year; and of Tea 5,318,123 lbs. against 5,796,388 lbs. in the season ending June 1863.

Still, except for the cloud overhanging the Inland Sea business, foreigners recognised the decided improvement in relations that had taken place; and there was no reason to apprehend any immediate trouble, if things were allowed to take their course. Everything looked cheerful. The presence of the military, added to that of the Navy, imparted wonderful life to the place. Picnics were got up; small sporting events ashore and afloat were set on foot; excursions within the ten *ri* radius were taken with scarcely a thought of danger, (although all were careful to carry their revolvers in case of need); and care seemed banished from the place. All was gay; all was hopeful; I wish I could say all was sound. But in my next chapter I have a tale to tell that I would willingly avoid.

CHAPTER XXVI.

ARRIVAL OF H.B.M.'S XX REGIMENT.—ULTIMATUM RESPECTING SHIMONOSEKI.—THE TYCOON'S DIFFICULTIES.—PEACE DISPATCHES FROM EARL RUSSELL ARRIVE TOO LATE.—JAPANESE VISIT EUROPE FOR EDUCATION.—RETURN OF ITO SHIUNSKE AND INOUYE BUNDA.—BEARERS OF A LETTER TO THE PRINCE OF CHOSHIU FROM THE FOREIGN MINISTERS.—CONVEYED TO THEIR PROVINCE ON BOARD H.M.S. "BAROSSA" AND "CORMORANT."—ILL SUCCESS.—THE INEFFECTUAL APPEAL ON BEHALF OF CHOSHIU TO THE MIKADO.—THE ATTACK ON THE PALACE.—OWARI APPOINTED COMMANDER-IN-CHIEF TO PUNISH THE CLAN.—INDIGNATION AGAINST CHOSHIU IN YEDO.—HIS YASHIKIS BURNT.—SUDDEN RETURN OF THE ENVOYS.—THEIR AGREEMENT WITH FRANCE NOT RATIFIED.—DEPARTURE OF EXPEDITION AGAINST SHIMONOSEKI.—FRIENDLY INTERCOURSE BETWEEN THE FOREIGN AND NATIVE SOLDIERS.—THE BATTLE OF SHIMONOSEKI.—DETAILS.—PEACE CONCLUDED.—THE INDEMNITY.—ALTERNATIVES PROPOSED BY FOREIGNERS AND REJECTED BY THE JAPANESE GOVERNMENT.—SIR R. ALCOCK ORDERED HOME TO EXPLAIN MATTERS TO THE FOREIGN OFFICE.

In July 1864, the remainder of H. M. XXth Regiment under the command of Lt. Col. H. R. BROWNE, arrived from Hongkong, and at once took possession of the new barracks built for them on the British Consular Reserve on the Bluff.

The departure of the forces for the demolition of the Shimonoseki forts, and the opening of the Inland Sea was freely spoken of, and the foreign ministers sent an *ultimatum* to the Yedo Government, that if, within twenty days, no satisfactory steps were taken, the fleet would be set in motion. The Japanese with whom foreigners came in contact had, in common with all their countrymen, an overweening opinion of the prowess of Choshiu. They believed that any force that could be sent against the clan would meet with certain destruction. They were often too polite to say so in plain terms; but they shook their heads ominously; and it may well be supposed their sympathies were with their own countryman.

The Tycoon at this juncture was in a peculiarly trying position. All his Ministers were in the sulks, and under the plea of illness absented themselves from their duties: so that practically he might be said to be without a Ministry. And worse than this, he narrowly escaped an attempt to poison him. The quiet, therefore, that had prevailed for several months seemed about to give place to further turmoils of a very serious character.

At this very time, whilst troops were arriving, and the foreign ministers and naval and military authorities were making all kinds of preparations for a struggle, Earl RUSSELL was dispatching from London to Sir RUTHERFORD ALCOCK, instructions, "not to undertake any military operation whatever in the interior of Japan"; and further, stating that the Home Government "would indeed regret the adoption of any measures of hostility against the Japanese Government or princes, even though limited to naval operations, unless absolutely required by self-defence." These instructions arrived too late to be acted upon.

It will be remembered that when the country was

closed against the admission of foreigners, a similar prohibition was issued against Japanese leaving it to visit other realms. This prohibition was so rigidly acted upon, that even sailors who had been driven away by adverse winds, and had been picked up at sea by foreign vessels and brought back to Japan, were very hardly dealt with. Some were not allowed to land, and others were severely punished.

But about the end of 1863 certain young samurai belonging to various clans, obtained permission from their chiefs and, I suppose, the Government, to go to Europe for the purpose of education. Of these some had actually entered the service of foreigners, accepting even menial employment, with the view of picking up instruction and information that they felt their countrymen were deficient in. Two Choshiu men Ito Shiunske and Inouye Bunda, were of the number. These two young men, on arriving in England and seeing the material prosperity and immense resources of the country, left their friends and returned to Japan, it was said, with the intention of informing their clan of the futility of opposing such power; and arrived in Yokohama just as the fleet was waiting for final orders for its departure.

This fact being represented to the foreign ministers, it was resolved, with the consent of the Government, to send two English men-of-war with these gentlemen to Shimonoseki with letters to the Prince of Nagato from the foreign ministers, in hopes that their representations might be effectual in inducing the clan to act more prudently, and to cease its inimical proceedings towards vessels passing the Straits. On the 21st July, accordingly, H. B. M. Ss. Barossa and Cormorant were dispatched, having on board, besides the two native gentlemen alluded to, Messrs. Enslie and Satow, of H. M. Civil service.

It was asserted by some that the object of the ships was to see if the forts would fire into them; but it was not so. The two messengers were landed out of reach of the guns; and, assuming the garb of doctors, made their way to Yamaguchi, where the prince of Nagato and his son were residing. Their reception was not unkindly; but the answer they had to take back was unfavourable. The consequence was that the ships returned to Yokohama, and the warlike excitement increased.

The month of August was one of great activity on the part of Choshiu. A strong and fervent appeal was made to the Mikado, to acknowledge the loyalty of the clan, who, it was asserted, had only acted in obedience to the orders they received; and, to reverse the decision by which the prince and his son were forbidden to enter Kioto. The appeal was unsuccessful, and then it was that the attempt was made to obtain by force of arms what could not be acquired by gentler means. All the daimios around the Court, including HITOTSUBASHI, AIDZU, ECHIZEN, SATSUMA, set themselves in array against them; and such was the consternation in Kioto that there was a general exodus of the population.

The Choshiu men now made the attack on the palace, already alluded to; and, after very determined fighting, were defeated. Other bands belonging to the clan endeavoured from various centres to force their way to the capital, but in each case unsuccessfully. These operations brought on a crisis. It was determined to chastise the clan, and bring it back to its allegiance. The Prince of Owari—one of the Gosanké—was appointed Commander-in-chief; the troops of Satsuma and twenty other clans being ordered to place themselves under his command. It was also decided that the Tycoon should himself take the field, and his hatamotos and their retainers were ordered to hold themselves in readiness.

In Yedo, the intelligence of the violence committed at Kioto aroused intense indignation against the clan. It possessed three *yashikis* within the O-shiro (castle) precincts, besides two in the suburbs. These were immediately invested by the Shogun's forces. A proclamation was issued that Choshiu being recusant against the established Government, and his adherents having caused disturbances in Kioto, steps were to be taken to bring him to order, unless guarantees were given for his future loyalty.

In the midst of all these stirring events, the Envoys who had gone to Europe suddenly returned. They had gone no further than Paris, when, utterly failing in the objects of their mission, they decided to visit no other country. They had made an agreement, however, subject to the Shogun's ratification, that at the end of three months the Inland Sea should be free; and should be kept so, if necessary, by force acting in concert with the French Naval Commander. An indemnity also was to be paid to France of 140,000 dollars, of which 100,000 were to be paid by the Government, and 40,000 by Choshiu.

The fleet was to have sailed on the very day following that of the return of the mission, but was now ordered to wait until the decision of the Shogun's Government was known. It was to the effect that the ratification was impossible; for the provisions could not be carried out. The Envoys were imprisoned and not released for many months.

Before the fleet sailed a very earnest request was sent by the Shogun's Government to the allied Ministers that they should not as yet take any hostile steps; explaining the great difficulties which beset the Government, but trusting that "the foreign representatives would rely upon the action of the Tycoon's Government, and take no steps themselves to force the passage." All this was unheeded. On the 28th August the expedition started. I well remember the circumstances attending the embarkation of the Royal Marines. They were to be conveyed to Shimonoseki on board of H. M. S. Conqueror, which had brought them to Japan. The XXth regiment was drawn up on the French or western hatoba, and an immense crowd of foreigners and natives assembled to see them off. Many thought that the force about to be dispatched was altogether too small; and a feeling of sadness was expressed as Colonel BROWNE the commandant, who remained behind, shook the hand of Colonel SUTHER and wished him a safe and speedy return. The "Minden boys" (XXth) seemed to envy the "jollies" their luck in being selected for active service; but all imagined that they had a very much harder task before them than proved to be the case.

There was some apprehension felt that the departure of the fleet would encourage the ronins to make a descent upon the settlement: but really there was small chance of it; for besides the ships that were left, the French garrison consisted of 300 men; whilst the English had the whole of 2nd batt. of the XXth regiment, 167 men of H. M.'s 67th regiment, 263 men of the Beloochees, about 100 of the Royal Artillery and Engineers, besides the Legation guard. There would therefore have been very little chance for any such force as the ronins were likely to bring. In Yedo they continued to be very troublesome.

From the first the "red regiments," as the English soldiers were called by the Japanese, commanded a good deal of curiosity. The amount of drilling that went on all day long by one corps or another—soldiers or sailors

—was such as to astonish the natives; whilst every few days there were inspections or reviews, or long marches, in heavy marching order, for exercise as well as discipline. A little later, such was the friendliness that sprung up among the Japanese troops stationed at Nögé—about a mile from the foreign settlement—and our men, that the latter joined in these marches—and on one or two occasions in sham fights in the vallies around. By these means the men were kept in splendid health and discipline; in good trim for whatever call might be made upon them. Rifle matches were got up on the beach under the Bluff; and athletic sports became an institution. In these last the Beloochees particularly excelled.

But whilst foreigners were thus rejoicing in their strength and security, the Government continued to be full of anxiety and trouble. The daimios MATSUDAIRA YAMATO-NO-KAMI and ITAKURA SUWO-NO-KAMI, with many smaller officials, were degraded, because they had mismanaged the affair of notifying foreigners as to the Government's intention of closing the port of Yokohama.

I must now hasten to finish the story of Shimonoseki. Choshiu had given fresh offence during the month of August by firing on an American steamer, at Hagi, a place within his territories, where forts had been erected, at some distance from Shimonoseki. The merchant steamer Monitor had anchored there in hopes of obtaining supplies; but was soon convinced of the mistake she had made. The British Admiral was instructed therefore to take the castle of Hagi, but this does not seem to have been attempted.

On Sunday the 4th September, the fleet assembled at Himoshima, consisting of three French—the Semiramis with Admiral JAURES on board, the Dupleix and Tancrède; four Dutch,—the Djambi, Medusa, Metulen Kruis and Amsterdam; one American, the Takiang, a small merchant steamer which had been chartered for the purpose, on board of which Lieut. Pearson U. S. N., 50 men and a Parrot gun, had been embarked; and nine British—the Euryalus with Admiral KUPER, Tartar, Perseus, Conqueror, Barrosa, Leopard, Argus, Bouncer and Coquette.

At 4 P.M. on the 5th the signal to "engage the enemy" was hoisted on the Euryalus and Semiramis, and in half a minute the engagement became general, the forts returning the fire with immense spirit. The batteries ashore were eight in member; the Chofu; the Ravine; the Maita-mura (three); the Sato; the Kybuné Point, and the Stockade. For half an hour no effect seemed to be produced by the artillery from the ships; but then symptoms began to show themselves of the work they were doing. A battery was destroyed by an explosion caused by one of the Armstrong pivot guns; and at 4.34 P.M., the light squadron was directed to close on the batteries. Half an hour later the battery on Chofu Point was silenced, and several of the forts slackened their fire materially. At 7 P.M. the heavy squadron which had been keeping up a telling fire on the Maita-mura forts ceased for the night.

At this time Captain KINGSTON of the Perseus with his second Lieutenant Mr. PITT, Sub. Lieut. FROUDE, Mr. COCHRANE, gunner, and twenty men, quickly joined by a boats' crew from the Medusa under Mr. DE HART, landed, and, driving the gunners from one of the forts, succeeded in spiking all its guns, 14 in number, threw the powder and shot over the parapet, and laid a train to the magazine (which, however, missed), under a severe fire of musketry from the paddy-fields and bush in the neighbourhood. It was well that this dashing feat was accomplished; for the next morning at 10 o'clock the Perseus got aground under this very fort, and her position would have been perilous indeed, had the guns been available and the men to serve them intact. As it was she lay aground all day, and was only relieved from her awkward plight at 11 o'clock on the following morning.

On the 6th the action recommenced. The Tartar and Dupleix, which were anchored under the Sato battery, were wakened up at daylight, to a sense of their situation, by a vigourous and well-directed salute, by which several men on both the ships were killed and wounded. At 7.15 A.M. the marines landed from the Conqueror, under Colonel SUTHER and Lieut. Colonels PENROSE and ADAIR. The Euryalus also landed her small-arms men and marines under Captain ALEXANDER. At 8, all the Maita-mura forts were in their hands, and the barracks in rear were on fire. The marines drove the enemy before them out of the batteries and spiked the guns. But the Choshiu men, though driven out, still attempted to resist, and towards evening made a spirited attack on the marines with five or six hundred men. In this gallant effort they were not successful; but Captain ALEXANDER was wounded by a bullet through his ankle.

Working parties from all the ships were landed on the 8th, with guards of marines to embark the guns from the batteries. At first great numbers of Japanese soldiers had returned to the batteries, but they speedily decamped. In the forts were found a number of Dutch books on artillery, several bows, an immense number of arrows, many muskets, and a map tracing out the position of the ships during the engagement up to the last moment before the flight of the draughtsmen.

About noon, Choshiu showed a flag of truce, under the protection of which an emissary—one of the two gentlemen lately returned from Europe, and who had been taken down in the preliminary trip of the Barossa—was received on board the Euryalus. He had been but a short time with the admiral, when a signal was made to hoist flags of truce. Capitulation was complete and unreserved. To convince the Admirals, however, that the emissary had powers to treat, and of the sincerity of the Prince, it was deemed necessary to have a letter to that effect under his own hand. Two days being necessary for this, it was agreed that actual hostilities should cease, but that the embarkation of the guns should be proceeded with. It was declared on the part of Choshiu, that he was not to blame. He had been only loyally acting up to the orders he had received—once from the Bakufu and repeatedly from the Mikado.

The Admirals expressed a desire to see the Prince, and settle everything personally with him; but this was impossible. He was living at a distance from Shimonoseki, in retirement, (virtually a prisoner), by order of the Court.

An interview with the chieftain being unattainable, he was made acquainted with the terms demanded by the Admirals. These included the promise never to rebuild the forts, or otherwise place any hindrance on the free passage of the Straits; and, the payment of a sum of money as a consideration for sparing the town of Shimonoseki and for the expenses of the expedition. The amount of this indemnity was to be settled by the foreign representatives and the Government of the Shogun. It was plainly stated to the young Envoy that if he did not return, or if no answer were received by the appointed time, the work of destruction would be proceeded with.

Punctual to the hour he returned, bearing the sign-manual of the Prince, agreeing to everything.

During his absence the guns from all the forts, 72 in all, were placed on board the various ships of the squadron, the Japanese from the town offering their aid as if they were glad too see the last of neighbours that had been the means of bringing danger so near to them. During the operation, not a two-sworded man was to be seen.

The amount of the indemnity decided upon by the ministers was $3,000,000; the payment of which the Yedo Government undertook, saying that they would collect it from Choshiu.

The French and English Governments, but particularly the latter, were desirous that instead of a pecuniary payment, the Japanese Government should open another port; or throw the port of Hiogo open to foreigners at an earlier period than that last fixed for it. The Dutch and American Ministers, (the latter of whom claimed an equal share in the spoil with the others, contending that the moral influences of his coöperation, and not the actual force he was able to send, was to be estimated), preferred receiving the actual money. All, however, acquiesced in the proposal of the British Cabinet, and the opening of Shimonoseki or some other port was strenuously urged upon the Government, but as steadily refused. Had it been agreed upon a great deal of heart-burning and acrimonious feeling would have been avoided, all to the advantage of Japan.

The opening of Niigata, of which so much was expected, has shown how little foreign trade was to be benefited from an open port on the west coast; and the experience of the commercial advantages to be derived from Hiogo and even of Osaka itself, has proved how comparatively limited the trade with any ports in that region would be. The probability is that for a while it would have been a useless concession; for very few foreigners would have cared to settle there whilst the troubles between the clan and the Government continued.

By agreeing therefore to this alternative, the Government would have got off very easily. No money would have had to be paid; and if trade had arisen, it would have benefited the country. As it was, they were not able to pay the first instalment of $50,000 until the following August, nearly a year after the event; and when difficulties prevented the punctual payment of the later instalments, which the foreign powers were always willing to remove in the simple way described, the foreign proposals were proudly rejected, and the money was gradually, at very long intervals, paid. The final proposal was, that, if the Mikado would ratify the treaties, consent to the opening of Hiogo and Osaka at once, instead of eighteen months later, and to a revision of the tariff on a basis of 5 per cent., two-thirds of the indemnity—$2,000,000—should be foregone. But the opening of those ports one day earlier than had been agreed upon they would not think of. And when the treaty was ratified, and the revision of the tariff agreed to, though Sir Harry Parkes pressed the third provision on their consideration and urged its acceptance, it was replied that "the indemnity they were quite prepared to pay. It would severely tax their resources, but they decidedly preferred to meet this obligation, rather than consent at once to the opening of Hiogo and Osaka."

The last payment was not made until the middle of 1874, just ten years after the battle of Shimonoseki.

As a matter of course the various Governments approved the action of their Ministers after the signal success of the allied squadron; but Sir Rutherford Alcock, having been ordered home to give personal information as to the actual state of affairs in Japan, now made preparations for his departure.

CHAPTER XXVII.

THE CHANGES THAT HAVE HAPPENED SINCE THE BATTLE OF SHIMONOSEKI.—EFFECTS OF THE BATTLES OF KAGOSHIMA AND SHIMONOSEKI ON THE CLANS OF SATSUMA AND CHOSHIU.—BITTERNESS OF CHOSHIU AGAINST THE YEDO GOVERNMENT.—THE BRAVERY AND PATRIOTISM OF THE CLAN.—ADOPTION BY SATSUMA AND CHOSHIU OF FOREIGN ARMS.—DESIRE OF THE TYCOON TO DO THE SAME, BUT UNWILLINGNESS OF MANY OF HIS RETAINERS TO USE THEM.—PRESENT PREJUDICE OF FIGHTING MEN IN FAVOUR OF THE SWORD.—THE SWORD AND THE RULE THAT IT SHOULD NOT BE UNSHEATHED EXCEPT TO SHED BLOOD.—A PERSONAL REMINISCENCE.—ONE MORE PROOF OF THE DEADLY CHARACTER OF THE SWORD.—EXCURSIONS OF FOREIGNERS.

It is difficult to realise that all I have been hitherto recording happened so few years ago. Is it possible that only fifteen years have elapsed since the battle of Shimonoseki? Where are all those who took part in it? Where those who were the principals in all the negotiations preceding it? Sir RUTHERFORD ALCOCK has since left his mark as British Minister at Peking, and, having retired, is now constantly before the public in connection with some learned society, or some scheme for the advantage of China or Japan. His colleagues of 1864 have also retired into private life, and are no longer heard of. But how is it with the Shogun?

The Gorojiu?

The Prince of Nagato and his son?

The seven Kugé?

The young men who went to Scotland for their education?

And how is it with the Mikado?

Where are the ronins?

Where the guards who were employed to keep them in check?

Where are the daimios?

The hatamotos?

The two-sworded retainers of whom we were wont to speak as the dangerous classes?

Where is the Bakufu, or Government of the Shogun?

Where the Dairi—the Court of the Mikado?

There is no Shogun.

There is no Gorojiu.

The old Prince of Nagato is probably dead, for he is never heard of. His son lives as a noble in a pleasant foreign-built house in the suburb of Shinagawa.

Of the seven Kugés, one, SANJO SANEYOSHI, is Daijo Daijin, or Prime Minister of Japan; and has been so since the year 1868.

Every one of the youths who went to Scotland occupies now some important position in the state. Of the two who returned to warn their chief—ITO is the Minister or Secretary of State for Home Affairs; INOUYE BUNDA is Minister for Foreign Affairs.

The Mikado no longer simply reigns—He governs!

The ronins are no more—they and the guards absorbed either in the ranks of commerce, or other industrial workers. Very few now either carry a sword or follow a military career.

The daimios are private gentlemen, with the rank of noblemen.

The hatamotos (upholders of the flag) no longer possess status or privileges. They are but as influence or ability may place them.

The two-sworded men have long lain their murderous weapons aside, and 'dangerous classes' are only spoken of as a memory of the past.

The Bakufu is as if it had never been; and the Dairi with its curiously mysterious inner life at Kioto has given place to a Court in Tokio, whose activity and personal influence (especially that of the Empress) shed blessings over all the land.

Such changes have taken place within the fifteen years of which I have yet to treat. How these changes have been effected is now my principal theme.

The effect of the battle of Kagoshima I have already described. It led to a distinctly improved appreciation of foreigners by the Satsuma clan, who turned their attention at once to the best means of obtaining foreign appliances both of war and commerce.

On Choshiu, the effect of the battle of Shimonoseki was only seen by foreigners, in the material fact, that the clan was rendered powerless for further aggression against ships entering the Inland Sea.' Beyond that fact, there was nothing that brought the clan and foreigners within notice of each other: but, unhappily for the clan, being at logger-heads with the Government, its troubles did not close with the departure of the foreign squadron.

The bitter feeling entertained by all the clansmen against the Government was intensified a hundred-fold by the events I have been recording; and severe as the lesson was that they had received from foreigners, they were determined to fight à outrance whatever troops of their own countrymen were sent against them. Brave fellows! It is impossible not to sympathise with such warriors, malgré all their old opposition to us. Unlike other clans I could name, they were never mere swashbucklers. In Yedo the people all liked Choshiu men as much as they dreaded the samurai of Satsuma. They fought openly and nobly in support of their patriotic convictions.

When the allied squadron set forth for Shimonoseki, all the men in it, and every man, civil or military, left behind, felt that the foe about to be encountered was worthy of their steel. And though the victory was more easy than had been anticipated, this fact has never been disputed:—that, to the present day the Choshiu clan has maintained its right to be classed with the bravest and noblest in Japan.

One circumstance that always appears to me worthy of notice with regard to Satsuma and Choshiu, is, that both of them practically acknowledged the superiority of foreign appliances in war, by obtaining rifles and ammunition, and largely arming their men with them, adopting, at the same time, as far as they could, foreign drill and discipline. The Shogun was desirous of doing the same; and some regiments that occupied barracks in the neighbourhood of Yokohama, were very creditably instructed. But in the fight with Choshiu that was about to take place, many of the samurai to whom rifles were offered, refused to use them, or to undergo the new drill, preferring to trust to the old bows and arrows, the trusty sword, and the tactics of Old Japan.

And even now the true Japanese warrior clings to his sword. In the recent Satsuma rebellion, in some of the fights it was found that the imperialists who were wounded with sword-cuts were nearly as numerous as those who received bullet wounds.

It used to be a prevailing notion that no samurai might unsheath his sword except to shed blood. This is an exaggeration. Doubtless it was well, that among a class so fiery and so regardless of life as the samurai were, there should be some kind of restraint on the too impulsive beings; but the laws of IYEYAS, made expressly for the guidance of the samurai, have no such provision. The great TOKUGAWA chief very clearly defined the duty of every samurai to uphold the honour of his class; but he did not instruct them to become butchers.

Shortly after my arrival in Japan, I remember meeting in a friend's house, a yakunin who had come upon some business for his prince; and observing that he had taken his sword from his belt, and placed it on the ground by the side of his chair, curiosity induced me to ask to be allowed to look at it. My friend, no doubt in mere cajolery, told me to leave it alone, as it was a rule with Japanese never to allow the sword to be unsheathed without shedding blood.

The yakunin, seeing that I hesitated to touch the weapon, on hearing this, kindly took it up, unsheathed it, and handed it to me to look at, pointing out with pride that it was a remarkably fine blade; and then added in fair English:—" Mr. ———— pays me a poor compliment when he tells his stranger friend that the sword I consented to his examining could not be returned to its sheath unless dimmed by blood."

After a little time, when the business on which he had come was concluded, he turned to me again and said, as he pointed to numerous samples of rifles and ammunition and brought his hand down on a revolver case—

"You see I have more confidence in Englishmen than they have in me. I come into a room full of destructive weapons without suspicion. And, as he was about leaving he seemed to be unable to get the remark out of his head. "Mr ———— and I understand each other;" he remarked. "I know he only said that in fun: but some Japanese would not understand him, and would think it cowardice." He again wavèd his hand round to the specimens of fire-arms and said " So many!" and then touching his sword-hilt, his last word as he joined three or four attendants who had been waiting for him outside, was—"One!"

This occured in Nagasaki, shortly after the battle of Kagoshima, and the man was an officer of Satsuma.

But although he might thus speak of the foreign weapons outnumbering the single sword just restored to his girdle, its deadly character was not one whit inferior to them. Of this one more sad proof was given before the close of the year.

The excursions of foreigners were usually confined to three or four special routes : viz., in one direction to the temple of Dai-Shi-sama at Kawasaki, to reach which the Tokaido was traversed for about eight miles; and in the opposite direction to the caves of Totsuka, and the temples at Fujisawa dedicated to Ugio Shonin—both on the Tokaido; besides the most frequented of all— by Kanasawa to Kamakura, the ancient governmental capital of the empire, to DAIBUTSZU the great bronze image of BUDDHA, which all foreigners made it a principal object to see; and to Yenoshima, a kind of holy isle about five miles distant from Kamakura.

To these three latter places there were several routes. One was by the Tokaido and by branch roads from Totsuka and Fujisawa to Yenoshima and Kamakura; but the most favourite was by bridle-paths over the hills to

Kanasawa, some of the views from which were surpassingly beautiful.

The journeys were most commonly made on horseback, as most of the residents had ponies of their own, and there were plenty of livery-stables from whence suitable animals could be hired by visitors. As yet, with the exception of the Tokaido, there was no road fit for carriage traffic, and no wheeled vehicles had been introduced. The only alternatives to those who did not like riding, were the ordinary bamboo cango, (a very uncomfortable kind of conveyance), or walking.

In addition to the naval and military officers, who, as new comers, were naturally as curious with regard to the country and people as others had been, there were constantly visitors from Shanghai and Hongkong. Excursions were very numerous; for all the places mentioned possessed features of interest; history and beauty of scenery combining to render them attractive.

Kamakura, especially, has a place in Japanese history which most foreigners know as a general fact. As, however, it was founded by YORITOMO, whom I have more than once spoken of as the originator of the dual system of government, I will give in my next chapter, some particulars of the city and its founder, before passing on.

CHAPTER VIII.

A BRIEF ACCOUNT OF YORITOMO, THE FOUNDER OF WHAT IS CALLED SHOGUN-KE, AND ALSO OF THE CITY OF KAMAKURA, WHERE HE APPEARS TO HAVE REIGNED AS SHOGUN FOR TWENTY YEARS.

KAMAKURA.—DESCRIPTION AND HISTORY.—YORITOMO ITS FOUNDER.—YORITOMO'S DESCENDANTS HOJO YOSHITOKI.—RECAPITULATION OF THE FOREGOING.—YORITOMO'S SUCCESSORS, AND END OF THE DYNASTY.—KAMAKURA NO LONGER THE GOVERNMENTAL CAPITAL.

[*The following account was written for me, by Mr.* HECO, *a native of Japan, but an American citizen, in the year 1865.*]

YORITOMO was the son of YOSHITOMO and his wife TOKIWA GOZEN. He had two younger brothers, NORIYORI and YOSHITSUNE.

In the era of Heiji the first, or about 712 years ago, YOSHITOMO (the father of YORITOMO), and a daimio named KIYOMORI, fought against each other. After years of discord YORITOMO was ordered by his father to take command of his army and to levy war against his enemy; at the same time he received a family sword called "Higé-kiri-Maru," and also an ancient suit of armour.

With these YORITOMO went forth to battle, but was unfortunately defeated. Soon after he was captured by his enemy, MUNEKIYO, and exiled to Cape Idzu. This occurred in the era An-gin the first, or about 700 years ago, when he was only fourteen years old. In this strange country, he found a friend in a daimio called HOJIO TOKIMASA, who adopted him as his son, and subsequently gave him his daughter in marriage. He had not long been married, when he removed to Kamakura, which had become his property in the following manner.

It was first settled by his ancestor HATCHIMAN TARO, YOSHI-IYE, who, having received an order from the Mikado to go to Oshiu and subdue the rebellious princes ABENO, MUNETO and SADATO, on his way thither he stopped at Kamakura, and built a small temple and worshipped there. Thenceforward the place became known as the property of GENKE or house of GENJI,—that to which YORITOMO belonged.

YORITOMO's first act was to remove the temple of Hachiman-gu from Uiga-hama to Tsuruga-oka—its present site. Having accomplished this, he began to build palaces and official residences, and quickly gave the place the appearance of a city. In those days the Japanese nobles seem to have been quite as prolific in rebellious lords, as any portion of Europe in the middle ages. Ten years later, we find YORITOMO ordering his two brothers named above, to go against the prince KISO YOSHINAKA, who had rebelled against the Government of the Mikado at Miyako, and to subdue him. Having successfully effected their object, by subjugating the prince, they went further and made war with the house of HEIKE (their fathers enemy, KIYOMORI) at Ichi-no-tani near Hiogo, and drove their enemy from the castle and territory.

KIYOMORI and his followers escaped westward through

the Inland Sea, and occupied the Island of Yashima and the northern edge of Shikoku. To these places YOSHITSUNE and NORIYORI followed, and in the first month of the era Bunji the first (about 690 years ago) NORIYORI crossed to Shikoku from Nagato and landed his forces, whilst YOSHITSUNE landed with his army at Sanuki in the second month. A naval engagement ensued between the contending hosts. A month later and KIYOMORI was completely repulsed; Yashima Castle was taken; and from that period YORITOMO, the Shogun, began to rule the empire of Japan, as military chief, and head of all Government affairs, yet acknowledging the supremacy of the Mikado.

YOSHITSUNE, returning to Kamakura, was not well received by YORITOMO. In fact, on his arriving at the outer gate of the city, he was not admitted. For certain slanderous reports had come to the ears of the Shogun, and representations made to the effect that YOSHITSUNE was working secretly for his own aggrandisement, and had in view the dethroning of his brother and reigning in his place. Not finding the cordial reception he had expected, and being refused entrance into the city, he went to Oshiu, and died at Koromogawa. Some say, he crossed to the Island of Yezo where he was deified by the people under the title " Gikei Dai-miyo-jin." A few years later YORITOMO ordered his brother NORIYORI to leave Kamakura, and repair to Cape Idzu, and then and there to commit *hara-kiri* in the temple of Shu-san-ji. Thus the two brave and noble brothers of YORITOMO were treated by him for whose interest and glory they had done so much. Both were expelled and died in a most lamentable manner. Seven years after the death of his youngest brother, 678 years ago, YORITOMO himself died at the age of fifty-three, leaving two sons, the eldest of whom YORI-IYE succeeded to his father's throne.

The personal deeds of YORITOMO are not dwelt upon by

the authorities I have had the opportunity of consulting, but his dynasty seems to have been most unhappy. YORI-IYE, soon after succeeding to his father's throne, fell dangerously ill, and retired from the direction of public affairs for a time, after placing 38 provinces west of Hakoné under the charge of his brother SANETOMO, and 28 east of Hakoné under ICHIBATA KIMI, his eldest son. That same year he died at Idzu, and the father-in-law of YORITOMO went with his son and assassinated ICHIBATA KIMI—so that the whole empire fell into the hands of YORI-IYE's brother, SANETOMO. He was thus the third of the dynasty, and reigned 17 years. He had several narrow escapes from assassination—but at length met his death through the direction of none other than the regent of the empire—the brother of YORITOMO's widow. On a certain day the Shogun went, accompanied by all the daimios, to visit the temple of Hatchiman. The plot was to be carried out by the instrumentality of another. The regent excused himself from attendance on the pretence of illness: for if he were present, it would be his duty to carry the sword of the Shogun and follow immediately behind; and in case any injury happened to his master he would be held personally responsible. The plot was well laid. The Shogun's nephew was persuaded to kill his uncle in revenge for the death of his father by the Shogun's hand; and the regent Hojo urged it not only as a justifiable act of retribution, but also, because, if successful, he, being the only heir, would of course succeed to the throne. The young man, Kugiyo, lent a willing ear to this advice. He went to the temple Hatchiman and waited under a tree (the tree is still there), near the central stone steps of the temple. Having offered his prayers, the Shogun was returning about dusk, when he was suddenly attacked by Koogiyo, who sprung up from his hiding place and stabbed him with a dagger.

The treacherous regent, hearing that Koogiyo had accomplished the fatal work, sent troops, as if to avenge the Shogun's death, and killed his poor dupe, declaring that he had rebelled against the person and Government of the Shogun. Thus the race of YORITOMO was extinguished. It comprised but three reigns and endured only forty years.

It is satisfactory to know that HOJO YOSHITOKI, although he contrived to put an end to the legitimate YORITOMO dynasty, did not succeed in his design of becoming himself Shogun. The other daimios would not permit it, and he found it impossible to do so in opposition to them. He therefore advised his sister (YORITOMO's widow) to send for a successor to Kioto. In reply to this application, she received a child for adoption in the person of a son of Kugé Kam-Paku MITCHI-IYE, named YORITSUNE, who was only two years of age at the time. Thereupon HOJO made the child the head of the Government of the Shogun, and himself continued regent and for many years the actual ruler of Japan.

I have thus shewn how the legitimate dynasty of the Shogun YORITOMO, the founder of the city of Kamakura, came to an end in three reigns, comprising a period of forty years: and it was seen that envy, hatred, malice and all uncharitableness had played their part from the first. The world, during the six thousand years of its existence, has but one general characteristic in this respect, and all ages, all countries and all peoples, civilized and uncivilized, have borne witness to the fact. YORITOMO himself appears to have had greatness thrust upon him by the achievements of his brothers—but when they had successfully wielded their swords in his service, he feared lest they should snatch his high estate from him, and themselves enjoy what their bravery had secured for him. He banished both, and they died in exile—the younger performing *hara-kiri* by YORITOMO's orders. The immediate successor was his eldest son—YORI-IYE—but he through illness was forced to divide the rule between his younger brother SANETOMO—and his son ICHIBATA KIMI; the latter was murdered by order of his great grandfather (the father of YORITOMO's wife) who thus hoped to clear the way for his own lineal male descendants. In this however he was disappointed, SANETOMO—the younger son of YORITOMO assumed the Shogunate over the whole land and reigned seventeen years. Treachery seems to have been inherent in the family; for the brother of YORITOMO's wife inveigled SANETOMO's nephew and apparent heir to murder him, and then caused his dupe to be put to death—thus cutting off the last lineal descendant of YORITOMO—and hoping himself to assume the office of Shogun. The Council of daimios not permitting this, his sister, by his advice, sent to Miako, whence the Mikado sent a child two years old for her adoption, who was placed at the head of the Government as Shogun—and the traitorous HOJO YOSHITOKI became Regent and actual ruler of the country.

Such is a recapitulation of the history of YORITOMO and his legitimate male descendants as given above. The adopted child was named YORITSUNE. When he arrived at the age of 13—the Regent HOJO made him marry the daughter of YORI-IYE the son and successor of YORITOMO. The lady had reached the advanced age of 33. This remarkable match was made by HOJO only to blind the eyes of others, and induce the world to believe that he was no enemy, but on the contrary, a fast friend and faithful servant of the dynasty. He managed, however, to keep the reins of government in his hands during the whole reign of YORITSUNE, and on the Shogun reaching the age of 20—made him retire to Kioto, where he died before he had reached his fortieth year. The Regent applied again to Kioto for a successor, and a youth of 10 years old called YORITSUGU was sent, who died when only 18, at the Mikado's metropolis.

For the third time, the Mikado was appealed to, and a successor was found in the person of a son of the Mikado named MUNETAKA SHINNO. He was still so young that HOJO continued to hold the office and exercise the functions of Regent. (It was early in this Shogunate, that the law was enacted that no more than five Chinese junks should be allowed to come yearly to Japan, and and that if more came, they should be burnt or otherwise destroyed.)

At the age of 33—MUNETAKA SHINNO died, and his son KOREYASU SHINNO occupied his place.

It was in this reign, the seventh from YORITOMO, that the Portuguese first visited the country. Our chronicle states that they came with a fleet and arrived at the island of Kiushiu. They brought a letter from their Government to the Shogun, to the effect that their sovereign was desirous that Japan should come under Portuguese protection and be dependent. KOREYASU SHINNO was extremely indignant on hearing such an impudent communication, and ordered that they should be driven away from the country. The order was executed, and having put to sea, they were overtaken by a typhoon which sunk all their ships, and of all who had reached Japan only three men were saved to return to Portugal and tell the sad news of the fate of their companions.

Kamakura still continued to be the residence of the Shogun and consequently the seat of Government. On the death of KOREYASU, his son become the eighth Shogun who had governed from thence, and nothing of importance occurred during his reign; but in that of the ninth, MORIKUNI SHINNO, the army left Kamakura for Akusaki and destroyed the castle and confiscated the property of a rebellious daimio KUSUNOKI. At the time of the capture the prince himself was absent, and only a few of the retainers were there, and thus the victory of the Shogun's troops was easy and complete. Having effected this the army marched against another prince, MORIYOSHI SHINNO, and took the castle at Yoshino in the province of Yamato. Proceeding further to a place called Chihaya in Yamato, they came front to front with KUSUNOKI, and this time they suffered a repulse. This was the beginning of a series of misfortunes. In the following month a daimio, AKAMATSU ENSHIN, attacked Miyako, and, as in duty bound, the Shogun's army hurried to defend the metropolis and the Mikado. It was unsuccessful in a pitched battle with AKAMATSU, and the daimios OWARI-NO-KAMI and ASHIKAGA were ordered to go against the insurgents. They fought a battle, in which OWARI was killed: whilst another disaffected prince, NITTA YOSHISADA collected an army, and, taking advantage of the absence of the grand army of the Shogun, marched upon Kamakura. The city was taken without difficulty, and from that period ceased to be the Shogun's capital.

These nine reigns are called by the Japanese the YORITOMO dynasty—but our account will cause it to be fully understood that the six last Shoguns were only grafts upon the family tree, by the appointment of the Mikado and by adoption. Throughout the whole of the latter period the Regency continued in the HOJO family —and in every Shogunate they were the real directors of affairs.

The dynasty of YORITOMO then, and the Regency of the house of HOJO—extended over a period of about 154 years. It is a little over 500 years since they came to a close—and for a considerable period the grand empire was divided into two sections, North and South. For a long series of years War raged between the two divisions —but at length the former was victorious, and its ruler ASHIKAGA TAKA-UJI became Shogun over the whole land. But Kamakura was no longer the capital—and it gradually sunk in importance, and became only remembered for its former glory—the Hatchiman and one or two other temples and the Image of DAIBUTSZU— which to this day attract numberless pilgrims to worship at their shrines.

CHAPTER XXIX.

ANOTHER TRAGEDY.—ATTACK AT KAMAKURA ON MAJOR BALDWIN AND AND LIEUT. BIRD.—MANNER OF THE ATTACK.—CONSTERNATION THROUGHOUT THE SETTLEMENT.—DETERMINATION.—THE FUNERAL.—JUSTICE.—THE ASSASSINS CAUGHT AND DECAPITATED.—FIRST DOUBTS OF FOREIGNERS AS TO THE TRUE CULPRITS CLEARED UP.—SHIMIDZU SEIJI.—PROCES VERBAL.—SENTENCE.—PUBLIC EXPOSURE IN THE STREETS OF YOKOHAMA.—THE EXECUTION GROUND.—THE EXECUTIONER.—THE PRISONER'S DEMEANOUR.—HIS ANATHEMA AGAINST FOREIGNERS.—HIS DEATH ; AND THE EXHIBITION OF HIS HEAD FOR THREE DAYS.—CAPTURE AND DECAPITATION OF HIS MISERABLE ACCOMPLICE.—FATAL FRACAS IN THE YOSHIWARA.—A FRENCHMAN KILLED, BUT WITHOUT MALICE PREPENSE.

AND here I have brought my readers to the spot where another of those cold-blooded, treacherous assassinations took place, of which so many have been recorded.

On the 21st of November, two English officers, Major BALDWIN and Lieutenant BIRD, both of H. M. XXth Regiment, having visited Yenoshima and DAIBUTSZ', turned into the road that led from the cross-roads to the sea-shore ; and had hardly entered it when they were attacked by two men, each of whom, selecting his victim, made sure work by making the assault from behind, with those dreadful swords whose sharp edges and heavy substance rendered their gashes so deadly.

MAJOR BALDWIN, who was riding behind, had not time to use his revolver. The assassin rushed out upon him, and with the fateful upward stroke, cut him from hip to shoulder, dividing the spine, so that he fell at once from his horse, dead. Lieut. BIRD appears to have drawn out his revolver and fired one shot at the assailant of his companion, when he himself was assaulted by the second villain, and mortally wounded. It appeared from the testimony given at the inquest, that he was not actually killed on the spot; for when the village authorities were informed of the catastrophe and went to him, he was able to tell them his name, and that they were English officers. Suspicion for a moment fell on the officials; that they had cut the thread of poor BIRD's life in order that he might tell no tales. But it was dispelled eventually by the capture of the actual murderers. In truth, with such wounds as both of them received, it was quite impossible they could have lived long. They were very numerous and most of them fatal.

The consternation spread through the settlement by this occurrence exhibited itself in a quiet, resolute determination to have the affair investigated to the bottom. Sir RUTHERFORD ALCOCK was on the point of departure for Europe; but he at once laid the matter before the Gorojiu in such a manner as shewed that there must be no trifling this time. The culprits themselves must be found.

And they were found.

The bodies were removed from Kamakura and brought to Yokohama. The funeral took place the following day, and was certainly the most imposing that had ever been seen in Yokohama. In addition to draughts of men from the ships, and from each military corps ashore, all the officers who could be spared from duty, and all the civilians resident in Yokohama, besides many Japanese high officials, were present. It was a most impressive ceremony throughout, but it was rendered the more so by the solemn intensity of feeling which pervaded every breast in that vast assembly. It was not a cry for vengeance that was subsequently raised. It was a demand for justice. And justice was done.

Both of the assassins were captured; and both were decapitated. The first was taken just before Sir RUTHERFORD ALCOCK left; and as it was the first occasion on which any murderer of foreigners was brought to justice, he may well claim it as one of the beneficial results of his decisive policy.

There were many doubts expressed by foreigners, but more still by Japanese, as to whether the first prisoner taken was actually one of the guilty. It was openly alleged that he was a culprit doomed to death for another crime; and only represented to foreigners as one of those who had taken part in the assault on the Kamakura victims, in order to deceive them, and satisfy them of the intentions of the Government to bring all such villains to justice, and of their power to punish them. The perusal of the following *Procès Verbal*, signed by Mr. FLOWERS, H. B. M.'s Acting Consul, and Mr. SATOW, will, however, set all such doubts at rest:—

PROCES VERBAL

Of the recognition of SHIMIDZU SEIJI, *one of the murderers of Major* BALDWIN *and Lieut.* BIRD, *by the Japanese witnesses* SEI, KANEKITCHI, *and* ICHIBE, *at the Japanese prison, Tobé, on the 27th December, 1864.*

"Under instructions from H. M. Chargé d'Affaires, we proceeded to Tobe, at 1 P.M., for the purpose of being present at the recognition of the criminal by the above-mentioned witnesses, and on our arrival found the witnesses assembled.

"It was arranged that the witnesses should view and observe the features and person of the prisoner from behind a screen; an arrangement which the sliding partitions of Japanese rooms rendered perfectly easy.

"The prisoner arrived from Yedo about 4 P.M., and was immediately placed so as to be fully exposed to the observation of the witnesses.

"When a sufficient time had elapsed to enable the witnesses to speak to the identity, they were separately interrogated, and respectively made the following statements:—

"SEI—(a widow—who keeps the sweetmeat stall at the gate of . Hajiman)—declared that she recognised the prisoner to be the man who laid the hat on her bench, before going to the temple.

"KANEKITCHI—(a lad 11 years of age, residing at Miura),—declared that he recognised the prisoner as the man who with drawn sword attacked the first foreigner.

"ISHIBE—(the keeper of the KADOYA tea-house at Totsuka)—declared that he recognised the prisoner as one of the two samurai, who, on the night of the 22nd of the 10th Japanese month, came on to his premises and imperiously demanded food.

"Whereupon we proceeded into the room where the prisoner was, and the following questions were put and replies received, through the undersigned E. SATOW as interpreter:—

"'Are you indeed SHIMIDZU SEIJI?'

"'Yes: my name is SHIMIDZU SEIJI.'

"'Are you one of the men who killed the foreign officers at Kamakura on the 22nd of the 10th Japanese month?'"

"Yes: I killed one of the foreign officers at Kamakura."

The last question was repeated in a somewhat varied form, and the prisoner rejoined:—

"'Without doubt I am one of the men who killed the foreigners at Kamakura. But I have something to say about the manner in which I have been examined."

"At this point the Japanese officers rushed in, and

ordering the prisoners to be silent, requested that the interrogations might cease; and the undersigned Acting Consul, considering the satisfactory character of the recognition, and the subsequent acknowledgment of guilt, rendered it unnecessary to proceed further, we retired to the next apartment.

"The prisoner looked pale from confinement; but did not exhibit on his person or countenance, any marks of exhaustion or ill-usage.

MARCUS FLOWERS,
Acting Consul.
ERNEST SATOW,
Student interpreter."

The sentence passed upon this wretched man was, that he should first be exposed through the streets of Yokohama, then decapitated, and his head subsequently exhibited on the public highway.

Accordingly, about 5 P.M. on the 30th December, he was placed, tightly bound, on a pack-horse, and led through the streets both of the foreign settlement and the native town. A board was carried before him; on which was his sentence, written in large characters, such as all could read. A sufficient number of officials of the lower grades walked in the procession; which was augmented every minute, by scores of natives and foreigners.

His demeanour was that of a most determined and rabid hater of foreigners. Throughout the whole route, he sung at the loudest pitch of his voice, sentences full of his abhorrence of them, and calling on his countrymen to do as he had done. He was even addressed by foreigners, and replied to them, glorying in his deed. He partook of refreshment at one tea-house in the native town; and it was quite evident, that, whatever were the feelings generally prevalent as to foreigners, there was a strong sympathy felt for him—hardly to be wondered at, considering the manly way he played his part throughout.

The procession moved out, and went to the Execution

Ground, just above the Tobé prison; but it was now quite dark, and not possible for the military to see the decapitation that night. So as this was deemed to be a most important part of the proceedings, he was removed to the prison, and, much to his own chagrin, spared in life for another night and morning.

At nine o'clock the next morning, the XXth Regiment, the Marines, and the Artillery, were formed in three sides of a square, opposite the spot where he was to suffer, and a very large majority of the residents occupied the ground within the enclosure.

Ordinary executions were quite frequent. They took place within the precincts of the Tobé prison, in a small paved square, enclosed by black boarded palings. Those who hear of decapitations, in lands where it is almost unknown, or who judge of such things by the accounts handed down from the middle ages, and picture to themselves all the paraphernalia of the axe and the block, with the half brutalised, masked executioner, have nothing before them at all assimilating to a decapitation in Japan. It is done so unceremoniously, and in such a matter-of-fact, easy, off-hand way, with that marvellous cleaver, the sword, that it produces no emotion. Generally the prisoners are sufficiently drugged to prevent their being actually conscious at the last of what is taking place. Their sentence is read to them; and they are at once hurried off, their arms bound tightly behind them, to their death. A hole about three feet square and four to six inches deep has been prepared; on one side of which they are made to kneel. They are supported and hurried in, blindfold, by two gaolers, who, in days gone by, used always to be of the *yéta* class; and while these men placed the condemned on his kness, bent his head forward, and bared his neck and shoulders, the executioner poured a little water on his sword with a small ladle, from a bucket close at hand, and every preparation was complete. The executioner, baring his arms and tying the sleeves back in a manner peculiar to Japanese, raised his sword, and in a moment, with one fell swoop, the work was done. The head fell into the hole, the body over it; and those whose duty it was, huddled trunk and head into a mat bag prepared for them, and all was over.

But special criminals were dealt with elsewhere. The crucifixions, for instance, for such crimes as the murder of a husband or a father, and the burnings alive which in some cases expiated the crime of arson, took place on special execution grounds; and on one of these SHIMIDZU SEIJI was now to yield his life.

The site was particularly well chosen; for it was the highest point of the table-land above the Tobé, and very spacious and open withal, except at the back, where the pine trees closed it in. On the present occasion a fence had been placed around a sufficient space to accommodate all the foreigners likely to put in an appearance; and forms had been placed for the European and native officials. The hour appointed was 10 A.M., but it was near 11 before a norimon with a few prison attendants was seen wending its way from the prison, along the narrow winding paths between the fields; and shortly it arrived on the ground. The bars of the norimon were removed, and the murderer got out nimbly, bound as he was, and bowed to the native officers. Evidently he had not been drugged; for, when the men came forward with a cloth to bind his eyes, he pleaded so earnestly that he might be spared this humiliation, that the officer granted his prayer; and he immediately walked lightly and jauntily to the hole, and knelt in front if it, before the attendants had time to lay hold of him to guide him in the usual manner.

The executioner of the day was a young man, at whose side the regular executioner was standing. SHIMIDZU asked him to wait a moment. He then threw himself back on his haunches, and sung a verse containing a terrible imprecation on foreigners; then, placing himself in position, the attendants adjusting his clothes, he looked up at the executioner, and asked if he was sure of his skill; remarking that he had a very thick neck. The executioner seemed a little taken aback by this; but after the utterance of one more most discordant, passionate howl against foreigners, the doomed one bent his head forward, and said, "Now." In an instant the sword flashed through the air; but, alas! although certainly death accompanied the first blow—the spinal chord was severed and the head fell forward—yet it took two more slashes actually to sever it from the trunk.

As the sword fell the first time, the artillery discharged one gun, which it is not improbable the assassin may have heard as the last sound, ere his senses failed him.

All was over. The heroism with which the man met his death, awakened in many breasts a feeling of compassion—or rather of sorrow that if such a man must die by the sword, it had not been in a better cause.

The execution ground is about two miles from the settlement of Yokohama; but as foreigners returned to their own homes, they found at the Yoshida bridge, at the entrance of the native town, the ghastly head, moist and bleeding, impaled on an iron spike, the neck embedded in clay, on a kind of low gallows or stand, attended by guards, appointed to watch it and see that it was not touched by the natives; and there it remained for three days—the inscription of the crime and the sentence being placed in front of it.

It is a remarkable fact that, ever since then, all Japanese who have assaulted foreigners have been captured, and have been dealt with according to law. And it is very certain that, in every case, the actual culprits might have been taken had proper efforts been made; and had there been no fear of consequences.

I will no further refer to the capture and decapitation of the companion of Shimidzu, which took place two or three months later, than to say that the spectacle was in every way the very opposite to that displayed in his case. A poor, tortured victim, so heavily drugged that he could not keep his eyes open whilst waiting a few minutes (as he had to do) for the arrival of the British officials: with difficulty supported to the fatal spot, and unable to support his head as it was bent over the hole. In his case the work was well and cleanly done by the proper executioner; and everyone who witnessed it sorrowed to see such a mean and pitiable exhibition.

But justice was satisfied; and for a considerable time, such cowardly lamentable personal attacks ceased.

Towards the end of the year, a *fracas* took place in Yokohama which had a fatal result. Some French sailors, in a state of intoxication went to the Yoshiwara, the immoral quarter of the town. A quarrel arose between them and a number of the people, and they were obliged to fly, pursued by many of the exasperated natives armed with missiles and weapons of various kinds. Unhappily one Frenchman was killed on the spot, and another severely wounded. But this was one of those deplorable cases that arose solely from the folly of the sufferers themselves; and had not the slightest taint of political animosity attaching to it.

CHAPTER XXX.

PROPOSAL TO ESTABLISH A CHAMBER OF COMMERCE.—APPARENT NEED OF SUCH AN INSTITUTION.—INTERFERENCE OF JAPANESE OFFICIALS IN EVERY TRANSACTION.—VISIT OF FOREIGN REPRESENTATIVES TO YEDO.—YOKOHAMA AND LITERARY INSTITUTIONS.—MUNICIPAL.—GOOD FEELING BETWEEN THE JAPANESE AND FOREIGN TROOPS.—FIELD DAY IN PRESENCE OF HIGH FUNCTIONARIES.—ANOTHER INCIDENT.—JAPANESE MAKE THE ROAD BY HOMOCO VALLEY AND MISSISSIPPI BAY.—THE RIFLE RANGE.—IMPROVED RELATIONS AND DEPARTURE OF ROYAL MARINES.—DIPLOMATIC CHANGES.—DETERMINATION OF TYCOON TO PUNISH CHOSHIU, AND OF THE LATTER TO RESIST.—SATSUMA TO ASSIST CHOSHIU ; BUT THE SHOGUN NEVERTHELESS RESOLUTE.—HE IS TO PROCEED TO OSAKA BY LAND.—REVIEWS 100,000 TROOPS AT COMABA.

A FEW incidents of a less exciting character call for notice, ere we take leave of the year 1864.

On the 26th October a meeting was held at the residence of Mr. CHARLES RICKERBY, the manager of the Central Bank of Western India, to discuss a proposition for the establishment of a Chamber of Commerce in Yokohama. Mr. KINGDON presided.

The proposal was brought forward by Mr. RICKERBY, who considered that the time had arrived when such a Chamber would be useful. The trade of the port had indeed become so considerable as to render it a necessity. He had himself seen within eighteen months, no less than five cases go before the Consulate, which would have been more satisfactorily settled by a Chamber ; and he mentioned a variety of matters in which the action of the Chamber would be called for.

Mr. MARSHALL, though doubtful whether this was the best time to start the project, moved, " that a committee be appointed to ascertain the views of the community." And this having been passed, the meeting adjourned.

It really did seem that the services of such an institution were seriously needed. The obstructions placed in the way of trade by the Japanese officials were vexatious to a degree.

It was asserted by the Japanese merchants, and it was strictly true, that not a transaction of any sort between them and foreign merchants was unknown and entirely uncontrolled by the local officials. Quantities, prices, profits, losses, were all noted by them, and the inquisitorial system was carried so far, as to interfere materially with the course of trade.

The obstruction to the entrance of Silk in particular, continued, notwithstanding all that had passed upon the subject, between the Government and the Consuls. Indeed it now assumed so marked a character that the Representatives of the United States, Holland, France and England, deemed it necessary to visit the Gorojiu together and impress upon that august Council, the absolute necessity for some decided improvement. They went up accompanied by a portion of the fleet—not intentionally as a menace; but it appears that this fact acted as a very efficient spur: for the moment it was ascertained that they were so attended, the Gorojiu hastened to send orders to remove all restrictions on the importation of silk into Yokohama.

It has often been a matter of surprise to new comers and visitors to Yokohama, to find that the settlement has remained so long without a public literary institution of any kind. This has not arisen from want of appreciation of the need of it. Two have been launched, but, through mismanagement, have fallen through. The first was called into existence in December 1864, and had an ephemeral existence of some six months.

Before the end of this year an effort was made to get the Municipal Council re-started. A meeting was held, and a preliminary committee appointed to "enquire as to the best method of forming a Municipal Council." The result was seen in the following spring.

As an evidence of the good feeling prevailing between the Japanese and foreign troops, I may mention, that in the middle of October some of the Japanese troops quartered at Nögé, about two miles from the settlement, were reviewed by their own officials on their ordinary drill-ground, Sir R. ALCOCK and several foreign officials being present.

The next day, there was another review on a more extensive scale, upon the small lot of vacant ground in the Swamp Concession, in rear of the German Club. It was a novel sight, and one that will not easily be forgotten by those who witnessed it. The English, United States, and Dutch, Ministers were present: the Consuls, and the bulk of the foreign residents. Of course there was also a great crowd of Japanese.

The Japanese soldiers marched on to the ground, under the command of KUBOTA SENTARO, the brigadier in command of all the Japanese troops in and around Yokohama.

Of English troops there were of the XXth 500 men ; Royal Marines 330 ; 67th 140 ; Beloochees 130 ; Artillery 55 ; Engineers 22 ; and Military train 12 ; —in all 1189 rank and file, in addition to their officers.

At 11 A.M. SAKAI HIGA-NO-KAMI, Vice-Minister and member of Gorojiu, TAKEMOTO AWADZI-NO-KAMI, confidential agent of the Tycoon and principal Minister for Foreign Affairs, SHIBATA HIGA-NO-KAMI, Commissioner and Minister for Foreign Affairs, and the two Governors of Kanagawa, arrived, with a large gathering of officials.

I have already alluded to this review in chapter XIV.

From this time onwards pleasant episodes of this, or an equally friendly, character, were constantly taking place between Japanese and foreigners ; and so far as Yokohama itself was concerned, it might have been supposed that the events which had so recently passed, had never been. No distrust was observable on either side ; and life went on from day to day as if foreigners were welcome guests, and the Japanese generous and appreciative hosts.

One simple incident occurs to me. I was walking with a friend, in the spring of 1865, in front of one of the native guard-houses on the Bluff. Several of the soldiers were evidently making preparations for something out of the common, and one, beckoning to my companion and myself to approach, made us understand that they were about to have a sham fight, at the same time inviting us to remain as witnesses.

At the moment of our arrival they were drawing lots for sides. There were a number of strings, some with white and some with red ends. The uncoloured ends of the strings were held to each of the would-be competitors, and everyone as he drew one or the other, became attached to the party displaying that colour. He then took a piece of baked clay painted of his particular colour, and fixed it across the top of his head, which it was shaped to fit. Then, equipping himself in the ordinary defensive articles with which they used habitually to practice fencing and sword exercise, umpires were appointed, and the belligerents took their positions opposite to each other.

There were eight on either side. They fought with the ordinary two-handed wooden swords with which all Japanese samurai practised. The object was to break their opponent's clay head-piece; and he whose distinguishing badge was so fractured was considered dead, and the umpires conducted him from the field.

The fight commenced. There was a good deal of feinting before they came to close quarters. At last two or three on each side were hard at it, the rest watching eagerly and excitedly, as if biding their time.

Now one, who had not as yet joined in the fray, seemed to think he could finish one of the engaged of the opposite party by rushing in behind and taking him at a disadvantage whilst defending himself from, or attacking, his foe in front. Quick as thought this was discovered by the disengaged on the other side, and a warrior flew to meet the new-comer and foil his threatened attack. Thus gradually all joined in, and the *mêlée* became general.

There was a good deal of excitement about it, even to lookers-on; for the sword play, after its kind, was excellent, and evidently all the belligerents were adepts.

The greatest good humour prevailed among the combatants. Not a scowl was seen, nor a growl heard, beyond the ordinary ejaculations inseparable from Japanese athletic competitions.

At length all were vanquished but two on one side and one on the other; when, being pressed hard by his foes, the one retired backward along the pathway, ever with his face to his adversaries, and bravely fighting as he fled.

On the pathway were two British Naval officers, one of whom stepped aside and let them pass—the other ran along the path—to get out of their way. This incident amused the Japanese intensely; they fairly screamed with laughter, evidently imagining that he fled from supposed danger.

Presently the single warrior stumbled over the bank, and was obliged to jump down into the field about three or four feet below the path. His pursuers immediately belaboured him unmercifully, and we could not help thinking it a great misfortune for him that his clay casque was so tough, for the blows must have hurt him considerably. He continued to defend himself still as well as he could; but it was a relief when the umpires stopped the unequal strife: declaring him a hero, but his side fairly vanquished.

The game, if we may so call it, was repeated again and again throughout the day, and gave a sort of weak idea of what the old style of fighting was among the Japanese.

Outside of the settlement, the Japanese did bestir themselves in our behalf. By making a good carriage road from Yokohama to Mississippi Bay by the Homoku valley, round over the hills above Negishi, and reentering the settlement by Ishikawa and the Swamp Concession, they hoped they would provide an inducement for foreigners to confine themselves to it, and to leave the Tokaido unvisited.

It had this effect to some extent, as the residents largely adopted the road for their daily constitutional rides, and many family men procured carriages of different kinds from Shanghai and elsewhere. Thenceforward wheel traffic became quite common.

The Japanese also caused one of the deep bays in the Homoco valley to be laid out as a rifle range. It was bounded by two long spurs of high land, the hill at the extremity of which was cut and faced, and when the targets were placed, formed one of the best Rifle butts in the East. The broad space between the spurs was further defined and bounded by a deep ditch on each side, for a distance of about a thousand yards. It was to be used indiscriminately by Japanese and foreigners; and a portion of the ground, when drained and properly grassed, was used as a race-course.

The relations between Japan and the Western Powers were deemed now to have changed so decidedly for the better, that the Royal Marines were ordered to hold themselves in readiness to embark on board the Conqueror, and proceed home. But two companies of the 11th Regiment were ordered to Japan from Hongkong.

News arrived in the month of May that Sir RUTHERFORD ALCOCK would not return to Japan. He was promoted to Peking. Sir HARRY SMYTHE PARKES K.C.B., was to replace him in the land of the Rising Sun. Dr. WINCHESTER was to go to Shanghai as H.B.M.'s Consul; and Dr. MYBURGH was appointed Consul at Yokohama.

It was now reported that the Tycoon had decided to confiscate the dominions of the Prince of Choshiu, as an equivalent for the $3,000,000 which he had undertaken to pay to England, France, Holland and the United States. But Nagato prepared to resist him to the last extremity.

It was understood that the Tycoon himself was about to head his forces and to attack the rebel in his own dominions.

It was also stated that the powerful Satsuma clan had promised its assistance to Choshiu; but that this fact did not deter the young Generalissimo of the empire—who was fired with the desire of proving himself a worthy descendant of the redoubtable Gongen-sama; well able to maintain by force the sacred rights attached to the throne which his great ancestor had won by conquest for his family.

It was arranged that he should proceed from Yedo to Osaka by land. A few days before setting forth, he reviewed at Comaba, (the site where the Agricultural College now stands), 100,000 troops, of those who owed him personal allegiance; and who were to march forthwith to take part in the struggle with Choshiu.

CHAPTER XXXI.

EVIDENCES OF JAPANESE ACCEPTANCE OF A PROGRESS POLICY.—INCIDENT THAT PROVED IT TO THE AUTHOR.—PROCLAMATIONS OF THE TYCOON BEFORE STARTING FOR THE WEST. GENERAL PROCLAMATION.—PROCLAMATION TO THE GOROJIU.—THE TYCOON'S PASSAGE THROUGH KANAGAWA, AS WITNESSED BY FOREIGNERS.—APPEAL OF THE TYCOON FOR SUPPLIES TO DEFRAY THE EXPENSES OF THE PRESENT EXPEDITION.—CIRCUMSTANCES SHOWING THE TEST HIS RETAINERS WERE PUT TO IN THEIR SYMPATHY WITH CHOSHIU.—MANY PLEAD SICKNESS.—MATZ'DAIRA IDZUMI-NO-KAMI'S REPLY AND ITS EFFECT.—LETTER FROM A COLONEL OF ARTILLERY IN THE ARMY TO HIS BROTHER IN YEDO.—PERIL OF TYCOON EN ROUTE.—PLOT FOR HIS ASSASSINATION AT DZEZE DISCOVERED.—ONE OF THE RINGLEADERS EXECUTED IN YEDO.

My readers will now be struck with the decided evidences of the readiness of the Japanese for the acceptance of the progress that has since this time so rapidly developed itself among them.

One of the first incidents that awakened me to the recognition of it, was, a visit I had, in my capacity as editor of the *Japan Herald*; which showed me that a comprehension of the power of the Press was actually extending to the officials of the Government.

The gentleman who called upon me was then very young. He was passing through one of the schools for foreign languages; and was also undergoing military drill with his companions, under foreign instruction.

With the utmost modesty he begged my pardon if he was taking an unjustifiable liberty, and hoped I would not betray to any one his having come to me. He then told me that he had received instructions from the officials (of his clan as I understood) to see me, and to mention that the Envoys who had been incarcerated in Yedo during the month of August in the preceding year, for their non-success in their mission to France, were still in confinement; and further to ask me to mention it in the newspaper with a recommendation that they should be released.

I said I would certainly comply with the request, and assured him also that his visit should be a secret; and that he need be under no apprehension on that account.

Accordingly I made it the subject of a leading article on the following Saturday, (June 24th 1865), and had no expectation of hearing anything more about it. If I remember rightly, there were only about half a dozen copies of the paper at that time subscribed for by Japanese.

I cannot recollect how long it may have been after the article appeared, when I received another visit from the same young gentleman, for the purpose of thanking me, and telling me that the appeal in the foreign newspaper, had been successful.

Surely no better evidence of the change that was at hand, could be given than this:—that the influence of the fourth estate was acknowledged.

The gentleman who thus called upon me in 1865, is

now a very influential man in the estimation both of foreigners and of his own countrymen. He is one of the most able, consistent and earnest friends of solid progress—not of mere change for change's sake—among the Japanese; and is intimately connected with some of the most marked and useful efforts for effecting good feeling, and pleasant and profitable intercourse between Japan and foreigners.

The Tycoon having now resolved to head his forces against Choshiu, the subjoined proclamations were issued:—

GENERAL PROCLAMATION OF THE TYCOON :—

"One of the maxims of GONGEN-SAMA was, that 'if a single motive is sufficient to determine an individual to act, a public man ought not to enter upon a resolution without having ten good reasons; and that where a private man only foresees one inconvenience, a public man ought to foresee ten.'

"Our ancestors and ourselves have always been faithful to this maxim; and it is partly because we have been directed by it, that we have been accused by our friends, —devoted to us but yet impatient—of sluggishness, whilst our enemies have blamed us for acting too hastily.

"If we have deserved censure from our friends, at least we are able to silence our enemies.

"We are now about to begin the most just war, and to inflict upon a rebel the most merited punishment, ever recorded in our annals. The crime, or rather the crimes, of MORI DAIZEN, are so patent, that none would venture to make any defence for him. As to those who wilfully would call them in question, we would simply reply to them by letting them known the acts of Mori. His very bad heart manifested itself at the very time when difficulties and intrigues almost deprived us of the rights of our ancestors, and threatened to overthrow the Government. Mori was at that time so much more guilty, that he was conspiring in the most hypocritical way. Ever since, he has not ceased to carry on intrigues in the court of the Mikado, audaciously misrepresenting and calumniating our intentions, when he could produce no facts.

"He has in a most vile manner deceived many of the Kugé, although they were favourably disposed for the new state of things. Owing to very difficult times, measures and precautions having been taken throughout the Empire, often very vague and as little precise as the circumstances which caused them would permit. These were for MORI a pretext for manifesting his bad character. He attacked inoffensive vessels belonging to the countries having a treaty with Japan. These ships had in no way provoked such an aggression. MORI pretended to justify this uncalled-for aggression by general orders issued by the Mikado and ourselves. We apparently took for good these explanations, but in order to avoid for the future such misunderstandings, we sent to MORI DAIZEN, an Ometsuké with many other officers both enlightened and prudent. MORI caused them to be murdered in the most treacherous manner, and dared afterwards to assert that such a murder was not to be imputed to him. It is a thing unheard of—to say that the chief is not responsible for the faults of his subordinates.

"Meanwhile the intrigues of MORI in order to disturb the minds of the Mikado and high Kugé, were becoming more and more bold. But that which is not seen in stormy weather is distinct when the sky is serene. The character of MORI was at last unveiled. Wise daimios baffled his underplots. It was soon known at Kioto that MORI was not even so much as a skilled impostor. MORI, being discouraged, attempted to seize the person of the Mikado. Kioto was burnt, and ten thousands and tens of thousands of families shed tears on account of the perversity of one man. In this very case, MORI DAIZEN hypocritically lied, and disowned his own people and their actions.

"About this time, foreigners, being fatigued by the hostile aggressions of Choshiu, so repeatedly renewed, and very much wearied with our clemency towards him, attacked Shimonoseki, in spite of our exertions to prevent them from going to the Inland Sea. MORI was thus a double danger to the Empire, drawing, as it were, with his own hands, calamities upon our people, both from within and without, and trying to involve us in serious difficulties which my Government alone is able to appreciate.

"The punishment of MORI was therefore resolved upon. Powerful daimios and hatamotos started up at our invitation to chastise a rebel. It is, however, very difficult to believe in the radical perversity of a man, and our OWARI and the other chiefs of the army were deceived by a feigned repentance. The heads of certain *karos*—whom MORI had caused to be beheaded, because they could no longer help him in his aspiring views, were sent to them with the express promise that the castles of Yamaguchi and Hagi should be destroyed; and that MORI, father and son, would come to Yedo, to hand over his estates to my Government. He laughs now at the honesty of OWARI and ETCHIZEN, and at our indulgence. The Mikado and our faithful ones are urging us not to delay any longer a chastisement so well merited. Therefore we would be deficient in our office, should we not proceed to inflict at once upon a rebel, a punishment demanded by the whole Empire.

"When GONGEN decided upon a war, he never said beforehand 'I shall do this,' or 'I shall not do that.' It is also the principle we adhere to; but we cannot discover at present, any harbour where the rebel may retire for shelter to wait until 'fair weather allows his navigating the open sea.

"The 10th of the 1st year of Kayo."

THE TYCOON'S PROCLAMATION TO THE GOROJIU.

"MORI, having violated the greatest of our laws—that which is the base of the Empire—viz., having profaned and burnt the capital, Kioto, having set at naught the authority of the Government, and being besides guilty of many other crimes and misdemeanours, we have resolved to punish him, as a lying traitorous rebel, dangerous to all the Empire, ought to be punished. We shall leave on the 16th day of the 5th month, at noon. Everyone in Yedo must continue his occupations. The Samurai will do his duty with more energy; the Hiakusho (peasant) should fearlessly work in the fields; the Cho-nin and Shokunin, (merchant and artisan), all shall comport themselves as if we were still in our palace. Those who are at the head of the |Government having our entire confidence, must see that our will is conformed to, which is, that peace and security reign over all. Yedo and all the provinces that understand the duties of true Japanese, are happily free from ronins. Those who have escaped the sword of our brave SAYEMON-NO-JO have retired to Choshiu to help the chief of the rebels. If my absence be longer than last year, all the arrangements must continue the same. It is customary that, in the absence of the Tycoon, the laws be more rigid, and delinquents punished more severely; but this time, to prove our goodwill and the confidence we have in our people, we have given orders to our Government that nothing be changed. This is a new proof of our affection for all subjects throughout our dominions.

"To be communicated to the Governors of the city of Yedo, and of all our provinces and towns, &c., &c."

The two incidents that follow—the starting of the Tycoon for the west, to punish the Prince of Choshiu, and the call upon the country for contributions in support of the expedition, will shew in a vivid manner how such things were managed in those days. Although so few years have sped, I shall hereafter have to describe how vastly different things are now.

The Tycoon passed through Kanagawa in the early part of June, on his way to Osaka. In compliance with a request suggested by a correspondent of the *Japan Herald*, and made by the British Acting Consul, the Governor of Kanagawa appropriated a plot of ground near the road, from whence foreigners might view the procession. It was the first time such a concession had been made to foreigners, and was doubly gratifying, from the fact that the requisite permission had been sought from Yedo and granted; and it afforded another proof of the good feeling now existing.

It was only notified by circular in the morning; but from nine o'clock A.M., until 2 P.M., there was a continuous stream of foreigners from Yokohama to the appointed spot. Many persons made a regular picnic of the occasion, and a better locality could hardly have been selected.

It was on a small knoll, under the shadow of fine umbrageous trees, separated from the Tokaido by about fifty yards, at a spot where for a hundred and fifty or two hundred yards, there was a cessation of the buildings, and, consequently an uninterrupted view.

To those who arrived early the uncertainty of seeing anything, and the idea that the straggling parties of soldiers and baggage carriers might be all that was to be seen, was a little tiring—for the army of the Tycoon marched very differently to European armies. Fully accoutred retainers of daimios strolled along, apparently without object—sometimes in twos and threes, and even sometimes singly. The baggage was carried by coolies in the ordinary manner in which private gentlemen have their personal baggage conveyed—but except that the stream was a little more continuous, it hardly indicated anything much out of the common.

At last, however, a clearing of the road by order of the vice-Governor of Kanagawa himself, who arrived on horseback, put everyone on the *qui vive*. It was a pleasant incident, too, that the people were driven away specially from such positions as would have obstructed the view of foreigners. The vice-Governor then dismounting, remained near us, until all had passed.

About two o'clock, a distant beating of drums was heard, and shortly afterwards, the vanguard of the Tycoon's escort came in sight. There were two drummers in front, who were immediately followed by the commanding officer of the Infantry body-guard, on horseback.

Next came several small field howitzers drawn by single led ponies.

Then followed a regiment of about six hundred men, four deep, armed with Enfield rifles and bayonets. Their dress was a curious hybrid between Japanese and foreign. They were in heavy marching order, with knapsacks, and each had drinking utensils, &c. These men marched with the greatest regularity, and evinced good drilling at least to that extent.

They were succeeded by another regiment preceded by about twenty drums. The dress and arms of this corps were purely Japanese—and the variety of colours in their tunics presented a very gay appearance.

The immediate body-guard came next, preceded by a large lacquered box containing the arms of the Tycoon. To this box, all the native officials and spectators kowtowed, as in duty bound.

The cavalcade was ended by a body of about twenty richly caparisoned horsemen, all men of the highest consideration: and in the midst of them rode the Tycoon. He was pointed out as a young man, the central figure of the brilliant group: his surcoat light buff embroidered with gold, with a large *mon* or crest on the back.

The enormous expenses the Government had been put to by the frequent movement of troops, the purchase of steamers, and of foreign arms and ammunition, quite exceeded the ordinary revenue at its disposal. The following appeal therefore was made by circular, calling for money to defray the charges of the present expedition.

" To the Head-men.

" For some years, the expense of protecting the coasts, and also of repairing and building the Tycoon's palaces; besides that incurred during the last three years—in which the Tycoon has been twice to Kioto, to visit the Mikado—has been very great. But now he is again about to leave Yedo, upon an expedition requiring more money than ever.

" Therefore—

" Let it be known in Yedo, Osaka and all the provinces belonging to the Tycoon, that they must give to him as much as they can. And particularly tell the merchants of Yedo, who are always with the Tycoon, and whose presence renders their business more safe, and very much larger, than is the case of the other provinces; and who, although they so profit largely by him, do nothing for him in return, they ought to contribute a portion of the profit they have been making for so long a time.

"The circumstances are now different to those formerly existing. The Tycoon has really not money in anticipation of the present crisis. So inform the merchants and shopkeepers that they must provide as much as they can. And order the head men (kocho) to write out the names of contributors and the amounts they give, and send the list to TACHI CHINA. It is to be hoped that all will do their utmost; but let these headmen know that if they do not exert themselves in persuading all to give liberally, they will be punished.

"The money shall be paid back in ten years by instalments of so much a year—or so much a month—from next year.

"Let this be explained to every one."

Many circumstances occurred on the route, to prove that the innate loyalty of the samurai to their chief was on this occasion put to a severe test. Many of the retainers of the Tycoon would gladly have been spared the necessity of attacking Choshiu; but none dared to stand boldly forward and say so.

At Fujisawa, Oiso and Odawara, large numbers of them pleaded sickness and asked to be allowed to return to Yedo.

MATSUDAIRA IDZU-NO-KAMI, the member of Gorojiu told them they were not fed, housed and clothed, by the Tycoon during peace, in order that they might sit at home at ease in times of trouble; but that they might defend and maintain the rights of their liege lord when assailed. 'Let then,' said he, 'those who are too ill to proceed, go and be examined by the doctors accompanying the army; but understand: that whilst those who are really unwell shall be allowed to go, any who are proved to be shamming shall be decapitated.' The result was magical. There was not a case of illness in the camp after that.

A letter from a Colonel of Artillery in the Tycoon's force to his brother in Yedo was kindly placed in my hands a few days later. The following is an extract from it :—

"The Tycoon's army, (his own retainers), as it left Yedo, consisted of 70,000 men. Of this number 10,000 were altogether equipped and drilled in the European style. This force, say the best judges, is the kernel of the army, and that on which the Tycoon more especially reckons for the final success of the struggle, if it really comes to be serious. Then there are 50,000 men belonging to ten very powerful daimios. These latter left the capital some days before those of the Tycoon; and among them are some few companies— how many it is difficult to say—more or less perfect in foreign tactics. Thus the whole force amounts to 120,000 men."

On the march to Osaka the Tycoon narrowly escaped imminent peril. The daimio HONDA SHIZEN-NO-SHO had planned that on his arrival at Dzézé, the chief town of Oömi, an attempt should be made on his life. The accounts varied greatly as to the manner in which this was to be carried into effect. One was, that the daimio had arranged that the roof of the house in which he lodged should fall in and crush his august guest and all who might be with him. Another report was that the place was to have been undermined, and all were to be blown up.

But whatever the means, there is no doubt of the fact; for a well-known official in Yedo, SHIMONO TATSUGORO, chief of the Fire brigades, was executed by being transpierced by lances while lashed to a wooden cross; his crime being that he was to have been an active agent in the execution of the plot.

CHAPTER XXXII.

EXCLUSIVELY MUNICIPAL.

I WILL now devote a chapter exclusively to Municipal affairs in Yokohama. It will have a certain interest for those who have been, or are, residents; and perhaps not for them only. It is, under any circumstances called for by the fact that in many respects our Municipality acted as leaven which is still working actively in Japan.

I need not stop to describe the original municipal institutions of this remarkable empire. In their way they were wonderfully perfect and effective for the people in the old state of society; but they were not suited for the altered conditions under the new *régime*. They have had to be much modified; and this has been done, not by clearing them away root and branch, but by judicious pruning, and by grafting-in sprigs from foreign institutions. Thus they still have a healthy and ever improving system in the government of their cities, towns and villages.

As instances, the Police force and Sanitary boards may be mentioned. There were formerly no policemen, properly so called. Now the organisation of this force is one of the most perfect in the world. Its nucleus was certainly that about to be mentioned, as established by the Municipal Council of Yokohama.

All Japanese cities were drained according to the lights they possessed. But it was only surface drainage, and very primitive indeed. The grading of the roads and their construction were on the simplest principles ; and the question of health hardly entered into the minds of those whose duty it was to attend to these things.

But the operations commenced by the Road and Sanitary committees of Yokohama produced their effect ; and never was anything more advantageous to a half-civilized nation, than was that of having imposed upon it, for its credit's sake, the necessity of continuing the beneficial work of these committees.

The failure of former municipal attempts has been mentioned. The cause was a simple one—want of means to carry them out. It was hoped that if the Japanese Government would hand over a good slice of what they received from the land-rents, a very much better chance of success existed ; and this they agreed to do.

That municipal institutions could flourish in the far East was proved by the example of Shanghai. There similar difficulties had existed to those found here : but they were surmounted by the good sense and unanimity of the people, fostered and promoted by the foreign Consular board. It has never been satisfactorily explained why the same powers could not be obtained for a Council in Yokohama as were granted to Shanghai; but nothing is more certain than that they were not; and that the condition of the two places has always therefore formed a marked contrast. Shanghai is justly termed a model settlement. It is a small well-governed republic, of which its residents are justly proud. Yokohama is the very reverse; and it seems inconceivable that the foreign settlement, with its fine houses, its excellent society, and its wealth as compared with the native settlement, is in darkness at night whilst the Japanese town is brilliantly lighted with gas.

Early in the year 1865, a great effort was made to establish the municipality on a firm and solid basis. The Japanese authorities consented to give up twenty *per cent.* of the money received from land-rents and the Consuls consented to hand over to the Council all license-fees and fines, and to delegate to them certain powers (which it was thought they had a right to do), that seemed likely to aid them materially in successfuly working the much desired institution.

In strict right the Japanese ought to have done most of the work the Council was required for, according to the very terms of the land regulations. But their ideas of road-making, draining and policing, differed widely from those of foreigners. It was, therefore, a relief to them to have these duties taken off their hands. They were quite willing to give any authority that they possessed over to the Council, and it would have been well if this had been availed of; and, better still if they would have given up one half instead of one fifth of the land-rents.

At a public meeting of the land-renters, held on the 7th March, which was very largely attended, Mr. KINGDON, who had always been one of the most zealous advocates for municipal self-government, and an active worker in improving the sanitary condition of the settlement, occupied the Chair. Several previous meetings had been held, at which he had also presided. His opening address on this occasion, well described what had previously been done, and how the wishes of the community had been thwarted. He said :—

"It will be remembered that at the first general meeting of the land-renters held on the 10th December 1864, it was decided that a certain number of delegates should be appointed by each nationality, proportionately to the number of tsubos held by them. Delegates were elected by all the nationalities except the American, and they met; but in consequence of the misunderstanding which had prevented the American citizens from appointing their delegates as others had done, it was felt by the other delegates that they could not proceed to business. At the same meeting a letter was received from Colonel FISHER, the U. S. Consul, informing the delegates that Mr. BLYDENBURGH had been duly elected the committee-man by the American citizens, and upon this letter being before them it had been decided to address the American Consul to the effect that the delegates had not assembled then to elect committee-men, inasmuch as the late resolution of the Consuls as to the formation of a Municipal Council could not be acted upon by the community, and that in consequence of no American delegates having been elected, no discussion on the method of forming a Municipal Council had been entered on. He had therefore addressed a letter to Colonel FISHER to this effect; but to that letter no reply had been received. Another meeting was held on the 20th February, when a deputation was appointed to wait upon the Consuls, to explain the views of the community, to ascertain the intention of the Consuls, and to endeavour to obtain a withdrawal of their decision upon the method of forming a Municipal Council. In compliance with this resolution, Mr. PIQUET, Mr. BRUYN, Mr. GRAUERT and himself had met the Consuls by appointment a few days before, but the result was not satisfactory; for it was then understood that on its appearing to the Consuls that their decision was not generally concurred in, the others were willing to cede their opinions to that of the community; but the American Consul thought that inasmuch as, on his recommendation, a committee-man had been elected, he could not, considering his own dignity and that of his people, allow that election to remain unheeded. It was well understood that if a Council were formed, it must partake of the national character, because the Consuls would not, or could not, yield the resolution he had alluded to, so long as it was insisted against by one of their body. He would urge upon the meeting the daily increasing necessity for pushing forward the formation of a Municipal Committee, as— one additional reason—if this were not done there would be no means of checking the number of Chinese continually coming here, and of regulating their conduct."

In the discussion that ensued, Mr. SCHOYER (American) said, that

"He had formerly differed altogether from his friend Mr. HALL, in the opinion that a Municipal Council could not be made to work; but he had since gone into a minute calculation on the subject, and was partly inclined to reverse his former opinion. It appeared that the present income, besides money in hand would be $6,000 *per annum*, which would do little more than keep the drains in order, and light the place. A police would be very expensive. Were the land-renters willing to submit to a tax of one eighth *per cent.* on imports and exports, and to a land tax? If this were answered in the affirmative, then a Municipal Council might be set going; if in the negative it would be a farce."

Mr. KINGDON replied:—

"Mr. SCHOYER has omitted one very important *item* of income:—the $12 a month paid for the licenses of the grog-shops. At present we had a constabulary in the settlement. It was true it is a very small one; but it is entirely supported by that Consul who had the least authority over, or income from, the grog-shops. The British Consul received only $74 a month from this source; yet out of this he kept up the only constabulary we had."

These few extracts will shew pretty clearly the state of affairs. It may be mentioned with reference to the Chinese, that the reason for the feeling that had sprung up with regard to them, was not that which actuates their opponents in the United States. No one feared to suffer by their competition; and had none but the more respectable classes come, there would have been but little objection to them. The lower orders, however, flocked over in great numbers; the quarters of the foreign settlement that they quickly filled became an eye-sore from the filth in which they lived; and it was feared that it would become a hot-bed of disease and the source of some dire epidemic, unless some control were exercised over it. The Chinese had no treaty, and consequently no Consul; and they were under no authority but the Japanese, who left them very much to themselves.

There was yet another objection made to them. They were suspected of supplying the thieves who had latterly committed numerous depredations in the settlement; and they certainly had many gambling dens opened. So that they were very undesirable neighbours in a variety of ways.

At the meeting alluded to, the delegates having resigned, Mr. PIQUET (French) said that:—

"Although, having but little money at command, we might perhaps be able to do only a little good, yet we should endeavour to do all we could. He had therefore prepared the rough draught of a scheme which he would like to be considered.

It was as follows:—

"Whereas it has been agreed in the General Meeting of land-renters, on the 10th December 1864, that the Municipal affairs of this settlement should be managed by one general Municipal Council:

"Whereas the Municipal right is generally derived from property:

"Whereas each nationality represented in this settlement is entitled to participate in the Municipal right in proportion to the importance of its property:

"Whereas the respective property of each nationality consists of the following number of tsuboes.

English 44,939
American 19,550
French 13,205

Prussians.............................. 7,591
Dutch 8,008
Portuguese 3,139
Swiss 872

"Whereas it is desirable that municipal regulations and taxes be voted by a large representation of land-renters; and it is important for the proper management of business that the executive power of the municipality be vested in a small number of persons.

"Whereas the municipal authority can only be enforced by the sanction of either the Japanese Government or the Consular board :—

"It is proposed—

1.—"That the General Municipal Council of Yokohama be composed for a term of one year, of

11	......	English.
5	......	Americans.
4	......	French.
2	......	Dutch.
2	......	Prussians.
1	......	Portuguese.
1	......	Swiss.
26	......	in all.

2.—"That the said Municipal Council elect for whatever period of time they may think advisable, an executive Committee of three to five persons chosen among those of their own members whom they judge best qualified for that position.

3.—"That the Municipal regulations and taxes be voted by a majority of the General Municipal Council.

4.—"That the executive Committee give the Municipal Council a quarterly account of their management of the Municipal funds, and, in the case of their not being supported by a majority of the Council, they resign their commission.

5.—"That the above preliminary steps to the constitution of a Municipality be submitted for approval to the Consular board."

This scheme, although it had one or two objectionable features, commended itself generally to the good sense of the meeting; and it was agreed to consider it clause by clause. The result was that after a few emendations it was passed in the following shape :—

1.—As above.

2.—" That the Council be authorised to form a code of rules and regulations for the Government of the settlement."

3.—" That the Council be empowered to appoint an executive committee of not less than three of their number to superintend the execution of the Municipal ordinances."

4.—" That Municipal regulations shall be voted by a majority of the General Municipal Committee.

5.—"That the Municipal Council shall publish a quarterly account of the expenditure of the Municipal funds."

6.—" That Mr. PIQUET and MR. SCHOYER be deputed to inform the Consuls of the proceedings at this meeting, and to request them to proceed to elect the members of the Council from their respective nationalities."

There now appeared to be ground for hoping that some sort of organisation for the good government of the settlement, would be effected. Although all that was desired was not to be attained, yet there seemed a probability of securing all that could be *reasonably* looked for. Some doubts were entertained as to the Consuls legally delegating certain of their powers. As to taxing and rate levying that was evidently impossible—for they did not possess such powers themselves. Anything of this kind must necessarily be voluntary on the part of the residents; and unanimity on such a subject was not likely to be realised. Nine-tenths of the community might gladly submit to a small taxation to secure the advantages of good municipal government, but the action of the remaining one-tenth would upset the whole. However, to the broad principles of the present scheme all present gave their votes unanimously; and it remained to be seen whether any powers could be obtained by any means, for general taxation; and how far the land-renters would allow themselves to be bound, for the general good, by the decisions of a majority.

The result of an interview with the Consuls was favourable; and the election of members was proceeded with. The gentlemen chosen were :—

English—Messrs. MACPHERSON, BARBER, WILLGOSS, MACDONALD, KEMPTNER, KINGDON, I. J. MILLER, CORNES, HOPE, JOSEPH, ELIAS ;—but Messrs. MACPHERSON and HOPE declining to serve, Messrs. RICKERBY and G. R. DAVIES were elected.

American—Dr. HEPBURN, Messrs. SCHOYER, SCHULTZE, GAY, BENSON.

French—Messrs. LEJEUNE, PIQUET, DEVEZE, CLIPET.

Prussian—Messrs. GRAUERT, SCHNEPEL.

Swiss—Mr. H. MORF.

Dutch—Messrs. BRUYN and HEGT.

The Portuguese did not elect any member.

All being thus completed, the first meeting of the new Municipal Council of Yokohama was held in H.B.M.'s Consular Court room on the 9th June 1865. There were 21 members present. Mr. SCHOYER was called to the chair, and Mr. KINGDON acted as secretary.

The Committee that had been appointed to frame an organization, brought up its report. Its propositions were entertained separately—as follows :—

1.—"That there should be a permanent Chairman.—Carried.

A permanent Secretary.—Carried.

2.—"That there should be a Finance Committee consisting of the Chairman and Secretary and that the duties of this Committee should be:—To collect from the Consuls and all other sources the funds accruing to the Municipal Council; for the disbursement of which the signatures of both members of the Committee should be necessary.—Carried.

That the funds of the Council shall be deposited

in a chartered Bank by the Financial Committee in trust for the M. C.—Carried.

The Bank to be selected by ballot.—Carried.

3.—"That there ought to be a *Police Committee*, consisting of three members of the Municipal Council, whose duties should be:—To organize a constabulary force, and to carry into execution such laws and regulations as might be adopted by the Council.—Carried.

4.—"That there ought to be a *Sanitary and Road* Committee, whose duty would be:—To put and keep in repair all the streets, roads and drains in the settlement, and to carry out such works for the sanitary improvement of the settlement as might be authorized by the M. C.—Carried.

5.—"That both the these Committees should propose such expenditure of monies, and should suggest to the Council such laws and regulations as they might consider necessary for the proper administration of their respective departments.—Carried.

6.—"That the power of granting licenses should remain with the M. C., and not with any special committees.—Carried.

7.—"That all elections for offices and for the Committees should be made by ballot.—Carried.

8.—"That a regular meeting should be held on the first Tuesday of every month, in order to receive the reports of the different committees, and to transact all necessary business.

Amendment proposed:—

"That there shall be a general meeting called by the Chairman during the first seven days of every month.—Amendment carried.

9.—"That no meeting of the Council should be considered valid, unless attended by 13 members of the Municipal body; the majority of whom would be sufficient to carry any measures.—Carried.

10.—"That the minutes of all the meetings should be published in one of the local papers, provided that there be no expense incurred.—Carried.

Mr. SCHOYER was elected Chairman.

Mr. RICKERBY offered to act as Hon. Sec.—Accepted.

Police Committee elected:—PIQUET, GAY and BRUYN.

Sanitary Committee:—KINGDON, CLIPET, HEPBURN, BENSON and MACDONALD.

It was agreed that all meetings be regulated by parliamentary rules.

Carried, that a Committee be appointed to inform the Consuls of the organisation of the Council as well as that the Finance committee has power to receive funds from their hands; and moreover to ascertain the amount of funds at the disposal of the Municipal board.

Finance Committee elected:—PIQUET, KEMPTNER, BRUYN, MORF, HEPBURN, GRAUERT.

At a meeting on the 10th June, 22 members being present, Messrs. PIQUET, MILLER, KINGDON, GAY, and HEPBURN were appointed a Committee "to report on the best way of bringing the Municipality into working order."

At a Meeting on the 7th July—20 members present.

Mr. SCHOYER made a statement as to the resources and requirements of the Municipality.

"Money received from Consuls—over $10,000.

"In addition there is a monthly income of $300 from licenses: to which are to be added the sums collected from fines.

"Current year's income will probably be—
 From Landrents 6,000.00
 ,, Licenses and fines 4,000.00
 ,, Surplus of former years......... 4,000.00

 Total for year ending June 1866 $14,000.00

"Next year will not materially differ, as new Swamp land-rents will come in.

"A large portion of this sum will be expended in payment of Japanese labour. The Council must determine how to obtain Ichibu exchange to aid in these payments.

"The 20 *per cent.* of the land-rents is entirely inadequate. It was clearly the duty of the Japanese to have sewered, graded and cleansed the settlement. They should now place at our disposal the means to carry out these objects."

The following is an extract from the Report of the Police Committee :—

"It is understood that the Commander of H. B. M.'s troops stationed here, will allow the present constabulary force at the British Consulate to be kept up, and a like force will be established at the French Consulate. The respective Consuls of the nationalities just named, have kindly offered to give their constable instructions to patrol the streets, and to arrest offenders against the ordinances of the Council, and generally to preserve order in the settlement.

"Your Committee then propose to appoint a superintendent and three sergeants, who, together with the Consular Constables, will compose a sufficient force for present purposes.

"The estimated expense of the organization is about $470 a month. * * * *

"The present scheme will remain effective only so long as men from the foreign regiments are available, and the Council must be prepared at any time for their withdrawal."

The first ordinance of the Municipal Council was regarding dogs running dangerously at large. These had been for years a great nuisance and annoyance to the public. At least one fine boy, a son of Mr. J. C. Jaquemot, had fallen a victim to hydrophobia from having been bitten by a rabid dog. So that as the hot weather approached this was a very important matter.

The next ordinance forbade the slaughtering of animals (intended for food) within the Foreign Settlement of Yokohama.

The third forbade the storing of explosive substances within the settlement; and as Mr. Hegt had a hulk, the *Nassau*, moored in a safe position in the harbour, specially for such purpose, this was a boon to all, and an inconvenience to none.

Shambles for the slaughter of animals for food, were provided at Homoco, on the sea-shore, a most convenient site about a mile from the settlement by land and less by water.

Mr. James Armstrong, Sergeant of H. B. M's. Commisariat department, received the appointment of

Superintendent of Police at a salary of $80 a month; but through ill-health he was obliged to resign, and Mr. GEORGE T. JURY was appointed in his stead.

It was resolved to have nothing to do with Ichibu exchange.

But the Municipality which had thus started so spiritedly began soon to shew symptoms of flagging. The July meeting had but fourteen members present—just one more than sufficed to make a *quorum*; the August meeting, though specially convened by the chairman, according to the rule, saw but eight put in an appearance —so no business could be done. It must be confessed, however, that it was an ill-chosen day, being a field day of the XXth Regiment; and in such communities these occasions engage the attentions of all, to the exclusion of everything that is not actually imperative.

But another fact began to be apparent. There was evidently a design in the minds of some of the members to organise an opposition, simply with the view of providing full discussion of every proposal that came before the Council. It was thought that there might be too much unanimity; and that measures ran the risk of being passed without due consideration. The intention was good; but it seemed a pity to impart so "porochial" an appearance into the little band of twenty-five excellent and practical gentlemen, who already had their work cut out to spare time from their business avocations to attend to the duties imposed upon them.

But there was yet another difficulty that presented itself in a shape as unexpected as it was unsatisfactory. The Council had received certain authority from the Consuls. Or, as the Chairman put it to a meeting specially called to take the matter about to be recorded, into consideration:—"At present we have a charter from the Consuls. And," he continued, " we proceed to make ordinances in accordance with the terms of that charter, and on passing them to the Consuls for their ratification, find them altered, and published as the acts of the Municipality in direct opposition to the meaning and intention of the board. He had good reasons for believing that the British, the French and the American Consuls, were willing to do all they could to give effect to the ordinances of the Council—but the other Consuls, representing but a small portion, comparatively speaking, of the community, opposed and caused the alteration and publication of one of the ordinances."

The fact was, that the Board of Consuls did alter the very first ordinance of the Council—the "Dog ordinance." By the charter they evidently had a perfect right to do so; but it was thought that at least they should have sent it back to the Council for reconsideration. It happened that the shape in which they published it was one that had been discussed in the Council, and negatived by a majority of 11 to 3. This therefore was a very serious matter. It was proposed to call a meeting of land-renters, and take their views on the subject; but this was opposed, as likely to lead to the stoppage of the Council altogether. It was finally agreed that a deputation should be appointed to meet the Consuls, and remonstrate with them on their having altered and passed as edicts, certain ordinances agreed to by the majority of the Municipal body elected by the land-renters of Yokohama. But this had very little effect.

A meeting of land-renters was eventually called, and was largely attended. It was held in the Court room of the British Consulate on Monday the 21st August; and Mr. F. HALL (WALSH, HALL & Co.) was called to the chair.

Mr. SCHOYER stated the objects of the meeting. He was very animated in the delivery of his speech, and, as they were the last words he ever uttered, my readers will bear with me if I give his final peroration. He said:—

"If we have no power to conduct the affairs of the settlement what is our position? I deny *in toto* that we have no power. We have full power over every indecent act although no power to punish." "But" he added with increasing warmth, "we will remove them, Sir, and take the responsibility. If Japanese are found, obscene or endangering the lives of others, the Municipal Police shall arrest them and take them to the Consuls, or, if they prefer it, to the Japanese authorities themselves. Why should Consuls tell us that which a child might say? It is mere school-boy talk. Our very nature gives the right, and it is sheer folly to talk in such a manner. Ladies, within the last ten days, have been insulted: and their lives endangered by bettoes furiously riding; and I say it shall be put down. Obscenity to be tolerated? And in places too, where ladies are promenading with their children? The very notion is absurd! and for any Consul to say that we cannot prevent it, is a gross insult to our common sense." (The Consuls had refused to sanction an ordinance on this subject also.)

Mr. SCHOYER resumed his seat, and Mr. KINGDON rose to reply—when the meeting was startled by Mr. SCHOYER apparently fainting. Great excitement naturally arose—Dr. HEPBURN immediately presented himself to give the benefit of his medical skill, and all eager to do what they could—but it was of no avail. In a few minutes it was apparent that RAPHAEL SCHOYER —was dead.

Mr. A. O. GAY (American) was elected Chairman,—and Mr. J. ALLMAND JUNIOR was elected member of the Council, in place of Mr. SCHOYER.

The land-renters passed a vote of confidence in the Council, and encouraged them to go on and do their best for the welfare of the community. It was therefore resolved to send a deputation to the Consuls, to "complain of the infringements of the charter granted to the Municipal Council, and requesting a fuller definition of the powers delegated, so that no such difficulties might arise in the future."

It was suggested that if the Consuls had no powers that they could delegate to the Council, they should be asked to apply to their respective governments on behalf of the Municipality. But this was not done.

The explanations that took place between the delegates and the Consuls were satisfactory: and thus ended a very unpleasant business, that seemed at one time likely to cut short the thread of the Council's existence.

Subjoined is a copy of the charter granted by the Consuls to the Council :—

CHARTER.

"Referring to the minutes of a meeting of the Consular body and the delegates of the community, held at the French Consulate 8th May 1865, copy of which is attached hereto, which resulted in the election of twenty-six members, as therein proposed, the Consuls, in order that there shall be a clear understanding of the powers delegated by them, enter in to the following arrangement with the delegates representing the community.

1st.—"That the Council shall have the whole charge of Superintendence of roads, streets and drains, and power to make all necessary Regulations for Sanitary purposes, and to organise and maintain a Police force, and to form Rules and Regulations for the good order of their own proceedings and discussions; and to propose for the necessary sanction of the several Consuls, all Municipal Regulations either with respect to foreigners or Japanese which it may be desirable to enforce.

2nd.—" That the Council shall appoint the time for the annual election of Council-men.

3rd.—"That the Council are to have the exclusive power to great licenses for Public-houses, or such other purposes as they shall deem necessary: and the fees arising from such shall be collected by them for Municipal purposes. It is understood that this shall not interfere with the licenses previously granted by the Consuls, or either of them, and which are now in force, but that these shall not be renewed by the Consuls after expiration of their present term.

4th.—"That all regulations framed by such Council for the repair and keeping in order of streets, drains and roads, and, in fact, all the votes for the expenditure of funds at its command, shall not require to be submitted to the approval of the Consuls.

5th.—"That Regulations involving Police fines and taxes must be submitted to the Consuls, as by their means alone such regulations can be enforced.

6th.—"That the Consuls will hand over yearly to the Council, all monies reserved, or to be reserved from the land-rent due to the Japanese Government, understood now to be 20 *per cent.*, as well as the funds previously reserved, and now in their possession, for the past year.

(Signed in duplicate),   MARCUS FLOWERS,
H.B.M.'s Act. Consul.

,,   P. CHEVREU RAMEAU,
H.I.M.'s Consul.

,,   GEO. S. FISHER,
U.S. Consul.

,,   G. F. PLATE,
H.N.M.'s Consul.

,,   VON BRANDT,
H.P.M.'s Consul.

,,   R. LINDAU,
Swiss Consul.

,,   N. P. KINGDON,
H.M.F.M.'s Act. Consul.

But though the difficulty with the Consuls was thus satisfactorily got over, others had to be faced, that required all the patient thoughtfulness and energetic resolution that could be brought to bear upon them.

The principal of these was the shortness of funds; and how to raise the money sufficient for all that it was declared necessary to undertake. The fixed income for the year was exactly known, and it was found to be insufficient by one half for the works proposed. There was but one method by which more could be raised; and that was by levying some tax or rates upon the community;

but this could not be done without their consent. It was also seen that in order to obtain general acquiescence, and ready payment of any such rates or taxes, the suffrage must be greatly extended; and this became a subject of serious discussion. Hitherto the land-renters only had votes, and they only were eligible for members of the Council. The public justly said:—" This is all well, so long as they are willing to pay all expenses, and take all responsibilities. They claim all the landed property in the settlement. It is to their advantage, by judicious outlay, to make it as valuable as possible. But if they require us to help them they must allow us to participate in deciding the best methods of providing ways and means, as well as in paying the money when the decision is arrived at." And undoubtedly they were right.

With this question in full discussion, the first year of the Council's existence closed. The term for which the first members were elected was reached; and the public could but admit that they had done as well as could possibly have been expected.

The elections for the second year resulted in many changes. Some were inevitable, several members declining to serve a second term, and others either having left, or being about to leave, Japan. But strange inconsistency—the man, who of all others had been the most assiduous in raising the Council and in working for the good of the settlement, was left out. At the time, I wrote, and, (as he is still an honoured member of the community), I cannot refrain from quoting my own words from the *Japan Herald* of the 26th May 1866:—

" What the English renters can have been about in passing over Mr. KINGDON we are at a loss to conceive, unless, indeed, he no longer appears on the list as a land-renter. We cannot, however, allow him to leave the Council without reminding the community that for the successful formation and working of the Scavenger Corps—we are almost entirely indebted to him. How much this corps has added to the health and convenience of the public all must be aware. Since 1863, long before the Municipality was agreed to, he set to work—monthly collecting the necessary funds from the residents; and often have we seen him at early morn, while half Yokohama was still sleeping, active in seeing the men were at work and doing their work well. When the Municipality came into existence, the Sanitary Committee found this corps in perfect working order; and we have come to look upon its efficiency as so pre-eminently the work of Mr. KINGDON, that we are really sorry that he will direct it no longer. Of course many others in the Council deserve all the credit their constituents could afford them; but too often, in elections of this kind, the best services are forgotten, the most assiduous labour left unacknowledged. It is to-day as it ever was—the public is the hardest master to satisfy: the slowest to perceive when it has a good servant: the most niggardly in rewarding when found: and the first to cast him aside to chafe under a sense of indifference and neglect."

Of all the members elected to the first Council, there remain only the following still resident in Japan.

Dr. HEPBURN, Messrs. GAY, SCHULTZE, MACPHERSON, KINGDON, WILKIN, MACDONALD, and HEGT.

And here for the present I leave this theme. Of the ultimate fall of the Council, it will be my duty to tell in the second volume.

CHAPTER XXXIV.

THE "JAPAN TIMES" STARTED.—CHAMBER OF COMMERCE.
—YOKOHAMA RIFLE ASSOCIATION AND TIR NATIONAL.—
YOKOHAMA ENJOYMENTS.—ICHIBOO EXCHANGE.—ARRIVAL OF
H.M.S. "PRINCESS ROYAL."—DEPARTURE OF ROYAL MARINES.
—H.B.M. SUPREME COURT.—CLOSE OF THE YEAR 1865.

In September 1865, was started the *Japan Times*. It was never publicly known who its proprietory consisted of, (although it was pretty generally, and, no doubt correctly, surmised); and it was represented as being under no special editor, but under a kind of editorial board of gentlemen, who met and decided as to its line of policy, articles, &c. Its projector, and certainly its real editor, was Mr. CHARLES RICKERBY, who, so far as ability went, lacked nothing. Had his tact been equal to his talent, the *Japan Times* might have become a power in the land; for, without question, it was well written; and it had excellent sources of information.

Mr. RICKERBY had been the manager of the first bank established in Yokohama; and in that capacity was a general favourite. Genial, liberal, fairly well read, hospitable, and public-spirited withal, he had peculiar qualifications for maintaining the leading position bank managers usually hold in commercial communities.

Retiring from this position, however, he purchased the printing plant and goodwill of a daily paper—the *Commercial News*, which had been running under the proprietorship of Mr. F. DA ROZA, a Portuguese subject, for some two years; but which had languished for want of a properly qualified editor.

Mr. RICKERBY made his arrangements, and brought out his paper, under the new title mentioned above.

But Yokohama owes to Mr. RICKERBY, perhaps in a greater degree than to any one else, the establishment of a Chamber of Commerce. It has already been told that the first meetings to consider the necessity for such an institution were held in his house; and he was the prime mover and advocate.

On the 8th November 1865, at a meeting which was considered private, the Chamber was established; all the gentleman then present enrolling themselves as the original members.

It is needless to say how useful to commerce the Chamber has proved. Combined action on the part of foreign merchants for the purpose of protecting themselves against the combinations of native merchants constantly taking place both in China and Japan, had never been found practicable; but the Chamber formed a means of securing unanimous action against the illegal obstructions placed in the way of business by the officials of the government, to which allusion has been so frequently made. The voice of the Chamber was likely to be attended to both by Consuls and Ministers, to a far greater extent even than memorials signed by several individual mercantile firms. As was said at the time, " great political questions always force themselves upon a minister's attention, but the ' little things,'—the ' 'tis buts,' of daily intercourse in the country, demand a notice that is never accorded to them; and these it would be the particular duty of the Chamber to take under its care."

I ought to have mentioned another institution which about this time sprung into existence—" The Yokohama Rifle Association." There was already a Swiss " *Tir National*," the members of which were confined to gentlemen of the Helvetian Republic. The Y. R. A., however, admitted all nationalities to membership; and for a number of years, held annual competitions, which were always spiritedly entered into by marksmen of all classes—from private soldiers up to the field officers, and to the leading members of our little society. Japanese even were invited to attend and compete; and it is worthy of remark that Colonel MURATA, now admittedly one of the foremost marksmen in the world; and the inventor of certain improvements in the rifle, which his government have adopted; first made his public appearances at the competitions of the Yokohama Rifle Association, and the annual fêtes of the Swiss *Tir National*.

On the formation of the Y. R. A., Lieut. HARRIS, of H. M.'s XXth Regiment, who, with many of his brother officers, joined it, wrote to the Wimbledon Association, and announced its birth. In reply he received the Society's Silver medal, to be contended for by members of the Y. R. A., subject to Wimbledon rules.

It was Lieut. HARRIS, also, who succeeded in reviving the Volunteers.

Races, regattas, sailing-matches, athletic sports, all had their turn; and thus it may be seen that as a community Yokohama was most singularly favoured in those days. It was not as yet split up into factions; it had no lawyers to create for it the character it afterwards obtained as the most litigious place in the East; and it had any amount of young blood, energy, and—what rendered these most available—plenty of money circulating. Ladies were increasing in numbers, imparting a charm that had long been wanting; and balls, picnics and country excursions, were frequent. Almost every one had his pony and made use of him. And the country around the settlement offered inducements—by the loveliness and variety of the scenery, and the friendliness of the country people—for pedestrian exercise, which was hardly ever omitted, day by day. Yes, in those days, it was a real privilege to live, and to enjoy life, in Yokohama.

The presence of the military and naval forces has been mentioned as socially advantageous. It was so in a variety of ways. In the first place, it was the extraordinary addition that the boo exchange made to them in doubling the pay of all ranks, that caused such an abundance of money to be circulated.

It will not be time thrown away if I give my readers a little insight into this 'boo exchange' business. I must premise that the Japanese, on the representations of Sir RUTHERFORD ALCOCK and his colleagues, on the termination of the weight for weight system at the close of the first year's intercourse, had agreed that all officials belonging to the Treaty Powers should be permitted to exchange dollars for native currency at its true value— viz. 311 boos for $100. There was no injustice to the country in this. On the contrary it was indirectly beneficial; for none spent money more freely with native shopkeepers than the class who would particularly benefit by the arrangement; and of course it gave them enhanced means of doing it.

The merchants preferred that all money dealings should be left to a regular course of exchange—depending on supply and demand; as it gave them greater opportunities for making money by speculating for the rise or fall; and, as a fact, the scarcity of boos was so great in comparison with the demand, that the price for a very long time fluctuated between 210 and 230 boos for the $100.

So long as there were only the officers of the legations and consulates to be supplied, all was plain-sailing enough. These gentlemen honestly exchanged the amount of their pay only; but when the forces put in an appearance and claimed the privilege of the exchange, it was gladly accorded to them, and it was agreed that each grade should be allowed to change a certain specific sum *per diem*.

Thus, taking the military:—Every commissioned officer was allowed to exchange, irrespective of his actual rank or pay—three dollars a day, at three boos for each dollar. Every private soldier and non-commissioned officer was allowed to exchange one dollar a day at the same rate. Had it been possible for each individual private to take his money to the Custom-house daily, and change the amount of his pay, it would have made a difference to him of no less than fifteen boos a month. For taking the average rate of pay at one shilling a day, it would amount to 30s. a month—@ 4/3 = $7.06 @ 3 boos = 21 boos 3 tempos. But he was entitled to change $1 a day—$30 a month— that is—in addition to his pay, he was entitled to the difference of exchange on $22.94 a month, which difference (supposing the current rate of exchange on the open market to be 235 boos *per* $100) amounts to about 15 boos. So that by the boo exchange a soldier's (or a sailor's) pay was actually nearly doubled. But where was a private soldier to get a dollar a day to exchange? Well! there was no difficulty of that kind experienced. It was all managed through the paymaster. The money was found—the exchange was taken: but he got the amount of his pay—and, in the first instance, that only, in native currency at the exchange of three boos for one dollar; the rest all went into what was called an "Ichiboo fund."

This fund originated thus. On the XXth Regiment arriving here, the amount over and above the exchange on the true pay, accumulated so fast, and to such an amount, that a meeting of the officers was convened, and it was decided to establish a general fund: from which, first, the exchange on the full pay of all officers receiving over three dollars a day should be made up, and then, the balance should be divided between the officers and men in shares proportionate to their pay, the soldier getting one share, a captain about thirty, a major about fifty-three shares, and so on. If any one will estimate the true pay of the officers and men at the exchange of three boos for $1—the dollar being fixed at s.4/3d., and then the rate actually drawn, it will be seen what was the advantage to each individual.

Now, let me on to other matters.

H. M. S. Princess Royal, bearing the flag of Admiral KING, arrived on the 7th August, and the Japanese had to admire the presence of two fine line-of-battle ships— the new arrival and the Conqueror—anchored in close proximity in the harbour.

The Royal Marines, who had been brought to Yokohama in the Conqueror, left in her for home on the 23rd August, having done good work during their presence in Japan.

On the 4th September a change of a most important kind was made in the administration of the law to British subjects.

Her Majesty's "Order in Council," substituting a Supreme Court for the Consular Courts in China and Japan came into operation.

There were to be one Judge, and a Law Secretary, besides the necessary officers and clerks.

Sir EDMUND HORNBY was appointed the Judge. He was to reside at Shanghai, where the ordinary sittings would be held. Mr. W. GOODWIN was the Assistant Judge. And either one or other would from time to time visit Japan as on circuit. Ultimately it was determined that the Assistant Judge should reside in Yokohama but in the meantime the Consul would act as Judge. The change worked well from the first. Sir EDMUND HORNBY, as an adept at organization, and possessed of immense energy and personal influence: and Mr. GOODWIN, as a man of sound and varied learning, and many accomplishments: were both admirably suited for the positions allotted to them; winning and preserving universal respect.

One provision of the "Order in Council" has produced a good deal of annoyance and opposition. It is that contained in clauses 114 to 116, which provide for the annual registration of British subjects, each renewal of registration costing the artizan and labourer one dollar, and all others five dollars. By many it is found to be a tax most unwillingly paid; but its non-payment means non-protection.

The year 1865 closed peacefully and pleasantly, so far as foreigners were concerned. It cannot be said that familiar intercourse with all ranks had been attained; but there were not wanting, symptoms of improvement even in this respect. Occasionally excursionists would return after a jaunt into the country and tell of having encountered a little incivility from samurai whom they met on the road. But it was very rare. As a rule the universal report was that they had been received with kindness and cordiality everywhere. By this time, such was the confidence felt by the residents, that not one in ten thought of carrying a revolver, unless when going on a particularly long journey ; or one that was little known and seldom traversed. Indeed everything betokened that the old dread might be set aside, and that a safe and agreeable intercourse might be looked for in the future.

The ratification of the Treaty by the Mikado, had the effect of strengthening this feeling of security. How this ratification was obtained shall form the theme of another chapter.

CHAPTER XXXV.

SIR HARRY PARKES, AND HIS PRACTICAL MEASURES.—THE RATIFICATION OF THE TREATIES THE 'SINE QUA NON.'—ACCORD BETWEEN FOREIGN REPRESENTATIVES.—TRADE BENEFITS BY THE GENERAL ACCORD.—EXPORT OF SILKWORM'S SEED, VIRTUALLY THE SALVATION OF ITALIAN SILK ENTERPRIZE.—SQUADRON ORDERED TO HIOGO.—STATE EMBARKATION OF MINISTERS.—PROCEEDINGS AT HIOGO, OSAKA AND KIOTO.—VISIT OF MEMBERS OF GOROJIU TO THE SQUADRON.—OCCUPATION OF THE OFFICERS OF THE LEGATIONS.—TEN DAYS GIVEN FOR A FINAL REPLY.—EXCITEMENT AT KIOTO.—THREATS AGAINST THE TYCOON AND THE MIKADO.—MIKADO REQUESTS THAT THE SQUADRON WILL LEAVE HIOGO.—DISGRACES TWO MEMBERS OF GOROJIU.—THE FOREIGN REPRESENTATIVES REMAIN FIRM.—LETTER WRITTEN TO THE MIKADO BY THE TYCOON OFFERING TO RESIGN, FORTUNATELY STOPPED.—IN ITS STEAD, DOCUMENT PREPARED ENTREATING THE MIKADO TO GIVE HIS SANCTION TO THE TREATIES.—THE TYCOON SENDS TROOPS TO KIOTO.—MIKADO STILL UNFAVORABLE.—TYCOON PROCEEDS TO KIOTO; ORDERS APPREHENSION OF DAIMIO'S OFFICERS, and ASSEMBLES REPRESENTATIVES OF DAIMIOS.—EXCITEMENT EXCESSIVE.—FOREIGN MINISTERS HOURLY INFORMED OF PASSING EVENTS—STILL FIRM.—CRISIS AT HAND.—FINAL INTERVIEW BETWEEN THE GOROJIU, HIGH OFFICIALS AND THE TYCOON, WITH HITOTSUBASHI AT THEIR HEAD, AND THE MIKADO.—THEIR RESOLUTION.—HITOTSUBASHI'S ACTION.—THE MIKADO YIELDS.—THE TREATIES ARE RATIFIED.—INSTANTANEOUS EFFECT.—LETTER OF THE SATSUMA CLAN TO THE MIKADO, PROTESTING AGAINST THE OPENING OF HIOGO, AND DEMANDING TO BE PLACED IN VAN OF THE ARMY TO OPPOSE IT.

His Excellency Sir HARRY PARKES landed in Yokohama on the 18th July 1865.

Mr. GRIFFIS, in his excellent work "The Mikado's Empire," says :—

"To the English was reserved a quiet victory and a mighty discovery, second to none achieved on the soil of the mysterious islands. English scholarship first discovered the true source of power, exposed the counterfeit government in Yedo, read the riddle of ages, and rent the veil that so long hid the truth. It was the English Minister, Sir HARRY PARKES, who first risked his life to find the truth; stripped the Shogun of his fictitious title of 'Majesty'; asked for at home, obtained, and presented credentials to the Mikado, the sovereign of Japan; recognised the new National Government, and thus laid the foundation of true diplomacy in Japan."

Sir HARRY could have done but little without his diplomatic colleagues. Sir RUTHERFORD ALCOCK and Mr. DE WITT were the first to arrive at a thorough conviction of the real nature of the power of the Mikado and the Tycoon respectively; although Mr. HARRIS had seen good reason to suspect it even before his treaty was completed. My readers will remember his threat that if there were further delays he would go to the metropolis, and negociate with the Mikado direct.

At the conference held at Yokohama on the 18th September, 1864, directly after the receipt of the intellegence of the battle of Shimonoseki,—Sir R. ALCOCK, M. LEON ROCHES, Mr. PRUYN and M. DE GRAEFF VON POLESBROEK being present,—it was suggested by each of these foreign representatives to TAKEMOTO KAI-NO-KAMI the representative of the Tycoon, that a favourable opportunity now presented itself for the Tycoon to urge on the Mikado the propriety of at once ratifying the treaties. "Hitherto," they said, "the Tycoon has always been considered as the treaty-making power in Japan, and the sole representative of Government in relation with foreign States. But if it continued to be demonstrated that the Tycoon had not the necessary authority, and was so completely over-ruled by a superior power in the State, as to be unable to prevent or resist orders for the rupture of treaties, however well-disposed he might be to maintain them, foreign powers would sooner or later have no alternative but to seek this superior power in the State, and make their own terms."

From this it will be understood that Sir HARRY PARKES would never think of appropriating the praise so generously bestowed on him by Mr. GRIFFIS. From the well-known energy of his character, it is quite likely, that, no sooner had he arrived at his post than he set vigorously to work to investigate the exact nature of the dual government. Sir HARRY had this advantage over his predecessor, that he was himself a fine Chinese scholar, and as all the best Japanese works on political and historical affairs are in the Chinese character, he may have been able, with a very little aid from his excellent subordinates, (the gentlemen of the English legation, who had studied the language, written as well as spoken, from their arrival in 1859 and onwards), to read, mark and inwardly digest, everything that could be found bearing on the subject.

He soon satisfied himself, beyond question, of this one great and fundamental truth—that whatever the Tycoon might be, the Mikado was sovereign of all. He may have argued with himself that the Queen did not intend, and was placed in a false position by being allowed, to enter into a treaty with any but the sovereign. He doubtless saw as clearly as anyone the weakness of the Mikado; and unquestionably he recognised that the strength of the Tycoon was passing away, and that nothing was hastening its annihilation so much as the fact of treaties having been made with foreigners, against the will of the Mikado.

It was manifestly quite impossible now to rescind the treaties. The foreign powers had acted in good faith in making them, and if they had been deceived by the governing officers of Dai Niphon, they could not allow themselves to be fooled and sent to the right about, merely because the Tycoon and his Government had done that which they ought not to have done.

It was well that the good accord between the diplomatic corps in Japan was sufficiently strong to allow of all acting together on this most important occasion. All agreed that it was of primary necessity that the treaties should be ratified. Sir HARRY considered that this must be effected whatever might be the consequence to the Tycoon. All the other ministers had a very strong sympathy for the Tycoon, who had endured so much for foreigners; but yet, on this point they held the same views, and all worked together to secure this great desideratum.

Locally, in Yokohama, trade was benefiting in a marked degree from the united and energetic action of the ministers. The restrictions that had been so perplexing were quickly disappearing. The export of Silkworm's eggs, so highly important to Europe at that period, became, (principally through the persuasions of of M. LEON ROCHES), a remarkable and permanent feature in the exports. That year, disease had destroyed nearly the whole of the silkworms of France and Italy; and Japanese was the only seed sent that was successfully cultivated, to replace them. It may be said that the Italian silk trade was saved from utter annihilation solely through Japan thus opportunely coming to the rescue.

But all these were trifling affairs beside the great and absorbing one of the Treaties. So now a united effort was to be made to settle this.

Towards the close of October it began to be rumoured that several of the ships of war in harbour had been ordered to hold themselves in readiness to start for the Inland sea, and the community was not long allowed to remain in ignorance of the reason.

On Wednesday the 4th November, early in the morning, a detachment of the 2nd Batt. of H. M. XXth Regiment marched down to the west *hatoba* under the command of Captain BLOUNT. A battery of Artillery also fell into position on the Bund, and there awaited the arrival of Sir HARRY PARKES, who was about to embark on board of H.M.S. Princess Royal, (a noble two-decker of 73 guns), to proceed with the ministers of France, Holland and the United States, accompanied by the combined squadron, to Hiogo, in the Inland sea. At 9.30 H.E. Mons. LEON ROCHES left the *hatoba* for the Guerriére frigate, the troops presenting arms, and the band playing "Partant pour la Syrie." A few minutes later, Sir HARRY—accompanied by Mr. EUSDEN the Japanese Secretary of Legation, Colonel BROWNE, and Messrs. McDONALD, SATOW and VON SIEBOLD—arrived at the *hatoba*, the soldiers receiving him with the usual formalities. Taking leave cordially of Colonel BROWNE and Mr. EUSDEN, His Excellency stepped into the boat, attended by Mr. McDONALD, the Artillery firing a salute, the band playing "God save the Queen." A second boat conveyed the interpreters, Messrs. SATOW and VON SIEBOLD, and directly they had all embarked the signal was made for the squadron to weigh. The Dutch corvette Zoutman, with M. VON POLSBROEK, H.N.M. Minister, was the first in motion; the Princess Royal not a minute later; and the latter, going ahead, led the squadron out of harbour in grand style. H.M.S. Pelorus, with Mr. PORTMAN the U.S. Chargé d'Affaires on board, was next ready, but waited to give the *pas* to the Guerriere with the French dispatch boat Kienchang in tow. Then came the Leopard, Dupleix, and Argus with the British gunboat Bouncer in tow. And in this order they were lost to sight.

All this display was thought necessary, in order to mark the great end the expedition had in view. The complete success the ministers met with shall now be told.

The importance of the events about to be recorded, cannot be over-estimated. The ratification of the Treaties entered into by the Tycoon and foreign governments, by the Mikado, would be the greatest stride towards progressive, pleasant and profitable, intercourse between Japan and other countries, of any that could occur. It was all-essential. It would be a new starting point. It would confirm Japan as a member of the comity of nations, and render the universal progress of the country and people certain.

The Tycoon and his Government had information of the intention of the foreign representatives to visit Osaka. On the arrival of the fleet, he was at Kioto, awaiting the final orders of the Mikado respecting Choshiu. On the very day on which the foreign ships dropped anchor off Hiogo, he received a *djien-baori* (war-dress) and a *tatchi* (war-sword)—equivalent to an order to take up his arms and set his troops in motion.

The foreign ministers at once sent officers to Osaka, with letters to the Gorojiu, in which was stated the requirements of the treaty powers :—viz.

1st.—" The Ratification of the Treaties by the Mikado.
2nd.—" The opening of Hiogo.
3rd.—" The Revision of the Tariff.

Two or three days afterwards the members of the Gorojiu came themselves to Hiogo, and had an interview with the foreign representatives. After relating what had been done to induce the Mikado to sanction the treaties,—after having repeatedly asserted that *without this sanction, the execution of the treaties was almost impossible,*—they added the declaration that the question was a very dangerous one, on account of the hostile feelings entertained by many towards foreigners. At the close of a very long conference, the Gorojiu promised to add their exertions to those of the Tycoon, and spare no trouble to obtain the imperial sanction: which, they said, was "as necessary to the Tycoon himself as to foreigners."

Accordingly, the following day, high officials were sent to Kioto. Meanwhile, the officers of the various legations were at work at Osaka, busily employed in explaining and illustrating the intentions and fixed resolutions of the representatives.

• Our ministers considered that a prompt and energetic diplomatic action was requisite to effect the desired end. The Gorojiu called again, and agreed with the ministers, that the utmost efforts of the Tycoon and his government were indispensable, and that no time should be lost in discussing the matter with the Council of the Mikado. Ten days were then given for a final reply.

Whilst these negotiations were going on at Osaka, Kioto was in an indescribable state. Emissaries of daimios rushed in, to counter-order the departure of the Tycoon. Ronins made horrible threats against the life of the Tycoon, and even against the Mikado himself.

The Mikado begged that the men-of-war should be removed at once, and declared he would not sanction the treaties. He then ordered the removal of ABE BUNGO-NO-KAMI and MATS'MAI IDZUMI-NO-KAMI from the Gorojiu, and took from them their title of Kami.

These two daimios were ordered at once to retire to their dominions, and to express their regret for the favour they had shown to the foreign cause.

The Tycoon and his government were stupefied at this *unexampled audacity of Kioto.* They thought that from such an act to the deposition of the Tycoon by the Mikado, the distance was small.

Osaka and Kioto were in a state of revolution. The foreign representatives were informed of all these changes, but they became more determined than ever —encouraged by the Tycoon and his ministers.

A letter was about to be sent to the Mikado, in which the Tycoon offered to retire; and begged that the Tycoonate might pass into the hands of HITOTSUBASHI, and the command of the army be entrusted to his relatives the daimios of Owari and Kishiu. In order to prove to the Mikado and his Court, that he was in earnest, he ordered the eight Japanese steamers at anchor before Hiogo, to move at once to Osaka, to be ready to convey him to Yedo.

Happily, this letter was stopped; and the Tycoon was told that it was a shame for himself, and a disgrace to his ancestors, to abdicate and to yield to a miserable faction, tyrannising over the Mikado and his Council, when he was at the head of an army of 300,000 men.

Another most remarkable document was therefore prepared and sent to Kioto. In this masterpiece of Japanese literature, the Tycoon entreats the Mikado to give his sanction. And to support his diplomatic note, he moved with 34,000 of his best troops to Fushimi, about eight miles from Kioto. There he sent for some members of the Mikado's Council; but the reply was, that the emissaries of the hostile daimios, and the ronins, were so enraged, that it was unsafe for them to undertake the journey. The Mikado, indeed, gave the Tycoon to understand that his presence was necessary to protect the sacred person.

The Tycoon at once proceeded to Kioto, with 2,000

troops, ordered some daimios officers, apparently ronins and in the employ of high members of the Mikado's Council, to be apprehended; and assembled all the representatives of the daimios actually at Kioto.

The excitement was great—the crisis fearful. The officers of the legations, sent to Osaka on a special mission, met only the stern and sorrowful faces of the Tycoon's followers, all more or less ready to perform the *hara-kiri*, should the Tycoon be compelled to retire. This painful excitement lasted three days. The representatives of the four powers, almost hourly informed of the state of affairs, were, during all this time, busily engaged day and night.

The Japanese fleet was now ordered to leave Hiogo and Osaka, and take refuge in the Bay of Youra.

The climax was hourly approaching. The member of Gorojiu, OGASAWARA IKI-NO-KAMI, throughout the whole of the night of the 22nd November, discussed with 36 deputies of the daimios the question of the sanction of the Treaties. He succeeded in persuading them; but there were invisible enemies round the Mikado, and he himself feared for his life.

At last, all the members of the Gorojiu, the great *metsukes* and high officials of the Tycoon, with HITOTSU-BASHI at their head, called on the Mikado, and prostrated themselves at his Majesty's feet. The Mikado was moved; but messages containing threats were brought in every minute, and the sacred emperor was still hesitating, when all the high officers declared they would die at once, should they not obtain what they were sent for. HITOTSUBASHI went so far as to take hold of the sleeve of the Mikado, respectfully swearing that he would not loose his hold until His Majesty sanctioned the Treaties. Finally, the Kuambaku—the first officer of the Mikado—

was directed to bring the BOOK OF THE IRREVOCABLE WILLS—and the sanction was given.

The change was instantaneous. Where all was fear and distrust, confidence and resolution became triumphant. All congratulated each other on the issue of their patient labours; all expressed the strongest confidence in the future; and they could well say with the utmost truth :—" We have accomplished a great work."

The European ministers did not themselves go to Osaka, but H.M. gunboat Bouncer went backwards and forwards every day with dispatches. The result was told in the following notification :—

MIKADO RATIFIES TREATY.—TARIFF TO BE ADJUSTED.— HIOGO TO BE OPENED IN 1868—EARLIER IF POSSIBLE.—AND THE INDEMNITY MONEY WILL BE PAID.

The following is a translation of a letter sent by the high officers of Satsuma at Kioto, to the Mikado, with reference to the opening of Hiogo. To this I would ask my readers to pay special attention; and to bear it in mind, when we come to the events of 1868.

" Although we do not exactly know the motives which have brought into the harbour of Hiogo the ships of the barbarians, still we have been confidentially informed that after a conference held between the same barbarians, ABE BUNGO-NO-KAMI and MATS'DAIRA IDZU-NO-KAMI, it has been agreed that Hiogo should be open, and satisfaction given to their demands within ten days; and that, on this occasion the Tycoon would come up to Kioto.

" Now, your Majesty is well aware that Hiogo is in the vicinity of your sacred residence, and a very important port in the Inland Sea. We are, for this reason, far from thinking that your Majesty will for a moment entertain the idea of allowing the opening of Hiogo.

" Since the American came and trampled on our land, the resolution of your Majesty has been immutable. That we all know, and admire more than any other of your subjects. We dare to say that we do not entertain serious anxieties on this subject.

"Still, it might happen that the statements made to Your Majesty should move your heart, and in exacting from you concessions, put your Empire in a danger and in an opprobrium unknown until our days, and which a thousand years would not repair.

"Nothing less than the submission, or the rebellion, of the hearts of the people, is at stake, and regrettable concessions would be the origin of immense calamities. We therefore humbly request Your Majesty, to convoke, at once, all the daimios; and, after having taken their advice, to cause the Majesty of Your Empire to shine, once for all.

"However, such a measure would take time, and it might happen that these barbarians should fatigue Your Majesty with their obstinate resolutions. Should they dare to act lightly, it would be the duty of Your Majesty to decree their expulsion. In such a contingency, although our infirm *yashiki* has but very few hands at present, according to the instructions of SHIUNI TAIYO OSUMI-NO-KAMI (SHIMADZU SABURO) we offer to form the advance guard; and, by fighting to death, we would endeavour to show our gratitude for all the favours with which we have been blessed in the Empire of Your Majesty.

"May Your Majesty deign to receive our request, and forgive its intrusiveness.

THE HIGH OFFICERS OF SATSUMA YASHIKI."

CHAPTER XXXVI.

AFFAIRS IN YOKOHAMA.—ARRIVAL OF THE FUSIYAMA.—FIRE IN YEDO.—SCHOOLS.—NATIVE PECULIARITIES.—PROFESSOR RISLEY.—MANY USEFUL SCHEMES AFLOAT.—GENERAL PROGRESS.

THE dawn of 1866 saw Mr. F. MYBURGH arrive from England, and enter upon his duties as H.B.M. Consul at Yokohama; Mr. MARCUS FLOWERS resuming the functions of Vice Consul, but leaving at the end of the month for Nagasaki.

It also saw the establishment of a Pony corps, followed a few months later by the resurrection of the Volunteers. Everything of this kind was very fitfully carried out. A fine spirited start would be made, and it looked as if such energy would be lasting, and carry everything before it; but it generally proved a mere fizzle, and after the first effervescence, became dull and quiescent.

Political matters were particularly unexciting. The Envoy of the King of Belgians indeed arrived, and visited Yedo with the view of feeling his way towards a treaty; and his reception was so far satisfactory that negociations were laid in train which resulted in the accomplishment of his wishes within a few weeks from that time.

But one event of a really interesting character I must mention; because it was the first time the barrier was fairly set aside, which had opposed itself obstructively to genial intercourse between natives of high birth and foreigners.

It was been mentioned that the construction of a good drive round by Mississippi Bay had been the means of inducing many to keep carriages. Amongst others, Mr. JOHN MAC DONALD, of H.B.M. Legation, had his—a handsome mail phaeton—in which he ordinarily drove two, but not infrequently four, Japanese ponies.

About the middle of January, a member of Gorojiu, MATSZ'DAIRA HOKI-NO-KAMI, visited Yokohama with several of the high government officials. He took occasion to congratulate the foreign ministers on the removal of all the old restraints that had existed before the ratification of the treaties—and even admitted how very difficult had been the position of the Tycoon and his government as standing between the foreigners and the Mikado: unable, in some sort, to tell either party the exact truth with regard to the other. But the most extraordinary circumstance connected with this visit was its *finale;* and we can hardly class it as among secondary affairs, indicating as it does the remarkable change in feeling in the Japanese mind towards foreigners.

MATSUDAIRA HOKI-NO-KAMI, acknowledged that until the ministers went up to Hiogo, he had never met a European. He was an elderly man, and one of the most polished even of the Japanese nobles. Before leaving for Yedo, he asked Mr. MAC DONALD, to drive him in his carriage to Kawasaki, as he would much prefer that mode of transit to returning in the steamer. Mr. MAC DONALD, having courteously assented, the steamer was despatched to Yedo, and MATSUDAIRA HOKI-NO-KAMI, with four others, mounted the vehicle. The legation guard under Captain APPLIN, and a number of his own attendants, accompanied them, and the whole route along the Tokaido presented a most extraordinary scene of excitement, the surprise of all grades being unbounded. This was really one of the most remarkable *coups* yet known in Japanese and foreign intercourse. The pleasure exhibited by all was extreme; and at Kawasaki they did not part without the warmest expressions of regard on both sides.

On the 23rd January, the Fusiyama, the first of the war-vessels ordered by the Japanese through Mr. PRUYN, the U. S. Minister, arrived from America.

A very few days revealed the fact that the government naval authorities were anything but proud of their acquisition. They expressed themselves plainly, in terms that showed their dissatisfaction with this specimen of what they were to expect the ships to be which they had fondly hoped would have been the real nucleus of their national navy. She was placed under the command of an officer of the French navy.

In Yedo a terrible fire broke out on the 28th January in Asakusa. In that district three daimio's *yashikis* were burnt, a great number of streets were laid in ruins, and the great outermost portal of the Temple of Kuanon-sama, was destroyed. Reaching the banks of the river Sumida, Adzuma-bashi (bridge) was partially burnt, and the fire, leaping across the river, (as broad here as the Thames at London Bridge), laid in ashes in Houdjo, four *yashikis* of daimios, many residences of hatamotos, and many streets. It was said that a hundred and fifty persons lost their lives, a hundred and seventy were wounded, and ten thousand houses were consumed in this terrible conflagration.

From Osaka, the news came that Choshiu had submitted to the Mikado and Tycoon, admitting himself to be in the wrong; and was awaiting their decision concerning him. It was thought that this would be lenient, as from the attitude of the clan it was evident that any harsh judgment would be resisted, and the renewal of the struggle would be immediate.

In former chapters I have spoken of schools for foreign instruction having been established. Long ago, while yet some of the American missionaries resided in Kanagawa, the government sent several young men from Yedo to be instructed in English; and more lately, schools had been established by authority, and under the protection, of the respective governors, both in Yokohama and Nagasaki, for the benefit, especially, of the sons of the higher classes. The school at Yokohama made wonderful progress; it now numbered over fifty pupils—young men, it must be borne in mind, not picked up by the way-side and entreated to come in, but—belonging to the upper class, and sent thither with the sanction and by desire of the government.

In addition to this government school, as it may be called, some of the wives of missionaries had classes of Japanese boys under instruction in English, and with much success.

The French school for the instruction of the sons of gentlemen, in active operation at Benten, had met with most satisfactory results, and was strongly supported by the Japanese authorities.

But now the Gorojiu was going a step further. It was about to erect school buildings in Yedo, in which a hundred young men of family should be taught. There were to be an English and a French department; and missionaries were applied to take charge of them.

This was the origin of the present university, now so familiarly known as the Kaisei Gakko. The time has not yet come for me to dwell on the subject of education at large. But it will form one of the most instructive and interesting chapters of the second volume.

Up to the time I have arrived at in my narrative, the progress in Japan had been slow; but little as it was, it had been accomplished under nearly insurmountable difficulties.

Still it was sure. And it was very marked. Those who resided here and saw it growing week by week, used to remark upon it as wonderful and interesting in the extreme.

The Japanese have always been noted for one peculiarity beyond all others—Inquisitiveness. They would quietly walk into a foreign dwelling-house, and ask to be allowed to see the rooms. It was not always agreeable; but they were rarely denied: and no doubt those who were thus favoured, reported all that they had seen—the size of the rooms, the elegance of the furniture, the brightness of the mirrors, the costliness of the plate, the luxuries of the bed-chambers, the cleanliness and comfort pervading the whole. Thus gradually a custom began to show itself, of native gentlemen having one room in their houses, furnished after a foreign fashion, with a handsome square carpet or rug in the centre of the room—over their own nice mats; a table covered with a gag cloth and chairs surrounding it, in the middle of the carpet; glass windows in at least one of the sliding sashes; and, sometimes, pictures and mirrors hanging on the sides of the room. Many began to eat meat and declare that they liked it; and all would drink champagne to any extent; thus giving the best proof of their approbation. As yet none dare appear openly in foreign costume. Any who did so would certainly have been roughly handled. But it was not long before they adopted them without fear. Indeed in a variety of ways, some large, some small, the forward movement as exhibited.

In concluding this chapter, one striking fact may be mentioned: viz., that, although children are nurtured from the maternal breast, up to an age when the children of Europeans are solidifying themselves with good butcher's meat, yet the native adult had, until lately, and many have still, an aversion to milk, all but unconquerable. It was years after the advent of foreigners to this country before the supply of good cow's milk was sufficient for their ordinary wants. The little that was obtainable was sold almost as a favour by the European butchers, who kept a few good Japanese cows, and did the best they could to accommodate their regular customers.

The first attempt at a regular dairy was made by Professor RISLEY, of whom I have already spoken as the introducer of ice among our Yokohama luxuries; and as the first introducer, also, of Japanese acrobats to foreign countries.

RISLEY was a man who never did himself justice. He was for some years a resident in Yokohama; but at one time of his life, his name was well known in all the great capitals of Europe and America. I remember him with his sons at the Strand Theatre in London in 1843, when his fame and success seemed carrying everything before him. Apart from his great strength and agility, and the wonderful pluck and cleverness of his boys, which enabled him to present an entertainment as attractive as it was at that time unique, he was peculiarly cut out for the kind of Bohemian life he had chosen. He was a wonderful rifle shot; a good billiard player; up to everything that lithe and active men most rejoice in. He knew thoroughly well the usages of good society, and could hold his own with high or low. His fund of anecdote was marvellous; and he could keep a roomful of people holding their sides with laughter, without the least appearance of effort, or the faintest shade of coarseness. Yet after his very successful European career, he did not manage to progress. His boys grew up, and became too big to be tossed about like playthings on the soles of their father's feet; and besides he wisely wished to placed them in a better sphere than that from which he had himself sprung, and accordingly sent them to be properly educated and to make their way as good citizens in America, the land of their birth.

He, however, saw no other means of earning his own bread, but by following his profession; and to this end, adopted another lad, who was not one whit less clever than his own sons had been. With him he went to Australia; and there found it was as much as he could do to make both ends meet. I saw him there in 1858, on the Bendigo diggings and at the Back Creek rush, at the latter of which he employed men to dig for him— but he told me that from his claim he "never saw the colour" (of gold).

The next time I met him was when he came, as the joint proprietor of a Circus, to Yokohama. This enterprise failed entirely; and he would have been left high and dry but for his remarkable energy and spirits. These gave confidence to many, and procured for him assistance; none entering more kindly and sympathetically into his schemes than Mr. G. S. FISHER, the U. S. Consul, and Mr. J. ALLMAND (an American merchant, resident in Yokohama, who had been with Commodore PERRY in his visits to Japan in 1853-4). These gentlemen not only listened to his proposals anent the establishment of a dairy in Yokohama, but they provided him with the means to set about it; and had he been content to make this his business, and stick steadily to it, he might long ere this have been a thoroughly independent man.

The dairy trade now has become an important one. There are in Yokohama alone two large dairies foreign-owned, besides several Japanese on a lesser scale. And in Tokio, the latter must abound; for, in all quarters of the city, milk is procurable at all times.

The reader will be amused to see Mr. RISLEY's own account of a difficulty that beset his first importation of cows. It will also show the real kindness of heart, which was his best characteristic.

On the 24th February 1866, the trim little regular trading schooner Ida D. Rogers, at that time the most favourite of the vessels that kept up communication between Japan and the United States, arrived from California, having on board Mr. RISLEY and the nucleus of his intended dairy—six fine cows and their calves. The little craft was noted for her rapid passages, but this unfortunately was unusually protracted. It lasted seventy days, and at one time there was a fear that the cattle would have died for want of water.

I took down the following from Mr. RISLEY's first interview with me when he called upon me to tell me of the safe arrival of his new importation.

"Waal! Got back you see; though I know the bettin' was against me—but we had a narrow squeak for it as ever you saw. But here I am! and I've got six as fine cows as ever were milked—and six fine calves too. But its God's mercy I've got them here; for I never was nearer losing anything in my life. Not a drop of water left—and they'd been on half allowance for several days. We were close to Yokohama a month ago—and blown right off to the north, and had to beat up against a dead head wind, and thought we should never get here. Waal! one day—I was wretched seeing the poor beasts licking the sides of their boxes and the deck, and lapping everything they could :—b'lieve me I could hardly stand it—I can't bear to see a poor dumb animal suffering—but—if you'd only seen the poor creatures! As I passed along in front of them they'd try to lay hold of me, as if to ask 'why don't you bring us some water?' I really hardly knew how to endure it. At last, I'd made up my mind that they must all die, and was only thinking whether I should throw them overboard or let them die—and not yet able to make up my mind—when God was merciful and sent a night's rain. I worked like a horse; and all that night I was employed in catching water—and I saved six thousand gallons—I did—all with my own hands! There! you may judge how I worked. Every bucket-full passed through my hands. Waal! You may smile—but it did, you know! and the cows were saved. I never was so relieved in my life. When the rain came, the ship was rolling terribly—and the Captain said 'Professor—don't you go forward—it's like tempting Providence—you'll be sure to go.'—'Waal!' said I,— 'I'm not very comfortable here, so if I must go I must— but the poor cows shall have some water first.' And so they did. You should ha' seen them before the water ran short! But they're splendid cattle—I picked them all myself from any quantity—and I flatter myself I know good milkers when I see them—all selected for dairy purposes you know—not for anything else—and they'll turn up trumps—you see!"

As a laudable, profitable and most useful enterprise, dairy farming has turned up trumps; but the professor could not settle down to attend to it. In the course of a few days, he was off to Tientsin for a cargo of ice, and ultimately both the dairy and the ice business passed into other hands whilst he rushed off to America and to England as the manager and part proprietor of a Japanese Acrobatic troupe—with which he imagined he should coin money. 'Yas, Sir! Yas! the biggest thing you ever saw in your life, Sir!"

Reverting to more weighty themes, it were well to notice the real state of affairs as more particularly affecting foreigners at this period.

The treaties having been ratified, the path for everything else was made smooth. The Japanese and foreign ministers were about to meet to discuss the tariff question, which had become of serious importance.

But at this time there were many schemes afloat— almost all of which have been carried out; and it is a most suggestive fact that they had all been undertaken by the Japanese Government before the ratification, and whilst they were apparently yielding to the pressing commands of the Mikado that they should drive foreigners from the country.

Thus, there was afoot a scheme for a dock. There was the mint project—which it was hoped to have so far completed by 1868, when Osaka was to be opened, that coincident with this event there might be an improvement in financial calculations.

Then there was the proposal for lighthouses on the principal points and headlands of the Japanese coast. No less than twenty three were proposed, and the matter was seriously being considered by the Japanese Government.

Already minting machinery and six lighthouses had been ordered in France; and shortly afterwards the Yokosuka Dock was commenced under the superintendence of French engineers, and with the pecuniary assistance of French financiers. The Government did not confine their orders to any one nationality; as yet

Great Britain hardly appeared to have her fair share of them. For instance—War vessels:—the Americans were to supply them—the *Fusiyama* being the first instalment. One had also been ordered in Holland. Guns, mint, lighthouses:—the French obtained their orders. Schools:—a Dutch surgeon superintended at Nagasaki their medical school:—and the establishments at Yokohama were, and at Yedo were about to be, presided over by French and American teachers. Officers were required to take charge of their foundries:—at Nagasaki they employed a Dutchman, at Yokohama a Frenchman. They wished that a naval officer should be placed on board the Fusiyama, to instruct their own officers:—the post was given to an officer of the French Navy.

It mattered not. All was on the right road; and those they engaged did their work well and faithfully. Ultimately, as will be seen, whilst each of the nationalities named increased the number of their people employed by the Government, England and Germany also supplied a large number of active and able servants, who helped forward the general work.

As regards minor matters in Yokohama, the place was still without any recreation ground. As long ago as 1864, it had been agreed between the governor of Kanagawa and Sir Rutherford Alcock, that the salt water swamp at the back of the settlement should be filled up, and converted into a race-course, surrounding a fine spacious area which was to be reserved for Japanese and foreigners alike. The race-course was to be rented to the race club at a fair sum, and the enclosure free for all recreative purposes.

It was really inconvenient having no such ground; for although the piece of swamp land between the original settlement and the canal, was being slowly filled in, and the portion thus reclaimed was used by cricketers and purpose: and arrangements can be made with a very experienced Japanese gardener, by which the garden could be always well stocked with the best plants, and the public supplied with specimens such as are now with difficulty obtainable. This is one of those schemes of permanent advantage to the settlement that all must heartily concur in."

And all did concur in it, and yet it fell through, and we had not a Public Garden until several years later.

On the evening of the 5th March, a very melancholy circumstance occurred. That night as Mr. BECKER was passing through Ota-machi, he saw a French sailor lying in the street. He stopped to examine him, and found that he was speechless, and had a frightful gash at the back of the head, which appeared to have been done by a blow with a bamboo or billet of wood. By the aid of some coolies the man was taken to the barracks of the British Military Train, and there he died in about two hours. It appeared that the man, in a state of intoxication had provoked some Japanese beyond endurance, violently knocking one of them down; and they attacked him. A comrade who was with him, but who was inoffensive, was not attacked or in any way molested; and it was quite clear that the deceased man alone was to blame.

It happened that just about this time there had been several cases of these riotous proceedings on the part of the soldiers and sailors in Japanese town, although, on the whole, the conduct of the men was good.

One day in H.B.M. Consular Court there were about half a dozen sailors and marines before the Consul, to answer more or less serious charges against them. One of them had amused himself scattering his enemies and clearing a street in the Japanese quarters, with a pole ten feet long. Another had been fighting with his comrades; a third with Japanese. A fourth had been riding furiously through the streets, and endangering the lives and limbs of all who passed. In every case they pleaded intoxication as an excuse. One of them said that as he could not get drunk on board, and he must do so somewhere, that being one of the first duties to himself of the British seaman, his only alternative was to avail himself of his leave on shore: and another said that he " came ashore on purpose to get drunk, and that, in his opinion, every sailor did the same." This caused immense merriment in the Court, and among the community, when it was reported in the newspapers; but the Japanese found that it was a kind of fun that they could have too much of. And more than once their annoyance got the better of their good nature, and the offenders had been severely handled.

In this case, although it was, at the worst, one of manslaughter, one Japanese was beheaded, and others punished—the Japanese laws making no distinction between "murder" and "man-slaughter."

The foreign residents felt this severity very acutely. They said that " the man who was beheaded, was not one of the dangerous classes. He was one of the common people who never greet foreigners but with respect, and who set a value on their presence. It must have been very strong provocation that roused his ire to such a pitch, as to make him, although not personally molested, call upon his countrymen around, to rise against their assailant." They also protested that "the excesses of sailors and soldiers had recently become almost unendurable; and as this had been repeatedly pointed out by the Press, their officers ought to have taken steps to control those, who, by their misconduct, not only disgraced themselves, but brought their respectable and well-conducted comrades, (happily, the great majority), into bad odour and contempt."

The *finale* was, that some of the foreign residents, taking into consideration the sudden bereavement of the man's widow, and to mark their sense of the conduct of the European sailor, in so deeply irritating her husband, as to excite him to the deed for which he suffered, raised, by subscription, a respectable sum of money, and presented it to her. It is probable that she never would have had so much money under other circumstances; and so small are the wants of the Japanese that she could have lived comfortably on the interest of it. Still it was a lamentable affair, and one that was universally regretted.

It must not, however, be supposed that these *contretemps* occasioned ill-feeling between the Japanese and foreigners. The former were quite able to discriminate between the good and the bad: and they knew well that in all communities both were to be found. They also saw how sincerely the foreigners deprecated anything like ill-behaviour towards them; and even that those who were the principal offenders, were kindly disposed towards them when they had their wits about them.

On the 21st March, an occasion presented itself for exhibiting the general good feeling between the English forces and the Japanese soldiery.

I have mentioned the "march-outs" and "sham fights" which the commandant, Colonel BROWNE, kept up pretty frequently—for the health, occupation and discipline of the troops. The day named may be well a red-letter day in the Yokohama calendar; and the proceedings are worthy of record. It was the first occasion on which Japanese and foreign troops paraded together.

Punctually at nine o'clock in the morning, the British troops from the barracks on the Bluff, marched on to the Bund, and took up a position at the extreme end (in front of Nos. 1 to 8). They consisted of a battery of Artillery, a detachment of the 11th, and the whole of the 2nd batt. XXth regiment.

To their right, formed in line, were the Japanese troops, in number about eight hundred; and, at their right again, the Mounted Volunteers (Pony corps).

With the troops there was a party from H. M. S. Pelorus, with one gun. The sight was altogether a most exhilarating one.

At about 9.30, H. E. Sir HARRY PARKES, K. C. B., with the Governor of Kanagawa, accompanied by Colonel BROWNE, Captain HASWELL R. N., and a brilliant suite, rode up and down the line; then, taking up a position at the end of the street which enters the Bund between Nos. 15 and 16, the whole marched past.

The Governor and His Excellency, having passed some mutually complimentary remarks and expressed their approbation to Colonel BROWNE and the Japanese commanding officer, separated; Sir HARRY promising to visit Homoku about 2.30 P.M., to see the evolutions of the troops.

The Japanese soldiers had evidently been very carefully drilled and disciplined: and both marched, and handled their rifles, in a masterly manner.

The Japanese troops with the English, and the Mounted Volunteers in the rear, now marched up the Kanasawa valley to Macpherson's hill, (a distance of six miles), and arrived there about noon. Here, in this lovely spot, they were allowed to break from the ranks, and partake of a hearty repast, which all were in a good state to enjoy after their walk. About 2 o'clock, the bugle sounded for the men to fall in and form in line; which was quietly executed by the English, and capitally followed by the Japanese, under the command of KUBOTA SENTARO, commander-in-chief of the native forces in

Yokohama. The order was then given to march to Mississippi Bay, the Japanese troops branching off to the right, the English to the left. The combined forces met at the Bay with loud greetings of *o-hayo*, (good morning), which seemed to gratify the Japanese officers and men, and led the former to exclaim that they were glad indeed to see their countrymen and foreigners on such friendly terms.

The march was now resumed to Homoku, the English and Japanese bands, (the latter drums and fifes only), playing alternately.

On arriving at Homoku, a portion of the blue-jackets were ordered to command the height on the left, and about a hundred Japanese, supported by a battery of the one gun from the Pelorus, to keep position in the valley. The battalions of the XXth, and a portion of the 11th, with the main body of the Japanese troops, were ordered to hold position on the right, just above the village of Homoku, supported by a battery of three guns, admirably placed in the midst of a clump of trees.

About 3 o'clock, Sir HARRY PARKES arrived on the field, and shortly afterwards firing commenced from the Pelorus battery, supported by the Japanese. The latter made a retreat, which was gallantly covered by the 'Plungers.' The forces to the right then opened fire, and the battle became general—lasting about ten minutes. The firing of the Japanese was very rapid, and evidently astonished many present. After the order had been given to 'cease firing,' the troops once more fell into marching order, and returned to Yokohama.

One unfortunate *contretemps* occurred just at starting. In passing between the guns, the horse of a sergeant ran against a soldier of the XXth, and drove him against the wheel of the gun-carriage. The man was sufficiently injured to require to be taken to the hospital. With this exception, there was not a single drawback throughout; and this was the more gratifying, inasmuch as the request that the Japanese should join in the field day, emanated from themselves.

But we were soon to lose the XXth regiment. On the 30th March, H.M.S. Adventure arrived, bringing up from Hongkong a wing of H.M.'s 9th regiment, under the command of Major Darling.

The 14th April saw the Adventure depart for Hongkong, with the left wing of the XXth and the detachment of the 11th, on board. The regiment was very much regretted by the residents. Other regiments followed, and English troops were not finally dispensed with until the year 1874. But the times became very quiet, and the boo exchange became of less value, and failed to give them such an increase of pay. The community, too, increased rapidly, and business became more absorbing. The consequence was that, with their departure, Yokohama became comparatively hum-drum; and the old social spirit has never revived.

On the 20th of April, the community had to mourn the death of Mr. JOHN MACDONALD, the senior assistant to Her Majesty's Legation in Japan. He was seized with paralysis as he was walking in the street, and never regained consciousness. He had entered the diplomatic service, and had come out direct to Japan, in 1859, when he joined the staff of Mr. ALCOCK the British minister, very soon after the opening of the port. He was only 28 years of age; a native of Inverness, and son of Mr. MAC DONALD, so often mentioned by the Queen, in her diary, as one of her trusty attendants at Balmoral. He was greatly liked, not only for his gentleman-like demeanour, but for his thorough amiability of character. It will be remembered that he was a member of the legation when it was attacked in 1861; and it was he who drove

Matsudaira Hoki-no-Kami, in his carriage from Yokohama to Kawasaki, as related in the previous chapter.

On the 24th April, Mr. C. Brennwald arrived as Consul-general for Switzerland, and Mr. Lindau sent in his resignation of the office of Consul.

On the 9th May, the Adventure returned from Hongkong with the remainder of the 9th Regiment, under Colonel Knox, who became the commandant of the garrison.

On the 9th, the remainder of the XXth embarked on the Adventure, and next day they were lost to Yokohama for ever.

One other circumstance I feel obliged to mention, as having occurred before their departure.

A Japanese soldier had, whilst drunk, drawn his sword, as two British officers were passing, and was only prevented from assaulting them by two of his sober comrades restraining him. He had been tried and sentenced to imprisonment. The man was a sergeant, and, in addition to his imprisonment, he was to be degraded to the ranks.

Colonel Browne, considering the good understanding hitherto existing between the Japanese and foreign soldiers, requested Sir Harry Parkes to apply for a mitigation of the sentence. On the 7th inst., therefore, Mr. Myburgh, the British Consul, attended by Lieut. Goldsmith of H. M. 2nd XXth, Fort Adjutant, Messrs. Satow and Von Siebold as interpreters, and escorted by a guard of the Military Train, went to Kanagawa barracks, Nogé, by invitation of General Kubota Sentaro. The Japanese soldiers were drawn up on parade, and the man brought forward. He was told that, on the application of the commandant of the British garrison, through Her Majesty's minister, his sentence was commuted, and he was to remain in confinement no longer. At the same time, to mark his general's opinion of his crime, that portion of the sentence that deprived him of his rank, would be adhered to.

On the regiment hearing of the kindness of the British authorities, they asked to be allowed to present arms to the Consul, which was permitted. So that, probably, this little affair may have been the means of strengthening the mutual friendly feelings, that it might have had the effect of dissipating.

On the 23rd May the Japanese Government issued a circular, which marked, more than anything else that had occurred, the advanced state of feeling, the real progress of ideas, that now existed in Japan. With this we may well bring our first volume to a close. It ran thus :—

NOTIFICATION.

"Persons wishing to go, in future, to any of the various countries beyond the sea, for the purpose of learning any science or art, or for objects of trade, will receive permission from the government on making application to this effect.

"The Government will, upon examination, grant a permit, with seal attached, to any such person. Let, therefore, the application be made out, giving the name of the petitioner, and stating clearly how he wishes to proceed, for what object, and to what country he intends to go. Retainers of daimios and hatamotos, should make their application through their master. Peasants and citizens through the Governor or Rent Collector of their place, or through the lord of the domain, to the proper department. In case any person should go abroad secretly, without a passport, he shall be severely punished. Therefore let everybody understand and observe this regulation.

"The above decree having been issued, it is to be

circulated and made known to every one, even to the ordinary people, in order that such as wish to go may make their application.

Government Office, May 23rd 1866."

It only remains to be told that the half year ending the 30th June 1866, to which I have now brought down my narrative, (and which closed the commercial year, or season, from July 1865 to June 1866), saw the completion of the new Tariff arrangement. The duties were generally on a *5 per cent. ad valorem* basis, though some special articles were to pay special rates, and some were to pass free. The Bonded system was adopted, and the Japanese Government purchased of the Dutch authorities the godowns on the lot originally given to that government for Consular purposes. The tariff was to come into operation with the commencement of the new season—on the 1st July.

The news from Kioto was uncertain. The terms offered to Choshiu were not replied to by that daimio, and on the 14th of the current Japanese month, seven days were given to him to accept the terms, or fight. The general belief was that he would remain silent; that war would be proclaimed against him; and that the Tycoon's troops would be immediately set in motion.

It was thought that Satsuma would openly remain quiet, but that he had already sent a small force to assist Choshiu.

It was pleasant, at this period, to be able to write as follows:—

"Thus, although there is much to be lamented, we think that the good greatly predominates—and as we have so recently expressed our convictions as to the effects that will most likely follow the recent diplomacy at Hiogo, we cannot but look forward with renewed satisfaction to the future. To us, the situation of our little world is paramount, and we do not see anything like gloom hanging over the aspect of affairs, in Japan. If the Japanese could only be brought to feel as kindly towards us as we feel towards them, there would be no country on earth more pleasant to sojourn in awhile, than this in which our lot is cast. But this state of things can only be brought about by time."

END OF VOLUME I.

www.ingramcontent.com/pod-product-compliance
Lightning Source LLC
Chambersburg PA
CBHW020536300426
44111CB00008B/693